THE CITY WALL
OF IMPERIAL ROME

I

PORTA APPIA, FINAL STAGE

The top story of the nearer tower belongs to period V. The rough block-work is a repair of period IV.
The marble blockwork belongs to period III. The Gates of periods I and II are hidden inside
the present structure.

THE CITY WALL
OF IMPERIAL ROME

AN ACCOUNT OF
ITS ARCHITECTURAL DEVELOPMENT
FROM AURELIAN TO NARSES

Ian A. Richmond

Foreword by Torsten Cumberland Jacobsen

WESTHOLME
Yardley

Originally published in 1931.
Foreword ©2013 Westholme Publishing

Westholme Publishing, LLC
904 Edgewood Road
Yardley, Pennsylvania 19067
Visit our Web site at www.westholmepublishing.com

ISBN: 978-1-59416-182-7
Also available as an eBook.

Printed in the United States of America.

FOREWORD

SINCE its publication in 1930, Sir Ian Archibald Richmond's *The City Wall of Imperial Rome* remains the essential work on the imperial fortifications of Rome. The continued relevance of the work lies primarily in its detailed and thorough scholarship and the importance of the subject. The narrative and composition is excellent, the language modern and it is very well illustrated. It is written in a style which is accessible to both specialists and general readers. The fact that the walls still remain the most imposing sight of ancient Rome only adds to the importance of the subject. For some years now, it has been very difficult to find a copy of this book, and it is therefore a great pleasure to reintroduce this reprint. The bibliography has been brought up to date and a short biography of Ian Richmond as well as a state of the scholarly research has been added.

My thanks goes to the Danish Institute in Rome for providing me accomodations and use of their library and to my guide in Rome, Claudia Cedrone.

THE WALLS THEN AND NOW

The Aurelian city wall of Rome was built between 271 and 275 in Rome, Italy, during the reign of the Roman Emperor Aurelian (270–275). It enclosed all seven hills of Rome as well as Campus Martius and the Trastevere district on the right bank of the Tiber. The riverside was certainly fortified along the Campus Martius, and probably elsewhere, although archaeology has not yet proven this belief.

The full circuit ran for 12.5 miles (19 km) and surrounded an area of some 5.3 square miles (13.7 km²). The walls were constructed in brick-faced concrete, 11.5 ft. (3.5 m) thick and 26.2 ft. (8 m) high, with a square tower on average every 100 Roman feet (97.1 ft./29.6 m). In the fifth century, the wall was renovated and its height was doubled to 52 ft. (16 m); it had 383 towers, eighteen main gates, and five posterns.

Rome had originally been protected by the old wall named after King Servius Tullius (578–535 BC), which had been built during the late fourth century BC. Since then, the wall had lost its purpose, and by the time of Emperor Augustus (27 BC–14 AD), the line of the old wall could not be traced. During the centuries of expansion and consolidation, Rome had little need of a city wall, and it was only during the crisis of the third century, that a city wall was again needed. In 271, Italy was threatened by Germanic tribes, who had crossed the borders in great numbers, and even defeated a Roman army at Placentia (modern-day Piacenza) in northern Italy, before being driven back.

Roman historian Aurelius Victor states that Aurelian's construction of the walls was a response to the new threat of barbarian invasion. Furthermore, it would also be a strong statement of the emperor's power and care for the capital in troubled times.

Despite the length of the walls, they were built in only five years, though Aurelian himself died before the completion of the project. To manage this, old tombs, private houses, garden walls and monuments were reused in the circuit of the wall, such as the Amphitheatrum Castrense, the Castra Praetoria, the Pyramid of Cestius, and even a section of the Aqua Claudia aqueduct near the Porta Maggiore. As much as ten percent of the walls are estimated to have been composed of preexisting structures.

The length of the wall was also its greatest weakness. The garrison of Rome—the Praetorian Guard, the *cohortes urbanae* and the *vigiles*—was very great, but still far too few to defend the walls adequately. Most likely, a token force would occupy the towers, and strong reserves would be brought up in the case of an attack. But the wall as Aurelian built it was not intended to withstand prolonged siege warfare. The barbarian tribes that it was built to defend against were not equipped or supplied for a regular siege. Instead, the wall would protect against a sudden assault or raid.

The wall was significantly enlarged and repaired in the times of Maxentius (306–312) and Honorius (395–423), when the walls and gates were heightened and the Tomb of Hadrian across the Tiber was also turned into a fortress, which was incorporated into the defenses. The increased height of the wall meant that more troops could be employed at any assault point, while fewer men were required to hold the walls. It was now able to withstand a real siege by experienced troops.

During the Gothic War in the middle of the sixth century, King Totila of the Ostrogoths (541–552), decided to destroy the walls to eliminate the Romans' ability to defend the city. According to the Greek historian Procopius, one-third of the walls were razed at the time, although a destruction on this magnitude cannot be archaeologically attested.

The Aurelian Wall continued to be the primary defences of Rome until September 20, 1870, when the Bersaglieri of the Kingdom of Italy breached it near Porta Pia and captured Rome. The walls continued to define the extent of the city, and a toll was levied at the gates until 1906.

Top, a contemporary photo of the breach in the Aurelian Walls created in 1870. Bottom, a cannon ball preserved in the wall from the 1870 bombardment. (*Claudia Cedrone*)

The Aurelian city walls are still well-preserved today, compared to other urban fortifications of the period, mainly due to their use as Rome's primary fortification until the nineteenth century. A small museum–the Museo delle Mura near Porta San Sebastiano (www.museodellemuraroma.it)–was established in 1989 and gives information on the walls' construction and how the defenses operated. The best preserved sections of the wall extend from the Muro Torto (Villa Borghese) to Cordo d'Italia and to Castro Pretorio, from Porta San Giovanni to Porta Ardeatina, from Porta Ostiense to the Tiber, and around Porta San Pancrazio.

FOREWORD

The collapse of a portion of the wall near the central station that occured in 2007.
(*Author's Collection*)

Unfortunately, as many other Roman monuments in Italy, the walls suffer from lack of maintenance. In 2001, a 100-foot stretch of the wall between Porta Latina and Porta San Sebastiano came down after a period of heavy rainfall. After several years, the damage was repaired, but again in 2007 another part of the wall fell down near the central station. This part has still to be repaired now six years later. It can only be hoped, that the Italian state will find money to conduct a thorough restoration of the walls, or more collapses will occur in the near future.

SIR IAN ARCHIBALD RICHMOND

Sir Ian Archibald Richmond (1902–1965) was born in Rochdale, Lancashire, on May 10, 1902, one of twin sons. His father was a medical doctor in Rochdale. Richmond was educated at Ruthin School in North Wales, one of the oldest public schools in the United Kingdom, and studied at Corpus Christi College, Oxford, 1920–24. His first publications appeared while he was still an undergraduate, such as a paper on "Ptolemaic Scotland" for the Society of Antiquaries of Scotland in 1921–22. With a third in honour moderations (1922) and a second in *literae humaniores* (1924), he was awarded the Gilchrist scholarship to the British School at Rome, the Craven fellowship, and a Goldsmiths' senior studentship.

FOREWORD

After graduating, he spent two years (1924–26) at the British School in Rome. Here he developed an interest in Roman military architecture and the operations of the Roman army in the field. This was to form the theme of his research throughout his life. Richmond's first book was the outstanding monograph, *The City Wall of Imperial Rome* (1930), illustrated by his own plans and isometric drawings. It was the main work of his residence in Rome and is still the standard work on the subject. While in Rome he also worked on the Mausoleum of Augustus and the Camp of the Praetorian Guards.

He gained practical archaeological experience working for the renowned archaeologist Mortimer Wheeler at Segontium in Wales and with F. G. Simpson on the Roman works at Cawthorn in Yorkshire. Richmond continued to produce publications, among others an article (in 1925) in the *Transactions of the Rochdale Literary and Scientific Society* on "The Roman Road across Blackstone Edge," which remains a central contribution to the subject. His achievements earned him a lectureship in Classical Archaeology and Ancient History at the Queen's University in Belfast, Ireland, from 1926 to 1930. Much of his summers he devoted to work on Hadrian's Wall, in conjunction with F. G. Simpson, R. G. Collingwood, and E. B. Birley, and was regarded as one of Englands' leading authorities on Hadrian's Wall and Roman military history and archaeology.

Richmond then returned to Rome as Director of the British School (1930–32) and worked on Trajan's Column, trying to understand the tactics and everyday life of the Roman army through the reliefs on the column. In 1932, Richmond had to retire because of ill health and for nearly three years he was without a post. Despite his condition, he put the years to good use, completing the great work *The Aqueducts of Ancient Rome* (1935), which Thomas Ashby's premature death had left unfinished, and contributing a series of important papers on the western sector of Hadrian's Wall to the *Transactions of the Cumberland and Westmorland Society*.

In 1935 he was appointed to a lectureship in Romano-British history and archaeology at Armstrong College in Newcastle, a part of the University of Durham. Here he would remain until 1956 with only a brief break for National Service. In 1938 he married Isabel Little, daughter of a wool merchant in Newcastle upon Tyne and later had a son and a daughter. Richmond was promoted to a Readership in 1943 and given a personal chair at the university in 1950, served two years as dean of the faculty of arts, and during his twenty-one years at Durham carried out numerous excavations along Hadrian's Wall and other sites in the vicinity. His work at Inchtuthil in Scotland continued until 1965, alongside his examination of the Roman fort at Hod Hill in Dorset until 1958.

In 1956, Richmond returned to Oxford University and the newly-created Chair of the Archaeology of the Roman Empire with a fellowship at All Souls College. During his time at Oxford, he taught and inspired many young archaeologists who would later achieve distinction. In his last years he turned his attention to the Roman siege works at Masada in Israel and at Numantia in Spain.

Richmond was known as a very dignified and eloquent public speaker. His speeches were notable for the elevation of their style and his deliberation when speaking. In private, he was a relaxed and humorous person, with a great contrast between his public and private images.

It is difficult to overstate his boundless energy and activity, and one of the best descriptions which has been quoted in several works are the words of Professor Sheppard Frere:

> "We must record the indefatigability of his labours in the service of archaeology and pay tribute to the wide horizons of his learning, and to the unfailing generosity which placed its resources at the disposal of all who asked. It was not an unusual experience to know that he was engaged on tasks A and B, either of which might strain the leisure of an ordinary mortal, and then to hear quite by chance from someone else how fully he was engaged on tasks C and D: yet all were done with equal thoroughness."*

His energy continued throughout his life, and in the fifteen years before his death, he managed three seasons of excavation at Lancaster, as well as the central study of Inchtuthil.

Richmond's major works included *Roman Britain* (1947) and the first volume of the Pelican History of England on the same subject (1955), reissued in 1963. He edited three successive editions of John Collingwood Bruce's *Handbook to the Roman Wall* (1947, 1957, and 1966). In 1949, he contributed together with O.G.S. Crawford a masterly treatment of the Ravenna Cosmography for *Archaeologia*. In 1958, he published his still-important *Roman and Native in North Britain*. With the late Robert Ogilvie, he produced a completely new *Commentary on Tacitus' Life of Agricola* (1967), which is still regarded as the standard treatment. Furthermore, he published papers on Queen Cartimandua, Palmyra and Masada, and was planning a book on Roman Spain. At the time of his death he had completed a

Journal of Roman Studies, Vol.55 (1965), pp. xiii-xiv.

FOREWORD

revised second edition of *The Archaeology of Roman Britain* by R. G. Collingwood, later published in 1969. His excavations at Hod Hill were published in 1968 and those at Inchtuthil in 1985. The great part of his work appeared in the publications of archaeological societies, particularly in *Archaeologia Aeliana* (Society of the Antiquaries of Newcastle upon Tyne) and the *Transactions of the Cumberland and Westmorland Antiquarian and Archaeological Society*, the *Proceedings of the Society of Antiquaries of Scotland*, and the *Journal of Roman Studies*. His major public lecture series included the Rhind lectures in Edinburgh (1933), the Riddell memorial lectures in Newcastle (1948), the Ford lectures in Oxford (1951), and the Gray lectures in Cambridge (1952). The Riddell lectures were published in the monograph *Archaeology and the After-Life in Pagan and Christian Imagery* (1950). The Ford lectures, on Britain in the third and fourth centuries, and the Gray lectures, on the Romano-British countryside, were edited by Professor Peter Salway and published in 1969.

Richmond also served on many national and local organizations. From 1944 he served on the royal commissions on historical monuments for England and Scotland, contributing much to their reports on Roman sites. He was elected a fellow of the Society of Antiquaries in 1931, served as director of the society in 1959–64, and was president from April 1964 until his death.

He was also an important figure in the Society for the Promotion of Roman Studies, and became president in 1958–61. He was elected Fellow of the British Academy in 1947 and received honorary doctorates from Edinburgh, Belfast, Leeds, Newcastle, Manchester, and Cambridge, and was a member of the German Archaeological Institute. He also served as president of the Society of Antiquaries of Newcastle and of the Bristol and Gloucestershire Archaeological Society. He was appointed Commander of the British Empire in 1958 and knighted in 1964.

Ian Richmond is considered one of the most accomplished Roman archaeologists of his time. He was as eminent in reassessing earlier discoveries as well as in conducting new research aims. His great knowledge and understanding of the Roman army made him an excellent excavator.

STATE OF THE SCHOLARLY RESEARCH

Despite its size and prominent position in Rome, the Aurelian Wall has received remarkably little attention from scholars. The wall has of course been noted through history, but the modern scholarly tradition on the wall began with the publication of *Le Mura di Roma* in

1820, written by the Italian archaeologist Antonio Nibby and illustrated by the British engraver Sir William Gell. In his book, he described the earlier walls of the city, including the one attributed to Emperor Aurelian by the ancient sources, and the historical background on the existing wall, which he believed was the work of Honorius. Nibby also gave a detailed description of the wall as it looked at the time, describing a clockwise circuit beginning from the vicinity of the Piazza del Popolo. Nibby's work was the first to try to identify all the construction phases of the Aurelian Wall from its origin to modern times, based on the literary and epigraphic traditions. Despite its mistakes, it was the foundation upon which later studies were built. The next really significant study came in 1930 with Ian Richmond's *The City Wall of Imperial Rome*. Immediately after its publication, it superseded all previous accounts and has since then remained the essential study on the ancient phases of the Aurelian Wall.

Of important work between Nibby and Richmond can be mentioned the British archaeologist John Henry Parker, who produced a great number of photographs of the Aurelian Wall and its gates. Some of them documented excavations, which have later been covered over, as well as parts of the wall which were torn down after the reunification of Italy in 1870, when Rome had become too constricted by the fortifications.

The German topographer Heinrich Jordan made a great topographical survey, and described the history of the walls, which he described to Aurelian, as well as a description of their remains. Jordan's work was considered the culmination of the scholarly tradition until the publication of Richmond in 1930.

The Italian archaeologist Rodolfo Lanciani was also one of the significant contributors before Richmond. His drawings of the Aurelian Wall in his *Forma Urbis Romae* is still the standard work now more than a century after its publication, and he published several articles on the wall. Like Parker, he also experienced the tearing down of parts of the wall, and documented the structural composition, which was revealed in this way.

The force in Richmond's book lay in its completeness. He combined literary, documentary, and artistic sources with archaeology and with his great personal acquaintance with the wall as it stood in his time. His main aim was to identify and date the major building phases and associate them with historical events. Few of his findings have later been challenged, although A. M. Colini was the first to place the heightening of the wall in the reign of Emperor Honorius, rather than in the reign of Maxentius, as Richmond believed.

FOREWORD

In the recent years, there has been a minor surge of interest in the Aurelian Wall. In the 1980s, Lucos Cozza began producing a series of articles describing various parts of the wall, which he followed in a clockwise circuit beginning in the south part of Trastevere. Before his death in 2011, he had described in detail about half of the remains of the wall. Cozza updated the findings of Richmond with new archaeological data and made a more refined typological framework for the study of late-antique and medieval masonry. He focused on the chronology and physical characteristics of the wall, and his architectural history covers the entire seventeen centuries of its existence, thereby supplementing Richmond, who focused on Antiquity.

Robert Coates-Stephens has also done important recent work, among others, the identification of the wall's previously unrecognized early-medieval phases.

In 2001, Italian architect Rossana Mancini published a historical "atlas" of the Aurelian Wall. The work contains colour-coded diagrams of the entire wall, showing the absolute chronology of the visible remains. The work gives a great overview of the current knowledge of the wall. The trend since Richmond is that most analyses have focused on the architectural history of the wall and the chronology of the various construction phases.

The most recent work is from 2011, when Hendrik Dey published his *The Aurelian Wall and the Refashioning of Imperial Rome, AD 271-855*, in which he turns to explore the relationship between the city of Rome and the Aurelian Wall during the six centuries following its construction in the 270s AD. In this period the city changed and contracted almost beyond recognition, as it evolved from imperial capital into the spiritual center of Western Christendom.

SELECTED BIBLIOGRAPHY AFTER 1930

Adam, J.-P. *La construction romaine. Materiaux et techniques.* Paris: 1984.

Aguilera Martin, A. *El Monte Testaccio e la llanura subaventina. Topografia extra portem Trigeminam.* Rome: 2002.

Amadei, E. Le porte di Roma. *Capitolium* 40. p. 553–62. Rome: 1965.

Bird, J., A. Claridge, O. Gilkes, and D. Neal. Porta Pia: Excavation and survey in an ara of suburban Rome, part 1. *Papers of the British School at Rome* 61, p. 51–113. Rome: 1993.

Brienza, M. and A. Delfino. "Il necessarium presso Porta Salaria a Roma". *Bulletino della Commissione Archeologica Communale di Roma* 107. p. 107–14. Rome: 2006.

Calci, C. and Mari, Z.. "Via Tiburtina," in Pergola, P., R. Santangeli Valenzani, and R. Volpe (eds.), *Suburbium*, p. 175–209. Rome: 2003.

FOREWORD

Cambedda, A. and A. Ceccherelli. *Le mura di Aureliano: dalla Porta Appia al Bastione Ardeatino.* Rome: 1990.

Cardilli, L., F. Coarelli, G. Pisano Sartorio, and C. Pietrangeli. *Mura e porte di Roma Antica.* Rome: 1995.

Caruso, G. and Volpe, R. "Le Mura Aureliane tra Porta Tiburtina e Porta Maggiore." *Bulletino della Commissione Archeologica Communale di Roma* 103. p. 76–78. Rome: 1989–90.

Cassanelli, L., G. Delfini, and D. Fonti. *Le mura di Roma. L'archittetura militare nella storia urbana.* Rome: 1974.

Ceccherelli, M. and M. G. D'Ippolito. "Considerazioni su alcune fasi costruttive di Porta Appia." *Bulletino della Commissione Archeologica Communale di Roma* 107. p. 87–106. Rome: 2006.

Ceccherelli, Alberta, A. Cambedda, and R. Motta. *Il Museo delle Mura di Roma.* Rome: 1990.

Ceccherelli, Alberta. "Il Museo delle Mura a Porta S. Sebastiano." *Bollettino dei Musei Comunali di Roma*, IV nuova serie. Rome: 1990.

Ceccherelli, Alberta and A. Cambedda. *Le Mura di Aureliano, itinerari d'arte e di cultura–via Appia.* Rome: 1990.

Coates-Stephens, R. "Quattro torri alto-medievali delle Mura Aureliane." *Archaeologia Medievale* 22. p. 501–17. Rome: 1995.

Coates-Stephens, R. "The walls and aqueducts of Rome in the early middle ages." *Journal of Roman Studies* 88. p. 166–78. London: 1998.

Coates-Stephens, R. "Le ricostruzioni altomedievali delle mure aureliane e degli aquedotti." Mélanges de l'Ecole francaise de Rome. *Moyen Age.* 111, 1: p. 209–25. Rome: 1999.

Coates-Stephens, R. "Muri dei bassi secoli in Rome: observations on the re-use of statuary in walls found on the Esquiline and Caelian after 1870." *Journal of Roman Archaeology* 14. p. 217–38. Portsmouth, RI: 2001.

Coates-Stephens, R. "Porta Maggiore: monument and landscape. Archaeology and topography of the southern Esquiline from the Late Republican Period to the present." *Bulletino della Commissione Archeologica Communale di Roma*, supplement 12. Rome: 2004.

Coates-Stephens, R. and A. Parisi. "Indagine di un crollo delle Mura Aureliane presso Porta Maggiore." *Analecta Romana Instituti Danici* 26. p. 85–98. Rome: 1999.

Coulston, J. and Dodge, H. (eds.). *Ancient Rome: The Archaeology of the Eternal City.* Oxford University School of Archaeology, Monograph 54. Oxford: 2000.

Cozza, L. (ed). "Muri portaque Aureliani," in G. Lugli (ed), *Fontes ad Topographiam Veteris Urbis Romae Pertinentes I*, p. 201–234. Rome: 1952.

Cozza, L. "Mura Aureliane, 1. Trastevere, il braccio settentrionale: dal Tevere a porta Aurelia-S. Pancrazio" *Bulletino della Commissione Archeologica Communale di Roma* 91, p. 103–30. Rome: 1986.

Cozza, L. "Osservazioni sulle Mura Aureliane a Roma." *Analecta Romana Instituti Danici* 16, p. 25–52. Rome: 1987.

Cozza, L. "Mura Aureliane, 2. Trastevere, il braccio meridionale: dal Tevere a Porta Aurelia-S. Pancrazio." *Bulletino della Commissione Archeologica Communale di Roma* 92, p. 137–74. Rome: 1987–88.

Cozza, L. "Le Mura Aureliane dalla Porta Flaminia al Tevere." *Papers of the British School at Rome*, 57, p. 1–5. Rome: 1989.

Cozza, L. "Mura di Roma dalla Porta Flaminia alla Pinciana." *Analecta Romana Instituti Danici* 20, p. 93–138. Rome: 1992.

Cozza, L. "Mura di Roma dalla Porta Pinciana alla Salaria." *Analecta Romana Instituti Danici* 21, p. 81–139. Rome: 1993.

Cozza, L. "Mura di Roma dalla Porta Salaria alla Porta Nomentana." *Analecta Romana Instituti Danici* 22, p. 61–95. Rome: 1994.

Cozza, L."Mura di Roma dalla Porta Nomentana alla Tiburtina." *Analecta Romana Instituti Danici* 25, p. 7–114. Rome: 1998.

Cozza, L. "Mura di Roma dalla Porta Latina all'Appia." *Papers of the British School at Rome*, 76, p. 99–154. Rome: 2008.

Cullhed, M. *Conservator Urbis Suae. Studies in the politics and propaganda of the emperor Maxentius.* Stockholm: 1994.

DeCarlo, L. and P. Quattrini. *Le mura di Roma tra realità e immagine.* Rome: 1995.

de la Croix, H. *Military Considerations in City Planning: Fortifications.* New York: 1972.

DeLaine, J. "The supply of building materials to the city of Rome," in Christie (ed.) *Settlement and Economy in Italy 1500 BC to 1500 AD* (Oxbow monograph 41), p. 555–562. Oxford: 1995.

DeLaine, J. "The Baths of Caracalla. A study in the design, construction and economics of large-scale building projects in imperial Rome." *Journal of Roman Archaeology* Supplement 25, Portsmouth, RI: 1997.

DeLaine, J. "Building the Eternal City: the construction industry in Imperial Rome," in Coulston and Dodge (eds), *Ancient Rome*, p. 119–41. Oxford: 2000.

De Seta, C. and J. Le Goff (eds.). *La città e le mura.* Rome and Bari: 1989.

Dey, Hendrik W. *The Aurelian Wall and the Refashioning of Imperial Rome, AD 271–855.* Cambridge University Press. Cambridge: 2011.

D'Onofrio, C. *Castel Sant'Angelo.* Rome: 1971.

D'Onofrio, C. *Castel Sant'Angelo nella storia di Roma e del papato.* Rome: 1982.

FOREWORD

Giovenale, G. B. "Le Porte del recinto di Aureliano e Probo." *Bollettino Communale* LIX, s. VII, p. 2–116. Rome: 1931.

Grazia Granino Cecere, M. and Mari, Z. (eds.). *Lexicon Topographicum Urbis Romae, Suburbium. Rome*: 2001–.

Hertz, L. E., "Roma. Aspetti della fortificazione fluviale." *Acta Hyperborea* 3, p. 297-310. Copenhagen: 1991.

Hobley, B. and Maloney, J (eds.). *Roman Urban Defences in the West*. London: 1983.

Johnson, F. "Who built the walls of Rome?" *Classical Philology* 43, p. 261–265. Chicago: 1948.

Johnson, S. "Late Roman urban defences in Europe," in Hobley and Maloney (eds.), *Roman Urban Defences in the West*, p. 69–76. London: 1983.

Krautheimer, R. *Rome, Profile of a City, 312–1308.* Princeton: 1980.

Lanciani, R. *Forma Urbis Romae.* Rome: 1893–1901. Reprinted 1988.

Lugli, G. *I monumenti antichi di Roma e Suburbio, I-III.* Rome: 1930-38.

Lugli, G. *La tecnica edilizia romana.* Rome: 1957.

Lugli, G. *Itinerario di Roma antica.* Milan: 1970.

Mancini, R. *Le mura aureliane di Roma. Atalante di un palinsesto murario.* Rome: 2001.

Marsden, E. W. *Greek and Roman Artillery. Historical Development.* Oxford: 1969.

Marsden, E. W. *Greek and Roman Artillery. Technical Treatises.* Oxford: 1971.

Pani Ermini, L. "Renovatio murorum: tra programma urbanistico e restauro conservative: Roma e il ducato romano." *Settimane del CISAM* 39, p. 485-530. Spoleto: 1992.

Pani Ermini, L. "Città fortificate e fortificazione delle città fra V e VI secolo." *Rivista di Studi Liguri* 59–60. p. 193–206. Genua: 1993–94.

Quercioli, M. *Le mura e le porte di Roma.* 2nd ed. Rome: 1993.

Rebuffat, R. "Les fortifications urbaines du monde romain," in Leriche and Tréziny (eds.), *La fortification dans l'histoire du monde grec*, p. 345–61. Paris: 1986.

Richardson, L. *A New Topographical Dictionary of Ancient Rome.* Baltimore: 1992.

Rizzo, S. "Le Mura Aureliane da Porta Pinciana a Porta Salaria." *Bulletino della Commissione Archeologica Communale di Roma* 95, p. 113–115. Rome: 1993.

Rizzo, S. "Le Mura Aureliane tra via valenziani e corso d'Italia." *Bulletino della Commissione Archeologica Communale di Roma* 95, p. 115–16. Rome: 1993.

Romeo, P. "Il restauro delle Mura Aureliane di Roma." *Bulletino della Commissione Archeologica Communale di Roma* 80, p. 151–81. Rome: 1965–67.

Scarpa, P. "Porta Asinaria." *Capitolium* 28, p. 87–92. 1953.

Sommella, P. "Le mura di Aureliano a roma (osservazioni generali)," in Rodriguez Colmenero and Rodá de Llanza (eds.), *Murallas de Ciudades en el Occidente del Impero Romano: Lucus Augusti como Paradigma*, p. 49–57. Lugo: 2007.

Sommella Beda, G. "Le mura di Aureliano a Roma. Esposizione documentaria organizzata dal Centro internazionale per lo studio delle cerchia urbane (C.I.S.C.U), a cura di Guiseppina Sommella Beda. Lucca: 1972.

Sommella Beda, G. *Roma, le fortificazioni del Trastevere.* Lucca: 1973.

Spagnesi, P. *Castel Sant'Angelo la fortezza di Roma.* Rome: 1995.

Todd, M. *The Walls of Rome.* Totowa, New Jersey: 1978.

Todd, M. "The Aurelianic Wall of Rome and its Analogues," in Hobley and Maloney (eds.), *Roman Urban Defences in the West,* p. 58–67. London: 1983.

Virgili, P. "Porta San Sebastiano." *Bulletino della Commissione Archeologica Communale di Roma* 90, p. 309. Rome: 1985.

Watson, A. *Aurelian and the Third Century.* London and New York: 1999.

PREFACE

FOR help in the studies which are described in this book the writer's first duty is to thank the Commissione Archeologica del Municipio di Roma, which generously gave permission for the work to be done, and followed that permission, in 1929, by the warmest co-operation, at Porta Ostiensis, through Sig. Dott. A. M. Colini. And it is a delight to recall the kindness of those whose land or houses abutted on the Wall and Gates: especially His Britannic Majesty's Embassy in Rome, and Signori Ciniselli (near Portae Appia and Latina) and Mazzaruti (of Porta Ostiensis).

Yet these debts, however thankfully acknowledged, are necessarily dwarfed by the claims of the British School in Rome. For there I received first encouragement to study the Wall, an encouragement supplemented by generous interest and help from the Directorate. The extent of Dr. Ashby's contribution may be gauged by a glance at the illustrations. My fellow-students in all Faculties co-operated in every kind of way, helping with surveys and discussing problems with the frankest and most lavish interest. These debts are acknowledged where they come, but two deserve special mention here. Mr. M. A. Sisson helped me not only in studying the complicated Castra Praetoria, when we were both deeply immersed in work, but in surveying Porta Appia, the toughest problem in Gate-evolution. Secondly, Mr. R. A. Cordingley has read through the whole of the text, and supplied many valuable counsels and suggestions during its preparation.

My financial debt is also large. To the Trustees of the Gilchrist Studentship at the British School in Rome and of the Charles Oldham Fund of Corpus Christi College, Oxford, I owe the possibility of work in 1924-5. My debt to my College continued in 1926-7, when I also became indebted to the Craven Committee of the University of Oxford, as their Fellow for 1925-7, and to the worshipful Company of Goldsmiths, as their Oxford senior Student for 1925. Subsequently, too, the Senate of the Queen's University, Belfast, enabled me to undertake a summer's work in 1927 and a further short season in 1928.

Finally, my thanks are due to the Delegates of the Clarendon Press for publishing this work, and to their officers for their help in its production, especially in the copying of my measured drawings for reproduction.

Belfast, 1930.   I. A. R.

CONTENTS

PART II. THE ARCHITECTURAL EVOLUTION OF
THE WALL

PART III. THE GATES

PART IV. HISTORICAL INTERPRETATION OF
THE REMAINS

LIST OF PLATES

FIGURES IN THE TEXT

GLOSSARY

Ancones: bosses to which ropes may be attached for lifting.

ARCHITRAVE: the moulded surround of doors, arches or windows.

ARCUATE LINTEL: monolithic lintel cut in arch form, with flat top.

BERM, OR BERME: space between wall and ditch.

Bipedalis: Roman brick, two feet square and about three inches thick.

COUNTERFORT: a large buttress.

COURSE OR COURSING: masonry built in continuous rows, each horizontal above the other.

CYMA: a moulding with double curve, or wave, on its projecting face.

EXTRADOS: the top, or outer edge, of a voussoir.

FRAME-DRESSING: the cutting of masonry with rough surface to a uniform plane at its edges.

HIPPED ROOF: a roof without a gable.

IMPOST: the member upon which an arch directly rests.

In litura: cut over an erasure.

INTRADOS: the bottom, inner edge or apex of a voussoir.

JOGGLED: masonry cut to fit vertical or horizontal jointing of unequal height or length.

MACHICOLATION: a projecting parapet, carried on small arches, supported on brackets.

MERLON: raised portion of indented (crenellated or embattled) breastwork or parapet.

NEWEL: the central pier of a spiral or 'dog-leg' staircase.

PUTLOG-HOLES: holes in a wall to carry the horizontal poles of a builder's scaffolding.

SHUTTERING: boarding which holds setting concrete or the sides of a builder's trench.

SKEW-BACK: the first voussoir above the impost of an arch.

Spina: the central pier of twin arches.

SPRINGING, SPRINGER: the first few members, or shoulder, of an arch.

SQUINCH: arch or lintel placed diagonally across a re-entrant angle.

TYMPANUM: the space between a door-head and the arch above it.

VANTAGE-COURT : enclosed court-yard behind main gateway, with secondary gate, —a barbican reversed.

VOUSSOIR: the wedge-shaped block which forms an arch.

LIST OF ABBREVIATIONS

A. J. A. = *American Journal of Archaeology.*

Atti Pont. = *Atti della Pontificia Accademia Romana di Archeologia.*

Audebert = British Museum, Lansdowne MS., 720.

B. C. = *Bulletino della Commissione Archeologica comunale di Roma.*

Boll. Inst. = *Bolletino dell' Instituto Archeologico di Roma.*

Bufalini = *Urbis Icnografia*, 1551.

C. I. L. = *Corpus Inscriptionum Latinarum.*

Corvisieri = *Archivio Romano di Storia Patria*, vol. i ; *Le posterule Tiberine.*

C. U. R. = *Codex Urbis Romae.*

C. Ved. = Bartoli, *Cento Vedute di Roma.*

De Rossi, *Piante* = *Piante icnografiche e prospettiche di Roma.*

Dessau = *Inscriptiones Latinae Selectae.*

Destr. Anc. R. = Lanciani, *The Destruction of Ancient Rome.*

D. U. J. = *Durham University Journal.*

Du Pérac = *Vestigij dell'Antichità di Roma,*

Essai = Homo, Essai sur le règne de l'Empereur Aurélien, in *Annales de l'École française à Rome*, 1888.

F. U. R. = *Forma Urbis Romae*, Rodolfo Lanciani.

Gell = Sir William Gell's engravings, for Nibby, *Mura di Roma*, 1820.

Gilbert = *Topographie der Stadt Rom.*

Jordan = *Topographie der Stadt Rom.*

J. R. S. = *Journal of Roman Studies.*

Maggi = *Icnografia della città di Roma*, 1625 (1744).

Melchiorri = 'Intorno al monumento sepolcrale di Marco Vergilio Eurisace', *Estratti dall'Album*, Anno V, p. 217, Roma, 1838.

Mon. Ant. = *Monumenti di Antichità.*

Nibby, *M. di. R.* = Nibby, A., *Mura di Roma*, 1821.

Nolli = *Nuova pianta di Roma*, 1748.

N. Scav. = *Notizie degli Scavi.*

Pauly-Wissowa = *Real-Encyclopädie des Altertums.*

P. B. S. R. = *Papers of The British School at Rome.*

Procop. *B. G.* = Procopius *de Bello Gothico.*

R. Arch. = Rivoira, *Roman Architecture.*

R. d. A. = *Rivista d'Artiglieria e di Genio.*

R. E. = *Ruins and Excavations of Ancient Rome*, Lanciani.

Ricciardelli = *Vedute delle Porte e Mura di Roma*, 1832.

Richter = *Topographie der Stadt Rom.*

R. Mittheil = *Römische Mittheilungen des Deutschen Archäologischen Instituts in Rom.*

Rossini = *Le porte antiche e moderne del recinto di Roma*, 1829.

R. Ved. = Egger, *Römische Veduten.*

Tempesta = *Urbis Romae Prospectus*, 1593.

T. P. R. = *Town Planning Review.*

Uff. = Collezione Uffizi di Firenze.

Uggeri = *Journées pittoresques*, 1828.

Vasi = *Delle magnificenze di Roma antica e moderna*, vol. i, 1747.

INTRODUCTION

THE AIM OF THIS BOOK AND PREVIOUS STUDIES

THE most recent description in detail of the great defensive Wall which Aurelian began to build round Imperial Rome in 271, appeared in 1821. To an English student it is a pleasure to record that this book[1] was the result of Anglo-Italian co-operation between Sir William Gell and Antonio Nibby: and, despite erroneous historical assumptions, Nibby's text will continue to be an extremely valuable and competent account of the actual remains. Its aim was to describe all the defensive Walls of Rome, as they appeared in the nineteenth century, with all their reconstructions. The present treatise is narrower in scope. It deals solely with the Imperial Wall, first collecting the literary traditions about it, and then examining the architectural evolution of the structure: finally, it attempts to establish contact between these two kinds of data, in the hope of working out a reliable architectural history of the Wall, from its first erection in A. D. 271 until the arrival of Narses in 552.

The method of treatment followed is in no way fresh; but it is new as applied to the City Wall, since the traditional mode of description has been the circular tour. Students always have been incited to walk round the whole circuit of the Wall, as tourists hasten round a picture gallery: and the process, unless often repeated, tended to bewilder rather than to sharpen their analytical faculties. In fact, this method became obsolete the moment analysis of the structure was required. Anatomists do not compare two arms by dissecting the trunk between them; no archaeologist should examine two pieces of contemporary work by dealing with the miles of irrelevant work which may separate them. In order to prepare a classification, of course, many such perambulations were required: but, if phases are classified, the student has only to visit a given spot and he will see for himself the conditions which obtain there. So the curtains, the towers and the Gates are now arranged typologically and not topographically. This book is, therefore, not a guide-book to the Wall, and those who wish to gain a swift impression of the monument in one tour will still be better served by the works of Audebert, Nibby, and Quarenghi.

It also seemed desirable to avoid the treatment which spoils Nibby's description of the actual remains. Into this very valuable account continually intrude unsound equations between historical

[1] Nibby, Gell, *Le Mura di Roma*, 1821.

records and actuality: indeed, historical adjectives often take the place of descriptions of the real structure. The Honorian style, for example, is often mentioned, but never clearly described. Yet actual remains form a special category of evidence, and are the premises upon which deductions about the Wall's history must be based. Any historical interpretation of these remains is a working hypothesis, to be discarded or corroborated by future students. Clearly, it is of vital importance to define the premises as precisely as possible, and to separate them from the deductions which are the next stage. And this belief has imposed the arrangement adopted for the book, by which the account of the development of the whole structure is completely free from any reference to the literary sources, while these sources in turn are discussed in isolation. Then, in a separate chapter, the two sets of data are combined in an interpretation, which attempts to satisfy all the facts known to present inquirers, but which at the same time remains a true working hypothesis, awaiting that verification which time and future inquiry alone can bring.

This consideration of the mutability of human notions should induce a tolerant attitude towards past accounts of the Wall, which were in their time the latest of their kind. But the important bibliography of the Wall, as is well known, is not large. The age of statistical accounts of the Wall lasted from the ninth to the fifteenth century, and its principal contributions to knowledge, the Einsiedeln List [1] and the List of Benedict of Soracte,[2] are somewhat less important, though not less tangled, than has been supposed. The long line of derivative documents is discussed in full below. The perambulation of Poggio and Antonio Lusco, made in 1431, was productive of remarks in Poggio's treatise *De Varietate Fortunae*,[3] which are sometimes valuable, and at other times confusing and confused. And they are surpassed in value by the careful description of Audebert,[4] compiled in 1574–8. This extremely detailed Itinerary eclipses all the other Renaissance accounts [5] of the structure, which are of very doubtful value indeed, and are chiefly concerned with the identification of Republican gate-names. Nothing approaching it in value is produced until the time of Nibby, in 1821. In the meantime, unconsciously useful work had been done by artists

---

[1] Published by Urlichs, *C. U. R.*, p. 78: a facsimile is illustrated by Hülsen, *Atti. Pont.*, Ser. II, vol. 9, Tav. xiii and p. 424; Einsiedeln MSS., 326, fol. 85 r. and v.: 86 r. Originally in the library of Pfäfers, De Rossi, *Inscr. Chr.* ii, 1, p. 9, and perhaps before that there was an archetype at Reichenau, as De. R. conjectures.

[2] *Mon. Germ. Hist.*, vol. v. = *C. U. R.*, p. 176.

[3] *C. U. R.*, pp. 242–3.

[4] Eugène Müntz, *Antiquités de la ville de Rome*, = B. M. Lansdowne MS., 720, fols. 229–73 v. The identification of the *Voyage d' Italie* as Audebert's was made by De Nolhac, *Revue Arch.*, Nov.–Dec., 1887, pp. 315–24.

[5] E. G. Fulvius, Nardini, &c.

in drawing the gates, beginning with Van Heemskerck,[1] in 1534, Dosio,[2] Asselyn,[3] Lyndenbergh[4] and Silvestre,[5] continuing with the artist of the Cadastro,[6] Preisler,[7] Vasi,[8] Cassini[9] and Caucig,[10] and culminating with the great series of engravings by Gell,[11] Rossini,[12] Uggeri[13] and Ricciardelli,[14] and the water-colour studies of Porta Tiburtina by J. Smith[15] and of Porta Maggiore by Marchese Melchiorri.[16] The City photographers also have followed the valuable lead of Parker[17] and of the Gabinetto Fotografico[18] in an inestimable way, and the productions of Chauffourier and Vasari call for special note here. There should also be mentioned the great plans by Bufalini[19] and Nolli,[20] and the very valuable panoramic views of Tempesta,[21] Maggi,[22] and Du Pérac.[23]

A very notable revival of interest in the Wall and Gates took place in the nineteenth century. For some time the work of Nibby remained the standard; indeed, it has not yet been completely superseded. But the study of the great topographer Jordan[24] surpassed both Nibby's work and much other valuable material as well, and must, indeed, form the basis of any critical study of the Wall. His criticism of the Einsiedeln List should, however, be checked with Gilbert's sage remarks[25] on the subject.

---

[1] Egger, *R. Ved.*, Taf. 2 = Hülsen-Egger, *Das Skizzenbuch von Marten van Heemskerck,* vol. i, 1913, pl. 8, Text, p. ix = Egger, *Krit. Verzeichniss,* 1903, p. 29, fig. 7. = Lanciani, *Destr. Anc. R.,* fig. 36.

[2] See Bartoli, *C. Ved.* lxx = Dosio, *Reliquiae* 32 = Uff. 2533.

[3] Jan Asselyn (1610–52); Egger, *R. Ved.,* Taf. 3.

[4] Egger, loc. cit., Taf. 4.

[5] *T. P. R.* 1924, vol. ix. 2, pl. 12, figs. 12, 13.

[6] Archivio dello Stato; Cadastro of Pope Alex. VII (1655–67): artist of these drawings is unknown.

[7] Johann Justin Preisler (1698–1771) = Egger, *R. Ved.,* Taf. 81.

[8] *Delle magnificenze di R. ant. e mod.,* vol. i, 1747.

[9] *Nuova Raccolta delle migliori vedute di Roma,* 1779.

[10] Franz Caucig, (1782–88) = Egger, *R. Ved.,* Taf. 82.

[11] *Le Mura di Roma,* 1821.

[12] *Le porte ant. e mod. del recinto di R.,* 1829.

[13] Uggeri, *Journées pittoresques,* 1828.

[14] Ricciardelli, *Vedute delle Porte e Mura di R.,* 1832.

[15] Victoria and Albert Mus. F. A. 582 = Ashby, *Top. Dict.,* pl. 44.

[16] G. Melchiorri, *Intorno al mon. sep. di M. Vergil Eurisace. Estratti dall'Album,* Anno V, p. 217, Roma 1838.

[17] J. H. Parker, *Historical Photographs,* folios 1 and 2.

[18] No catalogue: but see list of plates and figures here.

[19] L. Bufalini, *Urbis Icnografia,* 1551.

[20] G. Nolli, *Nuova pianta di Roma,* 1748.

[21] Tempesta, *Urbis Romae Prospectus,* 1593.

[22] Maggi, *Icnografia della città di Roma,* 1625 (1744). F. Ehrle, *Le piante maggiori di Roma,* 1915.

[23] Du Pérac, 1557, *Specimen urbis antiquae* ; 1574, *Urbis Romae Sciographia;* see also Du Pérac's *Vestigij di R.,* 1575.

[24] Jordan, *Topographie der Stadt Rom,* 1878–1907.

[25] Gilbert, *Topographie der Stadt Rom,* 1883–90.

The accounts of Becker,[1] Reber,[2] Middleton,[3] and Quarenghi[4] add little to the knowledge collected by Nibby, and the same is true of the more popular and less careful accounts of Burn[5] and Hare.[6] More valuable are the strategical studies of the military engineers Borgatti[7] and Sponzilli.[8] Among isolated treatments of particular detail, two articles by Lanciani, which deal with the Cinta Daziaria[9] and Porta Ostiensis West,[10] and another couple by Hülsen, which deal with the first-century boundary of Rome[11] and with Porta Ardeatina,[12] are of very special value. Lanciani's great Forma Urbis[13] supersedes all older plans of the Wall, with the important reservations that it is not always accurate in orientation and lay-out, especially at the Gates,[14] and that it is not to be trusted in dealing with Gates which have now disappeared. This said, it remains to praise it for its clear distinction between ancient and medieval work. Early in the twentieth century, Homo embodied in his *Essay on the Reign of Aurelian*[15] much of the available material for a study of the Wall: but his work is barely a *catalogue raisonée*, and is all too often inaccurate in detail; it also omits all the Gates, on the false ground that they are not Aurelianic. Mariani's paper,[16] on the Gates restored by the Commissione Archeologica in 1918, is of great value. Lugli's notes[17] on the part of the Wall embodied in the *zona archeologica* are short but useful. Those in search of up-to-date knowledge, fully annotated, will find it in Dr. Ashby's *Topographical Dictionary of Ancient Rome*.[18] Finally, the writer's own contributions to the problem, in short papers,[19] may be noted: they were written while this work was taking shape in his mind, and may be of interest to the student of the development of ideas.

In conclusion, it may be noted that this book is appearing at an opportune time in the history of the Wall, which, after long years of inactivity (due to fear of the enormous expense involved

[1] Becker, *De R. veter. muris et portis.*   [2] Reber, *Ruinen Roms.*
[3] Middleton, *The Remains of Ancient R.,* ii, p. 376.
[4] Quarenghi, *Le mura di Roma,* 1880.
[5] R. Burn, *Rome and the Campagna.*   [6] Hare, *Walks in Rome.*
[7] M. Borgatti, *Castel Sant'Angelo in Roma,* 1889; *Rivista d'Artiglieria e di Genio,* ii, 279; iii, 5; iv, 120 and 269, also, *Le Mura di Roma,* ibid., vol. ii, 1890.
[8] L. Sponzilli, *Rivista d'Artiglieria e di Genio,* vol. v, 1891.   [9] Lanciani, *B. C.* 1892.
[10] Lanciani, *B. C.* xx (1892), p. 92; *Mon. Ant.* i, p. 513.
[11] *R. Mittheil,* 1897, pp. 148–60.
[12] *R. Mittheil,* 1894, pp. 320–27.
[13] *Forma Urbis Romae,* by Rodolfo Lanciani, Milano, 1893–1901.
[14] For these details see the sections on the Gates,
[15] *Essai sur le règne de l'Empereur Aurélien,* Bibliothèque des Écoles françaises d'Athènes et de Rome, Fasc. 89; 1904, Paris.
[16] *B. C.* 1918, pp. 193–217, 'Lavori di sistemazione alle porte di Roma.'
[17] *La Zona Archeologica,* p. 317.
[18] *A Topographical Dictionary of Ancient Rome,* 1929.
[19] *Discovery,* August 1925; pp. 293–5; *B. C.* 1927, pp. 41–67; *P. B. S. R.* x, pp. 12–22.

in their repair) the Senate and People of Rome, through the
Commissione Archeologica, are now preserving. The Wall had
been for a long time in a ruinous state; it had also become a real
hindrance to the traffic of modern Rome. Now there has come
a praiseworthy compromise. The Wall is safe. It is breached,
but not razed, and further decay is satisfactorily arrested. In
many cases the work done has failed to satisfy critics, including
the writer.[1] Yet methods of restoration rarely win whole-hearted
approval, and every one who considers the problem in detail must
be grateful for the much needed repair. Especial thanks, moreover are due from 'ultimi Britanni' and other forestieri, who once
shared the Dominion of the Caesars, and now enjoy their legacy
without having to live on their graves.

[1] The methods used have been harsh; and occasionally the process has wiped away points
of real interest, as at Porta Asinaria, and Posterula Vigna Casali.

PART ONE

GENERAL FEATURES AND ANCIENT DESCRIPTIONS

I. THE WALL IN ITS PRESENT STATE

§1. THE RELATION OF THE WALL TO EARLIER BOUNDARIES AND DEFENCES OF THE CITY, AND ITS PRESENT CHARACTER

THE City Wall which we now see has nothing to do with any of the earlier defences of Rome (fig. 1). As will be shown in a subsequent section, it is of Imperial date. Accordingly, when the present Wall was built, the first known Wall of Rome, assigned by tradition to Servius Tullius, had long been out of use, having been hard to trace (δυσεύρετον) so early as the time of Augustus;[1] while memories of anything still earlier were surviving only in commentaries upon obscure place-names and in poetical traditions of Roma Quadrata. Again, the Imperial circuit is much wider in extent than the Servian, since it was designed to enclose as much as possible of the fourteen Wards (*regiones*) into which Augustus had divided the City (fig. 2). And although it followed the line of no earlier defensive structure, in surrounding so wide an area, it coincided, as De Rossi[2] and Lanciani[3] have shown, in part with a Customs boundary, which had existed as early as the elder Pliny's day, and which was supplied with Gates, or Bars, which went by the name of *Portae*. The Customs boundary itself, which is discussed most fully by Hülsen,[4] may just conceivably have been called *murus*. But its character was certainly totally different from that of a City Wall, as is proved by the erection, during the reign of Commodus, of boundary stones to define its position, 'propter controversias quae inter mercatores et mancipes ortae erant, uti finem demonstrarent vectigali foriculari et ansarii promercalium, secundum veterem legem semel dumtaxat exigundo.'[5] The course of the Customs barrier is not, indeed, known for the whole circuit of the City. But four boundary stones[6] fix points along it

[1] Dion. Hal., *Antiq. R.* iv, 12.   [2] *Archäolog. Zeitung*, 1856, p. 147.
[3] *B. C.* 1892, pp. 87–111. Pliny, *N. H.* iii, 5, 66.
[4] R. *Mittheil,* 1897, pp. 148–60. See my remarks, *B. C.* 1927, p. 45, n. 1. Comparison may be made with the modern concrete customs Wall on the west side of Turin.
[5] 'Because of the quarrels which had arisen between traders and the tax-collectors, that they may show the boundary for the taxes on transit and on goods for sale, which are to be levied strictly once, according to old-established law.'
[6] *C. I. L.* vi. 1016 c = P. Flaminia: ibid., 1016 b = P. Salaria: ibid., 31227 = P. Asinaria: *C. I. L.* vi, 1016 a = P. Esquilina: ibid., 779 and 8594 are not relevant here.

at the Imperial Portae Flaminia, Salaria, and Asinaria, and at a point near the old Servian Porta Esquilina. It may thus be regarded as highly probable that the Imperial Wall took the line of the earlier Customs barrier on the north of the City,

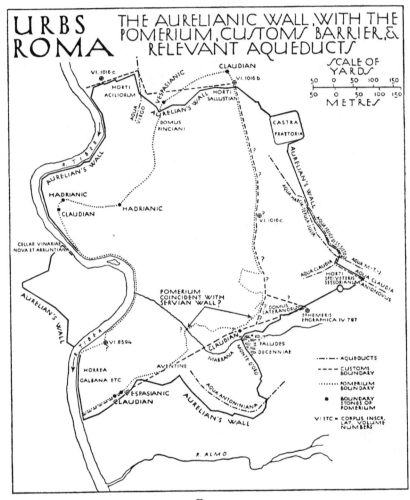

FIG. I

passed beyond it on the east, and regained it at some point[1] between the Servian Wall and Porta Asinaria. Once built, however, the new Wall was itself made to serve as the Customs barrier, and the dues were collected at the City Gates from that time until 1906. Presently, another boundary, of religious purpose, the *Pomerium*, was perhaps made to coincide with the Wall; but while the Customs boundary may have served as a guide to

[1] Perhaps Porta Maggiore, see note 9, p. 206.

those who laid out the Wall, the *Pomerium* can have dictated its course no more than a parish-boundary affects the construction of a defensive work to-day. So it is clear that among the boundaries and defences which the Imperial Wall eliminated, only the Customs barrier had any real influence upon the course which the new Wall took; and this was so, moreover, simply

Fig. 2

because the concern of both was to enclose the most valuable parts of the City. Apart from that, the general course of the Wall was determined mainly by defensive strategy, especially when divergences from the boundaries of Fourteen Wards were made. Strategy placed the Wall at the edge of the Paludes Decenniae, on the east side of Monte d'Oro, and at the northern lip of the Almo valley: as Procopius notes,[1] it governed almost entirely the salient of the Janiculum: it decided the location of Porta Flaminia, and the occupation of the eastern line of aqueducts: it dictated that the Wall should be divided so unequally by the Tiber.

[1] Procop. *B. G.* i. 19.

To-day the Wall still stands for more than two-thirds of its twelve mile circuit. It is yet a mighty Wall, faced with fragments of thin tiles in mortar, and provided with a core of tufa aggregate, bound together by a quick-drying cement of lime and pozzolana sand. It is twelve feet thick; in many places it is sixty feet high; and from it rectangular towers project for eleven feet at an average interval of one hundred feet. It was not everywhere of uniform construction, and types are dealt with below.[1] But the

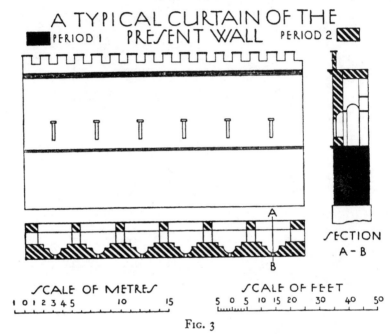

A TYPICAL CURTAIN OF THE PRESENT WALL
PERIOD 1   PERIOD 2

SECTION A - B

SCALE OF METRES
1 0 1 2 3 4 5   10   15

SCALE OF FEET
5 0 5 10 15 20   30   40   50

Fig. 3

general form is as follows (fig. 3). For twenty feet upwards from the footings it is solid. Above this point comes a gallery, or covered rampart-walk, lit by an open arcade at the back and protected in front by a thick wall, pierced with a varying numbei of loop-holes. On top of the gallery runs an open rampart-walk now robbed everywhere of its original parapet and merlons. The gallery and rampart-walk were connected with each other by stairs at each tower and were reached from the ground by stair-cases at the Gates. As has been seen, the Wall ran round the City for twelve miles in all: but the section on the west bank, in Trastevere, was quite short, and in order to link it with the main system, on the east bank, long and low River-Walls were con-structed. The River-Walls (see fig. 2) enclosed all the City bridges across the Tiber except the Pons Aelius, where, at an uncertain date, a special bridge-head fortress (see fig. 6) was

[1] *Vide* Part II, cap. 1.

built round the Mausoleum of Hadrian on the west bank in order to complete the defensive system.

Nine principal Gates are still to be seen of the original eighteen, and all but three took their names from the main roads they protected. They are variously built, but two types of tower (see figs. 17, 20) at present survive, one semicircular and tile-faced, the other quadrangular and stone-faced. There also remain four very similar postern-gates and two wickets, the former being neat structures (see Pl. XXII*a*) of a common Roman type, with travertine imposts and lintel, surmounted by one or more relieving-arches of *bipedales*. Even to-day the Imperial Wall and Gates are among the most memorable sights of Rome, and Hülsen acutely observes that no monument in the City impresses the visitor more deeply with Rome's ancient majesty and power than the Wall and Porta Appia, seen from the descent of *Domine quo vadis*.

The uniformity of the structure, however, is often broken, for consideration of both speed and economy prompted the builders of the Wall to incorporate therein any suitable building which lay in its course, either by modifying the older structure so that it might form part of the Wall's face, or by enclosing it completely as part of the Wall's core. In 1431 Poggio Bracciolini[1] was able to see more buildings treated thus than can be seen now. But many still exist, and Homo[2] has calculated that they take up one-sixth of the whole perimeter. This estimate, however, is too large, and the real proportion (see p. 64) is probably much nearer one-tenth. The structures themselves are very diverse in nature, and range from tombs, houses, park-walls, and aqueducts, to cisterns, porticoes, an amphitheatre, and a fortress: and it will be seen that their relation to the Wall is of real importance for dating its erection.

Most of the tombs (see Pl. II*a*) embodied in the Wall were already old when it was built. Some of them happened to lie by the side of one or other of the great main roads, where the Wall-builders intended to erect Gates. Accordingly, they were made to form part of the concrete core of the new gate-bastions, and all parts which projected from the finished structure were ruthlessly trimmed away.[3] This was the fate which befell the

---

[1] Poggio, *De Var. Fortunae* = Urlichs, *C. U. R.*, p. 243.   [2] *Essai*, p. 262.

[3] Not a little pietistic verbiage has been devoted to the treatment of these tombs, and the fact that the actual chamber often was not desecrated by the incorporation in the Wall has been assigned to religious scruples, even though there is an important exception at Porta Nomentana (cf. p. 94). But it should be observed: (*a*) that an intact building makes a good core for a concrete wall and saves time and material: and that (*b*) the builders of the Wall never hesitated to destroy parts of incorporated tombs which did not suit their purposes, e.g. the tomb of Eurysaces lost its front, that of the Platorini its back: (*c*) a folk who did not hesitate to use old tombstones for doorsteps, drain-covers, or latrine-seats, obviously had their religious scruples in excellent control.

late-Republican tomb of Vergilius Eurysaces,[1] in the central
tower of Porta Praenestina; so perished the tomb of Quintus
Haterius,[2] at the south tower of Porta Nomentana; while, at
Porta Salaria,[3] the monument of Cornelia Vatiena was built into
the west tower, and two more, those of Sulpicius Maximus and
an unknown personality, were covered by the east tower. In the
same way the Wall swallowed up other tombs. Examples occur
at the third tower[4] west of Porta Flaminia, at the postern (Pl. IIa)
west of Porta Appia,[5] and on the Porta Salaria-Pinciana sector.[6]
But the most notable are the well-known Pyramid of Gaius

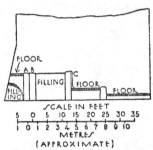

FIG. 4. House in Viale Montebello

Cestius,[7] and, at the back of the Wall in Trastevere, the tomb
of Aulus Platorinus,[8] which lost its rearward facing to make
room for the defensive work.

Houses utilized by the Wall-builders were treated no less
drastically than tombs. Between the Viale Montebello and the
re-entrant in the Wall at the North-west angle of Castra Praetoria, can be detected the remains of a large house,[9] provided
with *opus spicatum* floors and with water-cisterns, of which the
walls had been thickened at least once before the Wall was built
(see fig. 4). Here the low-level vaults were filled with concrete;
the Wall was carried right across the rooms; and then all projecting walls or floors were trimmed off, as at the tombs, on the
same plane as the face of the Wall. Houses visible from the
Vigna Ciniselli,[10] just west of the Porta Latina, were treated in
the same way, but only appear at the back of the Wall. Again,

[1] C. I. L. i, 1014–15 = vi. 1958.
[2] C. I. L. vi, 1426. Possibly the Haterius of Tac. *Ann.* iv. 61, cf. Cardinali, *Memorie Romane*, iii, p. 407.
[3] Henzen, *Boll. Inst.* 1871, 98–115 = C. I. L. vi, 1296, 33976.
[4] Bartoli, iv, pl. 388, fig. 681, 2 = Uff. 286 = Lanciani, *B.C.*, 1891, 140 = Egger, *Kritisches Verzeichnis*, pp. 69–70, fig. 15, p. 46, K. K. Hofbibliothek, Wien = Bartolomeo di Rocchi di Brianza.
[5] See below, p. 232.
[6] Lanciani, *B. C.* 1892, p. 106 = F.U.R. 2, 3.
[7] C. I. L. vi, 1374; see also p. 220 for the question of levels.
[8] *N. Scav.* 1880, pp. 127, 142.
[9] *B. C.* 1892, 66–88.   [10] Not described in any source examined by me.

when the modern Porta S. Lorenzo was cut through the ancient wall, to give passage to the tramway to the Basilica, an intact garden-wall came to light;[1] it was crowned with a lead-covered cornice, and embellished with niches, decorated with Anio incrustation,[2] in the style employed anew at the Renaissance. The niches even still held their statues, packed round with clay by the builders of the Wall. And so the structure, statues and all, was made to form part of the Wall's core. A little further south-wards, the front of a tenement-house[3] has been noted and figured by Gismondi and Calza (see fig. 5), while the Sessorian[4] and Lateran[5] Palaces were deprived of some rooms in the same way as the house of Viale Montebello.

West of the Tiber, the Wall cut across large porticoes[6] at both points where it descended to the river-bank; and at the northern-most point, where the Wall cut right across the *Cellae vinariae nova et Arruntiana*,[7] the builders made an older staircase-well serve as the foundation of a tower. Again, in the angle between the Wall and the east tower of Porta Ostiensis East, there is part of a niched structure (see fig. 19) which seems to have nothing to do with the gateway.[8]

Among park-walls and terraces incorporated in the Wall is the Muro Torto.[9] This formed part of the terrace of Horti Aciliorum, and is now almost completely masked by a retaining-wall; but it was open to view after 1820, as a drawing by Valadier and a photograph by Parker (Pl. II*b*) show.[10] There may also be added the Wall of Horti Sallustiani,[11] just west of Porta Salaria. The Horti Getae, in Trastevere, are not now to be included, since their site is uncertain.[12]

The aqueducts usually were included in the defensive scheme by building the Wall just in front of them, with its back touching their piers (see fig. 11). The object of the Wall-builders was to avoid leaving an aqueduct outside the Wall, where it would

---

[1] Lanciani, *R. E.*, p. 71; Petersen, *B. C.* 1889, p. 17, Tav. 1, 2 for the statues.

[2] A limestone incrustation formed round twigs and stones, and plastered on to walls to give a 'rustic' effect.

[3] *Mon. Ant.* xxiii, pl. v.   [4] *Mon. Ant.* i. 491.

[5] Ph. Lauer, *Le Latran*, p. 7 and fig. 6, p. 18.

[6] *F. U. R.* 39, 20. For Porta Portese, *N. Scav.* 1892, 116.

[7] *N. Scav.* 1880, 128–9: 140–1. This explains a rise in level assigned wrongly to the fourth-century accumulations by Lanciani, *B. C.* 1892, p. 111, contradicting his own paragraph, *N. Scav.* 1880, p. 141, par. 2.

[8] This was covered by the Honorian facing, at the junction with the Wall.

[9] Lanciani, *B. C.*, 1891, p. 138: used as wine-cellars.

[10] Lanciani, *R. E.*, p. 425, fig. 165.

[11] Missed by Homo, *Essai*, p. 242: this might be the wall mentioned by Tac. *Hist.* iii. 82 'ad Sallustianos hortos . . . flexerant. Superstantes maceriis hortorum Vitelliani ad serum usque diem saxis pilisque subeuntes arcebant'.

[12] Homo, *Mél. d'Arch. et d'Hist.*, xix. 1899, connects these gardens with those of Severus mentioned in *Hist. Aug.* Spartian *Vit. Sev.* iv, and assumes them to be near the 'porticoes' of Porta Septimiana. All this is quite uncertain.

provide cover or vantage, rather than to incorporate it as part of
the Wall. But in one short sector (see fig. 40) between the
salient east of Porta Praenestina and the re-entrant to the west
of Porta Labicana, the aqueduct piers are made to form part of
the Wall's face. This seems to imply the existence of merlons on
top of the aqueduct conduit at this point, as shown in prints [1] of
Porta Labicana-Praenestina. But the treatment of the aqueducts

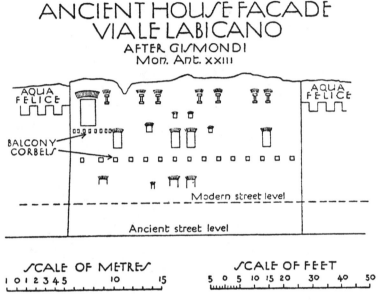

FIG. 5

involves more discussion than would be in place here, and is
described in a later section.

The arcades of *Amphitheatrum Castrense*,[2] which lies just west
of S. Croce in Gerusalemme and belongs to the Severan age,
were closed by the builders of the Wall in the same way as those
of the aqueduct at Porta Labicana and their piers were made to
serve as part of the face of the wall. It should be noted
that this monument once had three stories, as appears on a
sketch by Dosio,[3] and on a measured drawing by Palladio.[4]
Castra Praetoria, the Fortress of the Praetorian Guards, was
included at the north-east extremity of the circuit, but the relation
of this interesting building to the Wall is too complicated to be
summarized satisfactorily here. Before the Wall was built, the

---

[1] See fig. 41, pl. XX.
[2] A building of the Severan age, to judge from the brickwork, as Dr. Van Deman agrees.
Castrense = 'belonging to the Court.'
[3] Bartoli, *C. Ved.*, lxx = Uff. 2533 = *Reliquiae* 32 : see Hülsen, *Ausonia* vii, p. 14.
[4] Lanciani, *R. E.*, p. 386, fig. 146; from the Duke of Devonshire's collection.

a. A TOMB EMBODIED IN THE WALL IN VIGNA CASALI, L 11

b. THE MURO TORTO (Parker)

The Terrace-wall of the Pincian Gardens is in course of construction, A 1

fortress-wall had been much altered, as has been described by the writer elsewhere.[1]

Lastly, there are cisterns. Most of these occur between Portae Latina and Ostiensis East, where the Wall runs on high ground above the Almo Valley, and where deep wells or water rams are now required to supply the fields and vineyards. So far as can be ascertained this district was thinly inhabited in classical times, and was occupied chiefly by gardens and by cemeteries lining the arterial roads. In front of it lay the south-facing slopes of the Almo valley, still, under irrigation, a market gardener's paradise. Until the foundations of the Wall are everywhere uncovered, the number of cisterns which it destroyed here will be uncertain. But at the present time (1927) five of them are visible; they do not appear to have been very large, as such structures go, and resemble small garden-tanks rather than field-cisterns. The builders of the Wall wiped them out, and reduced them to foundation level, since they could not incorporate them usefully in the new structure.

§ 2. THE DATE OF THE WALL AS SHOWN BY INCORPORATED STRUCTURES

The buildings embodied in the Wall are of considerable interest, because the desire to incorporate them indicates that speed was required by the builders of the Wall, as well as economy in material. Yet, for archaeological purposes, perhaps their most important function is to provide a *terminus post quem* for the building of the Wall: and so the evidence from structures which provide the closest *termini* may now be considered. Four separate sections of Wall are involved: the Land Wall; the Transtiberine Wall; the River Wall; and the Mausoleum of Hadrian. Each of these might conceivably have a different date, like the Land and Sea Walls of Constantinople. They may therefore be treated in order.

(a) The Land Wall

In this sector *termini* are provided by the Lateran and Sessorian Palaces. When the south range of the Lateran Palace was cut through by the Wall-builders, the rooms which lay outside the line of the Wall were demolished, and the butt-ends of the palace-walls thus left were made to serve as buttresses. The rooms immediately behind the Wall were excavated in 1777, and produced stamped lead pipes of Ofellius Macrinus and Diadumenianus,[2] and of Iulia Mammaea.[3] Other rooms, below the Orti

---

[1] *P. B. S. R.* x, pp. 12–22.   [2] *C.I.L.* xv. 2, 7505.   [3] Ibid. 7336.

dei Penitenzieri, were excavated in 1742 and produced a pipe [1] stamped by the Imperial Patrimony of two Augusti, perhaps Severus and Caracalla. So it is clear that the rooms cut through by the Wall were used until well into the third century. Indeed, they cannot themselves be much older in date: for their visible walls are faced with bright straw-coloured tile-fragments, and built with closely-packed dark tufa concrete, both characteristic features of the Severan age.[2] Again, these Severan walls have received two additions before they ever became part of the Wall. Evidently, then, the rooms existed independently until well into the century, and so we get a *terminus post quem* for the building of the Wall that cannot be far off A.D. 250.

Very similar evidence has come to light at the Sessorianum —a Palace surrounded by a great park (*Horti Spei Veteris*) and scattered garden-houses (*nymphaea*). After the building of the Wall, which reduced the Park, the Palace was given by Constantine to his mother Helena. But, in an earlier age, it had been beloved and embellished by Elagabalus, and to that epoch may certainly be assigned two long walls, the easternmost continuing the line of the main wall of the Palace now S. Croce in Gerusalemme), which are cut by the City Wall at the first tower east of Amphitheatrum Castrense. They are described by Lanciani,[3] and figured by Hülsen.[4] This gives us once more a late Severan *terminus*. But there is another criterion. A garden-house belonging to the Park was also cut off from the Palace by the Wall; and it follows that the Wall must be of later date than this building. Unfortunately, the building no longer exists: but it is drawn carefully by Sangallo the Younger,[5] and resembles very closely other better-known third-century *nymphaea*.[6] It may therefore be assumed, with reasonable certainty, that this building is not earlier than A.D. 218–222.

The evidence from both the Lateran and the Sessorianum thus suggests that the Land Wall cannot have been built before the middle of the third century. This is, of course, in complete harmony with the literary tradition, that Aurelian first gave Imperial Rome a Wall. Indeed, without excavation it is hardly possible to get much closer.

(b) The Transtiberine Wall

Similar evidence dates the Transtiberine Wall. When the *Cellae vinariae nova et Arruntiana* were discovered to have been

---

[1] *C.I.L.* xv. 2, 7243.

[2] The similarity between this concrete and that of the Sessorian palace is striking.

[3] *Mon. Ant.* i, p. 491.   [4] *R. Mittheil,* 1896, p. 124.

[5] Lanciani, *R. E.,* p. 398 = Uff. 900.

[6] cf. *Minerva Medica*; Rivoira, *R. Arch.*, figs. 222, 221, usually assigned to the Horti Liciniani of A.D. 253 onwards.

cut through by the Wall, some important differences between the parts inside the Wall and those outside it were pointed out by Lanciani.

'È importante di osservare' he wrote,[1] 'che ambedue gli edifici non hanno subìto cambiamenti o restauri nei secoli sucessivi, e che tutte le parti scoperte nel corso degli scavi, spettano alla fabbrica primitiva ed originaria; cioè . . . agli inizi del secondo (secolo) per le celle vinarie nova ed arrunziana.   Dalla qual cosa parmi poter dedurre la conseguenza, che dopo le prime minaccie di incursioni barbariche, la zona estramuranea deve essere stata abbandonata alla rovina, invasa dalle torbide del fiume, e ridotta a coltivazione.   Ben diversa è la condizione degli avanzi, scoperti in quella parte della zona espropriata, che è racchiusa dentro la cerchia di Aureliano, cioè, fra questa ed il Ponte Sisto.   Rare e di niuna importanza sono le vestigie di manufatti della buona epoca scoperte: e questi meschini avanzi servono di sostegno e di fondamento a case private del secolo terzo, ristaurate e rifatte in epoche anche più vicine.   I pavimenti delle strade sono mal commessi ed irregolari, e tutto induce a credere, che questa parte della regione transtiberina, protetta com' era dalle mura, sia stata permanentemente abitata, anche dopo i grandi disastri dei secoli V e VI.'

Datable objects were also found.

'Si scoprirono, quindi, file di dolii, disposte parallelmente ai colonnati del portico (n. 10, 11) del che pùo dedursi che tutta l'area doveva essere ingombrata da questi recipienti, messi forse a quincunce . . . I dolii erano collocati sopra un pavimento di musaico a chiaro-scuro . . . I bolli di mattone son tutti del secolo secondo, predominando quelli delle fornaci imperiali; le monete incominciano da Augusto e finiscono con Massenzio'.[2]

These important discoveries were not applied to proving the date of the Wall, because it was not assumed at the time that any proof was required. They demonstrate that the building of the Wall completely destroyed the double portico of the *Cellae vinariae nova et Arruntiana*, and that by the end of the third century, when the ground inside the Wall had no doubt greatly

---

[1] *N. Scav.* 1880, pp. 127–8. For question of levels, see p. 226.

[2] 'It is important to note that neither building has undergone alteration or restoration during the centuries which followed, and that every part discovered during the course of the excavations belongs to the primary and original building; that is, to the second century, so far as the *Cellae vinariae nova et Arruntiana* are concerned. Hence it may be deduced that after the first menace of barbaric inroads, the land outside the Wall must have been left to ruin, invaded by river-floods, or reduced to cultivation. Very different is the condition of the remains found in that part of the expropriated tract which is enclosed by Aurelian's Circuit, that is between the Wall and Ponte Sisto. Scanty and unimportant are the remains of articles of good period discovered there; and those wretched remains themselves serve as supports and foundations to private houses of the third century, restored and rebuilt in still more recent ages. The street-paving is badly fitted and irregular; and everything induces the belief that this part of the Transtiberine Ward, protected as it was by the Wall, was permanently inhabited, even after the big disasters of the fifth and sixth centuries.' . . 'There were found, then, rows of *dolia*, arranged parallel with the colonnades of the portico, whence it may be deduced that the whole area must have been filled with these containers, perhaps arranged in quincunx-order . . . The *dolia* were set on top of a mosaic-pavement in black and white . . . Tile-stamps are all second-century, and mostly from the Imperial kilns; coins begin with Augustus and finish with Maxentius.'

increased in value, the foundations of the portico on that side of the Wall were buried and covered by private houses.[1] The list of coins from the curtailed buildings left outside the Wall, which runs from Augustus to Maxentius, suggests that some sort of life, not necessarily the kind which had preceded the erection of the Wall, continued there until the time of Maxentius. After that, activity from within them clearly ceased, and in the graceful language already quoted Lanciani has conjectured their fate. It is therefore established that the Transtiberine Wall was built not long before the close of the third century.

(c) The River Wall

Evidence from incorporated buildings is not available for dating closely the River Wall. But, for the sake of continuity, as in the next section, literary sources may be used. The River Wall is fixed as contemporary with the Transtiberine Wall and with the main Land Wall by the following passage in Procopius (B. G. i. 19):

ὅντινα δὲ τρόπον ʿΡωμαῖοι τοῦ ποταμοῦ ἐφ' ἑκάτερα τὸ τῆς πόλεως τεῖχος ἐδείμαντο ἐρῶν ἔρχομαι. πολὺς μὲν ὁ Τίβερις[2] παραρρέων ἐπὶ πλεῖστον τοῦ περιβόλου ἐφέρετο τῇδε. ὁ δὲ χῶρος οὗτος, ἐφ' οὗ ὁ περίβολος κατὰ τὸν ῥοῦν τοῦ ποταμοῦ ἀνέχει, ὕπτιός τε καὶ λίαν εὐέφοδός ἐστι. τούτου δὲ ἀντικρὺ τοῦ χώρου, ἐκτὸς τοῦ Τιβέριδος, λόφον τινὰ μέγαν συμβαίνει εἶναι, ἔνθα δὴ οἱ τῆς πόλεως μύλωνες ἐκ παλαιοῦ πάντες πεποίηνται, ἅτε ὕδατος ἐνταῦθα πολλοῦ διὰ μὲν ὀχετοῦ ἀγομένου ἐς τὴν τοῦ λόφου ὑπερβολήν, ἐς τὸ κάταντες δὲ ξὺν ῥύμῃ μεγάλῃ ἐνθένδε ἰόντος. διὸ δὴ οἱ πάλαι ʿΡωμαῖοι τόν τε λόφον καὶ τὴν κατ' αὐτὸν τοῦ ποταμοῦ ὄχθην τείχει περιβαλεῖν ἔγνωσαν ὡς μήποτε τοῖς πολεμίοις δυνατὰ εἴη τούς τε μύλωνας διαφθεῖραι καὶ τὸν ποταμὸν διάβασιν εὐπετῶς τῷ τῆς πόλεως περιβόλῳ ἐπιβουλεύειν. ζεύξαντες οὖν ταύτῃ τὸν ποταμὸν γεφύρᾳ ξυνάπτειν τε τὸ τεῖχος ἔδοξαν, καὶ οἰκίας συχνὰς ἐν χωρίῳ τῷ ἀντιπέρας δειμάμενοι μέσον τῆς πόλεως τὸ τοῦ Τιβέριδος πεποίηνται ῥεῦμα. ταῦτα μὲν ὧδέ πη ἔσχεν.[3]

So it emerges that the River Wall seemed to Procopius, who

---

[1] Procop. B. G. 1. 19, seems to refer to this building-development: καὶ οἰκίας συχνὰς ἐν χωρίῳ τῷ ἀντιπέρας δειμάμενοι: see passage quoted seventeen lines below.

[2] πάλαι for πολύς is adopted by Comparetti on the strength of the W and V combination of MSS., of which V (Cod. Vat. Grec. 1690) is the archetype. This seems unlikely, for it introduces a time-element which gives no sense here.

[3] 'I now proceed to tell how the Romans built the City Wall on each side of the river. The Tiber flows strong here, and runs past most of the Wall. But this place, where the Wall stops at the river-bed, is a gentle slope and too much open to attack. Opposite thereto, across the river, chances to be a great hill, where the City corn-mills have all been erected from old time, since much water is conducted thither in an aqueduct to the summit of the hill, and flows thence downhill with great force. So the Romans of long ago determined to surround both the hill and the river-bed opposite thereto with a Wall, so that enemies might never be able to destroy the corn-mills or to plan an attack on the Wall by crossing the river. Thus, they bridged the river here and joined the Wall up to the bridge; and building closely packed houses in the district across the river, they made the Tiber flow through the midst of the City. That was how things were.'

was thoroughly acquainted with the whole system, to be part of the same scheme as the Transtiberine defence. On tactical grounds this may be regarded as certain. The Tiber is not difficult to cross, except when running high in spring and winter, and it would have been against the usual Roman custom, and, indeed, ridiculously foolish, to leave the whole river-front open to enemy attack. But the description of Procopius [1] raises a further point of date. It states that Witiges, ἐπεὶ ταύτῃ οἱ πάλαι Ῥωμαῖοι θαρσοῦντες τοῦ ὕδατος τῷ ὀχυρώματι τὸ τεῖχος ἀπημελημένως ἐδείμαντο, βραχύ τε αὐτὸ καὶ πύργων ἔρημον παντάπασι ποιησάμενοι, ῥᾷον ἐνθένδε ἤλπιζε τὴν πόλιν αἱρήσειν.

As it stands, the text means that the Wall was here 'low and quite devoid of towers'. Yet sixteen towers are assigned to the sector between Portae Sci Petri in Hadrianio and Flaminia by the statistical account of the Wall embodied in the Einsiedeln List [2] not later than the ninth century. Since, then, the date of the statistical account is uncertain, a divergence between it and Procopius is of importance for determining the date required. Jordan, unable to make up his mind, suggested [3] either that the statistical account is late, and that the towers were added after the Gothic wars; or that it is early, and that the towers had vanished before the time of Procopius. Both these suggestions are unlikely. There was no special effort to protect [4] the river-front after the Gothic Wars, when Rome had become impoverished; and how could earlier towers have vanished by the time of Procopius (A.D. 536)? In the end, Jordan doubted the authenticity of the Procopian text, but suggested no emendation. It looks, however, as if there ought to be some basis of reconciliation between the two sources. And the following suggestion may be advanced, although any conclusion reached can form no basis for further argument. The sixteen towers mentioned in the Einsiedeln List were either spaced abnormally wide, or set at the normal interval, so that one piece of Wall was left without towers. So, can Procopius have written "βραχύ τε αὐτοῦ [MSS. αὐτὸ] καὶ πύργων ἔρημον παντάπασι ποιησάμενοι"; that is, 'they made a short stretch of it even quite devoid of towers'? The subsequent attempt to make the sentries blind-drunk with one skinful of wine (which could not be carried out wholesale) is thus confined to one spot, which, by coincidence, had few sentries. So, at least, the sense required emerges.

But, whatever the aspect of this part of the Wall, the date

---

[1] Procop. *B. G.* ii. 9. 'Since the Romans of old, trusting to the Tiber-channel, had built the Wall carelessly, making it low and quite devoid of towers, Witiges hoped to capture the City easily from this point.'

[2] Urlichs, *C. U. R.*, p. 78.   [3] Jordan, i¹, p. 381.

[4] This was, of course, quite a different proposition from Totila's little fortress at the Mausoleum of Hadrian, discussed below, p. 22.

seems certain. True, Procopius only specifies the builders as οἱ πάλαι 'Ρωμαῖοι; but he connects the River Wall with the fortification of the Janiculum, that is, the Transtiberine sector; and that sector, as noted above, is proved by the discoveries of 1880 to be third-century work. The exact course of this River Wall has not been discovered. It did not come to light when a quay[1] for unloading marble was discovered on the east bank of the river above Pons Aelius, and some topographers have therefore assumed that it was laid out irregularly. But the Roman river-embankment at this point, including the topmost walk, had three tiers;[2] and the quay was attached to the lowest tier, while the Wall must have been built on the highest. This would explain why the Wall was not discovered, and there is no need to assume that the course of the Wall was irregular.

(d) Hadrian's Mausoleum

Evidence of the kind used to date the main Land Wall and the Transtiberine Wall is once again lacking. But the Fortress of Hadrian's Mausoleum especially deserves consideration here, because it is closely connected with the arrangements for river-defence. Warning must also be given. A stock tradition has grown up about its date and form, which demands the closest examination.

The relevant passage is written by Procopius:

Ἐν τούτῳ δὲ Γότθων προσβολὴ ἑτέρα ἐς πύλην Αὐρηλίαν ἐγίνετο τρόπῳ τοιῷδε. Ἀδριανοῦ τοῦ 'Ρωμαίων αὐτοκράτορος τάφος ἔξω πύλης Αὐρηλίας ἐστίν, ἀπέχων τοῦ περιβόλου ὅσον λίθου βολήν, θέαμα λόγου πολλοῦ ἄξιον. πεποίηται γὰρ ἐκ λίθου Παρίου καὶ οἱ λίθοι ἐπ᾿ ἀλλήλοις μεμύκασιν, οὐδὲν ἄλλο ἐντὸς ἔχοντες. πλευραί τε αὐτοῦ τέσσαρές εἰσιν ἴσαι ἀλλήλαις εὖρος μὲν σχεδόν τι ἐς λίθου βολὴν ἑκάστη ἔχουσα, μῆκος δὲ ὑπὲρ τὸ τῆς πόλεως τεῖχος. ἀγάλματά τε ἄνω ἐκ λίθου εἰσὶ τοῦ αὐτοῦ ἀνδρῶν τε καὶ ἵππων θαυμάσια οἷα τοῦτον δὴ τὸν τάφον. οἱ παλαιοὶ ἄνθρωποι (ἐδόκει γὰρ τῇ πόλει ἐπιτείχισμα εἶναι) τειχίσμασι δύο ἐς αὐτὸν ἀπὸ τοῦ περιβόλου διήκουσι περιβάλλουσι καὶ μέρος εἶναι τοῦ τείχους πεποίηνται. ἔοικε γοῦν πύργῳ ὑψηλῷ πύλης τῆς ἐκείνῃ προβεβλημένῳ. ἦν μὲν οὖν τὸ ἐνταῦθα ὀχύρωμα ἱκανώτατον.[3]

---

[1] Marble quay, B. C. 1891, pp. 45–60.   [2] F. U. R. 14.

[3] Procop., B. G. i. 22. 'Meanwhile there came a second Gothic attack against Porta Aurelia in this wise. The tomb of Hadrian, Emperor of the Romans, lies outside Porta Aurelia, a stone's-throw from the Wall. It is a notable sight, made of Parian marble, in solid blocks fitted together without cramps; it has four equal sides, almost a stone's-throw long, and is higher than the City Wall; and on top are wonderful statues of men and horses, also of Parian marble. So the Romans of old made this tomb part of the Wall (for it seemed like a forework for the City), enclosing it with two walls reaching towards it from the City Wall. Indeed, it was like a lofty fore-tower of the Gate there, for the river-channel there was most suited to the purpose.'

THE FORTRESS OF HADRIAN'S MAUSOLEUM

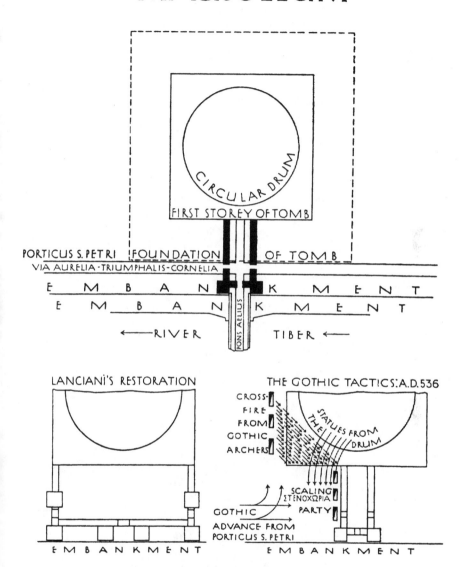

FIRST STOREY OF TOMB

CIRCULAR DRUM

PORTICUS S. PETRI   FOUNDATION   OF TOMB

VIA AURELIA · TRIUMPHALIS · CORNELIA

E   M   B   A   N   K   M   E   N   T

E   M   B   A   N   K   M   E   N   T

PONS AELIUS

←— RIVER   TIBER ←—

LANCIANI'S RESTORATION

THE GOTHIC TACTICS: A.D. 536

CROSS-
FIRE
FROM
GOTHIC
ARCHERS

STATUES FROM THE DRUM

SCALING
ΣΤΕΝΟΧΩΡΙΑ
PARTY

GOTHIC
ADVANCE FROM
PORTICUS S. PETRI

EMBANKMENT   EMBANKMENT

SCALE IN
FEET

5 0 5 10 15 20   30   40   50

1 0 1 2 3 4 5   10   15

METRES

FIG. 6

Then came a surprise attack by the Goths, directed from the Porticus Sancti Petri. . . . καὶ ἔλαθόν τε τοὺς ἐναντίους ἀγχοτάτω αὐτῶν ἥκοντες. ὑπὸ γὰρ τῇ στοᾷ κρυπτόμενοι ἦλθον, ἣ ἐς τὸν Πέτρου τοῦ ἀποστόλου νεὼν διήκει. ὅθεν δὴ φανέντες ἐξαπιναίως ἔργον εἴχοντο, ὡς μήτε τῇ καλουμένῃ βαλίστρᾳ χρῆσθαι τοὺς φύλακας οἵους τε εἶναι (οὐ γὰρ πέμπουσιν ὅτι μὴ ἐξ ἐναντίας αἱ μηχαναὶ αὗται τὰ βέλη) οὐ μὴν οὐδὲ τοῖς τοξεύμασιν τοὺς ἐπιόντας ἀμύνεσθαι, τοῦ πράγματος σφίσι διὰ τοὺς θυρεοὺς ἀντιστατοῦντος. ἐπεὶ δὲ καρτερῶς τε οἱ Γότθοι ἐνέκειντο, βάλλοντες συχνὰ ἐς τὰς ἐπάλξεις, καὶ τὰς κλίμακας ἤδη προσθήσειν τῷ τειχίσματι ἔμελλον, κυκλώσαντες σχεδόν τι τοὺς ἐκ . . . ῦ τάφου ἀμυνομένους, ἀεὶ γὰρ αὐτοῖς, εἰ χωρήσειαν, κατὰ νώτου ἐκ τῶν πλαγίων ἐγίνοντο, χρόνον μέν τινα ὀλίγον ἔκπληξις τοῖς Ῥωμαίοις . γένετο . . . μετὰ δὲ . . . τῶν ἀγαλμάτων τὰ πλεῖστα, μεγάλα λίαν ὄντα, διέ . . ον, αἴροντές τε λίθους περιπληθεῖς ἐνθένδε χερσὶν ἀμφοτέραις κατὰ κορυφ . . . ἐπὶ τοὺς πολεμίους ἐρρίπτουν, οἱ δὲ βαλλόμενοι ἐνεδίδοσαν.[1]

Certain textual points in the first passage may be mentioned. The sentence describing the new fortification is confused. The accepted reading is based upon the interdependent manuscripts from the Vatican (W, v, V) and a related manuscript of excerpts;[2] all other texts give an alternative reading, as follows: τοῦτον δὴ τὸν τάφον οἱ παλαιοὶ ἄνθρωποι, ἐδόκει γὰρ τῇ πόλει, ἐπιτειχίσμασι δύο ἐς αὐτὴν ἐπὶ τοῦ περιβόλου διήκουσι μέρος εἶναι τοῦ τείχους πεποίηνται. Now, while one part of the Vatican reading (. . . ἐπιτείχισμα εἶναι) τειχίσμασι is likely to be right, the other, περιβάλλουσι, followed by πεποίηνται, makes nonsense. Again, as between ἐς αὐτὴν ἐπί and ἐς αὐτὸν ἀπό the heterodox is more accurate, for it does not imply real connexion between the fortress and περίβολος across the river, but speaks only of walls running 'to the City, in the direction of the City Wall'. These discrepancies, however, do not affect the interpretation of the text so far as the locality of the walls is concerned. Either reading assigns to them the same position, between the front of the Tomb and the river. Finally, it must be noted that the fortress was enlarged by Totila,[3] τειχίσματι βραχεῖ ὀλίγην τινὰ τῆς πόλεως μοῖραν ἀμφὶ τοῦ Ἀδριανοῦ περιβαλὼν τάφον, καὶ αὐτὸ τῷ προτέρῳ

[1] 'The Goths came unseen as close as possible to their opponents. For they were hidden by the portico which stretches to the fane of Peter the Apostle. Thence they appeared unexpectedly and got to work, so that the guards were unable to use the *ballista* (for these machines do not fire missiles except directly in front of them), nor were they able to ward off the assailants with arrows, for circumstances were against them, because of the stout shields. Then the Goths applied themselves stoutly, raining missiles on the battlements, and were on the point of applying scaling ladders to the walls, for they had already all but surrounded the defenders of the tomb, who always got hit in the back if they came forward. For a short time the Romans lost their senses .. But afterwards ... they broke most of the statues, and, seizing the abundant stones, threw them off the top of the tomb on to the Goths, who gave in when hit.'

[2] Plut. ix. 32.

[3] Procop. *B. G.* iv, 33. 'Surrounding a small district of the City round the tomb of Hadrian with a short wall, and joining the latter to the previously existing wall, he erected a sort of castle.'

τείχει ἐνάψας φρουρίου κατεστήσατο σχῆμα. Accordingly, it may be this enlargement, rather than the original fortress, which is described in the Einsiedeln List. The whole fortification is there called the Hadrianium,[1] and is given *Turres VI, propugnacula CLXIII, fenestrae maiores forinsecus XIII, minores XVIII.*[2] This description has usually been applied to the original fortress, as by Lanciani. In fact, its date may well be later than Totila.

We may now return to the scheme of fortification described by Procopius. This is clear enough (fig. 6). The building[3] to be adapted rested upon a mighty vaulted foundation of concrete, which extended as far as the embankment wall of the river, and far beyond the building on other sides.[4] Its lowest story was square in plan and thirty feet high; and it was faced with Parian marble blocks, framed by a moulded base, pilasters at the angles, and a *bucrania* frieze at the top. The second story was a circular drum, rising above the square; it was at least forty feet high, and was surrounded at the top with large free-standing statues of stone. With the crowning features above this point the present inquiry is not concerned.

The square lower story was therefore fitted with merlons, and connected with the river bank by new embattled walls. The height of the new walls did not equal that of the lower story,[5] and so may be estimated at about twenty feet. They must have been pierced by at least two gates, as in medieval times,[6] one at the north end of Pons Aelius, to protect the Fortress from an attack by the river, and the other in the western τείχισμα, to give access to St. Peter's. The approximate position of the τειχίσματα can be recovered from the description of the Gothic attempt to capture the Fortress. This was carefully planned and almost succeeded. The Goths first decoyed the Commandant and part of the garrison away,[7] and then, approaching the Fortress from the west, stole along under cover of the Portico of St. Peter, armed with ladders and a large supply of arrows. When they had almost reached the Mausoleum unseen, they rushed forward, and got to work in such a way that the Roman *ballistae* could not be used, probably because the Goths were now within their sharpest angle of fire,[8] and therefore safe. The

---

[1] Urlichs, *C. U. R.* 78. See also Appendix I.

[2] For a discussion of these terms, see p. 47.

[3] Cf. S. R. Pierce, *J. R. S.* xv (1925), pls. xiii–xviii, pp. 75–103: M. Borgatti, *Castel Sant' Angelo in Roma*, 1889.

[4] These are no doubt the structures described by Theodore di Niem, discovered during the siege of 1378. T. di N., *de Schism.* i. 14, cited by Borgatti, loc. cit., p. 71.

[5] Procopius, *B. G.* i, 22, quoted above.

[6] See the views given by Hermanin, *Die Stadt Rom in XV. und XVI. Jahrhundert*, pl. XXXIX.

[7] Constantine had no doubt been decoyed towards Porta Flaminia, his other command.

[8] οὐ γὰρ πέμπουσιν ὅτι μὴ ἐξ ἐναντίας αἱ μηχαναὶ αὗται τὰ βέλη. See my discussion of the strategical significance of this statement in *D. U. J.*, xxv, pp. 399–405.

Goths were thus able to stand close to the Tomb, protected by their great shields against ordinary missiles, and thence they kept up a denuding arrow fire against the breastwork of the lower story, while some of them applied ladders to the western τείχισμα, which was the lowest obstacle before them. Procopius then records the important fact that the Gothic fire almost surrounded the defenders on the tomb, always hitting them *in the back* if they came forward. This is possible only if the τείχισμα was situated not at the south-east angle of the tomb, but a good deal farther east, near the head of Pons Aelius. And the point is demonstrated by the accompanying diagram (fig. 6), which shows not only that the Gothic attack was planned with great care, but that it was bound to fail. The garrison was saved by the final resource of throwing down the statues decorating the drum. For they then got up high enough to escape the murderous Gothic cross-fire, which enfiladed the south-west angle of the lowest story, and they had also found missiles large enough to crash through the great Gothic shields. This very fact once again proves that the Goths must have been standing well in beyond the corner of the Tomb; otherwise no heavy missile thrown from the drum could possibly have reached them; it therefore fixes the position of the τειχίσματα as shown. Once it is demonstrable that the τειχίσματα did not run down to the river from the Mausoleum, it is clear they must have formed a narrow bridge-head. No advantage is gained by putting them elsewhere, while the construction of two angles and a river wall is avoided, by placing them at the bridge.

This reconstruction is corroborated by a later passage of Procopius which describes the heroic defence of the fortress in A.D. 549, three years before the building of Totila's Castle: τῶν τε βαρβάρων, says Procopius,[1] ἅτε πλήθους τε μεγάλου καὶ στενοχωρίας ἐν αὐτοῖς οὔσης, πολλοὺς ἔκτειναν. Where was the στενοχωρία, the death-trap of the crowding Goths, if not in the long narrow space between the Tomb, the Tiber, and the fortified bridge-head?

In short, the defences of the Mausoleum in the early sixth century seem to have had much in common with the fifteenth-century fortifications round the Tomb, as shown on the drawings of the Codex Escurialensis (*c.* 1491), published by Hermanin.[2] Whether the Tomb was fitted with towers at the north angles is unknown, but it seems certain that they did not exist at the south angles, since the original decoration of the westernmost of these was undamaged until the restorations of Pope Alexander VI, in

[1] Procop. *B. G.* iii. 36. 'They killed many barbarians, for there were many and the spot was confined.'

[2] Hermanin, *Die Stadt Rom im XV. und XVI. Jahrhundert*, pl. xxxix = Egger, *R. Ved.*, Taf. 8, 9, = Egger, Cod. Esc., fols. 26 b; 30 b = Bartoli, *C. Ved.*, p. 29, fig. 5: cf. Cod. Barb. 4424, fols. 34, 35; 35 = Hülsen, *R. Mittheil.* vi, 1891, p. 145.

1492–95. Whether the medieval curtain wall and bridge-head towers followed earlier lines or embodied earlier structures is uncertain, for the *stemma* of Pope Eugenius IV,[1] noted by Borgatti on the west curtain, proves nothing about their origin. The chance to answer the question [2] was missed in 1892, when the foundations of the whole system of defences were uncovered,[3] and subsequently swept away or lost to sight. One more interesting point is raised by these conclusions. In the fortifications of the Mausoleum, as first described by Procopius, there was clearly no room for the six towers, or the galleried Wall, assigned to the Fortress by the Einsiedeln List. It is impossible to fit eighteen bays of gallery into the low walls running down to the river, and equally hard to fit in six towers when the angles of the fortress are excluded. So it looks as if the Einsiedeln List were describing a later addition to the scheme of fortification, such as Totila built:[4] something, in fact, which was more like a six-towered castle. At all events, no such fortification as the List describes will fit the strategy of the Gothic attack; the presence of towers would have altered the whole situation completely, and would have rendered such an attack impracticable.

These points, however, give no indication of the date when the building was first fortified. All that can be said is that Pons Aelius was the only bridge unenclosed by the Wall, if we except Pons 'Neronianus' just below it, which seems to have disappeared at least as early as the Constantinian age.[5] It is, therefore, hardly credible, from the tactician's point of view, that Pons Aelius was not fortified with the rest of the City, especially since the River Wall here stood well back from the water on the opposite bank, and might thus seem to be inviting attack. The provision of a bridge-head fortification was just as necessary for the defence of the City as the River Wall, and, since the latter is stamped as original by the narrative of Procopius, it might be expected that with it was built the Fortress of the Mausoleum.

Yet a much more definite belief has grown up about the date of this Fortress. Since the Fortress is described in the Einsiedeln List, which (quite uncertainly) Jordan conjectured[6] to be derived from Geometer Ammon's survey of the Wall, it has frequently been stated as fact[7] that the Einsiedeln List is a copy of the document in which Geometer Ammon described the Mausoleum fortress in 403. Again, since the date of the original construction

---

[1] Repairs in 1447, Borgatti, op. cit., p. 80: cf. stemma of Nicholas V of Porta di San Paolo.

[2] The preservation of Hadrian's precinct-gate (*N. Scav.* 1892, p. 422, fig. 8) may suggest that this was preserved in late R. fortifications: how else could it have remained ?

[3] Borsari, *N. Scav.* 1892, pp. 230–33: 412–28.　　　　　[4] Procop. *B. G.* iv, 33.

[5] Richter, p. 68, notes wisely: 'die zerstört worden ist spätestens bei Herstellung der Aurelianischen Mauer mit der sie . . . nicht zu vereinen war.'

[6] Jordan, i[1], pp. 346–7.　　　　　[7] e. g. Lanciani, *Mon. Ant.* i. 448.

of the fortress is uncertain, it has been assumed, on the last hypothesis, that a fortification must have existed by the time of Honorius; and thence the inference has been drawn that the fortress was perhaps built by Honorius. Presently, the element of doubt came to be omitted,[1] and the full statement emerged that Honorius built the Mausoleum-fortress, described by Geometer Ammon in 403. The whole statement, or any part of it, may some day turn out to be the truth, but on present evidence none of it whatever is entitled to reception as fact.

(e) Conclusions

The facts for the whole circuit have now been collected, and some conclusions may be drawn. The evidence from demolished buildings proves beyond doubt that the Wall on both sides of the Tiber was built after the Severan age, but before the close of the third century. The River Wall is connected with this system by Procopius,[2] and only the date of the Mausoleum-fortress remains uncertain. But even for the Mausoleum Procopius again gives a *terminus post quem* not earlier than the building of the River Wall: τὸν τάφον οἱ παλαιοὶ ἄνθρωποι μέρος εἶναι τοῦ τείχους πεποίηνται[3]. It may therefore be regarded as certain that, excepting the Mausoleum-fortress, the whole Wall was built in the same epoch, not before the middle of the third century, and not after its close. This conclusion is in complete harmony with the literary tradition, that Aurelian built the City Wall in A.D. 271–5, and it is of no small value, because it establishes the fact, upon which depends the place in history of the earliest constructional periods of the Wall, that the first-period work is Aurelian's. Otherwise it might be suggested, for example, that all or part of the first-period Wall is to be identified with the pre-Aurelianic customs-barrier.[4] That idea is quashed at once and decisively by this evidence alone, quite apart from other facts which bear on the question. Yet the scanty literary evidence alone would here be insufficient to refute such a theory, and only the union of archaeological and literary evidence makes the equation of Aurelian's work to the first building-period on the Wall irrefragably valid.

[1] Cf. Lanciani, ibid.=Lanciani, *R. E.*, p. 221=Platner, *Anc. Rom.*[2], p. 516. Ashby, Gilbert, and Richter are much more cautious.

[2] Procop. *B. G.* i. 19.

[3] Idem, *B. G.* i. 22, 'The Romans of old made the tomb part of the Wall.'

[4] It is important to establish this in view of the fact that Hülsen suspects a customs-wall (cf. modern Torino), although he is careful to specify that such a wall would have no defensive character. *R. Mittheil.* xii, 1897, p. 156. I agree: but the point to be established here is that this hypothetical customs-wall had nothing whatever to do structurally with that of Aurelian.

II. ANCIENT LITERARY SOURCES

INCLUDING TWO RENAISSANCE STUDIES

IN this chapter the early texts which bear upon the structural evolution of the Wall are collected and considered in detail. The collection, of course, in no way takes the place of a bibliography, for it deals only with the ancient Latin and Greek tradition and with two exceptionally valuable Renaissance descriptions. In the main this ancient literary tradition is neither detailed nor of great intrinsic worth. Much of it is redundant; other parts, which, if more precise, would have given fuller knowledge, will now remain obscure until that knowledge is won. Yet all the passages quoted do mention some definite period of construction or repair, with which may be collated phases in the architectural history of the Wall: and only thus does it become possible to ascribe dates to the evolution of the Wall on a scale that may help the historian. Herein lies the real and unchanging importance of the literary tradition.

§ 1. CLASSICAL LITERATURE

(a) *The Building of the Wall*

The accounts of the first building of the Wall are short, but precise and consistent, although they do not come from sources of great worth. There is, however, no need to doubt their truth, since they fit both the historical and the archaeological evidence. Also, they were written not very long after the first building of the Wall, and are therefore likely to be telling the truth. With this proviso, they may speak for themselves.

(i) 'Vopiscus', *Vita Aureliani*, 21, 9. (Finito proelio Marcomannico) 'His actis, cum videret posse fieri, ut aliquid tale iterum, quale sub Gallieno evenerat, proveniret, adhibito consilio senatus muros Urbis Romae dilatavit. Nec tamen pomerio addidit eo tempore sed postea.'[1]

(ii) Ibid. 39, 2. 'Muros Urbis Romae sic ampliavit ut quinquaginta prope milia murorum eius ambitu teneret.'[2]

---

[1] 'After the Marcommanic War was over, when it seemed possible that something like what had happened under Gallienus might recur, he enlarged the walls of Rome, after consulting the Senate. He did not, however, enlarge the Pomerium then, but later.' For Gallienus, cf. Zosimus, i, 37.

[2] 'He enlarged the Walls of Rome, so that its perimeter should contain approximately fifty thousand (murorum [ΤΕΙΧΕΩΝ] = walls: ΠΗΧΕΩΝ = cubits).' I owe to Mr. W. H. Fisher, Lecturer in Classics, University College of North Wales, Bangor, the valuable suggestion that since 'Vopiscus' was copying a Greek source he read τείχεων where πήχεων originally stood. This gets rid of the awkward *muros—murorum*: and it gives a circuit of some fifteen miles, sufficiently near for an approximation like 50,000 cubits. Anyhow, this

(iii) Chronograph of A.D. 354. Mommsen, p. 648, l. 8. 'Hic muris Urbem cinxit.'[1]

(iv) Zosimus, i. 49 ἐτειχίσθη δὲ τότε ἡ ʿΡώμη πρότερον ἀτείχιστος οὖσα· καὶ λάβων τὴν ἀρχὴν ἐξ Αὐρηλιάνου, συνεπληρώθη βασιλεύοντος Πρόβου τὸ τεῖχος.[2]

From the Latin sources other statements are derived. 'Vopiscus' gives rise to the following:

(v) Aurelius Victor, 35, 7 'Ac ne unquam quae per Gallienum evenerat acciderint, muris Urbem quam validissimis laxiore ambitu circumsaepsit.'[3]

(vi) Paulus Diaconus, *Hist. Misc.* x, Aurelian. 'Muris validioribus et latioribus Urbem saepsit.'[4]

From the Chronograph come

(vii) Orosius, *adv. Pag.* vii. 23, 5 'Urbem Romam muris firmioribus cinxit.'[5]

(viii) Eutropius, ix. 15 'Urbem Romam muris firmioribus cinxit.'

(ix) Eusebius, *Chron.* 'Romam firmioribus muris vallat.'[6]

(x) Cassiodorus, *Chron.* 'Romam firmioribus muris vallat.'

These repetitions do not increase the authority of the first four sources, from which they are taken. They count as copies, made by uncritical writers who were not using other corroborative material. Yet the whole mass of evidence shows that Aurelian surrounded Rome with a Wall which included a wider area than ever before. The size of that area, or the perimeter of the Wall, was once stated by 'Vopiscus'. But the text is now corrupt, and it is thus impossible to ascertain the original reading.

Byzantine sources contain a different tradition, first preserved by John Malalas,[7] whose work was finished about 573.

is much better than Becker's substitution of *pedum* for *passuum*, as the term understood. On the question see Becker, *de Romae vet. muris atque portis*, p. 112; de Rossi, *Piante icnografiche e prospettiche di Roma*, pp. 68–69. For πήχεις in Walls cf. Parvan, *Analele A. R.* xxxvii, p. 447: also, recently, W. H. Fisher in *J.R.S.* xix, p. 134.

[1] 'He surrounded Rome with Walls.'

[2] 'At this time was Rome walled, having had no wall before. And succeeding Aurelian, ... the Wall was completed in the reign of Probus.' The grammar of this sentence is very odd. I suggest that Zosimus was conflating at least two different sentences in his source, but to restore these is beyond our power.

[3] 'And lest what had happened under Gallienus should ever recur, he fenced the City with the strongest possible wall on a bigger circuit.'

[4] 'He fenced the City with stronger and more ample walls.'

[5] 'He encircled Rome with stouter walls.'

[6] 'He fortifies Rome with stouter walls.'

[7] 'Hardly had he begun to reign than he embellished the Walls of Rome, which were dilapidated with age. He himself presided over the work, and compelled the guilds of Rome to work at the task, and when the Walls were finished, in very short time, he made a sacred decree, that henceforward all the City guilds should be styled Aurelianic, receiving the distinction of the Imperial Name in return for their affliction and blows.' Homo, *Essai*, p. 222, note 2, thinks that Malalas's statement has no historical value (although he uses it!). True, the name 'Aureliani' and the story connected therewith may be an invention. But the fact of the employment of *collegia* seems likely enough: see Groag in *Pauly-Wissowa*

(xi) Ioh. Malal. *Chron.* xii, p. 299 (Dindorf.) ἢ μόνον δὲ βασίλευσεν, ἤρξατο τὰ τείχη Ῥώμης κτίζειν γενναῖα. ἦν γὰρ τῷ χρόνῳ φθαρέντα. αὐτὸς δὲ ἐφέστηκε τῷ ἔργῳ καὶ ἠνάγκαζε τὰ συνέργεια Ῥώμης ὑπουργεῖν τῷ κτίσματι, καὶ πληρώσας τὰ τείχη ἐν ὀλίγῳ πάνυ χρόνῳ, ἐποίησε θεία αὐτοῦ κέλευσιν ἵνα ἐξ ἐκείνου τοῦ χρόνου οἱ τῆς πόλεως πάσης ἐργαστηριακοὶ Αὐρηλιανοὶ χρηματίζουσιν. τοῦ βασιλικοῦ ὀνόματος λαβόντες τὴν ἀξίαν ὑπὲρ τιμῆς καὶ κόπων.

(xii) A Coptic translation of this passage by John of Nikiu vouches for the accuracy of the text as we have it. And there must be added,

(xiii) *Chronicon Paschale*, A.D. 632 τούτοις τοῖς ὑπάτοις (Τακίτου καὶ Πλακιδιανοῦ) Αὐρηλιάνου Αὔγουστος ἤρξατο τὰ τείχη Ῥώμης ἀνανεοῦν· ἦν γὰρ τῷ χρόνῳ φθαρέντα.[1] The affinity of these three passages is clear enough.

The use of collegiate labour described by Malalas was something new for Aurelian's day. But it is demanded by the magnitude of the task, and such organization later became the ordinary rule for large Government works, as the Codex Theodosianus proves. Nor was the principle in any way new in the third century, for regular employment of *collegia* in compulsory labour for governmental transport or provision-supplies was a century old and more, especially in Rome. Unfortunately, information about the condition of the *collegia* in the time of Aurelian is not available on any large scale, and it is therefore impossible to confirm the statement. But it is at least known that Aurelian was much interested in collegiate organization, and this was, in fact, the most natural solution of the labour problem, especially since Aurelian could not be expected to spare soldiers for the task. Finally, it may be noted now, and illustrated later, that the use of this kind of labour accounts for some odd departures from normal military design, which occur upon the original Wall, and which soldier-builders would hardly have brought themselves to make. On the whole, then, the story of Malalas may be accepted as true. And the fact that it reads as if the honorary title came on the completion of the work need not invalidate the whole account.

So this group of sources shows that Aurelian began to build the Wall in 271, after the Marcomannic campaign, before he journeyed eastwards to crush Zenobia, and that the work was completed by Probus. The task was entrusted to City *collegia*, presumably to those connected with building. Unfortunately, literature does not state in what year Probus completed the

V., p. 1375. The policy of keeping people and factions out of mischief by a building programme was well known in the Roman world. The coins Cohen vi, Aurelian 216–22, are hardly to be connected with the event, as Groag would suggest.

[1] 'While these were Consuls (Tacitus and Placidianus), Aurelianus Augustus began to renew the Walls of Rome. For they were dilapidated with age.'

building; but even if the work was finished in the first year of his reign, the Wall would have taken five years to build. Indeed, the time required to complete the work may easily have been longer than that,[1] although it is quite clear that the bulk of the work was done during Aurelian's reign.

(b) Maxentius and the Wall

The first Emperor to add a new feature to the Wall was Maxentius. A terse entry in the Chronograph of A.D. 354— *fossatum aperuit, sed non perfecit Maxentius* [2]—tells that he started to dig a ditch, but did not finish it. Apparently, the ditch was dug as an extra defence against Constantine at the close of the career of Maxentius. But the whole policy of Maxentius had always been intimately connected with the City Wall, as Otto Seeck has demonstrated in two cogent passages. The first [3] of these defines the policy. 'Bis zum letzten Augenblick hatte er an dem Plane festgehalten, den Angriff an der Aureliansmauer zerschellen zu lassen: noch während der Feind herannähte, hatte er begonnen sie mit einem Graben zu umziehen, der freilich nie vollendet wurde.' The second [4] illustrates the value of this plan of campaign. 'Dass Maxentius, der sein ganzes Reich dem vordringenden Feinde schutzlos preisgab, durch eine Schlacht die Mauern Roms werde schützen wollen, die sich schon selbst genügend schützen, lag ausser aller Berechnung; und blieb er ruhig stehen, wie er in den Kriegen gegen Severus und Galerius gethan hatte, so musste auch Konstantins Unternehmen zweifellos scheitern.' Any one who considers the reign of Maxentius in the light of these statements will perceive that they are not exaggerated; and it follows that much more than the literary sources mention may have been done to improve the City's defences. Indeed, a good archaeological case can be made for postulating a wholesale restoration at this time.

(c) The Honorian Restoration

Surviving literature assigns a great restoration to Honorius. The records are of two kinds: Claudian's Court-poem, *De sexto*

---

[1] Time-limits for ancient wall-building are difficult to estimate. At Constantinople five miles of low wall were erected in sixty days, *C.I.L.* iii, 734: at Verona five miles in eight months, *C. I. L.* v. 3329: at Syracuse 5½ km. of wall in twenty days by 60,000 workers, Diodor. xiv, 18.

[2] 'Maxentius dug a ditch, but did not finish it.'

[3] 'Until the last moment he stuck to the plan of letting the attack spend itself upon the Wall of Aurelian. Even while the enemy drew near, he had begun to encircle it with a ditch, which, indeed, was never finished.' *Untergang der Antiken Welt*, i, p. 124.

[4] 'That Maxentius, who gave up his whole Kingdom to the advancing enemy without a contest, would do battle for the City Wall, which already sufficed to protect itself, was in nobody's scheme of reckoning. And had he but remained quiet, as in the wars against Severus and Galerius, Constantine's enterprise must have miscarried without a doubt.' Seeck, *loc. cit.*; cf. *Excerpt. Vales. 6, 7.*

consulatu Honorii, and the inscriptions cut on three City gates
which commemorate a thank-offering of statues after the restoration. The verses were prepared [1] for the beginning of the year
404, and therefore recount events not later than the end of 403:

> Addebant pulchrum nova moenia vultum
> Audito perfecta recens rumore Getarum,
> Profecitque opifex decori timor, et vice mira,
> Quam pax intulerat, bello discussa senectus
> Erexit subitas turres cinctosque coegit
> Septem continuo colles iuvenescere muro

So the poem demonstrates that the Wall had been restored
between the time of Alaric's invasion, which happened in 401,[2]
and 403. This agrees completely with the inscriptions, which
were put up by the City-Prefect, Flavius Macrobius Longinianus.
For his predecessor, Albinus, was still in office on the sixth of
December, 402. The case for a restoration between November
401 and December 403 is therefore quite sound, and the three
inscriptions [3] which mention it tell that it involved the Gates, the
Wall, and the Towers.

The inscriptions themselves have not escaped vicissitudes.
One of them (1188), which belonged to Porta Portuensis, was
destroyed with the Gate in 1643 by Urban VIII. The second
(1189), from Porta Labicana, was dismantled and set up afresh
in 1838–9, near the old gate. Only the third (1190) is still in
its original position, on Porta Tiburtina. The actual texts of the
two surviving inscriptions differ slightly [4] from the accepted

---

[1] De VI cons. Hon. 529–34: date 404, Imp. Hon. VI., Aristaeneto Coss.
> 'New walls a beauteous mien did add to her,
> Made lately at the tidings of the Goths.
> Fear worked to swell her glory; wondrous change—
> Old age, which peace had nurtured, rent with war,
> Now built new towers, and by force revived
> The Seven Hills, forthwith begirt with walls.'

[2] Chronology demands 401–2 for the war. For discussion, see *Cambridge Hist. Essays,* xvii, pp. 175–80. But inscriptions and eclipses are decisive, see below, p. 33, n. 2.

[3] *C. I. L.* vi. 1188 (=31257), 1189, 1190. The Senate and People of Rome to the Emperor Caesars, Our Lords, the Unconquered Princes, Arcadius and Honorius, Victorious and Triumphant, Perpetual Augusti; for restoring the Walls, Gates, and Towers of the Eternal City, after clearing away immense debris; at the suggestion of the Right Honourable, Illustrious Count and Master of the Two Commands, Stilicho, in perpetuation of Their Name set up these statues. By the care of Flavius Macrobius Longinianus, Right Honourable, Praefect of the City, devoted to their Divine Majesties.

[4] 1189 (=Dessau 797): l. 2, DDNN : TRIVMFATORIB : AVGG. l. 4.
INLVSTRIS : COM . NOMIN░S, avoiding a flaw in the travertine. l. 6
CVRANTE : D of DNMQ is missing. 1190, Five lines, not six. l. 1. S missing:
l. 2. CAESS : ET : TRIVMFATORIB : l. 3. VRBI AE, ESTIS INMEN,
RVDERIB . E missing: l. 4. add SIMVLACRA C░░STITVIT. l. 5. before
V̄ · C̄ · , add ░ ; this is the end of the phrase *curante Fl. Macrobio Longiniano,* which was removed by rough scabbing, still visible on the stones, which are no late repair, as suggested in *C. I. L.*

versions. The text of the lost inscription, from Porta Portuensis,
depends upon the copies by Smetius and Pighi, of which Pighi's,
now in the Preussische Staatsbibliothek¹ at Berlin, is much the
better. It is a careful pen-and-ink drawing, showing the curtain
and the west tower, both much ruined. The inscription (fig. 37) is
on the gateway-curtain, and its left-hand end is partly covered by
a later thickening of the tower in stone. The text runs as follows:

S P Q R | IMPP. CAESS. D̄D̄Ñ Ñ. INVICTISSIMIS PRINCIPIBVS
ARCADIO ET HONORIO VICTORIBVS AC TRIVMFATORIBVS
SEMPER AVG̅G̅ | OB INSTAVRATOS VRBI AETERNAE MVROS
PORTAS AC TVRRES EGESTIS INMENSIS RVDERIBVS EX
SVGGESTIONE V̄C̄. ET INLVSTRIS | ▨▨▨▨NIS ▨▨ MAGISTRI
VTRIVSQ. MILITIAE ▨▨▨▨▨▨▨▨▨▨ AD PERPETVITA-
TEM NOMINIS ▨▨▨▨▨ SIMVLACRA CONSTITVIT | CVRANTE
▨▨ ▨▨▨▨▨▨▨ ▨▨▨▨▨▨▨▨ ▨ ▨ ▨▨▨▨▨ ▨▨▨▨▨
D̄. Ñ. M̄. Q̄. EORVM.

One error is obvious: at the beginning of the fourth line ▨▨▨▨NIS
should be ▨▨▨▨TIS—the last three letters of (comi)TIS. Otherwise the text resembles that of Porta Tiburtina (1190), except
that the ancient erasures have been made a little differently, with
less attention to the grammar of the long sentence.

Some minor points may be added. Although the letters of the
inscriptions are not strictly cut in litura, some of the blocks upon
which they are cut have been inscribed before. They once
served to describe other structures, whence they had been taken
as building-stones for the Honorian gates. They were there
built up roughly, and then dressed afresh, to a common plane;
but the dressing, as can well be understood, was not always
taken deep enough to hide every trace of the older letters,
especially if these did not lie where the new ones were to come.
With this treatment may be compared that of the marble and
travertine blocks of Porta Appia (see below, p. 129). So it comes
about that scraps of earlier inscriptions can often be traced by
keen eyes on the City Gates of this period. On the south transom
of the central window of Porta Tiburtina is a large M. At Porta
Labicana, just below the Honorian letters, TRIS COM ET MAG
VTRI, are traces of early letters, of which one is a D or an O,
while below STILICHON, on the next block on the right, IBI and
other illegible letters are visible. Perhaps these last formed part
of a funerary sentence 'hoc sibi vivus fecit'. At all events, there
can be little doubt that the blocks came from tombs near by, as

¹ Codex Pighianus=Preussische Staatsbibliothek, Lat. fol. 61, fol. 118. I desire here to
thank the authorities of the Library for permitting me to reproduce the drawing as fig. 37:
also the German Archaeological Institute, which secured a photograph for me.

did those from the tomb of Ofillius, which are built, upside down, into the south wall of the south tower of Porta Tiburtina.[1]

The whole Honorian text, however, is clear, and is to be read as follows in expanded form:

'Senatus Populusque Romanus, Imperatoribus Caesaribus, Dominis Nostris, Invictissimis Principibus Arcadio et Honorio, Victoribus et Triumfatoribus, Semper Augustis, ob instauratos Urbi Aeternae muros, portas, ac turres, egestis inmensis ruderibus, ex suggestione Viri Clarissimi, Inlustris Comitis, et Magistri Utriusque Militiae, Stilichonis, ad perpetuitatem Nominis Eorum, simulacra constituit. Curante Flavio Macrobio Longiniano, Viro Clarissimo, Praefecto Urbi, devoto Numinibus Maiestatibusque Eorum.'

From the text we may pass to its arrangement, which commands attention. As has been seen, the letters are not carved on a special slab of stone, but on the irregularly-coursed travertine blocks of which the curtains are built; and they are set so closely and carved so shallow that the usual vermilion paint must have been used to make them legible from the street below. The composition of the lines on Portae Tiburtina and Portuensis was exactly the same, which supports the probability that a standard draft was provided for the masons. S. P. Q. R., very widely spaced, heads all three inscriptions, while at the two gates mentioned the words fall into three long lines and one short one. At Porta Labicana, however, the arrangement is less happy. The closing words of the dedication, *simulacra constituit*, are arranged in one symmetrical short line. This is followed by the short phrase *curante . . . eorum*, which is given in a separate line, placed quite asymmetrically in relation to the rest of the inscription. An equally bad, if less glaring, arrangement exists at Porta Tiburtina. Here *simulacra constituit* is squeezed into the third long line, without regard to proportion: while the fourth line, once more containing nothing but the *curante* clause, has plenty of space. Finally, at Porta Portuensis, Pighi (fig. 37) shows that the *curante* clause was cut on the very voussoirs of the gateway, completely ruining the effect of the inscription, although there was plenty of room higher up the curtain.

This consistently bad composition, which always affects the last line, strongly suggests that in each inscription the said line was an afterthought, inserted as best might be. Chronological evidence proves this to be true. Dessau[2] has already noted that the inscriptions nowhere mention the Augustus Theodosius, and therefore cannot have been cut long after the second of February 402, when Theodosius was proclaimed Emperor in Constantinople. And the vote of Imperial statues which the inscriptions com-

---

[1] *C. I. L.* vi. 23381, now upside down, as *C. I. L.* omits to state.

[2] Dessau, 797=*C. I. L.* vi. 1189. This settles the date of the war and agrees with the eclipse-evidence (Seeck, *Forschungen* xxiv, p. 182).

memorate must have been made before then, since the Senate would not have honoured two Augusti in this way, to the exclusion of the newly-elevated third. On the other hand, the clause which mentions the City-Prefect Longinianus must be somewhat later: for on the sixth of December 402 his predecessor, Albinus, was still in office.[1] So, while the main part of the inscription evidently was carved not much later than February 402, when tidings of the new Augustus would arrive from Constantinople,[2] the final clause cannot have been added before December of that year. This not only explains the awkward spacing of the inscriptions, but also provides a reason for their odd distribution among the City Gates. An analysis of repairs shows that more Gates than the three which received inscriptions were refurbished at this time. Yet the vote of the statues for the City Gates must have included, if not every Gate, at least all that were repaired. But the inscriptions would be carved on the gates while the scaffolding for their new curtains was in position, and so would be decorating them long before the statues. If, then, the first part of the text of these inscriptions was composed and carved before the accession of Theodosius in February 402, it is clear that very few Gates could have received inscriptions by this time, since the restoration had only begun in November 401, *audito rumore Getarum*. After February the text became out of date and disloyal; it can thus have been carved no more, and the Gates which had not yet received it never would have it. Meanwhile, it may be noted, a new text to suit the altered conditions was not evolved, if for no better reason than that Alaric was advancing fast; *profecitque opifex decori timor*, as Claudian says. Nor were the statues set up. But after the victory of Pollentia, on Easter Sunday (6 April) 402, the Gothic danger was over. Honorius was due to visit Rome in 403, and the new City Prefect, Macrobius Longinianus, found himself in charge of three Gates, on which there existed inscriptions recording an official vote of statues to Arcadius and Honorius, at the suggestion of the all-powerful Stilicho, while no statue was yet in position. So he attended to the matter, supplying the statues, as the text states, and thus fulfilling an out-of-date vow. Naturally, too, he gave statues only to the inscribed Gates, since the addition of any more would have meant an extra statue all round for Theodosius and the alteration of the existing inscriptions. The hypothesis seems at least to explain the distribution of the inscriptions, the contradiction in dates which they contain, and the awkward spacing of

[1] Cod. Theod. vii. 13, 15 is addressed to Albinus and dated 6 Dec. 402. Nor can Longinianus have preceded Albinus, for A's predecessor is known in April 401, from Symmachus, *Ep.* vi. 40; and from Cod. Theod. xv. 2, 9, for 8 Nov. 400.

[2] Couriers would be using the sea or Via Egnatia, owing to Alaric's command of the Aquileia route.

their letters and lines. And we have only to add that after the death of Longinianus,[1] which attended the fall of Stilicho in 408, the names of both those notables were erased from Portae Portuensis and Tiburtina.

A further puzzle is the meaning of the phrase 'egestis inmensis ruderibus'. It is usually assumed [2] that this refers to the removal of rubbish which had been thrown at the foot of the Wall, and had caused a serious rise in level at the Gates and elsewhere. But in fact the change in level at the Gates between A.D. 271 and 401 was very slight, as has been proved by excavation at Portae Ostiensis East and Tiburtina,[3] and by chance discoveries elsewhere.[4] The accumulation of rubbish at the foot of the Wall, however, still remains a possibility. If other explanations are needed, two may be offered here. The operation might have to do with making an open space outside the Wall, by removing buildings which provided cover to an advancing foe. Or again, as happened in Constantinople,[5] the towers of the City Wall may have been let out to private citizens in times of peace for storage and similar purposes, on condition that the tenants kept them in repair, and evacuated them, if needed for military use. If the Wall and Towers of Rome had been virtually in private hands from 312 to 401 there would be much clearing to be done. None of these interpretations, however, can be regarded as certain, and it must be admitted that Time has robbed the phrase of its original significance.

Another event which may have taken place in this period is the survey of the Wall by Ammon the Geometer. The statement of Olympiodorus,[6] preserved by Photius, says that τὸ δὲ τεῖχος τῆς Ῥώμης μετρηθὲν παρὰ Ἄμμωνος τοῦ γεωμέτρου, καθ᾽ ὃν καιρὸν Γότθοι τὴν προτέραν κατ᾽ αὐτῆς ἐπιδρομὴν ἐποίησαντο, εἴκοσι καὶ ἑνὸς μιλίου διάστημα ἔχον ἀπεδείχθη. It is thus uncertain whether the invasion mentioned is one of Alaric's three, or that of Radagaisus; but it seems most likely that the intention was to contrast Alaric's first inroad with his second. The survey is also interesting, because it has been identified with the statistical account of the Wall, appended to the Einsiedeln Itinerary. This identification is examined in detail below: but it may be noted here that the perimeter given by Olympiodorus is wrong, and, even so, it does not occur in the Einsiedeln statistic, which does not give measurements, and which, as de Rossi noted, is quite unlike the work of a surveyor or geometer.

[1] Zosimus, v. 32.   [2] cf. Lanciani, *Destr. of Anc. Rome*, pp. 53–4; *B. C.* 1892, p. 111.
[3] See pp. 112, 176.   [4] See p. 226, n. 2.
[5] Cod. Theod. xv, 1, 51.
[6] Olympiodorus, frag. 43 = Photius, *Myriobiblia*, 80. 'The Wall of Rome, measured by Geometer Ammon at the time when the Goths made their former raid upon Rome, was shown to be twenty-one miles in extent.'

The interpretation of the literary evidence for the Honorian work is thus less easy than has been assumed. But criticism seems to make possible the following conclusions. A restoration of the City Wall, towers and Gates took place between A.D. 401 and 403: and there was a further operation, involving removal of rubbish or ruins, which (however obscure its real nature may be) is not connected with a rise in ground level at the Gates. This restoration was commemorated by inscriptions and by honorary statues on the Gates; but only Gates that were ready before the co-option of Theodosius II were inscribed. Finally, Longinianus, the City Prefect of 403, set up the statues on the inscribed Gates, and added a clause to the inscriptions to say that he had done so. As a result, he has often gained credit for the whole restoration, but the chronology of his career makes this impossible. Some credit must go to Albinus, his predecessor.

(d) An Edict of Theodosius II and Valentinian III

The possibility of further repairs to the Wall is mentioned in a general edict of Theodosius II and Valentinian III, entitled de Pantapōlis ad Urbem,[1] and dated to A.D. 440. The context is as follows:

'Ex illa sane parte totam sollicitudinem omnemque formidinem vestris animis censuimus auferendam, ut huius edicti serie cognoscat universitas, nullum de Romanis civibus, nullum de corporatis, ad militiam esse cogendum, sed tantum ad murorum portarumque custodiam, quoties usus exegerit, illustris Viri Praefecti Urbis dispositionibus ab omnibus obsequendum. Cuius ordinatio etiam in muris turribus et portis, quae sunt labefactata, restituat, ita ut a reparatione murorum vel omnium quae supra dicta sunt, nullus penitus excusetur.'

This passage has been taken to refer to a definite repair of the Wall. But it only indicates in fact that repairs might be pending. Here, however, it must be observed that the need for repairs no doubt came soon, for the Wall must have been badly shaken two years later by the earthquake which damaged badly large buildings [2] all over the City. But the Edict proves nothing about them, since its compilers could not foretell the event.

[1] Novellae Val. III, Tit. v. 'On the recall of General-dealers to the City. In that respect We have determined that all anxiety or fear shall be removed from your minds, that the public shall know from the course of this decree, that no citizen of Rome and no member of a guild is to be compelled to serve as a soldier, but only upon warding the Walls and Gates, as often as custom may demand, everyone obeying the dispositions of the Illustrious City Prefect. Whose order shall restore in respect of the walls, towers, and gates, which are ruined, so that no one whatever shall be excused from the reparation of the walls or of all aforesaid.'

[2] C. I. L. vi. 32086–32090: cf. also Paul. Diac. Hist. Misc. xiv, p. 961 (Migne).

(e) Theoderic's Repairs

The next restoration is assigned by literature to King Theoderic, and is mentioned in two letters of Cassiodorus,[1] written between A.D. 507 and 511.

(a) *Variarum* i. 25. SABINIANO V̄. S̄. THEODERICUS REX. Dudum siquidem propter Romanae moenia civitatis, ubi studium urbis semper impendere infatigabilis ambitus erat, portum Licini deputatis reditibus reparari iussio nostra constituit ut xxv. milia tegularum annua illatione praestaret.'

(b) *Variarum* ii. 33. 'ARTEMIDORO PRAEF. URB. 509–10. atque ideo universa pecunia, quae fuerat fabricis deputata Romanis et nunc Magnitudinis Tuae discussione constitit abiuratum cum nec reddita suo tempore nec docetur expensa resumatur sine aliqua dilatione vobisque ordinantibus iterum Romanis moenibus applicetur.'

(c) The same statement occurs in *Excerpta Valesiana*, 67. 'Et ad restaurationem palatii, seu ad recuperationem moeniae civitatis singulis annis libros ducentas de arca vinaria dari praecepit.'

These statements seem sufficiently precise, but it must be remembered that Cassiodorus and other late writers use *moenia* quite loosely, and not necessarily in the sense of defensive walls.[2] Nevertheless, the City Wall was probably included in the term, for Theoderic's stamped tiles have been found therein. It is, of course, always possible that some of these tiles may have been drawn from old stock or demolished buildings for use in repairs later than Theoderic's day; yet it is hardly likely that not a single one of the known groups found belonged to him. The stamps in question are of three kinds:

(1) *C. I. L.* xv. i. 1664. +REG͞D͞NTHEODE
RICOBONOROME

(2) *C. I. L.* xv. i. 1665 a. +REG͞DNTHEODE
+RICOBONOROME

(3) *C. I. L.* xv. i. 1665 b. +RĒGDИTHEODE
+RICOBOИOROME

---

[1] (a) 'Some time since, if only on account of the walls of the City of Rome, when there was an unwearied desire to spend upon the care of the City, Our decree ordered a repair, deputing the income from Portus Licini, to yield an annual income of twenty-five thousand roof-tiles.'

(b) 'And so all that money, which was deputed to Roman workshops and is now withdrawn by Your Magnitude's revision of accounts, since it was found neither to be rendered at the proper time nor spent, shall be resumed forthwith, and, at your ordaining, shall be applied once more to the walls of Rome.'

(c) 'And he ordered two hundred pounds to be given each year from the Wine Chest, towards the restoration of the Palace or towards the repair of the City Walls (buildings?)'.

[2] This was an old use, too: cf. Servius, ad *Aen.* ii. 254: Florus i. 1, 14: Vitruv. viii. 4, 24: Hülsen, *R. Mittheil.* 1897, p. 149, note 4; also Suetonius, frag. 'moenia publicorum sunt opera, aedificia privatorum'.

They have appeared in the sixth curtain east of Porta Asinaria,[1] and at Porta Flaminia.[2] As has already been noted, they do not occur in large numbers but in groups, so it looks as if the repairs merely consisted of slight refacing where this was needed. There is no reason to suspect that extensive repairs were undertaken or even required. For Gaiseric had met[3] with no resistance in 455; the siege of Ricimer in 472, which lasted[4] five months and involved much suffering, had been a blockade rather than an assault; while Theoderic came[5] to the City in 500 as an overawed visitor.

(f) Belisarius Prepares for the Siege of Witigis

During the nine years between the ruin of Theoderic's King-dom under Queen Amalasuntha (526–35) and the annexation of Italy to the Eastern Empire by Belisarius, the Wall seems to have got into a bad state—a further indication that Theoderic did not devote much attention to it. Belisarius, on taking Rome in December 536, set about immediate repairs, to forestall an at-tempt by Witigis to besiege and recapture the City. He was, in fact, following the policy of Maxentius, though with less support from the City populace than Maxentius at first received. The improvements made are described as follows by Procopius.[6]

αὐτὸς δὲ τοῦ περιβόλου πολλαχῇ διερρυηκότος ἐπιμελεῖτο, ἔπαλξιν δὲ ἑκάστην ἐγγώνιον ἐποίει, οἰκοδομίαν δή τινα ἑτέραν ἐκ πλαγίου τοῦ εὐωνύμου τιθέμενος, ὅπως οἱ ἐνθένδε τοῖς ἐπιοῦσι μαχόμενοι πρὸς τῶν ἐν ἀριστερᾷ σφίσι τειχομαχούντων ἥκιστα βάλλωνται, καὶ τάφρον ἀμφὶ τὸ τεῖχος βαθεῖάν τε καὶ λόγου ἀξίαν πολλοῦ ὤρυσσε.

The plan of the merlon with a traverse evidently resembled a capital letter gamma, its top-stroke lying along the front edge of the Wall, while the down-stroke ran back on the rampart-walk, protecting the defender's left side, and enabling him to dispense with a shield. Merlons of this kind were not new in the sixth century,[7] and they still exist on the Wall between Porta Ostiensis East and the Pyramid of Gaius Cestius, though these examples are not older than medieval times. But traces of similar structures appear in the Viale Labicano, where the front of the merlons has gone, while the traverse wall is to be seen in section; these may easily go back to the time of Belisarius. There is now no trace of the ditch, and no clue to its position is given by

[1] Suppl. Pap. Amer. Acad. R. i. 1905; Pfeiffer, Van Buren, and Armstrong.
[2] C. I. L. xv. 1. 1665 b, 27. [3] Jordanes, H. Got. xlv.
[4] Paul. Diac. Hist. misc. xv. 3, 4. [5] Excerpt. Vales. 65.
[6] B. G. i. 14. 'Belisarius himself looked after the wall, which was ruined in many places. He made each merlon angular, by building an addition to the left side of each, so that those fighting with assailants therefrom (fighting to their right on the wall) might be hit as little as possible. He also dug a deep and noteworthy ditch round the wall.'
[7] Cf. Pompeii: Durm, Baukunst der Römern, p. 439, figs. 494, 495.

subsidences over its filling, that fruitful indication which has been used with such effect on the Wall of Pius in Scotland.[1] Yet Procopius is not to be doubted when he speaks of one or even more than one ditch.[2] There was also a wide berme, which gave room[3] for a good deal of fighting between the Wall and ditch, and kept siege-engines well away from the Wall, so as to be within range of the defensive artillery. This was a late-Roman defensive theory which is discussed in detail below.[4]

Belisarius also took other less permanent measures against attack. For a time, since the danger was coming from the north, Porta Flaminia was shut, and its doors were backed by an infilling of large unmortared stones, ὅπως δὴ αὐτὰς μηδενὶ ἀνακλίνειν δυνατὰ εἴη.[5] The wall-towers received a complement of *ballistae* (Procopius calls them βαλίστραι), described so minutely as to identify them with the powerful Augustan form of machine. On the parapet-walk smaller machines,[6] σφενδόναις δὲ αὐταί εἰσιν ἐμφερεῖς καὶ ὄναγροι ἐπικαλοῦνται were fixed (ἐπήξαντο) to the merlons. These must have been small indeed, and not meant to shoot far, like medieval *trébuchets*. They were no doubt built into the new merlons, which provided a box-like frame for the wood-work of the simple machinery, as almost certainly at Constantinople. Finally, some remarkable contrivances, called 'wolves', were arranged at the Gates. They seem to have been quite temporary constructions, not so complicated as might be supposed, and not to be confused with a portcullis. Also, although they were called λύκοι, they were certainly not ordinary military *lupi*,[7] which were strong hooks, or 'wolves'-claws', for tearing down palisades; this emerges from Procopius' detailed description.[8]

ἐν δὲ ταῖς πύλαις λύκους ἔξω ἐπετίθεντο οὓς δὴ ποιοῦσι τρόπῳ τοιῷδε. δοκοὺς δύο ἱστᾶσιν ἐκ γῆς ἄχρι καὶ ἐς τὰς ἐπάλξεις ἐξικνουμένας, ξύλα τε εἰργασμένα ἐπάλληλα θέμενοι τὰ μὲν ὀρθά, τὰ δὲ ἐγκάρσια ἐναρμόζουσιν, ὡς τῶν ἐνέρσεων τὰ ἐν μέσῳ εἰς ἀλλήλους τρυπήματα φαίνεσθαι. ἑκάστης δὲ ἁρμονίας ἐμβολή τις προὔχει κέντρῳ παχεῖ ἐς τὰ μάλιστα ἐμφερὴς οὖσα.

---

[1] Macdonald, R. *Wall in Scotland*, p. 135.   [2] B. G. iii. 24.   [3] Ibid. i. 29.
[4] See also. D. U. J. xxv., pp. 399–405, where the theory is discussed by the writer in full.
[5] B. G. i. 19. 'So that no one should be able to force them in.'
[6] Ibid. i. 21. 'They are like slings and are called *onagri* (wild asses).'
[7] Equated with *harpago* and *in modo forficis dentatum ferrum*.
[8] 'And at the Gates they placed *lupi* (wolves), which they make thus. They set up two beams, reaching from the ground to the parapet, and place thereon spars, fitted together, some vertical and some horizontal, so that holes between the fitted pieces appear central and adjacent. And at each junction there sticks out a sort of beak, most like a stout ox-goad. The horizontal spars are fixed to the two upright beams, reaching down to half way from the top, while they make the beams to lean, bottom side up, against the gate. Then, when the enemy come near, those on top of the gate push the top of the beams, and the latter, suddenly falling upon the assailants, easily kill those whom they happen to catch with the points of the beaks.'

καὶ τῶν ξύλων τὰ ἐγκάρσια ἐς δοκὸν ἑκατέραν πηξάμενοι, ἄνωθεν ἄχρι ἐς
μοῖραν διήκοντα τὴν ἡμίσειαν, ὑπτίας τὰς δοκοὺς ἐπὶ τῶν πυλῶν ἀνακλίνουσι.
καὶ ἐπειδὰν αὐτῆς ἐγγυτέρω οἱ πόλεμοι ἵκωνται, οἱ δὲ ἄνωθεν ἄκρων δοκῶν
ἁψάμενοι ὠθοῦσιν, αὗται δὲ ἐς τοὺς ἐπιόντας ἐκ τοῦ αἰφνιδίου ἐμπίπτουσι τοῖς
προὔχουσι τῶν ἐμβολῶν ὅσους ἂν λάβοιεν, εὐπετῶς κτείνουσι.

It is clear that the instrument was a large and heavy harrow-
like machine, which leant against the outer face of the gateway,
ready to be pushed over on to the assailants, with a snap like a
wolf's jaw. Hence, no doubt, came its name, λύκος. A reconstruction thereof is simple to make, and it may be mentioned
that hunters of big game now give to a very similar trap the name
'dead-fall'.

These preparations enabled Belisarius to hold the Wall for
more than a year, until Witigis retreated in March 538. It did
not suffer really serious destruction at Gothic hands, although
there is reason to think that its tile facing may have suffered
considerably. The ditch, or ditches, saved it from the stroke of
the ram; and it was too high to invite the use of scaling-ladders.
In the end, therefore, Witigis met the fate of Galerius and Severus,
and the policy of Belisarius was crowned with success. The
repairs which must have followed the siege have been mentioned
already. They seem to be marked by distinctive work in coarse
block-and-brick work (*opus mixtum*).

(g) *The Destruction of the Wall by Totila and Further Repairs by Belisarius*

Seven years later came the siege of Totila. This was attended
by great misery owing to shortage of food, and was ended by
treachery on the seventeenth of December 546, when Porta
Asinaria was opened by Isaurian soldiers from a tower nearby.
In telling this story Procopius [1] describes how the gate was
fastened: τό τε ξύλον πελέκεσιν διαφθείρουσιν, ᾧπερ ἐνέρσει τείχου ἑκατέρου
ἐναρμοσθέντι τὰς πύλας ἐπιζευγνύναι εἰώθεισαν, τά τε σιδήρια ξύμπαντα, οἷς
δὴ τὰς κλεῖς ἀεὶ οἱ φύλακες ἐμβαλλόμενοι ἔκλειόν τε τὰς πύλας καὶ κατὰ τὴν
χρείαν ἀνέῳγον. Evidently the doors had a great wooden bar, which
brought them into line and kept them immovable, and locks
which linked them one to the other, as have the older college-gates
of Oxford or Cambridge. This was a common enough arrangement in the ancient world, and clear traces thereof exist at other
gates than Porta Asinaria.

Totila had already warned the Romans what he intended to do

---

[1] 'They destroy with axes the bar, with which they were wont to fasten the gates together,
fixing it horizontally in each wall, and also all the locks, to which the guards always applied
the keys, opening and shutting the gates at need.' loc. cit. iii. 20.

with their Wall, in a declaration to Deacon Pelagius, reported as follows by Procopius.[1]

λέγω δὲ ὅπως μήτε Σικελιωτῶν τινος ἕνεκα μήτε τῶν Ῥώμης περιβόλων
. . . τοὺς λόγους ποιήσεις. οὐ γὰρ οἷόν τε ἐστὶν . . . τόδε τὸ τεῖχος ἑστάναι. . . .
τούτων δὲ τῶν περιβόλων ἐντὸς καθείρξαντες αὑτοὺς οἱ πολέμιοι ἐς μὲν τὸ
πεδίον καταβαίνοντες παρατάσσεσθαι ἡμῖν οὐδαμῆ ἔγνωσαν, σοφίσμασι δὲ
καὶ παραγωγαῖς ἀεί τε καὶ καθ᾽ ἡμέραν Γότθους ἐκκρούοντες κύριοι τῶν
ἡμετέρων ἐκ τοῦ παραλόγου γεγένηνται. ὅπως τοίνυν καὶ ὕστερον μὴ
ταῦτα πάθοιμεν προνοεῖν ἄξιον. . . . προσθείη δ᾽ ἄν τις ὡς καὶ τὸν Ῥώμης
καθαιρεθῆναι περίβολον μάλιστα πάντων ὑμῖν συνοίσει. οὐδέτεροι γὰρ τὸ
λοιπὸν καθειργμένοι, πάντων τε ἀποκεκλεισμένοι τῶν ἀναγκαίων, πολιορκη-
θήσονται πρὸς τῶν ἐπιόντων, ἀλλὰ κινδυνεύσουσι μὲν τῇ μάχῃ πρὸς ἀλλήλους
ἑκάτεροι, ἆθλον δὲ τῶν νικώντων ὑμεῖς οὐ μετὰ κινδύνων ὑμετέρων γενήσεσθε.

This was naïve advice, backed by iron determination, and Totila kept his word: τοῦ μὲν οὖν περιβόλου ἐν χωρίοις πολλοῖς τοσοῦτον καθεῖλεν ὅσον ἐς τριτημόριον τοῦ παντὸς μάλιστα.[2] What was the extent of this damage? If the passage means that Totila tore down completely one-third of the whole circuit of the Wall, as is usually assumed, the statement is quite untrue. Any one who examines the Wall to-day can see very quickly that on the main Land Wall not even one mile of the original Wall has been pulled down and rebuilt since Totila's day. Furthermore, this view is confuted by Procopius' own account of the events which took place in the spring of 547. As soon as Totila had left Rome for Apulia, Belisarius, who was watching events from Portus, decided to re-occupy the almost deserted City. The whole success of this move depended upon the speed with which the ruined Walls could be refurbished, and it was found possible to put them into an emergency state of repair in twenty-five days. Rough as it was, this repair could never have been accomplished if one-third of the Wall was completely demolished. Finally, Procopius[3] says ex-

[1] 'And I tell you not to bandy words about a single Sicilian nor about the Wall of Rome. For it is impossible . . . that this Wall should stand. After shutting themselves inside these Walls the enemy would not come down to the plain and set themselves to do battle with us, but always repulsed Goths, even by day, with tricks and quibbles, and mastered us by trickery. It is therefore right to consider how we may not suffer this in future; . . . and one might submit that the demolition of the Wall of Rome would benefit you most of all. For thus in future neither party will be shut up or deprived of all necessities or besieged by assailants, but will take their chance in battle against each other, while you will be the victor's reward, without danger to yourselves.' loc. cit. iii. 16.

[2] 'So he destroyed in many places as much of the Wall as about a third of the whole.' loc. cit. iii. 22.

[3] 'And when he was unable to rebuild in a short time what Totila had destroyed of the Wall, he did as follows. Collecting the nearest stones at hand, he fitted them together in any order, without anything behind them, for he had no mortar or anything of that sort, if only he might save the face of the building. And he fixed a great quantity of stakes outside. He happened also to have dug deep ditches round the whole circuit before. . . . The whole force worked with all zeal, and in twenty-five days as much of the circuit as was ruined was finished in this manner.' loc. cit. iii. 24.

plicitly that the damage concerned the face of the Wall, as follows:

ἐπεὶ δὲ οὐκ οἷός τε ἦν ὅσα καθελὼν τοῦ περιβόλου Τωτίλας ἔτυχε βραχεῖ ἀνοικοδομήσασθαι χρόνῳ, ἐποίει τάδε. λίθους ἀγχιστά πη ὄντας ξυναγάγων ἐπ' ἀλλήλους οὐδενὶ κόσμῳ συνέβαλεν, οὐδὲν τὸ παράπαν ἐντὸς ἔχοντας, ἐπεὶ οὐδὲ τίτανον εἶχεν οὐδέ τι ἄλλο τοιοῦτον, ἀλλ' ὅπως μόνον τὸ τῆς οἰκοδομίας σώζοιτο πρόσωπον, σκολόπων τε μέγα τι χρῆμα ἔξωθεν ἵστησιν. ἐτύγχανε δὲ καὶ τάφρους βαθείας ἀμφὶ τὸν περίβολον ὅλον ὀρύξας πρότερον. . . . παντὸς δὲ τοῦ στρατοῦ προθυμίᾳ τε πάσῃ ταῦτα ἐργαζομένου πέντε καὶ εἴκοσι ἡμερῶν ὅσα τοῦ περιβόλου καθῄρητο τῷ τρόπῳ τούτῳ τετέλεστε.

On the view that the Wall was down for all its thickness in the demolished sectors this account will not make sense. No general could stop up four miles of broken Wall in the way described and expect them to resist attack. But suppose the Wall to have been undermined to one-third in depth, which may equally well be the meaning of τριτημόριον τοῦ παντός, and liable to collapse, then the conditions required by the text emerge, for the great stones described, even if built into the face of the Wall as dry masonry, would be quite sufficient to prop up the face, until the chance came to put in the mortar, nor would the repair be difficult to execute. This kind of construction is visible to-day in many parts of the circuit; and it is also clear that the big blocks used therein have been set loosely into position, and that the joints between them have been filled afterwards, sometimes in the most haphazard fashion. Long ago Nibby assigned this work to Belisarius, although he did not observe that the position of this filling shows the damage to have been confined to the lower face of the Wall. His identification seems certain, especially when considered, as below, in chronological relation to the other repairs of the Wall. But only when the implication about Totila's damage is accepted also does the Belisarian plan of campaign become completely clear. The method of repair was not a new one, and it had lately been used on the Walls of Pisaurum:[1] ὅσα τοῦ περιβόλου καταπεπτώκει, ὅτῳ δὴ ἀνοικοδομῆσαι τρόπῳ, λίθους τε καὶ πηλὸν καὶ ἄλλο ὁτιοῦν ἐμβαλλομένους, and there the question had obviously to do with the face of the Wall. It may thus be accepted that the damage done by Totila in Rome was not so serious as has been thought, and that it was confined to the face of the Wall.

When Totila returned to recapture the City the doors for the Gates were not ready, owing to the lack of workmen, and the entrances were defended by emergency palisades; three days' heavy fighting was needed to decide the question of possession. After this, the Goths retired to Tibur, and Belisarius had opportunity to fit iron-bound doors to the Gates before winter.[2]

[1] 'As much of the Wall as was fallen, should be repaired in this way, making it up with stones and mud and anything of the sort.' loc. cit. iii. 11. [2] loc. cit. iii. 24.

This is the last time that classical literature mentions repairs to the Wall of Rome. In 549 the City was betrayed once more to Totila,[1] again, too, by Isaurian troops. And when Narses arrived to effect its recapture,[2] after defeating Totila in the Furlo Pass, his army was not large enough to invest the City, nor was the Gothic garrison sufficiently big to defend it.[3] Totila therefore concentrated his forces round the Mausoleum of Hadrian, where he now built a castle.[4] There is no mention of repairs in connexion with either of these events, but Nibby was no doubt right in observing that, if Narses rebuilt bridges,[5] he probably repaired the City Wall.

Almost three centuries passed between this time and the building of the Leonine City in 849, and during the interval there were at least four Papal repairs, all the result of activity in the eighth century: by Sisinnius[6] in 708, by Gregory II[7] and Gregory III in 725–31, and by Hadrian I in 772.[8] Excepting Hadrian's, these seem to have been little more than botching, in spite of the high-sounding language which describes them. Finally, Leo IV in 849 did[9] some more extensive work, involving the restoration of fifteen towers; but at the same time he built the Civitas Leonina,[10] to protect the Borgo. The new towers of the Borgo, built in the latest machicolated style, were the outward sign that Rome's centre of authority had moved from the Palatine to St. Peter's. Nor is there further need to follow repairs in detail on the City Wall, for Papal styles of building become distinctive enough, even when unmarked by *stemmata*.

§ 2. MEDIEVAL DESCRIPTIONS OF THE WALL

From the prose writings of the late-Roman tradition it is easy to pass to the medieval statistical descriptions of the Wall.

(a) The Einsiedeln List

The best known of these statistics is appended to the Einsiedeln Itinerary,[11] a ninth-century pilgrim's guide, which once belonged to the library of the Monastery of Pfäfers in S. Gall. It gives a statistical account of the component parts of each section of the

[1] loc. cit. iii. 36. [2] loc. cit. iv. 32 = June 552.
[3] ὅλον μὲν οὖν τὸν Ῥώμης περίβολον διὰ μεγέθους ὑπερβολὴν οὔτε Ῥωμαῖοι ἐπιόντες περιβάλλεσθαι εἶχον οὔτε Γότθοι φρουρεῖν. iv. 33.
[4] loc. cit. iv. 33. [5] C. I. L. vi. 1199 = Pons Salarius, A.D. 565.
[6] Anastas. Bibl. *in Sisinnio.*
[7] Anastas. Bibl. *in Greg. II* = Frodoardus, in Muratori, *Script. Rer. Ital.* iii. 2, col. 67.
[8] Anastas. Bibl. *in Hadriano* = *Liber Pont.* c. 5.
[9] *Liber Pont.* c. 38. [10] Dedicated 27 June 852 = *Inscr. Chr.* ii. 326.
[11] Einsiedeln MS., 326, fol. 85ʳ etᵛ, 86ʳ: pedigree traced by De Rossi, *Inscr. Christ.* ii. 1, p. 9: once the property of Monast. Fabariense (Pfäfers in S. Gall), and copied from Reichenau MSS. Attention should be drawn to Hülsen's facsimiles, *Atti Pont.*, Ser. ii., vol. 9: p. 424 and Tav. xiii.

Wall, but no detailed analysis of its contents has been made public. The nearest approach thereto was provided by Jordan,[1] who eventually decided that the List was based upon a survey of the Wall as it existed in the time of Honorius. He also identified the document with the survey made by Geometer Ammon, assigned by Olympiodorus[2] to this period. The reasons for this important decision were, however, left quite vague, and Jordan never placed the view in a higher category than that of the *höchstwahrscheinlich*.[3] In fact his identification of the List (once dated to the fifth century) with Ammon's work, was no more than a suggestion, made in order to satisfy the impression that so detailed a list could hardly be work of the ninth century. But the suggestion was bold, and other commentators have been more cautious. Gilbert's verdict,[4] for example, puts the whole case in a nutshell. 'Uber die Mauer selbst haben wir eine in dem Einsiedler Reisehandbuch überlieferte genaue Beschreibung, die einen so durchaus sachgemassen glaubwürdigen Eindruck gemacht, dass die Annahme dieselbe enstamme einer offiiziellen Quelle unabweisbar erscheint.' Only a minute analysis will answer the question satisfactorily, and this is especially needed, since Jordan's opinion is now coming to be widely accepted as true, without further examination. Unfortunately, the Wall is seldom so complete as to permit a detailed comparison between it and the document. But in the document itself some important internal indications of a *terminus post quem* exist, and may now be considered in detail.

The first group of these concerns the Gates. If the adjective *clausa*, governing Porta Pinciana, belongs to the original text, the compilation is later than A.D. 537, for the Gate was still open then.[5] Similarly, if the omission of the Porta Chiusa is original,[6] the account must be later than 402, when the Gate was open, and received its fine stone front of Honorian type. Portae Septimiana and Ardeatina, which are also omitted, defy judgement, since the first was demolished in 1498 under Alexander VI, and the second in 1534 under Paul IV. But it should be noted that there is no

---

[1] Jordan, ii. p. 174.

[2] Olymp. frag. 43 = Photius, *Myriobiblia* 80.

[3] 'extremely likely': Jordan, ii. p. 170.

[4] 'We have a good description of the Walls themselves, handed down in the Einsiedeln Handbook, which creates an impression so thoroughly in accordance with the facts and so trustworthy, that the idea seems irrefutable that the Handbook descends from an official source.' Gilbert, iii. p. 13.

[5] Procop. B. G. i. 28 ἐξῆγε τὸ στράτευμα διά τε πυλίδος Πιγκιανῆς. 'He led the army out through the small Pincian Gate.' It may, indeed, have been open as late as the eighth century, if the cemeteries described by the source of William of Malmesbury (C. U. R. p. 87) as outside the Gate were reached through it. But then *clausa* is almost certainly an addition.

[6] This is most likely, else why was the Gate not left in the List and called *clausa* (shut)? Its form belongs, as will appear, to the third period, see p. 160.

reason for thinking that Porta Septimiana was an unimportant postern, which is the device used by Jordan to escape from the difficulty raised by the omission. The accuracy of other details can be submitted to some rough tests. The number of towers appears to be approximately right, but between the items and the total there is a discrepancy of two, which cannot be corrected now, because the Wall along[1] and beyond the Tiber has disappeared. Yet it should be noted, as has been proved in detail above, that the six towers assigned to the Mausoleum of Hadrian do not belong to the building as it existed before the time of Totila, and, if this discrepancy is real, the document cannot be earlier than 552. The merlons (*propugnacula*), which are the next feature in the List, do not exist in their original state anywhere on the upper rampart-walk, with which the List is undoubtedly concerned. They are, however, numbered in sections from Gate to Gate, and the proportion of these numbers is of considerable interest, owing to the astonishing differences involved. Six examples of this may be taken:

(1) 4 towers: 59 merlons.   (2) 6 towers: 164 merlons.
(3) 12 towers: 174 merlons.   (4) 16 towers: 782 merlons.
(5) 35 towers: 733 merlons.   (6) 57 towers: 806 merlons.

These remarkably discrepant figures may be interpreted in various ways, which it is helpful to tabulate as follows:

(i) It may be supposed that the towers in each section did not possess merlons. This interpretation will work for sections 1 and 5, giving a possible twenty merlons to each curtain, a figure well above the truth. But it will not work for 2, 3, 4, or 6; and it cannot be reconciled with the fact that on section 5 the towers undoubtedly always had merlons.

(ii) It may be supposed that only tower-merlons are counted. This might work for 1, 3, and 6, if the towers had no merlons at the back. It works well for 5; it is impossible for 2 and 4.

(iii) Equally unsatisfactory is any composite arrangement based on distribution between curtains and towers, for it will suit neither 1, 3, 4, 5, nor 6, though it might be just possible for 2.

(iv) No better result is obtained by postulating that only the wall-merlons or tower-merlons are enumerated, and that there were great differences in total and distribution upon different sections of the Wall. For although a unit of 14 will then work for sections 3 and 6 and one of 20 for 1 and 5, neither system will work for sections 2 or 4.

(v) Finally, some sort of working result might be reached by treating each sector independently. But this would involve assuming not only that in each sector the arrangements were

---

[1] The question of an apparent discrepancy between Procopius and the List in connexion with this Wall has already been discussed, see p. 19.

different, but also that the survey had been conducted on different lines in each place. This seems an impossible basis for a document whose purpose is clearly to collect information about the Wall in usefully summarized form.

When all these postulates have broken down, the following possibilities remain to be considered. Either the existing manuscript is hopelessly corrupt: or the List was compiled when the Wall was out of repair, and when, for that reason, there was no sort of uniformity between section and section. So far as the possibility of corruption is concerned, however, it has been shown that such figures in the section dealing with the towers as can be tested precisely, are likely to be corrupted in two instances at most, and, although the totals have become corrupted, the extent of this is not alarmingly bad. The conclusion that the Wall was ruined when the List was made therefore wins: and the List may be considered as an inventory compiled when the Wall was badly damaged, and presumably about to be repaired; *it is not a statement of its condition when complete.*

This view receives helpful support from a consideration of the latrines [1] (*necessaria*). These are still to be traced at numerous points on the Wall, by the remains of corbels and shoots, tucked away in the angles between the Wall and its towers; but there are not enough of them to compare with the Einsiedeln figures. Nevertheless, it is abundantly clear that the number given is incomplete, as follows from such arrangements as 29 towers— 2 *necessaria*, 24 towers—11 *necessaria*, 20 towers—4 *necessaria*, or 20 towers—17 *necessaria*. These figures are incompatible, unless an absurd divergence of planning from sector to sector is postulated. Two *necessaria* for twenty-nine towers is an especially insanitary provision; and it is greatly to be regretted that this particular sector, between Portae Portuensis and Aurelia-Pancraziana, perished in 1643; had it survived, there can be little doubt that actual remains would have confuted the evidence of statistics. Again, it is quite improbable that two successive sectors, with nine and six towers apiece, had no latrine. But these structures, which projected from the Wall on two corbels, were very liable to damage, and must have tended to decay even more quickly than the merlons. It will, therefore, be admitted that their odd distribution is quite explicable, if the Wall was out of repair when the List was made.

The *fenestrae* of the Wall raise other problems.[2] The meaning of the terms, *fenestrae maiores forinsecus* and (*fenestrae*) *minores*,

[1] This answers Jordan (ii. 169), 'ob sich solche necessaria noch nachwiesen lassen kann ich nicht sagen'. 'I cannot say whether such latrines are still recognizable.'

[2] The major problem is abandoned by Jordan (ii. 169). 'Mir fehlt das Material zur Entscheidung der Frage, welches die "grossen" and welches die "kleinen" Fenster seien.' A minor problem is outlined by him: 'unklar bleibt es mir (i. 349, n. 16) ob die gleich grossen

has been obscure. Commentators have usually assumed that both classes of fenestrae belong to the outer face of the Wall, *maiores* being the large windows in the towers, while *minores* are the small loop-holes in the towers and Wall. But this cannot be true, since the combined number is too great for the arrangement to have been possible at any time in the Wall's history. Indeed, the *fenestrae forinsecus* alone will include, in every sector but one, both the windows and the loop-holes. The other term, then, *fenestrae minores*, might be expected to cover the internal windows and the arches of the gallery, and this is, in fact, the only feasible solution when the List is confronted with the remains which it is meant to describe. Yet, if it is true, why are the arcade-arches and internal windows called *minores*, especially in contrast with loop-holes? Or, conversely, why are the loop-holes called *maiores*, when they are the smallest feature on the Wall? A possible, if not too obvious, explanation is a transposition of the two terms in the archetype by an extremely easy corruption, which actually occurs in one passage.[1] Then the contrast would be quite precise, and the text would read, *fenestrae minores forinsecus . . . fenestrae maiores* (*intrinsecus*, understood). *Forinsecus* cannot be the word transposed, for it is already attached to the larger quota, to which it properly belongs. When the transposed arrangement is used, the following result emerges, which, fortunately, can be tested by actual remains. On the sector Porta Latina–Porta Appia there are eighty-five rear arcades and windows; this is the number of *fenestrae minores* given in the List. The 58 front loop-holes now remaining fall 22 short of the Einsiedeln number, LXXX; but some of the Wall is now ruined, and the corre-spondence probably was once complete. The same probability holds for the damaged sector Porta Pinciana-Porta Salaria, where there are 156 *fenestrae maiores* as against cc, and 111 *minores* as against clx. Exceptionally the front of the sector Porta Metrobia –Porta Latina has an excess of loop-holes, 125 as against c. But many loop-holes on this sector were blocked up at an early date, and so the discrepancy vanishes, if the List were made at a later period. Nor does this deficiency permit the introduction of *fenestrae minores* as features on the outside of the Wall, for the total would once again be much too large.

This evidence helps considerably in determining the date of the List, when combined with the following facts. Internal or external *fenestrae* occur rarely on the original Wall. As a whole, they belong to the heightening of the structure, which took place

Fenster der Thorgallerien und der die Thore flankirenden Thürme mitgezählt wurden. . . . Die zu erwartende detaillirte Analyse der ganzen Mauer wird auch diese Fragen zu lösen haben.' In fact, the solution seems impossible owing to the imperfect state of the Wall: but I suspect that the Gates were not enumerated. [1] Line 11, fol. 85 v.

one stage before the restoration by Honorius, in 402–3. But the large windows of the towers (see below) were not converted into narrow loop-holes until one stage later still, when, as has been noted elsewhere, the chief arm of defence was the bow and not the *ballista*. So an incomplete List, which classes loop-holes on the Wall and the towers together without distinguishing them, presumably cannot have been compiled before the first occasion when the heightened Wall got out of repair. Nor is there, indeed, any reason why the inventory should not have been prepared in view of a much later repair than that. Anyhow, it is abundantly clear that it has nothing whatever to do with the Wall built by Aurelian and Probus.

We can now return to the question of Jordan's accuracy in identifying the Einsiedeln List, first, as an account of the Wall's state in 403, and, secondly, as the survey which, according to Olympiodorus, Geometer Ammon made about this time. The dating may be considered first. The existing manuscript of the List belongs to the ninth century. Jordan argued that it was a copy of an older document, and, since the list occurs irrelevantly at the end of a pilgrims' guide, Jordan was probably right. As for the age of this archetype, the architectural features which it describes cannot be earlier than Honorius; while omissions, apart from the addition of *clausa* to Porta Pinciana, make it later than 440, or, if the *Hadrianium* is Totila's Castle, later than 552. And the bad state of repair which the document reveals puts the date as late as possible. Jordan, however, uses as evidence only the fact about Porta Pinciana; and he wished strongly to identify the inventory with the early fifth-century survey by Geometer Ammon. So he postulated that the ninth-century copyist modified the text which he was transcribing, in order to suit the facts of the ninth century, and added *clausa* to Porta Pinciana. On the validity of this postulate[1] rests his whole case for the dating of the document, and it is not too much to say that the validity is fictitious. If the original document were known to be a work of the fifth century, the conclusion would not even be necessary; to make it outright in order to prove that the compilation was Ammon's would be logical chicanery.

Jordan was therefore cautious, and never claimed for his conclusion more than extreme likelihood: only his followers swallowed it whole.[2] But even the likelihood fades when the nature of the document is examined. Ammon, as de Rossi

---

[1] His other question (ii. 156), 'wer soll in 8ten Jahrhundert ausser den Thoren die Thürme und Zinnen, die Fenster, grosse und kleine, gezählt, oder wer an einen solchen Zählung Interesse gefunden haben?' is answered by a moment's thought. Any one repairing the Wall would need such an inventory, to check what had been done.

[2] e.g. Lanciani, *Mon. Ant.* i. 448; then Platner, *Anc. Rome*, p. 516.

cogently observed,[1] measured the Wall. This document has nothing to do with measurement. It is a List which enumerates the architectural features of the Wall at a time when they were far from complete. A record of this kind would no doubt be made whenever repairs were done, and would be compared later with a statistic of the finished work. Thus the scope of a given set of repairs would be clear, and a check thereof could be made. Ammon is not recorded to have compiled anything in the least like this, and this was not geometer's work. The character of the List does not therefore support the view that it was Ammon's, and, in suggesting that the conclusion was even probable, Jordan went farther than the facts allow.[2] The very possibility is in question; for the fact that Ammon measured the Wall in the early fifth century will not connect, on present evidence, with the fact that an inventory of the Wall was made at some time after 440 or 552; and further chronological evidence cannot be extracted from the document as it exists.[3] Jordan's case is therefore not proved.

The conclusions which the evidence permits to be drawn would seem to be these. The Einsiedeln List is copied from an inventory of the architectural features of the Wall, compiled when the Wall was much in need of repair: and it is reasonable to suppose that the List was made with a future repair in mind. As it stands it seems later than Belisarius, very possibly later than Totila. It therefore dates between 440 and the eighth century, and present knowledge will not give a closer dating.

(b) Chronicon Benedicti

There also exists a shorter statistic of the Wall which descended to medieval times. The relation of this to the Einsiedeln List is

[1] De Rossi, *Piante*, p. 71. 'Ma costui (=Ammon) misurò le mura, e l'icnografo dell' età di Carlo Magno . . . mai registra un passo od un piede . . . Ma qualunque sia di queste congetture la probabilità, non veggo perchè il computo . . . non debba essere stato fatto dagli architetti di quell'età, piuttosto che cercato negli scritti dal geometra Ammone. Della misura dell'anno 403, nè nella topografia einsiedlense nè in qualsivoglia altro documento latino ed occidentale trovo vestigio.'

[2] The pathetic desire to make every scrap of knowledge serve, be it the merest flotsam of ancient learning, is the bane of Quellenforschung: cf. note 4, p. 226, for an example by von Domaszewski.

[3] An intermediate theory may be mentioned; that the List was Ammon's, but revised by Pope Hadrian I in 772 (Lanciani, *B. C.* 1892, p. 89). This has been stated but never argued. No good reason exists why the whole List need not be early Papal, and it is arbitrary to hark back to Ammon. In stating the theory Lanciani has, I suspect, misunderstood De Rossi (*Piante*, cap. xi, p. 74) who thinks that the statistic, though not independent of map tradition, may go back to Pope Hadrian's restoration of the Walls and redistribution of church property: that, this being so, Hadrian sent a copy of his results to Charlemagne, and that so the information got to Reichenau, whence Pfäfers borrowed the MS. for copying. All this is ingenious conjecture. Lanciani, indeed, thought (loc. cit., p. 101) that *Pinciana clausa* gave the whole document to Pope Hadrian. But this cuts the knot, rather than unties it.

quite uncertain; but an argument for independence could be based on the facts that it includes only towers and merlons, and that the quotas of these differ in the two sources. The present account first appears, late in A.D. 968, in the Chronicle of Benedict of Soracte.[1] It then passed, by an unknown line of descent, into the Cemetery Lists and Descriptions of the City, and became steadily more corrupt in the process.

Benedict employed the material in the closing pages of his work, which lament the fate of Rome in 967 at the hands of Otto I. The effect is somewhat odd, and Benedict allowed his distress to get the better of his grammar. 'Ve Roma! Omnes tua moenia cum turris et pugnaculi sicuti modo repperitur. Turres tuarum tricenti octoginta una habuisse, turres castellis quadraginta sex, pugnaculi tui sex milia octo centies, portes tue quindecim. Ve Civitas Leonina! dudum capta fuistis, modo vero a Saxonicum rege relicta.' For our purpose, the passage suggests an archetype list something like this. 'Murus Romae habet turres cclxxxi, turres castellatas clvi, propugnacula vidccc, portas xv. And it is important that Benedict should have written the numbers in words instead of figures, which are so easily corrupted.

(c) The Cemetery Lists

The same source as inspired Benedict presumably furnished material in two manuscript cemetery lists, recently discussed by P. Guidi,[2] and thought by him to be independent of the Mirabilia.

(i) Cod. Vat. Lat. 3851, fol. 42. 'Murus Romae habet turres simplices ccclxxi, et turres castellatas xlviii, propugnacula sex milia dccc, portas xv, pusterulas xv, in circuitu vero eius sunt milia. Civitas Leonina habet turres xliiii, propugnacula mille ccccxliii, portas duas, in circuitu vero m.'

(ii) Escorial. S. III. 27, fol. 40 . 'Murus Romane Urbis habet turres simplices ccclxxi, et turres castellatas xlviii; propugnacula vi mil. dccc, portas xv, posterulas xv, in circuitu vero eius sunt milia.'

It will be noted that the number of towers is now reduced by ten, while two, and then three, new *turres castellatae* appear. This is no doubt due to corruption. *Posterulas xv* must also be introduced from *portas xv*. An original *v* may be suspected, in view of the next document to be quoted. The perimeter is nowhere stated.

[1] *Mon. Germ. Hist.* vol. v.=*C. U. R.* p. 176. 'Woe to Rome! Even now have all thy walls, towers and battlements been discovered. Towers of thine were three hundred, eighty and one, towers with castellations forty and six, thy battlements six thousand, eight hundred, thy gates fifteen. Woe to the Leonine City! Lately were you captured, now indeed abandoned by the King of the Saxons.'

[2] *Rendiconti della Pont. Accad. Rom. di Archeologia*, Ser. iii, vol. i, pp. 185–214.

(d) Descriptio Plenaria

The tradition then passes to the early medieval guides, of which the *Descriptio plenaria* is the first type, belonging to the twelfth century.[1] 'Murus civitatis Romae habet turres ccclxi, castella xlviiii, propugnacula vidcccc, portas xii sine Transtiberim, posterulas v. In circuitu vero eius sunt miliaria xxi, excepto Transtiberim et civitate Leonina.' Ten more towers have gone; *turres castellatae* are still firm at forty-nine; but the merlons have increased by one hundred.

(e) Graphia Aureae Urbis Romae

In the thirteenth century corruption and interpolation proceed, and the tradition assumes the following form.[2] 'Habet autem turres ccclxii, castella xlviii, arcus principales vii, propugnacula vidcccc, portas xxxvi, posterulas v. In circuitu miliaria xlii.' Here the number of Gates may have come in from the *Curiosum*;[3] the perimeter of the Wall is possibly a corruption from xxi, or xiii. One more ordinary tower appears, one less *turris castellata*.

(f) De Mirabilibus Urbis Romae

The handbooks of the next century present some new corruptions.[4] 'Murus civitatis Romae habet turres ccclxi, castella ⟨xlviii, propugnacula⟩, id est merulos, vidccc, portas xii, pusterulas v. In circuitu vero sunt miliaria xxii, exceptis Transtiberim et civitate Leonina, id est porticus S. Petri.' Here it seems certain that the words in brackets should be supplied. The *propugnacula* have returned to Benedict's standard; and the mileage mentioned is more reasonable, though still difficult to understand.

(g) Anonymus Magliabecchianus. 1410–15

The tradition which began in the tenth century ends miserably at the opening of the fifteenth.[5] 'Murus urbis Romae in circuitu habet turres ccclxi, castella quadraginta novem, propugnacula noningenta et sex.' The final corruption defies adequate comment.

The most interesting item in this series of documents is *turres castellatae*, which later became *castella*. These towers are secure in the tradition at least as early as the tenth century, and it is important to decide what their nature was. The possibilities are clear. Either the *turres castellatae* are a special type of tower on the Imperial Wall, with abnormal parapet and merlons; or they belong to another extensive fortification. But it has already been noted that Belisarius gave to the Imperial Wall a new and uniform

[1] C. U. R., p. 91. Six codices: (1) Cod. Vat. 3973: (2) Cod. Vat. Cenci. Cam., sine numero: (3) Cod. Cast. S. Angeli: (4) Cod. Archiv. Vat. Plut. xi: (5) Cod. Ottobon. 3057: (6) Cod. Bibl. Vallicelli.

[2] C. U. R., p. 113. [3] C. U. R., p. 27. [4] C. U. R., p. 126. [5] C. U. R., p. 149.

type of merlon with traverse, and, after that reconstruction, there is no reason to think that forty-six of its towers were equipped with a special type of top. The two main later restorations were by the Popes Hadrian I [1] and Leo IV,[2] and neither is recorded to have built anything so important as this: Leo, for example, rebuilt fifteen towers. The following line of explanation may therefore be suggested.[3] Forty-six is precisely the number of towers that defended the *Civitas Leonina*—forty-four in the circuit, and two beyond it, guarding the river near Porta Portuensis. All these towers were equipped with the newly invented machicolated parapets. They could thus be described very precisely as *turres castellatae*. It is therefore highly probable that the forty-six *turres castellatae*, which are not subtracted from the full number in the Imperial Wall, belong to the new defences of Pope Leo IV. Further, this view is corroborated by the *Descriptio plenaria*, which, in describing the Wall, makes special exception of the Civitas Leonina when giving particulars of the Gates and the perimeter, thereby implying that the Civitas is ordinarily to be considered as included. That the towers and merlons of this *civitas* are mentioned as well as the *turres castellatae* in the Vatican codex of the *Documento cimiteriale* means nothing more than the addition of a specially definitive rubric, added to classify an already obscure tradition.

It may thus be regarded as distinctly probable, as Guidi has already suggested, in editing the *documenti cimiteriali*, that Benedict and kindred compilers were using a ninth-century account of the Walls of Rome, perhaps drawn up by Leo's engineers. This was either a revision of the Einsiedeln List or, as is more likely, an entirely different statistic. Apparently the Wall was now in worse repair than when the Einsiedeln document was compiled, if the number of merlons given, 6,800 as against 7,020, is a safe criterion. Such, then, are the statistics of the Wall. On the whole, they raise more questions than they help to solve; and the Einsiedeln List has an especially deceptive air of completeness, which seems to have staved off hitherto a detailed examination of its contents, and has almost succeeded in making it a first-class authority.

§ 3. TWO RENAISSANCE STUDIES

(a) More important, if of less intrinsic interest, is the fifteenth-century description by Poggio Braccciolini, contained in his treatise *De Varietate Fortunae*.[4] There is no need to quote the

---

[1] *Lib. Pont.* c. 5.   [2] ibid., c. 38.
[3] cf. Gregorovius-Hamilton, vol. iii. p. 388.
[4] *C. U. R.*, pp. 242–3. 'Three gates have ceased to be in use, and are walled up. Two of these are of ancient structure; letters on one of which, between the Ostian and so-called

whole account, for its value varies considerably: but certain points call for comment here. The most mischievous error is the statement about the distribution of Honorian inscriptions

'Tres (portae) in usu esse desierunt, muro obductae: earum duae antiquae sunt structurae, quarum alterius inter Ostiensem et, ut dicitur, Appiam . . . portas, sicut in Ostiensi, litterae Arcadium et Honorium muros portas et turres urbis instaurasse, sunt documento: altera, inter portam Latinam atque Asinariam, literis caret: tertia inter Tiburtinam est et, quae hodie dicitur S. Agnetis, Nomentana.'

This statement seems precise, but it is condemned by the fact that quite certainly there never was any inscription of Honorius on Porta Ostiensis. Hülsen[1] suspected this, and an architectural study of the Gate establishes beyond all doubt that if an inscription of Honorius had ever been there, it would still be visible to-day. Poggio may, however, like Burn,[2] have mistaken Ostiensis for Portuensis. There is now no possibility of testing the statement that the Gate 'between Portae Appia and Ostiensis' (Porta Ardeatina) had such an inscription. But it must be noted that no other writer mentions the fact, and, since the three other similar and authentic inscriptions were both well-known and frequently copied, it might be expected that a copy of this one also would have occurred in some other source. The architectural form (see fig. 42) of Porta Ardeatina also strongly suggests[3] that no inscription ever existed there.

Yet Poggio had a keen eye for archaeological detail, as is shown by his detailed demonstration[4] of the fact that the Imperial

Appian Gates, prove, as at the Ostian, that Arcadius and Honorius restored the walls gates and towers. The other, between Porta Latina and Asinaria, has no letters. The third is between Porta Tiburtina and Nomentana (now known as Porta S. Agnese).'

[1] R. Mittheil. 1894, p. 326, and C. I. L. vi. 31257=1188.

[2] Burn's mistakes about these inscriptions are remarkable (Rome and the Campagna, p. 65).

[3] See below, p. 217.

[4] 'That the present Wall is not the ancient one (i.e. that of Servius) is shown by proofs. In many places public and private buildings, and small temples too, are embodied therein, and from time to time its foundations rest upon ancient ruins. From Porta Tiburtina for a long distance the aqueduct of Claudius the Divine is used as a wall; between Porta Tiburtina and Nomentana, for more than a thousand paces, the wall is taken round on top of a rectangular public building (now called the Vivaiolo), on three sides of which appear most lovely plastered walls, painted in various colours. Between Porta Flaminia and the Tiber a shrine is contained in the Wall; and there can be seen in many places blocked windows and doors of private houses, which serve as the Wall. Again, there are rotten and crumbling walls, which fall without being touched, of which the body is a mass of varied smashed pieces of marble and sherds of tile. I saw part of the Wall where the building material was taken from collected stones and fragments of marble: while on the outer and inner faces the wall was adorned with bricks polished like tiles. Indeed, the ancient building is so compact that it cannot be removed even by the strength of man without great labour. It may be added that there is no uniform method of building, but that it differs in many places; so that it is evident that the Wall was built neither all at the same time nor by one architect. That is what I mean about the City Wall, although it is thought older by many.' C. U. R. p. 243.

Wall could not be the primitive Wall of Rome, as many scholars thought in his day.

'Muros quae nunc sunt non esse antiquos argumentis monstratur; nam pluribus in locis publica privataque aedificia, sacella quoque, amplectuntur, et fundamenta quandoque veteribus ruinis superaedificata sunt. A porta quidem Praenestina longo spatio aquaeductus Divi Claudii pro muro habetur; inter Tiburtinam et Nomentanam, murus ad mille amplius passus circumducitur supra publicum quadratum aedificium (Piscinam [1] moderni vocant), cuius ex tribus partibus testudines pulcherrimae apparent, variis coloribus pictae. A porta Flaminia usque ad Tiberim sacellum moenibus continetur; conspiciuntur et multis in locis fenestrae portaeque privatorum resarcitae, quae pro moenibus sumpsere. Sunt praeterea muri fragiles ac putridi, ut, nullo impellente, labantur, quorum structura ex variis marmorum contritorum &c. tegularum frustris conglutinata est. Vidi ego partem murorum collectitiisque lapidibus marmorum quoque fragmentis materiem aedificandi sumptam; exterius interiusque ob decorem lateribus politis in modo testarum, moenia ornata. Prisca vero aedificia ita compacta sunt ut ne viribus quidem hominum disturbari absque summo labore queant. Non est insuper unica aedificandi ratio, sed multis in locis varia; ut plane constet nec uno tempore, nec ab eodem architecto, muros factos. Haec de Urbis moenibus, quoniam a multis antiquiora existimantur, dixisse velim.'

This passage shows that Poggio, whatever his other faults, could read palimpsests in mortar and brick as well as in ink. His notes are, indeed, an almost complete epitome of the present study.

(b) A hundred and forty-four years later, in 1575, the Wall was studied by a distinguished young Frenchman, Nicholas Audebert of Orleans,[2] whose manuscript is now in the British Museum.[3] His account is the earliest precise description of the structure that exists. All inscriptions commemorating restorations are carefully copied: postern-gates, and even the tiny wicket between the Bastione di Sangallo and the postern farther east, are enumerated in their proper place. The whole document has been published by Eugéne Müntz,[4] and often is of great importance for its description of details which have now vanished, as at Porta Flaminia; but it is too long, and not quite important enough, to be cited in full. All passages important for archaeology, however, are quoted in their appropriate places, and three[5] examples of the style and method are given here.

[1] An alternative for Vivaiolo, the medieval name for Castra Praetoria, see p. 184, n. 4.

[2] At first unconnected with this manuscript. Identified by De Nolhac, *Revue arch.* Nov.–Dec. 1887, pp. 315–24.

[3] B. M. Lansdowne MS. 720, fols. 229–273vo: dated 1574–8.

[4] *Antiquités de la ville de Rome.* Paris, 1886.

[5] (i) 'Via Portuensis, which led to the port of Ostia, whence this great road and also the port took their names. This gate is situated between the Janiculum and the Tiber, built with two arches in front, side by side, of large and very ancient quarried stone. One of them is blocked, and above it is the following inscription, readable, all the same, only with great difficulty.'

(ii) 'After this bulwark the wall and building of Paul III continue for 360 paces further, being in all 480 paces long. Then the ancient walls begin again, which (no more than

(i) fol. 238.

'VIA PORTUENSIS, qui conduisait au Port d'Ostia, d'où ce grand chemin et aussy la porte ont pris leur noms. Ceste porte est assise entre le Janicule et le Tybre, bastye de deux archades en front, et à costé l'une de l'autre, qui sont de grosse pierre de taille fort antique, l'une desquelles est bouschée et audessus d'icelle y a une inscription, telle qui suit, laquelle toutesfoys on list fort malaisément.'

(ii) fol. 244.

'Depuis ce boullevart continuent ces murailles et bastiment de Paul III, qui dure encores 360 pas loing, lesquelles ont en tout 480 pas de long. Puis après recommencent les anciens murs, lesquels (non plus que les précédents) n'ont point de fossé, tellement que l'on va tousjours près du pied d'iceux et en montant, où se trouve une petite porte bouschée, qui doibt avoir esté un GUISCHET de la ville.'

(iii) fol. 261.

'Après cela on trouve une tour forte antique à 230 pas, faisant un coin de ceste grande espace qui souloit estre Castrum Praetorium, contre laquelle est escrit de fort vieille lettre gravée en une pierre minée d'antiquité, ce qui suit. CM ▨▨▨▨▨▨ MEGNATIAE TRY'.

As a commentary upon the last passage, the following extract is taken from the writer's own note-book. 'Inscription in tower— *C. I. L.* vi. 32773; Ⓒ . . . . |NAT·|AET|RY|' The inscription is moulded on terracotta plaques, of which some have fallen since 1574: the letters are not easy to read, and the whole record speaks for its own accuracy. All the passages, in fact, need little further comment, and in conclusion may be quoted the verdict of Müntz.[1] 'L'auteur . . . fait preuve d'une rare précision: son temoinage permet à chaque instant de rectifier ou de compléter cela de ses contemporains . . . Ceci dit, je laisse la parole à l'auteur.'

those before) have no ditch, so that one walks always at their foot on ascending ground, where is a little blocked gate, which must have been a town-wicket.'

(iii) 'After that occurs, at 230 paces, a very ancient tower, forming one angle of this great enclosure, which ought to be the Castra Praetoria, on which is inscribed in ancient lettering, on a stone weathered with age, the following C M ▨▨▨▨▨▨ MEG-NATIAE TRY.'

[1] 'The author makes proof of uncommon precision. His evidence allows that of his contemporaries to be corrected or completed at every instant . . . That said, I let the author speak for himself.'

PART TWO

THE ARCHITECTURAL EVOLUTION OF THE WALL

I. THE CONSTRUCTION OF THE WALL

THE general design of the Wall has already been described. It is a solid structure, some twenty feet high and twelve feet thick, which carries a continuous gallery, defended by loop-holes facing the open country, and lit by a great arcade, with open bays facing the City. The gallery supports in turn a crenellated rampart-walk. This arrangement, indeed, is given by many text-books as the type in use at all points. But actually there are important sectors where its place is taken by other patterns, which have, for example, no gallery. These occur between the Porta Chiusa and Porta Tiburtina, between Porta Tiburtina and S. Croce in Gerusalemme, and between the Bastione di Sangallo and Porta Ostiensis East. Again, the older buildings which were made to serve as part of the Wall all receive their own special treatment. Finally, no writer in discussing the Wall has noted that the whole structure below the level of the gallery is really a complete and self-standing early wall, only about half as high as the composite structure of which it now forms part. And on sectors where no gallery exists, or where there is a second, lower, gallery, the Wall is early up to a corresponding height. On this basis classification may now proceed.

§ 1. THE WALL OF THE FIRST PERIOD, TYPE A

The simplest type of early Wall is twenty feet high, and twelve feet wide. It rests on a somewhat wider foundation, and it is built of brick-faced concrete.[1] Wherever the concrete (Pl. IV*a*) is visible to-day it is composed of light-brown tufa *caementa*,[2] laid carefully in rows, in pieces about the size of a tangerine on the

---

[1] I desire to acknowledge my special indebtedness to Dr. Esther van Deman and Mr. R. A. Cordingley in discussing the methods and types of concrete construction in use upon the Wall. Both of them have spent many hours cf valuable time discussing the matter, and we have now reached complete agreement upon all essentials, and, I trust, upon most particulars. Dr. Van Deman's discussion of Roman concrete construction is, of course, the essential treatise. *A. J. A.* 1912, pp. 230–51, 387–432.

[2] This is the Vitruvian term for aggregate material: the mass thus formed is called a 'crusta' or 'shell': but so are the faces called 'shells'. It is therefore handier to use *caementa*. Vitruv. ii. 8. 7 'sed nostri *celeritati* (N. B., I. A. R.) studentes erecta conlocantes frontibus serviunt, et in medio farciunt fractis separatim cum materia caementis. Ita tres suscitantur in ea structura crustae, duae frontium et una media farturae.'

outside of the Wall, but larger towards the middle. The material
is usually freshly quarried; and there is no suggestion that the
builders were using any kind of rubble which demolished buildings might provide. The facing is composed of broken roof-tiles,
which have furnished many stamps, very largely Hadrianic;[1]
not one of them is directly attributable to Aurelian's day. So the
builders of the Wall seem indeed to have followed the precepts[2]
of Vitruvius, that roof-tiles well tested by weather are the best
material for facing. Many of these tiles must have come from
old buildings, which were demolished to make way for the Wall,
or for the cleared space (*glacis*) just outside it: for thus would
easily be secured a large supply of old roof-tiles in good condition,
which no doubt enabled the builders to keep pace with the heavy
demand for the fragments.

That the solid Wall thus constructed was designed as a complete defensive wall, without any galleried super-structure, is
proved beyond all doubt by the fact that in thirty-five different
curtains[3] it is still possible to see merlons and parapet embedded
in its face (Pl. III: fig. 7) above the level of the floor of the
gallery. As can be seen at Porta Ostiensis East, these belong to
a breastwork which fronted an original rampart-walk, now forming the gallery floor. Accordingly, the gallery, or upper half of
the Wall, is a later addition, built on the old rampart-walk in
order to heighten the Wall. This addition is not to be thought of
as a change of plan, made while the building of the original Wall
was in progress; for the brick-facing of the gallery is always quite
different from original work in the lower portion; and, again, the
Gates, as will be seen later in detail, were remodelled thoroughly
at the time when the gallery was built, yet not before they had
been in use for a considerable period. It is therefore quite
certain that this smaller Wall had an independent existence, and
is, in fact, the original Wall of Imperial Rome. The reduction in
scale detracts less from the defensive value of the Wall than
might be thought. The effective height of the smaller structure is
some twenty-six feet, and it is doubtful whether many contemporary Walls were so thick. So it reaches a good standard in
size and type, and it will be seen that it was emphatically not out-
of-date for its period, as a larger wall would be.

From visible details it can be seen just how this earliest Wall
was built. The first task, after preparing[4] of plans, personelle,

---

[1] Lanciani noted this, *B. C.* 1892, p. 90: the question is examined in detail by Pfeiffer,
Van Buren and Armstrong, *Suppl. Pap. Amer. Acad.* i.; out of the sixth curtain east of
Porta Asinaria 37·14 per cent. were Hadrianic, as against 5·17 per cent. of Antonine and
5·18 per cent. of Severan date. Others were of later restorations.

[2] Vitruvius on roofing tiles. ii, 8, 19.

[3] i.e. Nos. B 9; D 5—19; E 11, 12; F 1, 6, 7, 10, 12, 13, 15; L 23, 24, 30, 33, 45, 46,
47, 48, 51; M 1.

[4] Arranged between the Emperor and the Senate; Vit. Aurel. c. 21. 9 'adhibito consilio

EARLY MERLONS
AND
BUILDING JOINTS

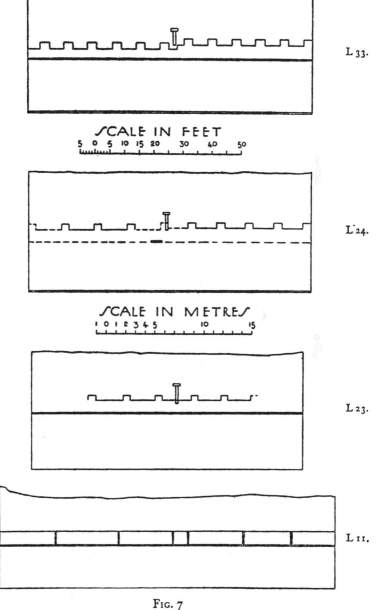

L 33.

SCALE IN FEET

5 0 5 10 15 20 30 40 50

L 24.

SCALE IN METRES

1 0 1 2 3 4 5 10 15

L 23.

L 11.

FIG. 7

and materials, was to dig a foundation-trench about thirteen feet wide. The depth of the trench varied according to the nature of the ground. But, as might be expected, few foundations are exposed, and it is difficult to generalize. In loose ground the trench was lined with rough wooden shuttering, of which the uprights were kept inside (as impressions in the concrete prove), in order to revet successfully the sides of the trench. Concrete or rough tufa packing was then placed within the frame, and allowed to harden, after which the framework might be withdrawn, or left in altogether. Sometimes, when the ground dipped quickly or undulated, the foundations are stepped, and left exposed, being faced[1] with tiles or tufa blocks, while their top remains at uniform level. When rock[2] came close to the surface, similar footings of faced concrete were provided.

The foundation thus prepared, a Wall of somewhat less thickness began to rise upon it, the difference in thickness being made up by one[3] or more[4] slight offsets, each of one course of bipedales. This change occurred about ground-level, and helped (if much less so than in modern construction) to spread the weight of the facing. The facings were of tile, broken to roughly triangular shape and set, smooth side frontwards, in quick-drying mortar. They were built up together for several courses, and the caementa, or aggregate, placed[5] very carefully behind them in the Vitruvian manner, as is shown by the accompanying photograph (Pl. III a). In the best work great attention was paid both to filling in the caementa behind the rough edge of the facing and to securing a really sharp angular back to each facing tile, in order to give the best possible bond. This, as Dr. van Deman has pointed out, is the whole secret of good Roman brick-facing. In several curtains,[6] toothed building-joints (Pl. IV b: fig. 7) may be seen, which indicate that the length of section laid down in one operation was between fifteen and twenty Roman feet, the breadth being, as said, twelve feet and the height between four and five feet. And it is noteworthy that in the Wall itself these joints are always regularly and carefully made, much more so than in the parapet.[7] Putlog holes are absent, so as to suggest either that all the work was done from the top of the Wall as it grew, or that the builders worked from double scaffolding, as shown on the Tomb of Trebius Justus.[8]

Senatus, muros Urbis Romae dilatavit': and 22. 1 'Transactis igitur, quae ad saeptiones . . . pertinebant, contra Palmyrenos . . . iter flexit.' The actual officer in charge of the Wall was the Praefectus Urbi, styled Praefectus Urbis in the Theodosian Codex and the *Novellae* of Valentinian III, and on *C. I. L.* vi. 1188–90.

[1] i.e. curtains C 11, L 10.   [2] i.e. curtains L 11, 13.
[3] i.e. curtains B 19, D 2.   [4] i.e. curtains G 6, L 51.
[5] *Vitr. de Arch.* ii. 8, 7; see note p. 57.   [6] Curtains D 1, F 8, L 11.   [7] Curtain L 24.
[8] For this valuable illustration see G. Giovannoni, *La tecnica della costruzione presso i Romani*, Tav. xxii = Rivoira, *Arch. Rom.*, p. 111, fig. 95.

Horizontally, the Wall is divided at irregular intervals by courses of large tiles, reaching back from the face of the Wall into the concrete core. The function of these bonders, in Aurelian's Wall at least, was to hold the two facings to the concrete core, and so to bind three separately-built units together. When the whole mass had hardened and become almost monolithic there were two dangers connected with these bonding courses. In an earthquake the Wall might swing on the horizontal course, which split its material. The facings might have failed to bond, and would be held on only by the bonders, thus giving the Wall a specious look of solidity. When the topmost stage was finished, a thick layer of finer concrete [1] was laid upon it to form the floor of the rampart-walk, and on the outside of the Wall was placed a small tile string-course [2] of two to four members composed of ordinary or specially-moulded tiles, and arranged with a care which depended upon the individuality of its builders. The result of these operations was a beautiful Wall, evenly built with maximum speed and economy, and likely to endure, as time has proved, for centuries. The only weak point was the bonding of the facing to the core, which was often rendered imperfect by the insufficient backward projection of the tile-fragments.[3] The style of this original brickwork varies very considerably from curtain to curtain, and at its best is extremely good. As a rule, however, rather short tile-fragments are employed, with thick but regular joints, both horizontal and vertical. This is to be compared with the refacing of the Porticus of the Baths of Caracalla, which is dated to Aurelian.[4] Bonding-courses are present, but are rare, and the tiles thereof very thin. The mortar is of good fine quality, though not so white as that of the second period.

The taste of individual builders, which gave different forms to the plinth or to the string-course of this original Wall, influenced still more the character of its breast-work and merlons, as is illustrated by the accompanying diagram (fig. 7). The following generalizations may be made from this evidence. The breastwork [5] varied in height from 3 ft. 6 ins. to 4 ft. 5 ins., and was faced with variant materials on different sections; sometimes [6] with tiles, sometimes [7] with roughly-squared tufa, and sometimes [8]

---

[1] Very rarely visible, but see curtains C 3, L 51, where the Wall has been cut through.

[2] By contrast, visible *passim*.

[3] A point discussed with me in great detail by Dr. Van Deman.

[4] Chron. of 334, s. v. Aurelianus: 'Porticus termarum Antoninianarum arserunt et fabricatum est.' My attention was called to this valuable parallel by Dr. Van Deman.

[5] See curtains L 24, 33.

[6] See curtain L 24 (Pl. III c).

[7] See curtain F 13.

[8] See curtain F 6.

with block-and-brick work (*opus mixtum*). Similar variations also
occur among the merlons [1] (Pl. III), which, as is natural, are as
thick as the breastwork in the single section, where both can be
measured. The spacing or setting-out of the merlons is not
uniform over the whole Wall; and there are different intervals
in the same curtain, as is quite comprehensible on a structure
of such vast extent. Again, the level of the merlons is sometimes [2]
stepped, while the string-mould sometimes [3] slopes (see Pl. V *b*),
when the Wall rises. Minor differences of the same kind appear
on the much shorter circuit of Castra Praetoria.

Nowhere was the top of the Wall reached from the ground by
means of ramps attached thereto. The gate-towers or postern-
towers provided the only means of access. In this matter comparison may be made with the Wall of Anthemius at Constantinople.[4]   The reason for this paucity of ascents, so sharply
contrasted with the normal fortress wall, is no doubt that town
walls did not enclose a wholly military population, of which every
member had to reach and man the defences at a moment's notice.
It was a vital factor in defence to prevent the appearance of
excited and irresponsible townsfolk on the rampart in moments
of crisis,[5] lest they should interfere with the all-important
military operations; while, in peace time, it was equally necessary
to prevent the guards on the Wall from pilfering or philandering
in the gardens or houses behind it. The requisite guard-duty
was organized by the Praefectus Urbi,[6] and sentinels could be
best controlled from the City Gates by the proper authority.

There are also points on the circuit where the configuration
of the ground seems to have demanded that the type of Wall just
described should hold up behind itself a large amount of earth.
The south slope of the Aventine, now the Quartiere di San Saba,
and the eastern edge of the Viminal, between Porta Tiburtina
and the Porta Chiusa, are the two most noteworthy sectors.[7]
Indeed, the latter sector provides one of the good views of the
front. But while the arrangements at the front of the Wall are
sufficiently clear, those behind it are obscure. So far as can be
seen from the upper parts now visible, the back of the Wall was
faced with tiles in the usual manner, which suggests, although it
emphatically does not prove, that internal and external levels
of the Wall were the same. It may be, then, that the early Wall
in these sectors was designed here on the same free-standing lines

---

[1] See curtain L 33.
[2] See curtain F 13; (fig. 7).
[3] See curtain 214: Pl. V *b*: cf. Salonika; Tafrali, *Topographie de Thessalonique*, pl. viii.
[4] Van Millingen, *Byzantine Constantinople*, Map.
[5] cf. Procop. *B. G.* i. 22: where the townsfolk misunderstood Belisarius.
[6] *Nov. Val.* iii, tit. v.
[7] i.e. curtains E 4–16.

as elsewhere. But if this is true, how did the great mass of earth get behind it, a mass which is now big enough to support, at the level of the rampart-walk, a road with tram-cars at the Quartiere di San Saba, or a broad boulevard south of the Porta Chiusa? Was the nucleus of this mass of earth a defensive bank, built behind the Wall and forming an additional rampart-walk, as in many third-century or fourth-century walls? Or was the Wall made to revet a natural rise in the ground, of which the edge had been cut back to receive the Wall? This is perhaps more likely, for the appearance of earth banks behind the walls at this late period is usually the relic of an earlier earthwork defence, as at Caerwent [1] and York.[2] Also, the Wall is the usual twelve feet in thickness, and Walls which serve as revetment to a purely artificial bank of earth, of which the extent and pressure is not great, are usually much less wide.[3] So it may be suspected that in these sectors the earth was the edge of a natural hillock, not necessarily arranged as a walk; that its edge was cut back to provide a proper bed for the Wall; and that the Wall was then built to usual thickness, partly because the earth was not affecting its defensive arrangements, and partly because the very weight of the earth demanded an extremely strong wall to bring its pressure to rest.

The same type of early wall was attached to the City Aqueducts (see fig. 11). In front of Aquae Marcia-Tepula-Iulia the plan of the early Wall was normal. It lay just in front of the low line of aqueducts, but on an increasingly divergent alinement. For there are incorporated in this sector of the Wall several structures already noted,[4] a house-front and ornamental garden wall, all of which stand well in front of the aqueduct. Further south, the aqueduct passes below ground, and it is therefore important not to confuse it with the high-level Acqua Felice [5] of Pope Sixtus V, which occupies the rampart-walk of the second-period Wall on the southern part of this sector. The Papal conduit was built in an age which not only knew that the defensive value of the City Wall was gone, but had already marked its realization of the fact by beginning to erect a series of interesting Bastioni for artillery defence, which have been studied in detail by Borgatti.[6] And so the Wall was made to support the Acqua Felice at the cost of nearly all its defensive value, not to mention the complete re-modelling of the south tower of Porta

---

[1] Caerwent, *Archaeologia*, lviii, pl. ix ; Dr. Ashby tells me that the wall really rests on a shelf cut in the bank.

[2] York, S. N. Miller, *J. R. S.* xv, pp. 177–8.

[3] Ward, *Romano-British Buildings and Earthworks*, pp. 49–51.

[4] See p. 13.

[5] Acqua Felice, dedicated 15 June, 1587.

[6] Borgatti, *R. d. A.*, 1890, vol. ii.

Tiburtina.   The ancient aqueduct, on the other hand, did not
interfere in any way with the defensive scheme.

The same treatment as that used for the Wall in front of
Aquae Marcia-Tepulia-Iulia was accorded to the long sector of
Wall attached to Aquae Claudia and Anio Novus (see fig. 11).
The first-period Wall was designed to run just in front of the
aqueduct, with its back touching the piers.   It is uncertain
whether the rampart-walk was widened by the addition of the existing platforms, set between the aqueduct-piers, which gave extra
width to the walk and resemble artillery-platforms; but it rather
looks as if this was not an original arrangement.   The setting-
out of towers in this sector has clearly been conducted from
either end, and the result is an oddly short length of curtain [1] in
the middle.

In fine, it becomes obvious that the aqueducts were not incorporated, as has been suggested,[2] in order to save building
material.   For they were left behind the Wall and did not form
part of it.   This is important, since these structures help very
largely to make the enormous total of distance saved in building
the Wall by the use of earlier structures, which has been reached
by Homo.[3]   When they are eliminated, the estimate is reduced
from one-sixth of the whole perimeter to something like one-
tenth or less.   The reasons which moved the builders of the Wall
to cling to the line of the aqueducts evidently were strategical
rather than economic.   The size of the City and the boundaries
of the fourteen Regions dictated that the Wall should run somewhere near these aqueducts, while the natural configuration of
the ground prevented its extension far beyond them.   It was
therefore essential that they should not command from outside
the defences of the City.   In that case, any active enemy could
denude the Wall of defenders by using the aqueducts as a
besieger's platform.   It is therefore erroneous to suppose that the
aqueducts lightened the builders' task.   Rather than that, they
complicated the problem of providing through communication
along the original Wall, and they introduced great difficulties,
which were never happily solved, when the Wall came to be
doubled in height in the second period.   The builders of the Wall
must thus have regarded the aqueducts much more as a necessary
evil than as a help.

§ 2   THE WALL OF THE FIRST PERIOD, TYPE B.

On the other hand, the short sectors of Aquae Claudia-Anio
Novus on either side of Porta Praenestina-Labicana were treated

---

[1] No. G 5, cf. no. L 35, in the great re-entrant of Quartiere di San Saba.
[2] Homo, *Essai*, p. 249: Lanciani, *R. E.*, p. 72.   [3] Homo, *Essai*, p. 261–2.

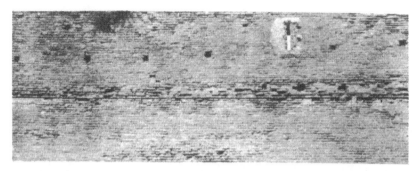

a. FIRST-PERIOD PARAPET AND MERLONS, CURTAIN L 33

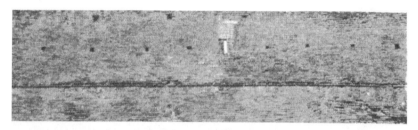

b. FIRST-PERIOD PARAPET AND MERLONS, CURTAIN L 23

c. FIRST-PERIOD PARAPET AND MERLONS, CURTAIN L 24

Note the putlog holes of the new structure in (*a*) and (*b*); and the Belisarian refacing of blocks in (*c*)

quite differently. Here the arrangement from the first was to use the aqueduct piers as part of the face of the Wall. But no platform was provided behind them, and so each piece of rampart-walk between the piers would seem to have been isolated, unless there originally existed some means of access thereto, constructed in wood, of which no trace now remains. Fortunately for the strategical value of the Wall, this awkward mistake only continues for a short distance on each side of the Gate.

§ 3. THE WALL OF THE FIRST PERIOD, TYPE C.

The clearest remains of a more strikingly variant type of early Wall appear between Amphitheatrum Castrense and Porta Asinaria (Pl. V*a*: fig. 8). This had a low base, visible in the curtain

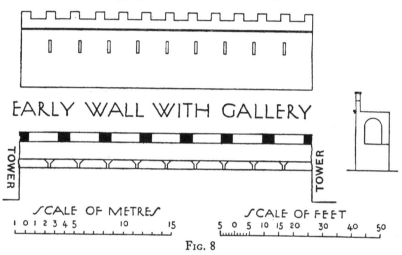

EARLY WALL WITH GALLERY

TOWER

TOWER

SCALE OF METRES
1 0 1 2 3 4 5   10   15

SCALE OF FEET
5 0 5 10 15 20   30   40   50

FIG. 8

of Porta Asinaria itself, where there is also a rather low gallery, roofed with a simple barrel vault, carrying the rampart-walk, parapet, and merlons. A complete section is therefore obtainable, but only two rear arcades belonging to it are now visible. Further rear arcades are to be seen in Wall-curtains to the east, though much obscured by modern dividing walls and by a tramway shed.[1] A front appears again in the second curtain[2] west of the Lateran Palace (see Pl. VI*a*). This Wall was, in fact, an early version of the type adopted widely for the second-period Wall, and when the gallery of the second Wall was built later on top of it, there were two arcades on top of each other, which were, however, never used together. The arcades of the first-period gallery were quite simply arranged (fig. 8); seven went to the hundred-foot curtain of the Wall; the arches had six four-foot piers, with two three-foot piers at each end, and this gave ten

[1] Nos. G 22, 23, 24.   [2] No. H 3 and Tower H 2, a most important combination

feet apiece for each arch. The loop-holes were spaced differently at a ten-foot interval.

Although visible examples of this kind of first-period Wall in Rome are confined to the sectors just described, it may be suspected that the same type of Wall existed elsewhere on the circuit. An original Wall of this type will account completely for the present state of the sector [1] east of Porta Pinciana, where the gallery floor of the second-period Wall is much too low to have belonged to the top of an early wall. It may therefore be suggested that this is the floor of an early gallery, and that the vault of the early wall has been removed, and replaced by a new gallery, which used the older piers as the base for its new ones, and so carried them to a great and disproportionate height. Similar curtains also occur at Porta Metrobia.[2]

§ 4. THE SCOPE AND VALUE OF THE FIRST-PERIOD WALL

The results of the analysis of the first period of construction may now be summarized. For the greater part of its extent, the first Wall was an extremely simple structure, notable only for its considerable thickness. Its height conforms to the standards of its time, and may be compared with the late second-century Wall of York,[3] the Wall of Chester,[4] and the estimate for Lauriacum.[5] But it was a free-standing wall in all its essentials, and did not depend upon an earthwork tradition. There was, in fact, no earlier earth bank to complicate matters of construction; and it is clear that the Trajanic[6] style, with stone facings retaining an earth filling, a style which was based upon earlier works in wood, had now passed away. This is, then, just the specification for a wall that military engineers might be expected to draw up at the close of the third century for the use of non-military builders; it is a simple and straightforward scheme, which involves no experiment.

On a few sectors, however, another type of wall was erected, with a loop-holed gallery, supporting a high-level rampart-walk. This was not an invention from the north-west frontier, but was an extremely old product of the Mediterranean world. Its advantages do not emerge except in times of closely concentrated attack, like that of Marcellus at Syracuse, when great damage can be done from the loop-holes with the Scythian bow or with the cross-bow. This distribution of this Wall varies considerably, and the total length, though not certain, is not great. But it has nothing to do with the need for intensified defence at any given

[1] Curtains nos. B 1–7.   [2] Curtains nos. H 14, J 1, 2.
[3] York, Miller, *J. R. S.* xv, p. 177.
[4] Chester, see Newstead, *Annals of Archaeology and Anthropology*, ii, pl. ix; very similar to York.   [5] Lauriacum, von Groller, *R. Limes in Österreich*, Heft xi, fig. 3.
[6] Evidence for this in Britain steadily crystallizes.

point. So it is perhaps best explained as the work of a particular gang of workmen,[1] or the contribution of some particular *collegium*.[2] Variants were almost sure to occur on a scheme of this magnitude, especially if it were being carried out by non-military labour as Malalas[3] suggests.

The tactical value of the Wall is covered by the remarks which have been made by Mr. R. G. Collingwood[4] about Hadrian's Wall in Britain. It is not a wall built for sustaining a long siege, and its defenders were not expected to fight from its top. True, its towers were primarily designed to accommodate powerful artillery. But this was meant to frighten foes away from the Wall, and was of very little use when they came near it, owing to the impossibility of depressing the angle of fire[5] sufficiently to hit them. Frequent sally-ports were required for the adequate defence of such a line. This fact, and not merely the traffic needs[6] of normal times, explains why twenty-eight gates were left in the twelve-mile circuit. So the Wall becomes a formidable barrier, and not a fighting platform, while its scope is clearly to shut chance bodies of undesirables out of the City, just as a frontier wall shut them out of the Empire. How well this conception, which follows entirely from the design, fits the historical circumstances of Aurelian's time, will be seen in the final chapter.

§ 5. THE WALL OF THE SECOND PERIOD, TYPE A

It was, no doubt, the galleried sectors of the first Wall which suggested to the second-period builders the happy method of doubling the height of the earliest Wall by crowning it with a gallery. But the galleried type, even on the original Wall, was no new invention. Defensive walls in which the rampart-walk is carried upon vaulted chambers or arcading are not uncommon in any age. The Walls of Punic Carthage;[7] the Wall of Perge in Pamphylia;[8] the Praetorian Fortress in Rome;[9] the Severan Legionary Fortress of Alba;[10] the outer Land Wall of Constanti-

---

[1] Cf. Salonae, where under M. Aurelius one gang did one curtain and tower (*C. I. L.* iii. 1979).

[2] Cf. Constantinople where the work was divided between the Greens and the Blues: *Patria*, ii, 58, p. 182, 7 (Preger).

[3] Malalas, *Chron.* xii, p. 299, (Dindorf).

[4] *Vasculum* (Andrew Reid, Newcastle-on-Tyne), Oct. 1921.

[5] See *D. U. J.*, pp. 399–406.

[6] While these were important, it is clear that they were subordinated to military demands. For streets blocked by the Wall see *F. U. R.* 2, 20, 39. Many cannot be marked.

[7] Appian, *Punica*, 95 διώροφον δ' ἦν ἑκάστου τείχους τὸ ὕψος, καὶ ἐν αὐτῷ κοίλῳ τε ὄντι καὶ στεγανῷ κάτω μὲν ἐστάθμευον ἐλέφαντες, ἱπποστάσια δὲ ὑπὲρ αὐτοὺς ἦν: cf. the modern use of railway viaduct-arches in towns, like Manchester or Leeds.

[8] Durm, *Baukunst der Griechen*, p. 209, fig. 182 = Niemann u. Petersen, *Städte Pamphyliens und Pisidiens*, vol. i, p. 61.

[9] *P. B. S. R.* x, p. 13, fig. 1.   [10] Lugli, *Ausonia*, ix. (1920), p. 225.

nople,[1] and a long line of Byzantine fortifications derived therefrom,[2] provide well-known examples. The series[3] goes back to Hittite Zindjirli or to Achaean Tiryns, and forward to Plantagenet York. But Philo and Appian both[4] attest that the erection of such walls was dictated by a desire, either for extra accommodation or for economy in material, and neither condition primarily concerned the Wall of Rome. Extra accommodation was not required: and the main problem was to give the new top the greatest lightness and stability rather than to economize in material: for the builders were fitting a sixty-foot wall on to a base designed for one not quite half as high. In most respects the solution of the problem adopted (see fig. 3) was entirely satisfactory. By building a galleried top, not only was a full-width rampart-walk obtained on top of the Wall, but the older and lower level was retained for use as well. Again, under ordinary conditions of siege warfare no battering-ram could be brought against the lightly-built upper portion, and the artillery of the Roman Age was not powerful enough to demolish it even by long and continued bombardment.[5] The strategic possibilities of the low-level walk, however, were very differently appreciated in different parts of the circuit, perhaps according to the resources, material and mental, of the gangs who built it. Three types (see fig. 9) of gallery were built, the first with six or seven loop-holes [6] (one to each bay), the second with two [7] (one to every other bay), the third with only one [8] (a central loop). All the loop-holes are of the same type, with vertical splays set in a niche; they are meant, it would seem, for the discharge of Scythian bows or of cross-bows (*arcuballistae*), since there was no room in the gallery for bigger machines.[9] But the different distribution of loop-holes in different sectors suggests that the defence was expected to be directed mainly from the upper rampart-walk, as in the siege of Witiges. The chief use of the gallery would then be the circulation of messages and materials. In this way congestion would not occur on the upper rampart-walk, where, as follows from the narrative of Procopius,[10] all available space would be needed for the spring-guns, their crews and their projectiles.

[1] Van Millingen, *Byzantine Constantinople*. Here the object was to save material and time.

[2] e.g. Butler and Littman, *Syria*, vols. ii a and b, *passim*.

[3] See the very valuable discussion in G. Bell, *Palace and Mosque of Ukhaidir*, pp. 106–110. For Zindjirli, p. 108.

[4] Philo, iii, 67; Appian, loc. cit.

[5] The possibilities of such a bombardment are illustrated by Sulla's work on the walls of Pompeii: see van Buren, *Mem. Amer. Acad. Rome*, vol. v, p. 110, pl. 60.

[6] Sectors A 24, 25, B, C 1, G 15–27, H 4–14, J, K, L 1–12, M.   [7] Curtains, L 13, 14, 30.

[8] Curtains, A 16–23, D 3, 4, E 1, 4, 5, 8, 11, 12, 13, F 4–11, L 23, 24.

[9] For the effect of such attack compare the fate of Marcellus at Syracuse: Livy, xxiv, 34, 8.   [10] Procop. *B. G.* i. 21.

The upper rampart-walk is about ten and a half feet broad, excluding the crenellated parapet in front. The original merlons of the heightened Wall seem to have disappeared everywhere, except on the first curtain[1] north of Porta Tiburtina, where two remain, embedded in medieval work. Here the width of the embrasure equals that of the merlon, and each merlon is capped with thin tiles. The walk which they protected was the chief fighting platform, on which small spring guns were placed, to create a barrage or curtain-fire, in contrast with the heavier artillery on the towers. The front of the walk was marked by a very massive tile string-course of many members: but of a parapet or rail at the back there is no trace.

The methods used in constructing this addition to the Wall were the same as those employed in building the original structure. But there are indications that the work was more hurried. The tiles for the facing (see Pl. III) are not nearly so carefully selected as in the original work; more mortar, strikingly clean, but of coarser quality, is used, with thicker and less regular joints: the bonding-courses of good tiles are absent; and less care is taken to get the face of the Wall quite true from section to section,[2] with the result that the junctions are ill-arranged, and invite those cleavages which strains have tended to create here and there. These faults, however, seem due to speed rather than to lack of skill, for some work of this period, notably that on the Gates (see Pl. XI*a*),[3] is of excellent quality. Here, in fact, just as in the original work, technique differs somewhat widely from Gate to Gate, or from section to section. And, although it is possible to detect a deterioration in the standard of the best (in the sense that the best work of the first period outclasses the best of the second), it is equally true that the best work of the second period is often superior to bad work of the first. These facts make it necessary to date the brick-facing of the City Wall by other than typological evidence (see below, p. 88).

The treatment of the first-period breastwork and merlons by the builders of the secondary gallery is of considerable intrinsic interest. For it reveals exactly why these features do not now appear among second-period work in every curtain of the Wall where second-period work survives in the right place. The treatment would seem to have been governed almost entirely by the number of loop-holes which it was proposed to make in the new gallery. For the setting-out of the new loop-holes was based upon quite different principles from the arrangement of the older merlons, and so the merlons, as the accompanying

[1] No. E 19. These were inaccessible for measuring.
[2] Notably curtains nos. L 9, 10, and Porta Asinaria.
[3] Cf. Porta Appia, but not Asinaria.

diagram (fig. 9) shows, always tended to interfere with the building of the loop-holes. This difficulty was met in various ways. At best (from the archaeologist's point of view), the merlons and the breastwork were preserved completely and built into the new Wall. And in such cases the horizontal braces for the new scaffolding were laid along the old breastwork top, often against a merlon's side, so as to leave a tell-tale line of putlog holes in the new Wall.[1] This wholesale incorporation of the older structure occurs most frequently between Porta Ostiensis East and

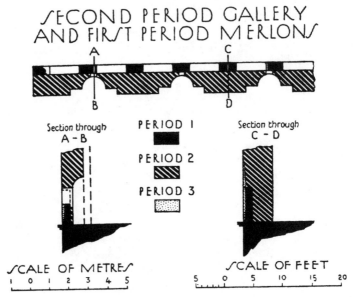

SECOND PERIOD GALLERY
AND FIRST PERIOD MERLONS

FIG. 9, from curtain M 1.

the Bastione di Sangallo, and to north and south of Porta Tiburtina. A closely similar treatment was to fill the gaps between the merlons with rough material, to add a low thickening wall behind them, and then to build the new wall upon the level surface thus gained. Examples of this treatment occur south of Porta Tiburtina,[2] at the postern west of Porta Appia,[3] and, in association with the first method, between the Bastione di Sangallo and Porta Ostiensis East.[4] Often, however, the building of the loop-holes in the new wall demanded the removal of merlons, for it was easier to knock off a merlon than to cut a loop-hole through it: and the position of the loop-hole was fixed precisely by the bays of the new gallery. This requirement, as might be expected, led to much more drastic alterations in sectors fitted with a full complement of loop-holes. Here it was impossible

[1] i.e. curtains, nos. L 23, 33; pl. IIIa and b.   [2] i.e. curtains, nos. F 1, 6.
[3] See p. 233, curtain L 10.   [4] i.e. curtain, no. L 33.

to retain the older merlons, and they were therefore swept away
—(half-way instances,[1] however, survive)—which explains why
they never occur on the Wall in connexion with the maximum
number of loop-holes.

In some places,[2] however, not only the merlons, but the
breastwork, were made to disappear. The reason for this is clear.
As may be seen on the important section now visible on the east
side of Porta Ostiensis East, the early breastwork was a thin wall
compared with the gallery front which was to take its place.
Consequently, a thickening always had to be built up behind it,
and only upon the wall as thus thickened could the new front be
built. But such a thickening provided a vertical cleavage in the
very foundation of the new structure; and, while a cleft of this
kind mattered little when the thickening was cut by only one
niche and one central loop-hole, it became a potential danger
that demanded serious attention when the loop-holes and niches
were many. For the niches (see fig. 9) in effect threw the weight
of the Wall on to a series of arcades, of which the piers required
flawlessly rigid foundations. To build them with an internal
vertical division would have been to invite disaster. This explains,
then, why the breastwork and merlons of the old Wall have been
completely removed in sections of this type. But almost everywhere the string-course, that marks the base of the first-period
breastwork and the level of the rampart-walk, still exists and
proves the existence of the older Wall: and it disappears only
when the Wall has been completely re-faced.[3] This happens
much more rarely than might be expected in so ancient a structure, and certain sectors of the primary galleried wall provide the
best examples.[4]

§ 6. THE WALL OF THE SECOND PERIOD, TYPE B

A very different type of Wall was built on top of those sectors[5]
of early Wall which are associated with a large earth backing.
The new heightening wall (fig. 10) was no more than six feet in
width, had no gallery, and was set on the front edge of the older
wall, so as to leave six feet behind for a lower rampart-walk.
Each curtain thereof was provided with a central loop-
hole, and its top was crowned by a thin parapet and merlons.
This gave a rather narrow upper rampart-walk, less wide than
the old Vitruvian[6] six-foot standard. Such is the arrangement
found at the Quartiere di San Saba. On the eastern side of the
City, south of Porta Chiusa, a very similar construction appears,

---

[1] i.e. curtains, nos. L 51, M 1.   [2] i.e. Sector B *passim.*
[3] i.e. curtains, nos. H 2, 10, 11.   [4] i.e. curtains, nos. G 15–26.
[5] i.e. Sectors E, L 36–50.   [6] Vitruv. *de Arch.* i. 5. 3.

but the new upper rampart-walk tends to be thicker and the lower one to be thinner. So it might be supposed, though the matter is in no way proved, that a greater width was obtained for the lower walk by the addition of an earthen mound behind it. Against this notion, however, it should be observed that the heightening wall in front of Aquae Marcia-Tepula-Iulia also followed this type, being a plain, narrow curtain-wall,[1] with no

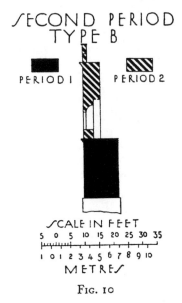

SECOND PERIOD TYPE B

PERIOD 1   PERIOD 2

SCALE IN FEET
5 0 5 10 15 20 25 30 35

1 0 1 2 3 4 5 6 7 8 9 10
METRES

FIG. 10

gallery, and the usual rather thin upper rampart-walk. Here no reason is apparent for the choice, since the Wall was neither hidden nor backed with earth. Loop-holes were reduced to one for each curtain. And on this sector, at a point where the Acqua Felice now rises high above the rest of the Wall, appear remains[2] of the distinctive merlons added to the Wall by Belisarius.

§ 7. THE WALL OF THE SECOND PERIOD, TYPE C

A further difference (fig. 8) occurs on the sector[3] of Aquae Claudia—Anio Novus. Here the rampart-walk of the first period must have been extended at the back by means of a platform built between the aqueduct piers, if this had not been done

[1] i.e. Sector F.
[2] i.e. curtain no. F 12.
[3] i.e. curtains, nos. G 2–7. For such buttresses at the back of thin walls cf. Aosta (Promis, *Antichità di Aosta*, Tav. iv) and Narona (*Schriften der Balkan-Kommission, Antiquarische Abteilung* V. Taf. ii. K. Patsch. Wien. 1907).

a. FIRST-PERIOD CURTAIN G 6, SHOWING FACING
AND CONCRETE

b. FIRST-PERIOD CURTAIN L 11; FACING AND BUILDING-JOINTS

already. For these platforms were now made to carry rearward buttresses supporting a new wall, which reached to the top of the aqueduct, and ran just in front of it. Loop-holes were arranged in a lower gallery formed by these platforms. The towers were placed so as to be accessible through the gaps between the aqueduct-piers. The upper rampart-walk ran level with the aqueduct conduit, but just in front of it, and it was reached by

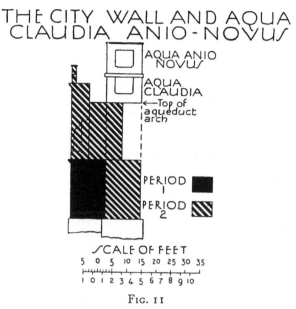

FIG. 11

staircases in the towers. There was therefore no need to walk on the conduit.[1]

§ 8. THE WALL OF THE SECOND PERIOD, TYPE D

A variation of the type just described must have existed to suit the peculiar conditions in the sectors east and west of Porta Praenestina—Labicana, where the Wall was built between the aqueduct-piers, and divided by them.[2] Its exact form is unknown, for the whole of the arrangement is blotted out by the Acqua Felice, and nothing of the ancient aqueduct is now left above the level of the springing of its arches. But the presumption is that the whole space between the piers was completely filled up, and that the conduit itself was crowned with a parapet and merlons,[3] and used as a rampart-walk. The danger arising

[1] The stopping of the conduit has nothing to do with the Wall, since it occurs outside it on the line of Claudia—Anio Novus at Porta Furba.

[2] Curtains nos. F 19, G 1.

[3] Cf. Porta Maggiore, as shown in the Cadastro; see p. 211.

from this ill-defended sector was met, however, by erecting, at its eastern end, a very large tower which was heavily buttressed in later periods,[1] doubtless in order to help it to withstand the recoil of the large *ballistae* or *onagri* which it carried. This is to be compared with the similar protection arranged for the weak re-entrant of Porta Metrobia.

§ 9. THE VALUE OF THE RECONSTRUCTED WALL

It remains to estimate the value of the reconstructed and heightened Wall. The great advantage[2] gained was the reduction in the number of defenders required. When the Wall had been lower its thickness had already defied the battering-ram, but its height was not proof against an attack with scaling-ladders. Its increased height now made it a mighty breakwater, against which wave after wave of attackers might surge in vain. This was in complete accordance with late Roman theory of town-defence.[3] Besiegers provided with the tackle of the ancient world had not the least chance of getting through the Wall unless they were allowed to carry out the most elaborate siege-operations. And they could be prevented from doing so by a minimum number of defenders, armed with bows or cross-bows for use against men, and with heavy *onagri* for the destruction of machinery. Furthermore, the provision of the gallery must have facilitated communications, especially upon sectors where there were few loop-holes to be occupied by defenders.

It must not be forgotten, however, that considerable lengths of second-period Wall had no gallery, and, instead of it, two narrow and much less efficient uncovered rampart-walks, although the Wall as a whole presented a similar outer face to assailants. These sectors therefore raise a special problem. They were clearly not constructed in the interests of efficiency. The type of structure does not reveal the purpose of design, nor does the distribution help, since the different sectors have no special feature in common. Three possibilities then suggest themselves. The scheme might be (*a*) the choice of one or more *collegia*, less well equipped to deal with the problem: or (*b*) it was the result of a desire for economy: or (*c*) there was need for unexpected speed in the later stages of building. But only poverty or haste

---

[1] e.g. in the period of travertine blocks in bands, and peperino blocks, possibly Valentinian III after the earthquake of 442. Tower F 18.

[2] Cf. the state of Rome in 552; Procop. *B. G.* iv. 33 ὅλον μὲν οὖν τὸν Ῥώμης περίβολον διὰ μεγέθους ὑπερβολὴν οὔτε Ῥωμαῖοι ἐπιόντες περιβάλλεσθαι εἶχον οὔτε Γότθοι φρουρεῖν.

[3] Cf. Constantinople, and my remarks in *D. U. J.* xxv, p. 399 sqq.

will adequately explain the badness and frequency of the type.[1]
These possibilities will be discussed afresh when connexions with
ancient literature are considered. They will provide a helpful clue
to the identity of their historical period.

[1] The specification to be followed might admit of improvements, furnished by the zeal
of the engineers or *collegium* in question: it would hardly admit defects in large quantity.
Again, it might be urged that the galleried scheme was an improvement upon this: but the
improvement could hardly have been an *afterthought* when the builders had the galleried
sectors of the first period to copy.

II. THE TOWERS AND THEIR EVOLUTION

§ 1. THE TOWERS OF THE FIRST PERIOD

ONE pattern of tower is found in association with the early Wall, with three uncommon variants. The ubiquitous type [1] was planned (fig. 12) as a solid rectangular block of tile or brick-faced concrete, twenty-five feet long, which projected eleven feet from the Wall, and reached as high as the rampart-walk, at which

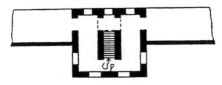

FIRST-PERIOD NORMAL TOWER

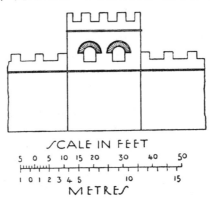

SCALE IN FEET

METRES

FIG. 12

level the external string-course of the Wall was continued round the tower. On the solid base thus gained there then arose a rectangular chamber, which included the rampart-walk in its breadth and was bounded by the usual two-foot walls, built to fit the *bipedalis* tile.[2] It was lit by two windows at the front, by one on each side, and by one at the back: all these windows had round heads, with voussoirs of *bipedalis* tiles, and in some towers [3] one course of tiles was laid round the extrados of the window-head, thus giving it definition. There is one quite certainly decorative feature to record: below the two front windows

---

[1] The type was, however, changed so much that it is desirable to quote numbers where the original type exists in fair order: these are nos. A 21, B 16, L 35, 36, M 22.
[2] This affair of standardization had much weight in the original planning of the towers.
[3] i.e. nos. A 21, B 16, M 22.

a small terracotta frame appears on one [1] of the towers, and no doubt it originally held a figured plaque, whose subject gave a name to the tower. The roof of the tower [2] is barrel-vaulted in three bays, the central one is narrow and covers a staircase which rises from the outer face and gives access to a flat battlemented roof. The stairs do not, however, begin too close to the front of the tower, and so give room, both to right and left, for a small *ballista*, arranged, it may be suggested, on a swivel,[3] for use at either the front or the side window. Circulation within the tower (fig. 12) could be conveniently arranged behind the *ballistae*,

FIRST PERIOD
TOWER FOR GALLERIED WALL

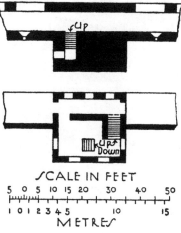

SCALE IN FEET

METRES

FIG. 13

and a direct through passage, aiding the speedy circulation of messages and material on the rampart-walk, was provided beneath the staircase-landing. Thus, whether the *ballistae* were considered as permanent fixtures, or whether they were put in position only in time of war, the tower seems to have been planned with their presence in mind.

A complete roof of the first period is nowhere to be seen on the Wall. But the existence of the staircase proves that it was flat and had battlements. Again, since neither the number nor the form of the merlons is certain, it is necessary to depend entirely upon analogy for a restoration of the top of the tower. The topmost features have disappeared either amid the havoc of

[1] No. L 36; cf. the *Casa di Diana* at Ostia.
[2] Cf. nos. L 36, A 21.
[3] Cf. the *ballista* mounting-slots in the towers of Burgh Castle (Gariannonum).

ancient and extensive restorations, or, if any survived[1] the Middle Ages, because of natural decay.

The first variation (fig. 13) of this plan was introduced in order to give access from the first-period gallery to the top of the tower, and so to the upper rampart-walk, by means of an extra set of stairs. The result was that the tower became much less strong in structure, since its base ceased at the low level of the gallery-walk, where was provided a through passage, and a staircase which climbed round three sides of the tower, and led to the uppermost chamber. Its tactical strength was also much diminished, for the new arrangement left no room for two *ballistae* on one floor, and one of the pair had to be placed below the stairs at gallery level. This deprived the gun-crews of that co-ordination which was all-important in defending the tower. Evidently, the designers of the scheme considered that this deficiency was outweighed by the advantage of having a loop-hole gallery in the curtain-wall, and so the building of the gallery dominated the whole plan. But the variation is nothing like general, since it occurs with the galleried Wall only on the sectors[2] Porta Pinciana—Porta Salaria, Amphitheatrum Castrense—Porta Asinaria, and Domus Lateranorum—Porta Metrobia.

Still rarer is the second variant type of tower[3] which contained stairs reaching to ground level behind the Wall. This provision is really confined to Gates of the third class, for example, Porta Asinaria and to posterns, for example, the postern of Vigna Casali, and no example is known of a staircase to the Wall independent of a gateway, an indication of how strictly access thereto was controlled. This staircase affected the upper arrangement of the tower in the same way as in the first variation: that is to say, a staircase led, round three sides of the tower, up to the level of the upper chamber, and a straight central staircase rose beyond it. The *ballistae* were therefore separated, as before.

Rarest of all variants (three[4] instances are known to-day) is the semicircular tower, substituted for a normal rectangular one. In two places the provision was governed by the way in which the Wall was planned. The first tower west of Porta Latina is thus fitted into an awkward re-entrant. The east tower of Porta Pinciana, which the plan of the Gate (fig. 30) shows to be really an ordinary Wall tower, is given semicircular form in order to leave adequate space for the roadway, which passes obliquely through the line of the Wall. Only the reason for the presence of the third semicircular tower (Pl. VI*b*), the first now left on the west of Porta Salaria, is uncertain. Provisionally, the writer is content

[1] On such towers as nos. L 35, 36, which were never heightened.
[2] i.e. Sectors B, G 15–27, H 2, 3.   [3] Towers nos. L 10, M 1.
[4] Towers nos. B 19, K 1, and Porta Pinciana, E. Tower.

to regard it as a builder's freak. The staircases inside these
towers were not complicated, since a galleried wall of the first
period was not involved. They were therefore simple central
flights, rising from the front and giving access to the roof as in
other towers.

Otherwise, there is no reason for supposing any other type of
tower to have been used in the first period. But it has been
suggested [1] that a peculiar form of bastion, with a broad flight of
steps leading up behind it, was designed for use on the earth-
backed sector of Wall between Porta Tiburtina and the Porta
Chiusa. There is grave doubt in this matter. The bastions in
question are ill-preserved, the steps are entirely modern; moreover, although the position of the ancient levels at this point is
certain, it is at least clear, from evidence at Porta Chiusa,[2] that
they lie far below the modern, and that therefore the arrangements
of access from the ground to the Wall must have been quite
different from those now visible: probably they conformed
closely to normal type. It is therefore reasonable to conclude
that, so far as is known, the earliest towers all round the circuit
had a uniform height and an almost uniform outward appearance,
while their plans differed only at staircases. In short, uniformity
of design, which is so marked a feature of the earliest Wall and
Gates, appears also in the earliest towers. If, then, towers of the
first period were as simply planned as the Wall which they were
designed to protect, what was their strategic value? This is
perhaps best illustrated by the statement about Palmyra by
'Vopiscus',[3] which may not be historically true, but which must
be based upon the tactical conceptions of the age. 'The City is
strongly fortified with towers, and in every tower there are two
or three *ballistae*.' Here was the defence by machinery which
was meant to break up a sudden attack or to smash hostile
siege-works. The reason for the lateral windows in the towers
thus becomes apparent. A study of the *ballista*[4] reveals that, without some very complicated adjustment, and particularly carefully
designed arrangements for dealing with a recoil, this spring-
gun could not hit at close range an objective below the level of
the barrel. For the normal trajectory of its missile was either
straight or parabolic. Ground immediately below the tower was
therefore dead, and so an isolated tower would be surrounded
by a space which its *ballista* could not cover. But when towers

[1] Homo, *Essai*, p. 278, fig. 7.
[2] See p. 183, fig. 35.
[3] Vopiscus, *Vit. Aurel.* 26, 2–5. The letter of Aurelian to Mucapor may be false; but it must embody the theory of the age. Philo (lxxxiii, 15) had worked out the theory on paper long ago.
[4] These remarks are based upon Lieutenant-General E. Schramm's, *Die Antiken Geschütze der Saalburg.*

were grouped close to one another (fig. 14), the difficulty of defence thus raised could be simply solved. The *ballistae*, which used the side-windows, would be designed to concentrate, not only upon the short piece of ground which separated the two towers (which also would have to be 'covered' by co-operation), but upon dead ground in front of the neighbouring towers as well. Only so would an adequate defence become possible.

It follows, then, that this type of defence depended for success upon a full complement of *ballistae*. This must have been extremely costly, for in Rome it implies a maximum of nearly

TOWERS AND BALLISTA TRAJECTORY

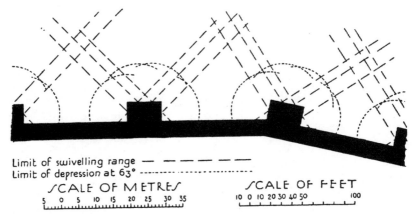

Limit of swivelling range — — — — — — —
Limit of depression at 63° ·············· ·············
SCALE OF METRES   SCALE OF FEET
5 0 5 10 15 20 25 30 35   10 0 10 20 30 40 50   100

FIG. 14

eight hundred machines,[1] and the life of even the Procopian type of *ballista*, with steel springs, was not long. Small wonder, then, that under Honorius artillery-men were replaced by the less costly archer, while the *ballistae* were regarded henceforward as movables, only to be used at vital points in times of siege, as under Belisarius.[2] But while the system lasted, and it was still in full use during the second period, it must have been one of the most magnificent and complete examples of the substitution of machinery for men in the Roman Empire. Only, however, while much wealth and high organization was still available can it have been possible to provide against the chance contingency of an attack at any point upon so vast a scale. In later ages the machines did not grow less efficient, nor were they less commonly used; but economy demanded that they should be moved about, and brought to bear at the points where they were required;

[1] There were 381 towers, according to the Einsiedeln List: each would have two machines: this is 762. Moreover, manufactories for these were not numerous; they were situated at Sirmium, Augusta Suessionum, and Augusta Treverorum. Schramm's machines, loc. cit., p. 76, lasted thirteen years and nine years, and the service would not be constant.

[2] Procop. *B. G.* i. 21.

V

a. CURTAIN G 22, FIRST-PERIOD GALLERY BELOW, SECOND-
PERIOD GALLERY ABOVE

The curtain has fallen away

b. TOWERS L 36 AND L 35; TWO FIRST-
PERIOD TYPES

and the risk of a surprise had to be taken when there was not the money to install that quantity of machines, which was the only sound insurance against such an event.

§ 2. THE TOWERS OF THE SECOND PERIOD

The second period, inaugurated by great changes on the Wall, witnessed correspondingly important changes at the towers. The older towers of the newly heightened Wall had to be adapted so as to fit a Wall now as high as themselves. Various solutions were chosen, but that most widely adopted [1] was to leave the towers alone (see Pl. V*b*) considering them as projecting *ballista*-casemates, which served for long-range shooting, while less effective missiles were discharged from the loop-holes of the new gallery in the Wall. But the deficient height of the towers robbed them of good outlook, and, in order to remedy the defect, a second solution was adopted (Pl. V*a*). The upper story of the primary tower [2] was removed down to the level of the springing of its round-headed windows. A new floor-level was then built at the height of the older flat roof, and on top of it was added an entirely new story, crowned by a hipped roof and loop-hole slits. This rose high above the Wall and gave the necessary vantage-point for a look-out post. Such towers occur near the Domus Lateranorum and east of the Bastione di Sangallo.

Much more common was the third arrangement (Pl. VII*a*) which stopped up the windows of the older tower [3] (especially those on a level with the first-period galleried walk), retained the old roof, but scrapped the parapet and merlons upon it; then was added a large chamber, covered by a hipped roof. Three round-headed windows pierced its front, and on each side was a further window and a door which gave access to the rampart-walk. Two windows existed at the back. Examples of this splendid type, used by Diocletian to decorate his Dalmatian palace [4] with great effect, are the *turris omnium perfectissima* and its companions, on sector B, between Porta Pinciana and Porta Salaria; and Dosio, [5] in giving such tops to the long line of towers west of the *Amphitheatrum Castrense*, shows that many once existed on the south side of the City also, which have now disappeared. This should emphasize the need for caution in estimating the original numbers of this class. It is significant that the Renais-

[1] See p. 253 for a further consideration of this point.
[2] i.e. nos. H 1, J 12, 13, L 12.
[3] i.e. nos. B 4, 18, G 15–20, the class of *Turris omnium perfectissima* B 14.
[4] Cf. also the pictures of the Wall of Susa on the frieze of the Arch of Constantine. In contrast, the towers of Trajan's Column. Rodenwaldt, *Die Kunst der Antike*, 579 & 649.
[5] Dosio, *Reliquiae* 32 = Uff. 2533 = Bartoli, *C. Ved.*, lxx. Cf. Jan Asselyn (1610–52), Leiden, P. d. R. U. no. 1860, shown to me by Mr. C. F. Bell.

sance panoramas[1] of the ancient City in restored form took
this type of tower for their standard schematic representation:
and the accuracy of their generalization is borne out by the views
of Tempesta[2] and Maggi,[3] which show the remains of the Wall
in their actual form.

The tactical purpose of this type of tower is sufficiently clear.
In essence, it is the primary scheme pushed a stage higher.
There still exists the arrangement of front and side windows
so as to suit a swivelling *ballista*; but an improvement has
been added, a central window, which serves as an observation-
post or 'crow's-nest'. How these windows were protected is
unknown. But possible devices are the Roman grilles,[4] usual
on ordinary windows which required protection, or the swinging
shutters common in medieval towers.[5] The pair of windows
holding the *ballista* would also need a device of the kind, for
although the iron-clad front[6] of the machine would fill one
window, one or other would always be vacant and in need of
protection. Below the level of the *ballista*-casemates most of the
available space is taken by staircases, connecting this floor of
the tower with the gallery, and these were lit by means of narrow
loop-holes instead of windows. The only decorations on the
tower are a string-course, continuing the line of that which marks
the upper rampart-walk, and an elaborate eaves-moulding with
modillions. But in many towers there still remains the earlier
string-course, marking the level of the primary *ballista*-casemate.

It would be interesting to know whether this type of tower
ever existed in connexion with the second-period Wall without
gallery, where the scheme of building was so much simpler than
elsewhere. But, unfortunately, no tower[7] on this sector is preserved above the height of the Wall. The fact, however, that the
lower windows were kept open suggests very strongly that the
towers here had battlements on a level with the top of the Wall,
and therefore did not receive any additional story. This was, at
least, the treatment reserved for many other sectors, where the
great towers did not get built.

The most striking feature of the second scheme is thus its lack
of uniformity. Whereas, on the one hand, certain towers are
remodelled on a magnificent and stately scale, other towers
(the majority) undergo as little alteration as possible. This
corresponds to the character of the first alteration on the Wall,
where some parts receive the elaborate and useful gallery, and
others the simple and far from efficient masking wall. It is also

[1] e.g. those of Ligorio, Cartaro, &c.   [2] Tempesta, 1593.
[3] Maggi, 1625.   [4] See Durm, *Baukunst der Römern*, pp. 348–9.
[5] e.g. the castle of the Count of Flanders at Ghent. Cf. Philo, lxxxi. 30, describing
such shutters; σεσιδηρωμένας γὰρ καὶ ἀμφιπλεύρους τὰς θυρίδας αὐτῶν ποιήσομεν.
[6] See Ammian. Marc. xxiii. 4. i.   [7] Nos. G 21–50.

clear that, although the worse towers go with the worse wall, they also occur elsewhere upon sectors of good wall. So the extent of inferior building was greater so far as the towers were concerned. This is explicable in two ways, which are not mutually exclusive, and may both be true. Towers take longer to build than simple curtains. If the scheme was proceeding at uniform rate, until the inferior standards were adopted, there would be more towers to finish than curtains. Secondly, the urgent matter was the wall-curtain,[1] for the towers were already high enough to suit even the new scheme; work on the curtains may therefore have been pushed ahead as a matter of urgency, while the conversion of the towers followed slowly, and ceased before it was complete. The significance of these observations, and their possible relation to History, are discussed later.[2]

[1] This is important in connexion with the question which came first, galleried wall or simple wall, in this reconstruction.
[2] See p. 252 sqq.

III. NECESSARIA

A VERY necessary if minor part of the defensive scheme was its sanitary accommodation, which is given a prominent place in the Einsiedeln List. But only one surviving *garderobe*, or *necessarium*,[1] was noted by Lanciani[2] and Homo.[3] It projects from the central loop-hole of the first curtain east of Porta Salaria, in the form of a tiny apse built on corbels, between which was arranged a hole in the floor. This example is, however, obviously late in date, since a loop-hole has been sacrificed to house it: and its form gives no clue to that of the original *necessaria*, contemporary with the loop-hole system. These almost every writer[4] on the Wall has neglected to describe, although their presence and type is attested in various sectors by twin travertine corbels, set close together at upper rampart-walk level, at the junction of the towers and the Wall. If proof were required (Pl. VIII*a*), a shoot in a buttress underneath one of these,[5] at the east end of the third curtain east of Porta Latina, demonstrates that the corbels were meant to support *garderobes*.

These *necessaria* belong, of course, to the Wall as heightened, and it is evident that they were built when the heightening took place, because their corbels are bedded carefully in the original concrete,[6] while the original facing is built up against them, and is not cut through by them. Not counting the apsidal structure at Porta Salaria, twenty sets of corbels can now be traced on different parts of the Wall; on one curtain[7] two sets occur next to each other: elsewhere five towers[8] in succession possess a set, or again, two[9] successive towers are fitted in the same way. The other examples are scattered. The reason for this odd distribution is not far to seek. The corbels lay at the upper rampart-walk level and were covered and held in place by the breastwork: when the breastwork disappeared, the corbels would tend to fall out; and, in

---

[1] The word is common in early medieval Latin, see Du Cange, s.v. *necessarium*. It is rare in classical Latin, but occurs in adjectival form, governing *locus*, in Gaius, *Inst.* iii, sect. 193. No doubt it was a common enough colloquialism.

[2] Lanciani, *B. C.* xx, 1892, p. 89, note 2, quoting parallels for the example at Porta Salaria (no. 4) and at S. Balbina on the Aventine.

[3] *Essai*, p. 280, fig. 9.

[4] The exceptions are Middleton (*Remains of Anc. R.*, vol. ii, p. 376), who divined their purpose: and Nibby (*M. di R.*, p. 317), who noted, on tower A 24, *due pietri sporgenti in fuori per gli appiombatori*; that is, he thought they were machicolations, which is impossible owing to their position and distribution and the shoots noted below.

[5] No. 16. The shoot is marble-lined, and this material, for obvious reasons, was frequently chosen for the purpose: comparison may be made with the examples photographed by Brogi (16892) on Porta Appia, and the beautiful two-storied example in the Marble Tower at Constantinople, of which the writer hopes to publish measured details.

[6] e.g. Nos. 12, 13, which are broken off. J 13–14.   [7] Nos. 5 & 6, G 19.

[8] Nos. 12, 13, 14, 15, 16, J 13–18.   [9] Nos. B 4, 5.

view of the fact that the breastwork is nowhere now in existence, the frequent absence of the corbels is less remarkable than their survival. It is thus important to note that the consecutive series described above suggest that originally the towers had at least one latrine apiece.[1]

The form of the *garderobe* itself was no doubt quite simple. A small projecting room was supported on a flat arch, carried in turn by the corbels, and a hole in the outer edge of the floor served the needs of evacuation. A row of three such buildings, and a fourth in ruin, is shown on Rossini's view[2] of Porta Tiburtina: these are roofed and do not look very ancient. The example drawn by Giovannantonio Dosio,[3] at the east end of the third curtain west of the Amphitheatrum Castrense, even if imaginary, may come nearer the truth. There the projecting floor is screened by a simple wall, equal in height to a merlon, and there is no roof: but the structure served its purpose, which was to protect an occupant of the convenience from the bow drawn at a venture. In later times[4] these tower-latrines received shoots beneath them, built up to the corbels from ground level. These were usually mere cesspools, and did not connect with any drainage system, with results which are better imagined than described. They can be compared with the *garderobe* towers in castles of the Norman age.[5] A more elaborate, and ancient, example exists on the third floor of Porta Appia.[6] Its complete relation to the rest of the gate need not concern us here. It opens from the lower landing of a small external staircase, leading from the west tower to the upper rampart-walk of the Wall, and is planned as a small tapering recess. The outer end of its floor is fitted with a gently sloping shoot, which discharges into the open air at the junction of the west tower and the Wall. But neither the method of sewage disposal nor the angle of the shoot were really efficient, as was practically demonstrated when the room was restored to use during the repairs of 1926. Other latrines appear at the same level on this Gate, in the northernmost west window and the easternmost front window of the west tower, and are shown on a photograph of the gate by Brogi.[7] But they are late additions, despite their carefully built and marble-lined shoots.

A terse criticism of the whole system seems desirable in view of current ideas about the excellence of Roman sewage disposal.

---

[1] Compare the discussion of the Einsiedeln Document, p. 46.

[2] *Le porte antiche e moderne del recinto di Roma*, tav. 7; *Cadastro di Alessandro VII.* shows also a little control-house, connected with the Acqua Felice.

[3] Dosio=Bartoli, *C. Ved.* lxx. See p. 81, n. 5.

[4] But the example at tower 129 (Pl. V) may be original. Here we have to do with the early gallery, and it may have been thought proper to guide the course of the sewage past the gallery when it was so low.

[5] Cf. Caerphilly.

[6] See p. 134: plan on fig. 21.   [7] Brogi, 16892: also Vasari's front view.

These latrines are arranged without any regard for the essential *desiderata* of sanitation. They only satisfied the most immediate requirement, to remove the offensive matter from the neighbourhood of the rampart-walk and the tops of the towers. 'Out of sight, out of mind' was the principle held, and the eventual disinfection or utilization of sewage never ruled the design of even the most elaborate Roman drains. The cruder and more dangerous forms of the system were part of Rome's legacy to the Middle Ages, and it has been reserved to modern science to devise the beneficial intricacies of the water-trap and sewage-farm.

IV. REPAIRS TO THE WALL AND TOWERS

AS might be expected, the Wall was repaired many times.[1]
But these repairs rarely went more than skin-deep, for the
core of the Wall was too solid to invite easy destruction. On the
other hand, the method of building the tile-facing, as a separate
and primary piece of construction, carried with it the following
risk. If the facing chanced to unite firmly with the *caementa*
behind it, all was well. But an insufficient union would make the
facing liable to break away under such conditions as extreme
changes in temperature, storm and wind, heavy bombardment, or
earthquake shock. In fact, this has often happened, especially
at the base of the Wall, which is the dampest and most exposed to
injury. The cause was clearly the insufficient backward projection
of the tiles, and the remedy was to fit on a new facing with the
tile fragments and mortar. Then, because the technique of such
patching tends to differ considerably from age to age, a distinctive
type of patching can be certainly recognized in many different
parts of the Wall. Usually, however, it is not possible to be so
sure of recognition as to classify the patch in relation to work
distributed over the whole Wall, and so a patch may only be
classified, chronologically, in relation to other work in its particular curtain—that is to say, it can be seen which of two or more
superimposed patches came first. In fact, common sense will
insist that typological evidence is only to be used in such classification with the very greatest caution, for in any age one workman
will patch badly and another well. Identification becomes easier
where the repair is a definitely characteristic piece of work, in
material as opposed to technique; and in certain places a combination of all the conditions mentioned above makes possible the
construction of a sequence of historical value, which none of
them in isolation could have enabled. But the lesson to be learnt
seems to be that each patch presents its own special problem,
which is not likely to be solved without careful reference to the
whole Wall, but is not always soluble after that.

Yet certain outstanding characteristics may be noted here.
The first repair on the Wall, that is to say, the heightening thereof, is everywhere to be distinguished from the later work, not
by the excellence of its technique, but by the light colour of its
mortar, in which the *pozzolana* has been washed very clean.[2]
This shows up well in comparatively wide joints, helping the
pink and red bricks to give to the Wall the golden colour which

[1] See the literary sources, p. 27 sqq.

[2] There is no doubt, Dr. Van Deman assures me, that the Romans washed the material
for their cement, thereby adding very greatly to its durability.

it has in sunlight. It is noteworthy that all these characteristics are shared by the Basilica of Maxentius.[1] There is also a superior class of facing belonging to the same period, which is clear at Portae Appia and Ostiensis East (Pls. XI*a*, XIII*a*). This is very carefully built, more so than that of the Basilica Maxentii, but bonding-courses therein are extremely rare, as in the arch of Malborghetto. This is a fact of considerable importance for chronology, since bonding-courses pass out of use in Rome early in the Constantinian age.[2] It creates a pre-supposition that on the Wall brick-facing provided with bonding-courses belongs to the Wall's earliest periods: and this holds true on all the sectors examined by the writer. Only work which can be assigned to the first-period, or the small class of very careful second-period work, which is reserved for special features, such as Gates, ever contains bonding-courses. This is a generalization, which the large amount of first-period work, and still greater quantity of second-period work, seem to make quite safe.

The work of the next periods,[3] to be detected clearly at Portae Appia and Asinaria, is distinguished by the presence of much coarse and dirty *pozzolana* in its mortar, by thick joints, and by the almost universal employment for facing of long and thin, or short and fat, flanges of roof-tiles. Among these tiles is to be especially distinguished a variety that has become very white, although the cause of this whiteness, whether firing or subsequent chemical action, is not clear. Again, while the tile-scraps of earlier periods, if often irregular in length and height, are usually alined to one another at the top or bottom, these tiles commonly show a tendency to fall out of line, and are laid with much bigger mortar-joints in proportion to their thickness than any group occurring earlier. These features seem common to all the brickwork of the fifth century, and, accordingly, the writer has felt that the character of the work itself does not enable a clear distinction to be drawn between the work of the Honorian period and that of Theoderic; any such distinction must be based upon other facts: for example, on constructional breaks.[4] Very distinctive, on the other hand, is a limited class of work, wherein brick-facing is associated with bands of long travertine blocks;

---

[1] For the Basilica see C. A. Minoprio's study, shortly to appear in *P. B. S. R.* xii.

[2] This change in fashion is sufficiently well illustrated by the Basilica Maxentii. Here the building of Maxentius contains regular bonding-courses, related to the putlog-holes: the additional north apse of Constantine contains none. Compare also Santa Pudenziana and Santa Maria Maggiore. For Malborghetto see Töbelmann, *Abhandl. d. Heidelberger Akad. d. Wissenschaften*, 2, 1915, pls. vii, xiv.

[3] It should be noted that this work is to be associated with serrate cornices of tiles, which have fifth-century associations in their rudimentary stage and continue later: see below, note 7, p. 114.

[4] It becomes clear at Porta Appia, owing to such breaks; but the distinction *per se* is not clear enough to use with absolute certainty.

a. FIRST-PERIOD TOWER H 2, FOR THE
GALLERIED WALL

b. FIRST-PERIOD SEMICIRCULAR TOWER B 19

and the place of this on Porta Appia[1] in relation to work of other periods (see fig. 21), combined with the fact that it is used else-where[2] in the construction of large buttresses for the Wall and towers (Pl. VII*b*), would strongly suggest that it is associated with repairs after the earthquake[3] of 442, which did serious damage all over the City. And repairs to the Wall were pending about this time, since they were foreshadowed in an Edict[4] of Theo-dosius II and Valentinian III, of two years before. If they were envisaged before the earthquake, some of them must have become urgent after it. So here the combination of historical facts with the distribution and character of a given repair enables a con-clusion to be drawn about its date with sufficient confidence.

The next distinctive repair involved a liberal use of a rough and somewhat irregularly coursed block-and-brick work, of very much cruder character than the similar work associated with the first period. Parker, in the rubrics of his photographs,[5] assigned this to Belisarius, without giving a reason for the identification. It should be noted, however, that this kind of work is confined[6] to the north and east of the City, and never occurs on the south. It can hardly be coincidence that the Gothic attack of 536 was concentrated exclusively[7] upon these points; and it would be pleasant to give Parker the credit for having recognized this, if it were possible to find any context in which he had noted it. In this distinctive block-and-brick work, then, may be recognized with some certainty a repair which followed the Gothic siege, and which would be executed by order of Bessas, the Byzantine general who held Rome until Totila's arrival, nine years later.[8] And it may be added that the work is matched by some extensive and very late repairs to Aqua Claudia on Via Valeria, at Osteria della Spiaggia,[9] and elsewhere, which fit a Belisarian date.

Traces of the first repair executed by Belisarius before the Gothic attack also exist in the merlons of Viale Labicano, but these can only be seen in section, and at all events are too few to serve as a criterion of that work. Complete merlons of this Hellenistic form, revived and introduced to Rome by Belisarius,[10] still survive between Porta Ostiensis East and the Pyramid of Gaius Cestius, but they belong to medieval times.[11]

---

[1] See p. 127, fig. 21.　　　[2] i.e. curtain no. J 19 ; towers nos. F 18, J 2, 3, K 6, 8.

[3] For evidence of the earthquake see *C. I. L.* vi. 32086–32090; Paul Diac, *Hist. Misc.* xiv, p. 961 (Migne).

[4] *Novellae Val.* iii, tit. v.　　　[5] e.g. nos. 4, 1217, 6.

[6] It is to be found nowhere west of Porta Asinaria.　　　[7] See Procop. *B. G.* i. 19.

[8] See Procop. *B. G.* iii. 13.

[9] I owe this reference to Dr. Ashby, who kindly permitted me to see his photographic collection for the aqueducts. Dr. van Deman draws my attention to Porta Furba.

[10] Procop. *B. G.* i. 14. See curtain F 12.

[11] This is shown by their construction in uncoursed tufa: I suspect Pope Nicholas V's hand here.

The final work of Belisarius, after the evacuation of Totila in 547, is the subject of a valuable description by Procopius,[1] quoted in full, with a contemporary analogy from Pisaurum, in the chapter on literary sources; λίθους ἀγχιστά πη ὄντας συναγαγὼν ἐπ᾽ ἀλλήλους οὐδενὶ κόσμῳ συνέβαλεν, οὐδὲν τὸ παράπαν ἐντὸς ἔχοντας ἐπεὶ οὐδὲ τίτανον εἶχεν οὐδέ τι ἄλλο τοιοῦτον ἀλλ᾽ ὅπως μόνον τῆς οἰκοδομίας σώζοιτο πρόσωπον . . . This work has been recognized for long in certain rough but solid masonry, put in to save the face of the structure, which occurs at many points[2] on the Wall (see Pl. IIIc). Its builders showed a marked preference for blocks of *tufo* and *peperino*, which were easy to handle and to fit. Later, in order to make the work permanent, some one united the blocks with mortar and rough tile-fragments. This must have taken place soon, and is therefore to be assigned either to Bessas or to Narses. Several towers[3] were also heavily reinforced with blocks of *tufo*, in order to strengthen their lower stories, perhaps in imitation of that earlier external thickening, or reinforcement, in brick and travertine, which seems to be connected with the provision of especially powerful artillery at the outer edges of weak re-entrants.

It is not intended that this inquiry should extend farther than this point. But two typical Papal styles may be noted, of which the first has yet to be dated. Dated parallels are wanted (*curet alius!*) for the rather rare but interesting refacing with *selce* street-paving blocks (see Pl. VIb), which occurs on two towers[4] and one curtain.[5] G. Lugli[6] suggests that it belongs to the time of the Saracenic invasions (846); Nibby[7] assigns it to the twelfth or thirteenth century, but gives no reason, although it might indeed be connected with the repairs of 1157. Finally, the uncoursed tufa facing, which is so frequent in repairs to the Gates and Wall, is dated to Pope Nicholas V, by a stemma (extant, but now illegible), which Audebert[8] luckily saw and copied at Porta Ostiensis East.

---

[1] Procop. *B. G.* iii. 24; Pisaurum, iii. 11.

[2] e.g. curtains nos. D 22, E 10, G 12, L 24, L 34, M 11.

[3] Towers nos. G 5, 6, 11, 13, H 1, 11, K 8, M 8, 10.

[4] Towers nos. B 18, K 1.   [5] Curtain no. A 24.

[6] Lugli, *La Zona Archeologica di R.*, p. 321: but he describes the facing, quite erroneously, as 'blocchetti quadrangolari di tufo'.

[7] *M. di R.*, p. 367.   [8] Audebert, fol. 243ᵃ.

b. REPAIR TO SECOND-PERIOD
TOWER K 8

a. SECOND-PERIOD TOWER
TYPE B: no. B 14

PART THREE

THE GATES

I. INTRODUCTORY

IT is now possible to pass to a study of the Gates. The disproportionate size of the two chapters which deal therewith is due to the quantity of material and its detailed character. No minute description of the Gates has yet been produced to which it is possible to refer and so to eliminate some of the description. And it is necessary to examine everything, in order to ensure that as little evidence as may be is left unrecorded. For the convenience of general readers, however, a recapitulation of conclusions has been arranged at the end of each section dealing with a Gate, and the whole significance of the evolution in type is discussed in Part IV, which is an attempt to relate the architectural evidence to historical contexts. This method is convenient for two reasons. Firstly, it enables the evidence to be assembled, unencumbered by the lengthy discussion necessary for assigning dates. Secondly, while opinions about dating may change, the architectural evidence upon which they are based exists for all to see. Thus it is desirable not to mix what may be transitory with self-evident facts: and the hope is modestly expressed that the account of the evidence may always be regarded as true and useful by those who make further study of the Wall and Gates, or revise conclusions drawn here about their history. So much for the account of Gates which still exist.

There then follows, as a separate chapter, an account of the vanished Gates, equal in number to those still extant. The most skilful pleader could not disguise this great loss, and there are one or two Gates whose fairly recent disappearance is a matter of great regret, for a fresh examination of them now would certainly have solved some important puzzles in the Wall's history. Yet some powerfully extenuating circumstances can be stated. Any student of town planning would be surprised that more Gates did not perish, during Rome's steady growth between the sixteenth and the nineteenth century, or during her exceptionally rapid increase in size in our own day. Again, even amid the numberless attractions of this Queen of Cities, pride and pleasure in the beauty of her Gates prompted artists to take an altogether exceptional interest in them. What other city can show within ninety years four[1] independent and almost complete series of gateway-views like those produced by Vasi, Gell,

---

[1] See p. 3, notes 8, 11, 12, 14.

Rossini, and Ricciardelli? This magnificent enterprise has made it easier to regain the true aspect of the vanished Gates of Rome than of any other important destroyed fortifications in Europe. And so, on comparing the conclusions from this inquiry with with those derived from examination of the extant Gates, it will be possible to observe that there is no disturbing contradiction, and that the phenomena visible to-day do much to give complete meaning to the evidence about the vanished Gates. The two sets of facts interlock without readjustment and demonstrate a consistent evolution, whose whole significance is considered in the final chapter.

II. EXISTING GATES

§ 1. PORTA NOMENTANA

THE present obscurity of Porta Nomentana is due to Pope Pius IV, who replaced[1] the ancient Gate in 1564 by the Porta Pia, in fulfilment of the scheme which substituted the Via Pia for the ancient Alta Semita. So Porta Pia came to be drawn by artists instead of the older Gate.

' On trouve au milieu des vieux murs ', writes Audebert,[2] 'la PORTA PIA, laquelle a eu ce nom depuis peu de temps à cause de Pie IV, qui feit metter bas l'antienne et rebastir celle de présent, faisant oultre cela dresser une rue à la ligne qui est merveilleusement longue, large et belle . . . ceste rue a près d'un mil de longueur, et est si bien dressée qu'on y va uniment sans monter ny descendre, combien qu'elle soit toute sur montagnes.'

At this time Porta Nomentana received a new battered brick curtain-wall, which completely masked,[3] or destroyed, the older curtain. This repair is recorded by an inscription, still *in situ*, PIUS IIII MEDICES | MEDIOLAN. PONT. | MAX. ANN. SAL. | M.D. LXIIII. Du Pérac's map,[4] which was made in 1557, just before the old Gate was thus eclipsed, gives to it a schematic aspect like that of Porta Salaria. This, however, seems to be conventional representation, which has to be checked by the extant remains. Bufalini's plan[5] (1551) adds little to our knowledge.

But, unfortunately, destruction did not end in 1564. The southern tower of the gate concealed an earlier tomb, which tempted nineteenth-century archaeologists; and so Major Zamboni pulled down what remained[6] of the tower (perhaps rather little), and disclosed the monument. Cardinali[7] tells the story briefly.

---

[1] See inscription quoted below: Uggeri, vol. xxx, pl. 9, gives a small view; otherwise I can trace no large illustration; cf. Jordan, i¹, p. 355, note 25.

[2] Audebert, fols. 262–3. 'In the midst of the ancient wall occurs Porta Pia, which has had this name only a short time because of Pope Pius IV, who laid low the ancient gate and built that of to-day. Besides that, he laid out in a straight line a marvellously long, broad, and beautiful street. . . . This street is more than a mile long, and is so well laid out that one journeys thereon uniformly, without rising or falling, in spite of the fact that it is all on hilly ground.'

[3] Judicious examination might reveal which: at present it is impossible to say.

[4] Du Pérac, *Urbis Romae Sciografia*, 1574.

[5] Bufalini, *Urbis Icnografia*, 1551.

[6] Cf. *M. di R.*, p. 325.

[7] *Memorie romane*, iii, p. 407 = C. I. L. vi. 1. 1426. 'Signor Ottavio Zamboni, major in the army of His Imperial Majesty the King of Austria, undertook an excavation at this monument at the beginning of the current year. On deepening it to twenty-seven palms, he found that here, as elsewhere, the actual City Walls, which are attributed to Aurelian by ancient tradition, are built upon remains of earlier date. Among these must certainly rank the tomb, already mentioned, which, from being a fair ornament of Via Nomentana,

'Il signor Ottavio Zamboni, maggiore nelle armi di S. M. I. R. A., intra-
prese uno scavo presso quel monumento sul principio dell' anno corrente
(i.e. 1827; I. A. R.), e, profondandolo fino a ventisette palmi, trovó che in
questo sito, come altrove, le mura attuali urbane, che attribuisconsi per
vecchia tradizione ad Aureliano, sono costrutte sopra avanzi di più antica
data, frai quali deve porsi certamente il nominato sepolcro, che, da bell'
ornamento della via nomentana, fu condannato a servire di fondamento
di una delle torri che difendevano la porta. Fra molte macerie, marmi,
travertini spezzati, di cui fu trovata riempiuta la volta, furono scoperti
alcuni de' grandi massi che rivestivano il sepolcro, alcuni frammenti di
marmo della sua decorazione che perlo stile debbono assegnarsi al primo
periodo dell' era cristiana, e due brami pure di marmo dell' iscrizione originale
del monumento. Dai frammenti sovracitati dell' ornato e da cio che rimane
è certo che il monumento . . . avea la forma di una grande ara sepolcrale
sormontata da due volute colla iscrizione di fronte, che diceva.' [1]

Q̱. HATERIVS . . . . O . . . .
SORTIT. TR. PL. PR. VII(vir epulonu)M.A. . . . . . .

To-day, therefore, the state of the Gate is pitiful (Pl. VIII*b*).
There remains only the shapeless ruin left by Zamboni on the
site of the south tower; the ancient curtain has completely
disappeared, and only the semicircular north tower is in fairly
perfect state. Such is the story of the Gate's decay; its present
state (fig. 15) may now be described in detail.

The courtesy of the British Embassy staff, whose garden
and mews abut on the Wall, enabled the writer to visit the back
of the north tower twice. It was thus possible to reach the top
chamber of the tower, and to discover, in a loft at a lower level,
beneath the butler's lodgings, some masonry and a vault. These
give a complete idea of the tower's arrangement.

The internal diameter of the upper chamber was twenty-two
feet; its walls were two feet thick (standard[2] *bipedalis* thickness),
giving an external diameter of twenty-six feet. The ancient vault
has now disappeared, and a modern roof, supported by a cross-
wall parallel with the back of the tower, now covers the rear
half of the room. It was impossible to examine the front of
the cross-wall, but the back of it did not seem old. The recesses

was compelled to serve as a foundation to one of the towers which defended the Gate.
Amidst the many broken stones, marbles, and shattered blocks of travertine, with which the
vault was found filled, were discovered some of the great blocks which encased the tomb,
some decorative fragments of marble, which, by their style, must be assigned to the first
years of the Christian Era, and two pieces, also marble, of the original inscription of the
monument. From the ornamental fragments mentioned above and from the remains
extant, it is certain that the monument . . . had the shape of a great grave-altar, crowned
with two volutes, with an inscription on the front, which said, Quintus Haterius . . . O . . .'
[1] *C. I. L.* vi. i. 1426: identified with Tac. *Ann.* iii. 57 'senex foedissimae adulationis',
a trait in character not surprising after his adventures in *Ann.* i. 13, 7.

[2] There is little doubt that the stock size of this useful tile, used as a bonder, or as a voussoir, frequently influenced the thickness of walls.

PORTA NOMENTANA

SCALE IN
FEET

5 0 5 10 15 20   30   40   50

1 0 1 2 3 4 5   10   15

METRES

NORTH TOWER
FIRST FLOOR

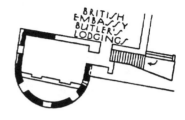

LEVEL ON STAIRS
HALF-WAY UP THE
NORTH TOWER

BRITISH
EMBASSY GROUNDS

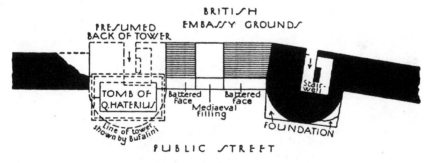

PUBLIC STREET

GROUND FLOOR

PERIOD 1
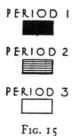

PERIOD 2

PERIOD 3

FIG. 15

therein were filled with rough filling of indeterminable date, and the whole structure is certainly to be explained as the result of a modern attempt[1] to make use of the tower for storage, leaving the front as a balcony for defence or, more probably, for contemplative enjoyment of Villa Patrizi.[2] The covered portion, now a box-room, receives light through a small hole cut in the outer wall at window-level; but anciently the tower was lit by three windows, with round heads, turned in *bipedales*. The west side and the springing of the north window remain, and straight joints, symmetrically disposed, mark the positions of two more. The north window is blocked with rough filling, which has been pierced once, patched once, and then pierced afresh, through the patch. Much of the back wall is of modern date, but there is nine feet seven inches of old facing at its south end. The floor is formed by consolidated rubbish and earth, and excavation therein should reveal the upper part of a staircase.

It is already possible to establish the precise position of the staircase from remains in the loft above the stables and coach-washing-yard. Here a minute search revealed, behind a pile of boxes and stacked timber, a narrow, barrel-vaulted passage, running east and west. Its north wall was irregularly cut in ancient concrete made of packed tufa; the south wall, against which had been built recently a little workshop forge, was covered with rough modern facing. This looked promising, but no wall-face confirmed the suspicion, based upon the position of the structure, that here was part of an ancient staircase-well. At the easternmost end of the vault, however, the required facing came to light on both sides of the passage; and it then became clear that much facing had been cut away on the north side of the passage; while it may be suspected that, on the south side, some facing and a turn in the stairs is hidden by a modern plaster wall, which has a somewhat different orientation from the older vault. The vault as a whole now turned out to be on exactly the same lines as the ancient tower, but set much out of centre. And so, in order to make room for stairs, another vault of the same size must have lain on the south side of this one. Close analogy permits the picture to be completed. If these vaults were separated by a newel as wide as that of the precisely similar staircase-vaults of the earliest Porta Appia,[3] the southern vault, just postulated, comes exactly central. So the staircase arrives centrally in the top chamber of the tower, and is entered below by a central door. There can be little doubt that this arrangement is right. Further,

---

[1] As old, however, as 1828, see Uggeri, xxx, pl. 9. Cf. also the treatment of Porta Labicana's west tower.

[2] Villa Patrizi has now disappeared, and its place is taken by the Palazzo delle Ferrovie dello Stato.   [3] See p. 123, fig. 20.

a. LATRINE, WITH ENCLOSED SHOOT, SURROUNDED
BY A BUTTRESS, TOWER J 17

b. PORTA NOMENTANA

c. PORTA LATINA IN 1655–67
From the Cadastral Survey of Pope Alexander VII

a comparison of this staircase with those of Portae Appia and Latina[1] will show that the builders were allowed some latitude in planning their stairs. Those who cared for real symmetry in plan placed the newel central; love for external grace made others give the central position to the entrance arch. The stairs were kept to a normal width, and there can be little doubt that their number conformed to a standard. The height to which they were required to rise was twenty feet at this Gate, and they must have done it, as at Porta Appia,[2] with three flights and two turns. Above the chamber into which they led would come a vaulted roof, as in the east tower of Porta Ostiensis East,[3] and this would be pierced at the side by a small staircase leading up to a flat embattled top. In this way can be recovered, with fair confidence, the complete arrangement of the north tower of Porta Nomentana.

It may be taken as certain that the original height of this tower never was increased, as was that of the towers of Portae Latina, Ostiensis East,[4] and Salaria, because no thickening was added to the wall of the upper chamber, either outside or inside, as at all other existing gates on the circuit where additions took place. The existing two-foot wall is strong enough to carry one vaulted story, but it is not built to bear the pressure of another, even if the two were separated only by a wooden floor. This tower is, therefore, of considerable value because of the certainty about its internal arrangement. No gate-tower in Rome is more simply planned, and none is less affected by later alterations, although many are better preserved. This elementary simplicity alone would hint that the tower was of early date, and, with the question of date in mind, the exterior may be examined.

The tower stands upon a quadrangular base, faced with rather short dark-red tile-fragments, and considerably damaged at the outer angles. It is important to note that the top of this foundation is level with the offset which marks the normal foundation-level of the Wall, although here, being roughly faced with tiles, as described in a former section,[5] the top of the foundation must have been exposed. The plan of the structure is to be compared with the quadrangular (but unfaced) foundation below the semicircular tower west of Porta Salaria (see Pl. VI*b*). The exact point of transition from foundation to tower is now masked by recent refacing. But the refacing fortunately does not extend very high on the north side of the tower. Its place is taken by a beautiful surface, of which the fine quality has been insufficiently

---

[1] p. 101, fig. 17. [2] p. 123, fig. 20.
[3] p. 111, fig. 19. [4] Pl. XI*a* and *b*.
[5] p. 60. Notable is the mass of white cement on the NE. angle. This is modern bedding for the post of a pent-house, now removed, of which roof-marks were visible in 1926 on the Wall and tower.

appreciated hitherto. It is provided with three bonding-courses, separated from each other by twenty-nine ordinary courses. Then comes a decorative tile string of one member, marking the level of the upper chamber's floor, and this is followed by another of three members, at the level of the three window-sills. The triple arrangement of windows and the decorative string-courses recur at Porta Latina, and once existed at Porta Salaria, as is proved by drawings and a photograph of the Gate (see Pl. XVIII*a* and *b*). The excellent facing and the quiet good taste of the building put its general date beyond doubt. No such workmanship appears in Rome after the close of the third century, and, indeed, the technique of this resembles Severan work rather than Diocletianic: much third-century work is not nearly so good.

On grounds of style, then, the north tower of Porta Nomentana goes back to the middle of the third century. Its homogeneous structure proves it to be, without doubt, an example of an Aurelianic gateway tower. The type, moreover, can be recognized elsewhere on the Wall, and it always belongs to a first period whenever it occurs. So a link of real importance has now been established between the architectural remains and the historical tradition, for the earliest Wall is already proved to be Aurelianic, and now the emergence of the gateway type completes our knowledge of his work. True, more details of planning can be extracted from other early Gates on the circuit, but none of them exhibits forms so simple as here, or so much original facing.

Apart from the north tower, however, some general details can be extracted about the plan of the whole Gate. Round the tomb of Q. Haterius may be fitted, as is warranted by Bufalini's plan[1] (1551), another tower of the same type and size as that on the north, and the curtain between them must have been not less than thirty-four, and not more than thirty-six, feet long. This is shorter than the first-period curtain[2] of the one-way Porta Latina, which is forty-five feet long; but it comes very close to the thirty-six feet of the first-period curtain at Porta Tiburtina,[3] the next important Gate to the south. The fact that the first-period plans of Portae Appia and Ostiensis East conform to a standard[4] may even suggest that Portae Tiburtina and Nomentana once formed another standard pair. Finally, the method of screening a change of direction in the line of the Wall, by skewing a gate-tower, is of interest as an architectural trick. The device was employed elsewhere on the Wall; Portae Latina, Appia, and Ostiensis East provide some striking cases.[5]

Conclusions. On the basis of the facts recounted here, a re-

[1] Fig. 15.   [2] See fig. 17.   [3] See fig. 33.
[4] See p. 112.   [5] See figs. 17, 19, 20.

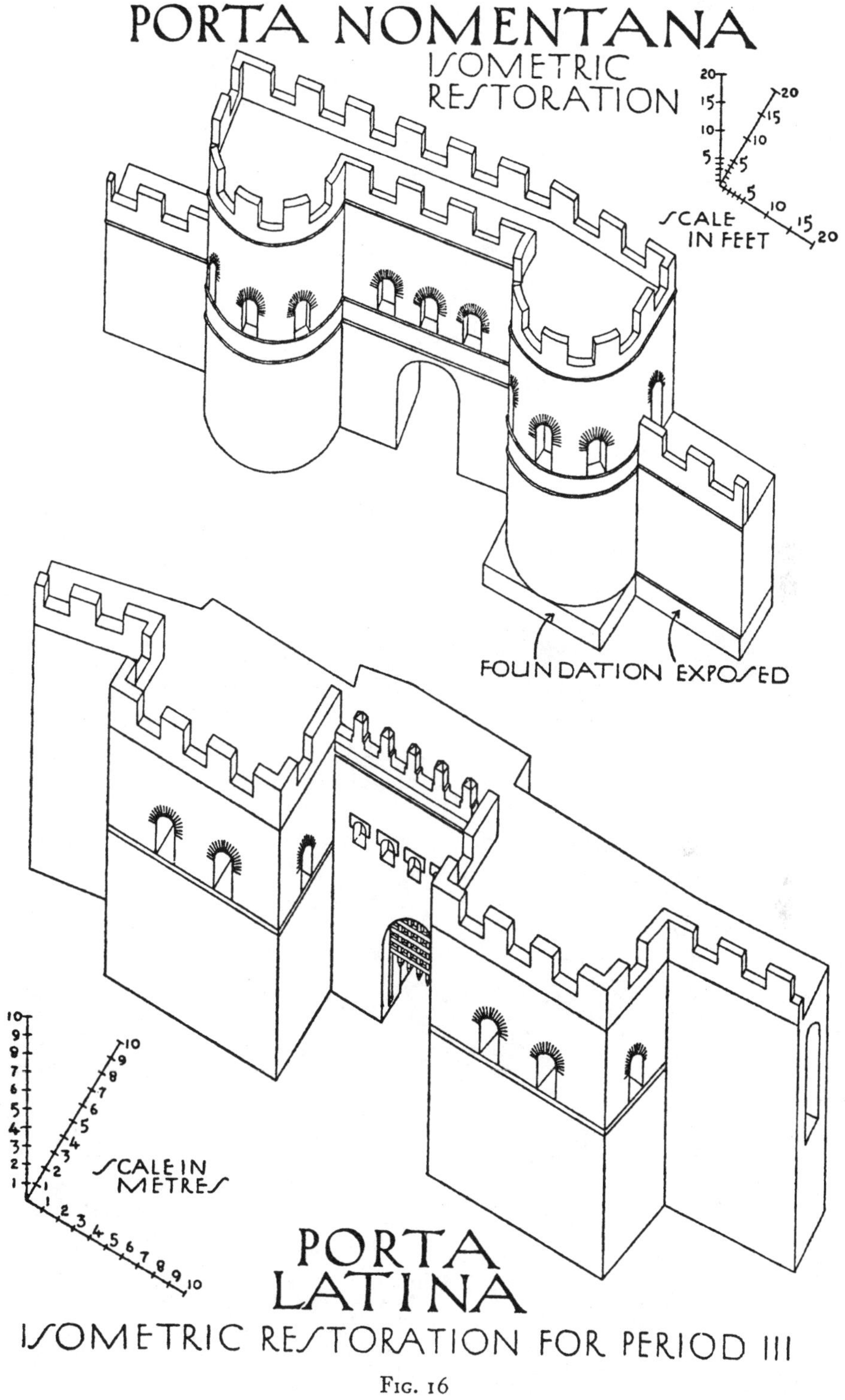

PORTA NOMENTANA

ISOMETRIC RESTORATION

SCALE IN FEET

FOUNDATION EXPOSED

PORTA LATINA

ISOMETRIC RESTORATION FOR PERIOD III

SCALE IN METRES

FIG. 16

stored elevation of the Gate has been constructed in isometrical form (fig. 16). The details of the windows are borrowed from the very similar Porta Salaria, and a thirty-six foot curtain has been provided, with an archway twelve feet wide and deep, following the triple motif of the tower windows. The mass of evidence for standardization of plans and elevations of the Gates built in Rome by Aurelian gives very fair certainty to this restoration, and readers in doubt are referred to the final chapter,[1] where the evidence bearing on this question is collected and summarized.

§ 2. PORTA LATINA

Time and man have treated Porta Latina (Pl. IX) more kindly than Porta Nomentana. It is still flanked by two semicircular towers, and between them runs an ancient stone curtain, which is too short for the available space, and is lengthened with tile-faced concrete at each end. All drawings of the Gate made before the end of the eighteenth century show that behind it there existed a walled court, which disappeared soon after that date, as Franz Caucig's sketch (1782–88) shows,[2] owing to a collapse of its rearward gate. Amid older documents, the Cadastro[3] of Pope Alexander VII (Pl. VIIIc) gives important details about the east tower and the top story of the curtain, which appear again in a larger drawing by Johann Justin Preisler[4] (1698–1771). After 1827, perhaps to save the expense of collecting the gabella, the Gate was closed, and was not opened again to traffic until 1906. In extant literature, the Gate is first mentioned in the Einsiedeln List,[5] and the Western Church Calendars[6] still associate with it the grim ordeal ascribed to St. John the Evangelist by medieval legend.

The structural history of the Gate may now be considered in detail (fig. 17), beginning with the eastern tower. This tower had been entirely rebuilt on old lines when the Cadastro was compiled and has been very considerably altered since then; before Preisler's day, for example, the staircase at the back had been removed. To-day, its most notable feature is its quadrangular base, which is faced with one course of great blocks, bedded in cement, on the west and south, and on the east by late brickwork, mostly hidden amid long grass. The usual belief is that this base is the remnant of an early tomb,[7] incorporated in the Gate. But that interpretation explains neither the late brickwork which forms part of it, nor the fact that the stonework, of which much

---

[1] Notably pp. 244–8.   [2] R. Ved., taf. 82.
[3] Archivio dello Stato.   [4] R. Ved., taf. 81.
[5] See Appendix I.
[6] Cf. Anglican Prayer Book Calendar, 6 May, S. John ante Portam Latinam.
[7] Cf. Ashby, P. B. S. R. iv, p. 13, and Lugli, La Zona Archaeologica, p. 320.

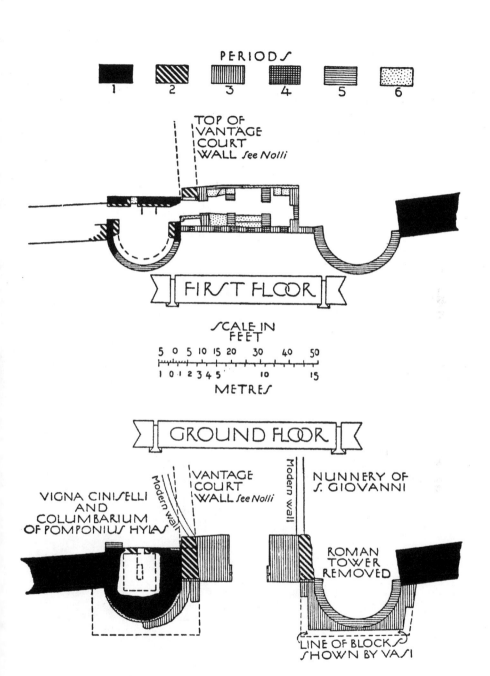

PERIODS

1   2   3   4   5   6

TOP OF
VANTAGE
COURT
WALL *see Nolli*

FIRST FLOOR

SCALE IN
FEET

5 0 5 10 15 20   30   40   50

1 0 1 2 3 4 5   10   15

METRES

GROUND FLOOR

VANTAGE
COURT
WALL *see Nolli*

NUNNERY OF
S. GIOVANNI

VIGNA CINISELLI
AND
COLUMBARIUM
OF POMPONIUS HYLAS

Modern wall

Modern wall

ROMAN
TOWER
REMOVED

LINE OF BLOCKS
SHOWN BY VASI

PORTA LATINA

FIG. 17

more was seen by Vasi[1] (1747) and Gell[2] (1821), is bonded
carefully with the stone curtain. Again, the edge of the curtain
is left toothed for its whole height, so it was clearly intended
that a whole wall of stone was to stand on the same line as this.
Finally, a similar quadrangular base exists at the west tower, and,
although none of its masonry is left *in situ*, the concrete core or
bedding[3] still remains, while a brick-faced wall marks its eastern
edge, and is bonded into the stone curtain. There is no doubt
whatever that the structure has been built round the semicircular tower, and not beneath it.

Any explanation of the bases therefore must suit both. Two
possibilities are eliminated first. It seems evident that tombs are
out of the question. Nowhere else on the circuit do the builders
permit any tomb to project beyond a gate-tower in this way;
and the western quadrangle is built round the tower, and not
underneath it, as a tomb must have been. Nor are they quadrangular foundations for semicircular towers, as at Porta
Nomentana, for they would not then be faced with stone, they
would project less far from the towers, and less high above
ground-level. Finally, their bonding with the stone curtain shows
that they belong to some special addition to the towers.[4] In
fact, they compare with the later quadrangular bastions (figs.
20, 36), which encased early semicircular towers[5] at Portae Appia
and Flaminia. Why they were left in this unfinished state is,
however, another question, to be discussed in greater detail elsewhere. Here it is sufficient to note the point that they were
unfinished, as is proved by the ancient brick-faced wings added
to the curtain when the stonework did not come. Thus is explained the curtain's present disproportionate appearance.

The western tower is very largely ancient. It rises to some
forty feet, and has a semicircular front, with a diameter of
twenty-six feet, the scale of Porta Nomentana. But much patching in modern fashion hides the ancient facing at the base of the
tower, and only at the junctions with the Wall and curtain do
small pieces of excellent brickwork remain (Pl. IX*b*) decorated
with two string-courses typical of the earliest period at Porta
Nomentana. On the west, one bonding-course is visible, and the
north side of the west window can be detected, together with
the springing of its round head, and some voussoirs. Below the
window there is also some good secondary facing; then all is
merged in more modern work. But the position of the window,

---

[1] Pl. ix.   [2] Pl. xxiv.

[3] Some of the bedding on the front of the tower is shown on Moscioni, fot. 22321, where
the Gate is called Porta Capena, and on Chauffourier, fot. 732 *a*, where this time the Gate is
called Porta S. Paolo.

[4] I am indebted to Mr. M. A. Sisson for first pointing out this explanation.

[5] See pp. 124, 191.

the twenty-six foot diameter of the tower, and the two decorative string-courses, establish the useful fact that the first-period tower at Porta Latina precisely resembled the north tower of Porta Nomentana[1] in size and outward aspect. Again, a blocked doorway and window at the back of the tower show that at first it had stairs of exactly the same plan as those at the first-period west tower of Porta Appia.[2] This elucidates the original aspect of the upper story of the tower.

Before visiting the interior of the tower, the writer had hoped to detect the arrangement of the stairs inside the upper chamber. But the room turned out to be choked by rank vegetation and collapsed ruins. Only a large central mass of concrete hinted that stairs had led from the centre of the tower to the roof, and two windows in the back wall, arranged symmetrically on each side of this mass, seemed to corroborate this view. The question is, however, settled by a drawing in the Cadastro (Pl. VIIIc) and by Vasi's engraving,[3] for both sources show the stairs as postulated, reaching as high as the top of the stone curtain. The same sources also show how the roofing was effected. The staircase had its own small barrel-vault and the tower was roofed by two barrel-vaults at each side of it. But it is important for the history of the Gate to note that these vaults were not supported completely on the original tower wall. They spring from a thickening wall, added on the inside of the original wall. Only a fragment of this wall now remains. When complete, it ruined the old scheme of windows and led to the substitution of loop-holes in their stead.[4] Again, it is demonstrable that this thickening, and the rebuilding of the top of the Gate, which went with it, are contemporary with the building of the gallery on the Wall; for the thickening wall is carried right round the end of the original outer tower wall, in order to bond with the gallery-pier next to the gate, and its brickwork is precisely the same as that of the gallery. So at Porta Latina, as will be seen[5] to have happened also at Porta Appia, the addition of the gallery to the Wall clearly involved a complete reconstruction of the upper part of the gate. Thereupon, the early towers, designed in the simple manner of Porta Nomentana, passed out of use for ever.

The method of access to the new tower was also new. The older stairs were not retained, and their window was blocked with brickwork, exactly like that of the gallery and thickening wall. Some of the new stairs, leading to the new and higher roof, which reached slightly higher than the new upper rampart-walk

[1] See Pl. VIIIb; fig. 15.
[2] See fig. 20. As at Porta Appia also, the door, from which the facing has disappeared, looks as if it had been put to secondary uses in medieval times.
[3] See Vasi, pl. ix.
[4] Cf. Porta Ostiensis East, fig. 19, pl. XIa.   [5] See p. 124.

of the Wall, have been considered already.[1] It is clear that they
were arranged in relation to the older stairway only in so far as
they were not built across its vaults. And so the alteration shows
a considerably more intelligent appreciation than will appear at
Porta Appia[2] of the structural soundness to be gained by building
in relation to the earlier remains. Connexion between the first
floor of the gate and the ground now was maintained in a new
way.[3] Slightly to the east of the tower, in the back of the curtain,
which at this point continued the line of the back of the tower,[4]
was cut a great doorway, later blocked twice with different fillings
of rough late concrete. This door once led out on to the vantage-
court wall, represented to-day by a small piece of thick cement
core, preserved at a lower level, and from the wall stairs would
lead to the ground-level. The doorway can have nothing to do
with the original arrangement of the tower or curtain since its
bipedales voussoirs cut into the edge of the first tower, which is
still marked by a straight joint. This joint has survived, in a
remarkable way, an evident re-facing of the tower after the arch
was added, a re-facing of which the tiles cut across certain
voussoirs of the arch.

The chronological relation of this door and of the vantage-
court wall to the stone curtain is also certain. Neither the door
nor the wall can be later than the curtain, since the west end of the
last-named is left toothed in order to fit against the vantage-
court wall, as at Porta Appia. And the curtain must, in fact, be
later than they, since the west end of its tile-faced upper story
is skewed, in order to fit the doorway and passage beyond it, as it
would not have been if both elements had been planned at once.
The doorway, and the vantage-court wall on to which it led,
therefore belong to a secondary arrangement, while the stone
curtain belongs to a third constructional period. This corresponds to the history of similar features at other gates.[5]

So the curtain may now be examined in detail.[6] It is composed
of robbed blocks of all sizes, which have been inserted and
trimmed on the spot, for this is the meaning of the bosses which
appear on the stones, as is explained in the section dealing with
Porta Appia. The reason for a marked change in orientation of
the west half of the curtain is not quite clear. But it may be that
the curtain at both ends was set at right-angles to vantage-court
walls which were erroneously thought to be parallel, and that the
miscalculation was not noted until the building was well in hand.

[1] See above, p. 103.   [2] p. 124.
[3] The strategical reasons for this change are discussed below, see p. 119.
[4] See fig. 17.   [5] See pp. 119, 138, 168, 180.
[6] I am grateful to Mr. G. H. Wedgwood, sometime Rome Scholar in Etching and Engraving, for help in measuring this part of the Gate: the upper part I measured alone with
rods.

IX

b. PORTA LATINA: TRACES OF THE FIRST-PERIOD WEST TOWER

a. PORTA LATINA; THIRD-PERIOD CURTAIN

Such a mistake could well be made in the restricted area of a vantage-court, whence the change in alinement of the Wall to the west, which ought to have shown the want of parallelism, would not be properly visible. Otherwise the arrangement at ground-level is quite simple. The front of the gate was closed by a portcullis,[1] which moved in slots that can still be studied in detail; behind it lies a long deep archway, in which great gates were fixed just behind the portcullis, with slots for hinges and a bolt-hole for a great bar, as may still be seen. Noteworthy is the fact that the size of this arch (12 ft. 1 in.) is almost the same as that of Porta Pinciana (12 ft. 5 in.), just as the Porta Chiusa (13 ft. 6 in.) pairs with Porta Tiburtina (13 ft. 2 in.), and Porta Appia (14 ft. 2 in.) with Porta Ostiensis East (14 ft. 4 in.). These correspondences may suggest that in this period the Gates were fitted with stonework in pairs.[2]

On both faces of the portal the main arch is surmounted by a relieving arch of unique type. Lugli[3] was the first to recognize the function of these arches; and the truth is that at this point the main arch has to carry great weight, especially at the front, where there is the portcullis-slot behind it. The unique point[4] is that the relieving arch is interlocked with the main arch below it, and that the two arches thus work in unison. The peculiar irregularity of the intrados and extrados of the voussoirs in the relieving arch strongly suggest that the stones formed part of an earlier arch (whether belonging to the Gate or not) which have been re-assembled in new position. This would account for the very unsatisfactory joggling of the adjacent masonry. The employment of the relieving arch is, however, a constructional improvement. But the upper arch would have done its work much better had it been completely independent. Moreover, the relief was needed: the main arch of Porta Salaria,[5] which had no relief, fell out of place.

The upper story of the curtain has a stone front wall and a tile-faced back one, and from inside the Gate it can be seen that this whole floor has been severely damaged by fire at an unknown date. It is, indeed, quite surprising that some of the stonework continues to stand in its badly cracked and calcined condition. The portcullis-slot has been covered over in medieval times, and the hoisting arrangements are not now visible. The extremely

[1] Portcullis arrangements for this type of gate are shown on p. 136, fig. 23.
[2] See p. 259.
[3] Lugli, La Zona Archeologica, p. 320. Grisar, on the other hand, thought an earlier arch had been torn out: see Roma alla fine del mondo antico, pp. 544–5, figs. 159, 160. This is impossible, as a glance at the Gate will show.
[4] During a brief visit to Rome, Mr. R. G. Collingwood walked with me from Porta S. Paolo to Porta Asinaria: it was of the greatest value to me to discuss these points with him. [5] See p. 187, pl. XVIIIa.

rough building of the stonework shows how block was placed
upon block, regardless of exact fitting, except towards the front,
and even there trimming was often needed. The stone front was
crowned by a moulding, cut in odd lengths, as if it had once
decorated an adjacent many-sided tomb. At both ends of the
curtain the stonework stopped short of the semicircular towers,
and was left toothed. Ancient brick-facing fills the gap, but is
not well preserved. Round the west window, however, it exhibits
irregular coursing and whitish tiles, which are both associated
with fifth-century brickwork on the Wall. On the west, again, it
is not bonded with the early tower wall, and must therefore have
been built when the stone-facing scheme did not materialize;
that it is not earlier is shown by the fact that its window is not on
a level with the first-period windows or second-period loop-holes
of the west tower, but is built to match the third-period stone-
built windows of the curtain. This brings the scheme of the
stonework at this gate, as well as its chronology, into line with
Portae Ostiensis East, Tiburtina, and Appia, where stone curtain
and stone-faced towers were added together, one period later than
the provision of a vantage-court.[1]

The back wall of the portcullis chamber was built of tile-faced
concrete, and its roof was arranged, as at Porta Tiburtina,[2]
in three barrel-vaults, with their axis parallel to that of the gateway arch. The easternmost vault is modern, and not quite on
ancient lines. Originally, the central bay was large enough to
take the portcullis and its simple machinery of pulley-blocks.
The two side rooms then could be used either for *ballistae*, or as
look-out chambers, or for the storage of spare tackle. The windows at the back of the gate were drawn[3] by Preisler—who did
not, however, completely understand their architectonics. But
he drew enough to make certain that the arrangement was two
windows for the small east vault. The arrangements in the west
vault and in the larger central one are not clear, but the drawings
of Preisler and of the Cadastro hint at something symmetrical.

On top of the portcullis-chamber came the rampart-walk,
at the same level as the upper walk on the Wall. It had, no doubt,
a low coping, in line with the foot of the stone merlons, which are
of that distinctive tapered type used in the Honorian[4] restoration
of Porta Tiburtina. Such merlons are ornamental rather than
defensive, and their connexion with the decoration of the Gate is
discussed in the section dealing with Porta Tiburtina. In order
to make them useful for defence, medieval builders built round

[1] See figs. 19, 33, 20.   [2] See p. 171, fig. 33.
[3] R. *Ved.* i, taf. 81.
[4] It is legitimate to speak of this restoration as Honorian, since it is a fixed point in
chronology, rendered certain by *C. I. L.* vi. 1190. See p. 170.

them parapets of normal type, and this explains how they have been preserved to our own time, like the pedestals on top of Porta Aurea at Split.[1] Preisler's drawing shows that, in the Middle Ages, a very considerable side-wall was also built on the east end of the curtain, which belongs, to judge from the distinctive arrangement of the putlog-holes, to the same scheme of building as the restored east tower.

One more point remains to be discussed about the dating of the stone curtain. It resembles closely the inscribed curtains[2] of Honorius at Portae Tiburtina and Praenestina, and its stone-

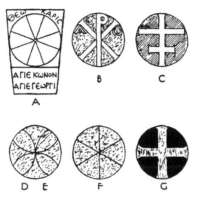

Fɪɢ. 18. Crosses and Chrisms from stone gates. ᴀ, Porta Appia;
ʙ, ɢ, Porta Latina; ᴄ, ᴅ, Porta Pinciana; ᴇ, ꜰ, Porta Ostiensis.

work has much in common with work[3] at Portae Pinciana, Ostiensis, Appia, Salaria, and the Porta Chiusa. It has often, indeed, been assigned to Belisarius,[4] because it is decorated with a Greek cross and chrism. Yet it should be noted that these symbols are of early form, and not of the kind usually associated with the sixth century. This is also true of the similar (fig. 18) incised wheel-crosses and chrisms of Portae Ostiensis East, Appia, and Latina, and of the Latin cross on Porta Pinciana, which goes back to the fourth century. The whole question of dating these symbols on the Gates therefore needs revision. Leclercq,[5] and Petrie,[6] in discussing similar types elsewhere, will not allow that they were in fashion after the middle of the fifth century, especially in Rome, where the catacombs[7] provide a rich dated series for classification. As for the practice of decorating City Gates with

[1] See Anderson, Spiers, and Ashby, *Architecture of Anc. R.*, pl. lxxxi.
[2] See pl. XVI*b* and fig. 39.   [3] See pls. X, XII, XVII, XVIII.
[4] This view was started by Nibby, and is copied afterwards, notably by Grisar, Tomasetti, and Ashby.
[5] Cabrol, *Dictionnaire d'Archéologie chrétienne*, s.v. *chrisme*.
[6] Petrie, *Ancient Egypt*, iii, 1916: article pp. 102–9: figure, p. 103.
[7] Cf. also De Rossi, *B. C.* 1872, p. 51, for the chrism.

crosses, it was in full vogue at Constantinople[1] by 412. Again, while the inscription on Porta Appia ΘΕΩ ΚΑΡΙϹ | ΑΓΙΕ ΚΩΝΟΝ | ΑΓΙΕ ΓΕΩΡΓΙ is usually thought to be Belisarian, the incised cross associated with it is of early type.[2] Here the choice of saints' names is peculiar. S. Conon was not noted as a military saint, as Tomasetti states,[3] and dedications to him are uncommon. But he suffered at Iconium under Aurelian, and this might be the reason for the choice. Or, again, some one connected with the building may have had a special connexion with Iconium. S. George, on the other hand, was one of the most popular saints of the fourth century. Important churches of this date are dedicated to him as far apart as Esdra (Nabatea), Naples, and Salonika.[4] A century later he had become so widely esteemed that Pope Gelasius[5] was compelled to issue, in 494, a warning against fictitious accounts of his life and character. So this inscription may very well be much earlier than 536. The theory that the inscription, the crosses, and the chrisms must record the Belisarian restoration of the Gates was apparently started by Nibby, and has since been copied uncritically. Actually, the view seems to be wrong so far as the crosses and chrisms are concerned; and with them goes the inscription, unless it is, indeed, a later addition to the cross which it adorns.

Conclusions. The evolution of Porta Latina may now be summarized. There are three clear stages of development. The earliest Gate had two semicircular towers entered from the ground by doors in their backs, like those of Porta Nomentana. They were connected by a curtain of which little is known: but it may be quite safely assumed that the curtain was not built of stone, since none of it was left behind the Gate at either side of the later stone curtain. There was probably only a single arch, since the curtain was only forty-five feet long, which is eight feet shorter than the fifty-three-foot curtains of two-way Gates. It was, however, some nine feet longer than the curtains of the one-way Portae[6] Nomentana and Tiburtina, and the reason for this extra length is not clear. But it may well be connected with the provision of a more elaborate façade or larger arch for an ancient and important road like Via Latina.

In its second stage the Gate underwent important changes, matched all round the circuit of the Wall. The towers received a new and higher roof, of which the flat embattled top rose some-

---

[1] Cf. Lietzmann, Die Landmauer von Konstantinopel, *Preussische Akad. d. Wissensch.* 1929, *Phil-Hist.* K. 2.   [2] Grisar, loc. cit., fig. 159, draws the cross wrongly.
[3] Tomasetti, *Campagna Romana,* ii, p. 35: cf. *Lives of the Saints,* Baring-Gould.
[4] S. George; for the Churches, see Rivoira, *Architettura Lombarda.*
[5] Pope Gelasius: E. von Dolschutz, *Das Decretum gelasianum,* pp. 9, 273-4. I owe this reference to the kindness of Dr. Cameron of the B. S. R.
[6] See pp. 95, 171, figs. 15, 33.

what above the upper rampart-walk of the newly heightened Wall. The back of the Gate was completely altered by the addition of a courtyard, of which the walls blocked the old access to the towers. These were now entered from the courtyard wall, to which flights of steps must have been attached. The significance of this is discussed in another context.[1] What happened to the curtain of the Gate in this period is quite uncertain, but it very well may have undergone no change, since the difference in the upper levels could be reconciled simply by flights of stairs.

The third period saw the building of the stone curtain. This was a mighty work, built in great blocks, in Syrian[2] style, and what remains of it now is clearly part of a bigger scheme than ever materialized. Stone-faced towers, of which only bases came into being, were to have been built, and the collapse of the scheme is testified by the half-finished aspect of the Gate to-day. Porta Tiburtina now gives the best idea in Rome of what the finished gate was intended to look like (see also fig. 16), but Constantinople[3] provides still more perfect examples of the type. The new gateway was provided with a portcullis, which hardly needed to enter the portcullis-chamber even when raised to full height. If the scheme had been fully carried out, Porta Latina would have been one of the most impressive gates in Rome.

Traces of later pre-medieval work can hardly be said to exist. The blocking of three front windows looks late-Roman, but may be much later since they are shown open in the Cadastro: that of the back windows of the west tower is more likely to be ancient. It seems, however, that Porta Latina did not suffer much late damage, with the reservation that nothing is known about what may have happened to the east tower. Certainly it was not in the fighting line during the Gothic sieges, which damaged so greatly certain other gates, and no fighting is connected with it in medieval literature. Hence comes its comparatively good preservation.

§ 3. PORTA OSTIENSIS EAST

This noble Gate is usually called Porta Ostiensis, but the final adjective is added here in order to call attention to the demolished, but very important, Gate which lay[4] close by, on the west side of the Pyramid of Gaius Cestius, and shared the Ostian traffic with this, its more splendid sister. For whereas Porta Ostiensis East spanned the south-west road from the obsolete Servian Porta Raudusculana, the smaller gate took all the heavy traffic

[1] See p. 119.
[2] See p. 259. The style is perhaps rather that of the Near East in general than of Syria, and it may have some bearing upon the choice of saints.
[3] See p. 261.   [4] See p. 220.

from Servian Porta Trigemina and the Tiberside warehouses.[1]
True, the name of the small gate is unknown; but it spanned the
primitive *via Ostiensis*, and therefore has a good right to be called
Porta Ostiensis West, so as to emphasize the importance of this
double line of traffic. But the smaller gate had a short life.[2]
In the Constantinian age the great Gate was already serving
both routes. There is therefore no doubt that it is the main
Gate, which Ammianus Marcellinus[3] mentions in recounting
the transport of the new obelisk to the Circus Maximus, under
Constantius II. At this time, too, the Gate was still known as
Porta Ostiensis. But presently the increasing wealth and fame
of Saint Paul's Basilica outside the Wall gave the Gate a new
name,[4] Porta Sancti Pauli: and a great portico,[5] like that of
Saint Peter on the *via Cornelia*, came to shade one side of the hot
and dusty road between the Gate and the far-famed church.
To-day, Porta Ostiensis is one of the best-preserved Gates in the
City (Pl. X). Its curtain is flanked by two semicircular towers,
with three stories apiece, of which the lowest and topmost in the
east tower are blind, while in the west only the third now has
windows or loop-holes. Both towers were much thickened at the
base between the time of the Cadastro (1655–67) and Vasi.[6]
Their parapets and merlons have been much altered, and belong
to some time after 1655–67, when the Cadastro shows machicolations, which have been drawn[7] also by Hendrick van Cleef
in 1550. The stone-faced curtain has a tile-faced upper story,
containing a portcullis-chamber, and crowned by a rampart-walk,
with a small sentry-box, or guard-house,[8] at each end. Its lower
story is of stone, with an arched gateway and portcullis. Behind
the Gate is a walled court, entered by twin rear arches, of which
the easternmost has long been blocked.[9] The walls of the court
are medieval in date, but the east still exhibits ancient brickwork at
its north end. Our knowledge of this Gate, however, has recently
been materially increased by excavation. Late in 1928, the
Municipality of Rome, acting through the Commissione Archeologica, Ufficio X and Dottore A. M. Colini, began to excavate
the rear court. When the excavations were in progress, the
writer went to Rome and was permitted to measure and describe

---

[1] See fig. 2.   [2] See p. 220, also *P. B. S. R.* x, p. 21.
[3] Amm. Marc. xvii. 4. 12 'per portam Ostiensem piscinamque publicam Circo inlatus
est Maximo.'
[4] Cf. Procop. *B. G.* ii. 4; iii. 36 πύλη ἡ Παύλου τοῦ ἀποστόλου ὁμώνυμός ἐστι.
[5] See Lanciani, *F. U. R.* 44.
[6] Vasi, pl. xi.
[7] *C. Ved.*, tav. lxii.
[8] These are classical, not medieval, as Bartoli suggests, see text to *C. Ved.* lxiii, a
mediocre view by Canaletto.
[9] This took place before the restorations of Nicholas V, in 1451, which were made to
fit one arch only, see below, p. 120.

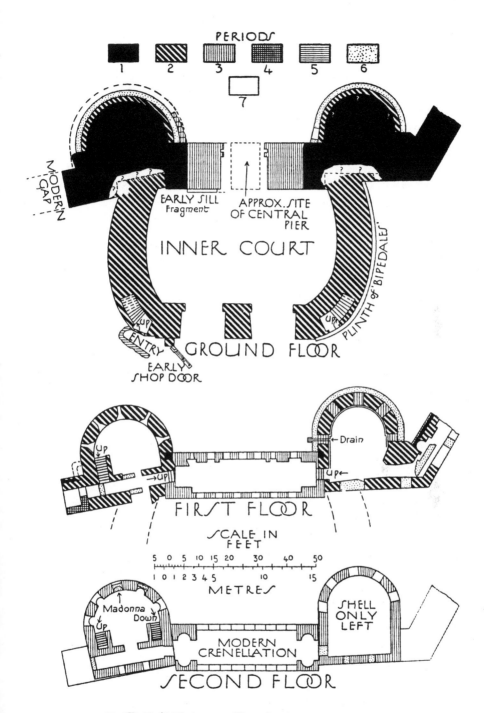

PERIODS

1 2 3 4 5 6

7

MODERN GAP

EARLY SILL Fragment

APPROX. SITE OF CENTRAL PIER

INNER COURT

PLINTH of 'BIPEDALES'

UP

UP

ENTRY

EARLY SHOP DOOR

GROUND FLOOR

UP

→Up

Drain

Up←

FIRST FLOOR

SCALE IN FEET

5 0 5 10 15 20   30   40   50

1 0 1 2 3 4 5   10   15

METRES

Madonna Down

Up

MODERN CRENELLATION

SHELL ONLY LEFT

SECOND FLOOR

PORTA OSTIENSIS

Fig. 19

the new material, while doing his best to offer suggestions in return. To the writer the work was of especial interest, since it gave the opportunity to prove the value of suggestions about the early form of the Gate which he had published shortly before, at the Municipio's request. All the forecasts came true, and to the generosity of the Municipio is due the present complete account of the Gate. It is, however, none the less necessary to record the unfailing courtesy of Signor Mazzaruti and his family, who dwelt in the eastern house in 1926, and allowed me free entry through their private rooms to all parts of the ancient structure before the Municipio resumed possession of the building.

An architectural study of the Gate (fig. 19) is best begun from the curtain, for there the remains of the earliest structure are clearest. To-day this curtain has a lower story of stone, and an upper one built in tile-faced concrete. But a glance at its front discloses that remains of an early stone curtain are embedded therein, which are not connected with the present design of the Gate. At each end of the upper tile-faced story can be seen the ragged ends of the earlier stone structure, crowned by a moulding and parapet, of which similar fragments are embedded, at the same level, in each of the present towers (Pl. XIa). Furthermore, it is evident that this earlier work exists in each end of the stone lower story, and its blocks are to be recognized by their special coursing and tooling, and by the distinctive way in which they have weathered (Pl. X).

Still further details about the character of this earliest curtain can be extracted from a closer examination of its rearward face. The length of the original curtain is given by its back, of which the ends, in early stonework, lie farther west and east than those now visible in the front. In order to prove, then, that the front originally had the same dimensions, the Municipio, at my request, had a hole made in the east tower, along the face of the curtain. This passed beyond the medieval skin of the tower, and then beyond one ancient skin, finally reaching the primary wall of the tower at the point required. The early curtain thus has exactly the same over-all measurements as that of Porta Appia.[1] It is also certain that it had twin arches, built to match those of the vantage-court behind it; for in 1929, when the vantage-court was excavated, two courses of the east jamb of the eastern arch and the threshold, little worn, came into view, with dimensions which correspond exactly to those of the double arch of Porta Appia, as the writer had forecast.[2] These coincidences are not likely to be the work of chance. Already there have been emerging standard main measurements for early gate-towers. Now comes a complete correspondence in the over-all dimensions of two early curtains,

[1] Cf. fig. 20.   [2] See B. C. 1927, p. 59.

X

PORTA OSTIENSIS EAST, BEFORE 1888

Note the first-period block-work in the upper story of the curtain: it emerges again at the base of the lower story with a joggled jointing

suggesting clearly that stereotyped plans were being used in the building of the Imperial fortification of Rome. The general lines and aspect of the earliest curtain may therefore be recovered with certainty. It was a twin-arched two-story structure of stone, crowned by a moulding and parapet.

The history of this early curtain is to be deduced from its relation to the gateway towers. The outer walls of these towers, as will appear in detail below, were secondary constructions; but they were built up against the stonework of the upper story of the curtain. This stonework was almost entirely removed when the curtain received its present brickwork upper story, and only the end blocks of stone, which were bonded far in behind the secondary tower walls, were left, as being very difficult to extract. If, however, the stone curtain was being removed when the brickwork secondary walls were being added to the towers, it would have been the simplest of operations to remove these stones, and to get the very much better bond which the junction of two structures in brickfaced concrete would afford. Even more striking is the treatment of the moulding, which came below the early parapet. This does not occur in the brickfaced curtain, but small pieces were left bonded in behind the additional walls of the towers, and were also trimmed off flush with the new face of the towers. But when these faces were built the mouldings can only have been left in behind them because they were needed on the curtain; the trimming is a later operation, performed when the first stone curtain was not wanted. This, again, assigns the rebuilding of the stone curtain to the third period in the history of the Gate. So it is clear that the first-period curtain, with twin arches, did not disappear in the second period, and that only in the third period was it reconstructed completely on the lines visible to-day.

The new work, it may be noted, has much in common with the third-period reconstructed curtain at Porta Appia. Both Gates were given a lower story of stone and an upper one of tile-faced concrete. And the single arch, which took the place of the twin arches at each Gate, is sufficiently uniform in size (14 ft. 4 in. at Porta Ostiensis as against 14 ft. 2 in. at Porta Appia) to suggest that the alterations at each Gate were planned by one architect. Again, the portcullis arrangements at both Gates were of exactly the same size, as may be tested by any one who compares the plans. Noteworthy, then, is the appearance of a Latin cross and chrism, set within incised circles, on the key-stones[1] of the single arch at Porta Ostiensis, which there is no reason to consider other than original. The level of the road which passed through this curtain is discussed in connexion

---

[1] Cross on the front, chrism on the back, keystone, fig. 18.

with Porta Ostiensis West.[1] Here it must be noted that the excavations have demonstrated that the difference between it and the earliest level was very small.

The tile-faced portcullis-chamber has been considerably damaged in medieval times by the insertion of loop-holes.[2] In front it received light from six windows,[3] set close together; and above the central pair, in a niche with stepped roof, were fixed three stone corbels, pierced horizontally, which held the pulley-blocks for raising the portcullis, as explained fully in the account of Porta Appia.[4] The back wall contained six windows also, and the whole chamber was vaulted with a long barrel-vault. All the windows were reduced at some time to loop-holes.

Above the portcullis-chamber ran an uncovered rampart-walk, which sloped considerably from front to back, as at Porta Appia. At each end thereof was a little guard-house, provided with two-niched seats. This gave accommodation for a posse of four guards in all. Two *contubernia* would thus complete the four night watches. These sentry-boxes are pleasingly distinctive little structures, and occur now in Rome only at Porta Asinaria,[5] although they may, of course, once have existed on other gates. Between them run parapets, surmounted by merlons, and there can be little doubt that these, though not original, preserve the original arrangement. A notable decorative feature of this third-period curtain is a serrate string-course of tiles, which appears elsewhere on the Gate, and gives to its lines a pleasantly rich appearance. It is situated at rampart-walk level, and is best preserved at the back of the curtain. The appearance of the serrate string-course in the Roman world as an architectural feature is not early, and is dated by Rivoira[6] to the fourth century. But the dating of SS. Cosmas e Damiano, on which the *terminus a quo* depended, has been changed[7] since Rivoira wrote. The *terminus* is now given by the eaves of S. Stefano Rotondo, which are not earlier than Valens and Gratian, though a serrate stone-moulding occurs on the north tower of the west gate of Diocletian's palace[8] at Split. The late date, however, is distinctly preferable for brickwork, in view of dated examples elsewhere. At Ravenna the serrate string-course appears on S. Giovanni Evangelista[9] (*c.* 425), and the Mausoleum of Galla Placidia[10] (*c.* 440): at Salonika it occurs on Eski-Djuma[11] (*c.* 425), on

---

[1] See p. 220.   [2] The round window shown by Cassini, tav. 50, is imaginary.
[3] Schultze's description, *Bonner Jahrb.* 118, p. 343, is in error here.
[4] See p. 136.   [5] See fig. 29.
[6] Rivoira, *Lombardic Architecture*, pp. 25-6.
[7] Whitehead, *A. J. A.*, ser. ii, vol. xxxi (1927), p. 18. Mr. Whitehead and I were able to have some very useful discussions about brickwork, and our comparisons would have been productive had he only remained in Rome longer.
[8] Personal observation.   [9] Rivoira, loc. cit., p. 27, fig. 34.
[10] Ibid., p. 31, fig. 41.   [11] Ibid., p. 17.

S. Demetrius (425–95), and, in highly developed form, on Hagia Sophia[1] (c. 495): at Sofia, it occurs on the well-built church of S. Paraskeva.[2] This rather late date goes well with third-period reconstruction at Porta Ostiensis, as becomes apparent when the date of that period is discussed.

The east tower may now be examined. It is much enlarged at its base by external thickening, now built in medieval brick, but once constructed in stone. Pope Alexander's Cadastro (Pl. XI*b*) shows six courses on the west side of the tower, of which the lowest can still be seen embedded in the modern street; and, although the drawing shows the stonework to be much ruined, it demonstrates quite clearly that the whole bottom story of the tower was once faced with stone. Nor is the period of this stone-work in doubt. The piece still visible is designed to fit on to the third-period stone curtain, and the drawing in the Cadastro shows that the purpose of this design was to give a uniform appearance to the whole lower story of the gateway, clothing it all in gleaming white stone—an aesthetic conception[3] which gives rise to even greater splendour at Portae Appia and Flaminia.

Inside this third-period skin lie the outer-walls of two earlier semicircular towers. One of these walls, two feet thick, is now visible. The other came to light in 1929, when, at the writer's desire, it was sought at the east end of the front of the curtain-wall, in the lowest story of the tower. It belongs to a curved tower, and, granting that this tower is planned on the usual lines, it will be seen, from the plan, that it has the standard twenty-six foot diameter[4] which is typical of the first period of Portae Latina and Nomentana. It then becomes clear that, on the first floor, the inner line of the tower wall, though not of first-period construction, is on first-period lines, since it corresponds to the standard twenty-two foot diameter. It is possible, therefore, to restore here with every confidence a first-period tower-front, built upon standard lines.

It remains to consider evidence for the early staircases, and for the relation of the tower to the Wall. It is not now possible to see an early doorway, like those of Portae Latina and Appia, at the back of this tower, because the earliest back wall is concealed by later work. This is proved by the fact that the present back wall of the east tower is built up against the end of the early stone curtain, parapet-moulding and all, in such a way as to show that the stonework really goes back much further, achieving thus a form like that of the early stone curtain at Porta Appia. The present wall must therefore be screening an earlier one, against

[1] Ibid., p. 9, fig. 2.
[2] Personal observation: I was able to check the facts at Salonika some weeks before.
[3] See p. 260.   [4] See pp. 94, 103.

which the stonework was built. And the position of this early wall had, no doubt, everything to do with the very peculiar way in which the City Wall is now attached to each side of the Gate. At the west tower, where the arrangement is still standing to almost full height, the Wall turns sharply outwards just before it reaches the Gate, and forms a quarter-circle buttress in the angle between Wall and Gate. The same arrangement once existed at the east tower, but only the lowest of its brick-courses remain, though the mark of its junction with the tower is shown to a great height by the ending of the second-period facing on the tower. At the back of the Gate the Wall must have turned inwards in some corresponding way in order to meet the first-period rear wall of the towers. In the large-scale plan (fig. 19) of this feature a curve has been supplied, and it will be seen that the position of the first-period back walls is fixed by evidence from the west tower. This shows that the early stone curtain had exactly the same backward projection as that of Porta Appia, and that the present back wall of the tower was built up against the earlier core to standard *bipedalis* width. Finally, the first-period east tower now corresponds in every over-all measurement to the first-period standards of Portae Nomentana, Latina, and Appia. It may therefore be assumed that it had a staircase of standard type, which passed out of use in the second period, when the vantage-court wall was built.

The reason for this odd method of joining the Wall to the Gate is evidently concerned with alinement.[1] The curtain was meant to break back from the line of the Wall. Instead, it is built level, an alinement which must have been arrived at by mistake. How, then, did the mistake arise? Were the first-period towers built too far forward? Or was the error made by the builders of the Wall, in joining the Wall to the Gate? Neither of these solutions can well be true, since the mistake was made on both sides of the Gate. So it looks as if the curtain was built first, in mistaken alinement with the Wall, and that the junction between the Wall and the gate-towers had then to be joggled, by the introduction of the quarter-round projections. This involved the least change in lay-out.

The later history of these projections is clear enough. In the second period of construction they were still retained at the front of the gateway, but demolished at the back, when the towers were thickened so as to run flush with the Wall. Then came a third period, which saw the addition of a thick stone facing to the towers. This almost hid the quarter-round projections, which were therefore put out of use, for they were no longer

---

[1] As an extreme case Fano may be adduced, see R. Schultze, *Die römischen Stadttore*, Bonn. *Jahrb.* 118, p. 302, Taf. xiii. But here a vantage-court may be in question.

needed when the tower had already been extended behind. The eastern one was cleaned away, where it was not covered by masonry; the western was left half-removed, and remains in that state to-day: and at both ends the Wall received a new front, built straight.

These conclusions make it possible to understand the construction of the second story of the east tower. It becomes clear that, in the second period, when the position of the back wall was changed, the whole upper story of the early tower must have been removed. Not even the early upper walls can be thought of as embodied in the second-period structure, since the new windows were much more numerous than the old standard permitted. The new vault also was provided with special skylights, for ventilation and extra lighting, with which the first-period towers of the Gate were not equipped, as is shown by the west tower, where the first-period windows, three to the semicircle, are covered over by a thickening wall of the second period on the outside. So the present arrangement of this story of the east tower belongs to the second period. At this time also the staircase had to be planned afresh. After the reorganization there was no lower staircase, such as occurs[1] in the early towers of Portae Nomentana, Latina, and Appia: instead, the Gate was entered by a door from the vantage-court wall, which is bonded into, and so contemporary with, the second-period thickening wall at the back of the tower. The new doorway led into a new and roomy passage, behind the front room, which took the through traffic between the Wall and Gate, as at Porta Appia.[2] From this story a staircase, arranged in the side of the main chamber, led up to the next level, by means of a passage over the rear corridor, and two flights of stairs. This probably once served to give access to a flat embattled top belonging to the second-period tower.

The third story was a third-period addition, contemporary with the building of the new stone curtain. This is proved by the fact that it has an exactly similar serrate moulding of tiles employed in its decoration. The brick-facing also resembles that of the curtain's upper story: in contrast with the second-period work the tiles are shorter and fatter, less well laid, and un-provided with bonding-courses. A great deal more mortar in relation to tiles is also used in building the window-arches, and, in the face of the wall, a Greek cross formed with tiles should also be noted, as an indication of late date.[3] The new story was lit by five windows, arranged to suit the front aspect of the Gate, and fitted with semicircular niches and loop-holes. The central

---

[1] See figs. 15, 17, 20.   [2] See p. 123, fig. 20.

[3] Cf. the brickwork of Pope Simplicius (Grisar, *Roma alla fine del mondo antico*, fig. 117, p. 389) on S. Stefano Rotondo: the idea fits well enough with fifth-century apotropaic beliefs.

window was at some time filled up, and covered with a charming picture in fresco of the Virgin Mary, regrettably damaged by pencilled scrawlings. This will belong to the Greek hermit *cella Muroniana*, described by Grisar,[1] and it may be compared with the Madonna to be seen in the Wall-gallery of Vigna Casali, west of Porta Appia.[2] The roof was vaulted in the same way as that of the second-period chamber below it, but it had no skylight, and its flat top was crowned by a parapet and merlons. Indeed, at least two sets of merlons go to form those which are now to be seen. But neither can be older than the time of the Cadastro, when machicolations were in existence.[3] The present set has therefore been marked on plan, and the other omitted. This completes the description of the east tower.

Of the west tower the earliest second story is better preserved, but the roofs and floors of its third and fourth stories are ruined, and, without special apparatus, it was impossible to climb to their level. Their plan, however, was completely comprehensible from below, and their position in the history of the Gate is sufficiently clear. As at the east tower, the Cadastro shows round the base of this one a stone casing, now replaced by modern thickening which rises rather higher than the floor of the second story. Above this point there can be seen a secondary facing, built against the moulding of an early stone curtain in exactly the same way as at the east tower, and terminating at the elaborate serrate string-course which marks the base of the third-period addition.

That the outer wall of the second story indubitably belongs to the second period is proved by the existence, on the inside of the tower, of a wall which is built in a quite different and better style of brickwork. This wall is also pierced by windows which do not come through to the outside of the Gate. The early tower thus defined is, however, three feet less in internal and external diameter (19 ft. and 23 ft.) than any early tower so far described, and the reason for this abnormality in size is not clear. It cannot be connected with adjusting the error in the west junction between Wall and tower, since it makes no improvement therein, and, anyhow, an adjustment could have been made without a change of the kind. In default of any other explanation, it may be suggested that the reduction in size was meant to disguise another peculiarity of plan. Any one who has approached the Gate closely enough to appreciate its aesthetic value cannot perceive the whole semicircle of the east tower, because it is planned askew. On the other hand, all of the west tower was visible, and if it had been built to normal size it would have

[1] Grisar, *Civiltà Cattolica*, 1902, *Memorie sacre della Porta Ostiense*.
[2] Lanciani, *R.E.*, p. 69, fig. 30.   [3] See pl. XI*b*.

looked very much bigger than the east tower. Was the west tower therefore built smaller than usual in order to avoid this illusion? Roman mural painters were quite used to playing tricks with perspective, and one of this kind certainly seems to have been adopted with the third-period windows of the east tower.

In the second period, then, the tower received its present external thickening, and a new cobbled floor, as revealed in 1929. It was also increased somewhat in height in order to suit the gallery of the Wall, of which the upper rampart-walk must have run straight on to the battlemented flat roof of the tower. The means of access to the tower from the vantage-court wall is not now clear. But a gap in the wall seems to mark where a door, covered by a flat arch of which one voussoir is to be seen on the outside of the Gate, has been torn out. To suit the new rise in level of the chamber, a staircase to the roof was arranged on the west wall, and the position of the window in the adjacent rear wall of the tower was altered.

Of the topmost story, added in the third period and marked by the serrate tile-moulding at floor-level, only the east rear angle is left standing to full height; the upper part of the rest is a later restoration, as old as Vasi's time.[1] It is possible to see that this story was added after the Wall-gallery had been built, since it overlaps the junction thereof with the tower. Access to the new roof of the tower was achieved with two flights of stairs and a passage, as is shown by marks on the inner side of the back wall of the tower, and by a window remaining in its east side, just above the little sentry-box on the curtain. Outside, a late external staircase was added to give access from the Wall-gallery, but otherwise both towers had the same architectural history.

Behind all the features so far described lay the vantage-court. The plan of this was revealed completely in 1929. It appears that the Roman court followed closely the lines of the medieval structure now visible, and, of course, embodied the extant double arch as its back gate. But its walls were much thicker, since they contained in their thickness two staircases, one on each side of the Gate. These were entered from the City by special small doors (fig. 19), which were not controlled from the inside of the court. Tile-stamps[2] on the treaders of these stairs were of the Hadrianic date so common on the Wall. The position of the stairs, moreover, helps to decide the purpose of the court-yard. Evidently it was not defensive. If the courtyard had been meant to isolate the Gate like a castle, access to the towers would have been controlled from inside the court. In fact, it now becomes clear that the courtyard was not accessible from the

[1] Vasi, pl. xi.
[2] C.I.L. xv. 1179: three examples, kindly furnished by Dr. A. M. Colini.

Gate or the Wall, except quite indirectly. Its function, then, can have had nothing to do with defence: and the only reasonable possibility that remains is that it provided quarters for the City customs officials, as buildings at Porta Appia[1] also suggest. Finally, it becomes evident how the present medieval courtyard, dated by Audebert[2] to Nicholas V, 1451, took its present shape. In 1410 the Gate was seized by King Ladislaus, and assailed by the City-folk with bombards. No doubt these ruined the stair-cases, the one weak part in the ancient structure, and so, when the courtyard came to be rebuilt, the medieval builders used the inner wall of the staircase as their outer wall, as can be seen on the east side of the Gate to-day.

The twin arches at the back of the Gate were obviously con-structed in considerable haste, with robbed blocks of traver-tine, irregularly coursed. The coursing is different on each side, and the two systems are joggled in the central pier. The vous-soirs are fairly well cut, but they differ in depth and some have slipped a little. The roughness of the building is not a criterion of late rebuilding, and may well be entirely due to employment of robbed material in their hasty initial construction. How the wall above the arches was finished off is obscure. At present it is occupied by Pope Nicholas's embattled curtain-wall and tower, provided with a wall-shrine of the Madonna.

Conclusions.—Such is the material available for reconstructing the history of Porta Ostiensis East. In outline the story runs as follows. The Gate began as a rather low structure, with semi-circular towers as high as a great double-arched curtain, of severely plain stonework. The curtain of Porta Praetoria at Regensburg[3] (Castra Regina) must have looked very like this, just as its towers, though built in stone, closely resemble the towers of this Gate. The windows in the stone curtain were probably of quite simple pattern, with round heads, not unlike those erected later by the third-period builders at Portae Latina and Tiburtina. It is notable that the west tower was narrower than the eastern, although it had the same projection; and it is suggested, provisionally, that this was meant to correct the illu-sion in perspective likely to be caused by the skew plan of the Gate. Two quarter-round projections at the angle made by each tower with the Wall corrected a mistake in planning there. Otherwise the gate closely resembled the first Porta Appia.[4]

In the second period, when the gallery was added to the Wall,

---

[1] See p. 138.
[2] Audebert, fol. 243; cf. Manetti, *Vita Nicolai V*, lib. i, col. 92 'Urbis moenia . . . multis locis concinnatis propugnaculis novis . . . generose admodum et utiliter reparavit.' The money of the Jubilee year went to this.
[3] Personal observation.   [4] See p. 140, fig. 24.

a. PORTA OSTIENSIS EAST

The first-period work in the upper story of the curtain at its junction with the tower

Porta di S Paolo per di fuori

b. PORTA OSTIENSIS EAST IN 1655–67

From the Cadastral Survey of Pope Alexander VII

Note the stone facing of the lower stories of the towers

the earlier towers were insufficiently high and deep to suit the new arrangement. They were therefore heightened, thickened externally, and provided with a system of loop-holes, in harmony with the new fashion for second stories at the Gates, and connexion with the Wall's gallery was improved by new corridors. The early staircases completely disappeared, and, in order to reach the towers from outside, stairs, accessible from the City by special doors, were built into the heart of a new vantage-court wall. The courtyard was entered from behind by twin arches, matching the two arches still retained in the front curtain. Thus the external aspect of the new Gate was not so very much changed, except that every one would note, with a pleasurable sense of security, how much higher the Wall reached on each side of it.

Security was still further increased in the third period, when it was decided to replace the first-period twin arches at the front of the Gate by a single arch with a portcullis, as at Porta Appia. Now also, the long low lines characteristic of the original curtain were broken by the construction of the new arch and of six windows in the curtain above it; each tower received a new story, and the curtain was crowned by guard-houses, which give rich interest to its outline. Finally, the bases of the towers received a casing of white travertine, matching the curtain. True, these decorative features were somewhat austere, but they go to show that the work of the third period, if primarily utilitarian, had its aesthetic side.

Ancient remains do not carry the story further, for subsequent constructions are medieval. But Procopius[1] tells the part that Porta Sancti Pauli had to play in the Gothic wars, a role shamed by Isaurian treachery, and not even relieved by dramatic incident. But the Gate received little damage, for it was not in the main line of attack, and only in the fifteenth century did its back receive serious harm, from the bombards which expelled the garrison of King Ladislaus.[2]

§ 4. PORTA APPIA

The three Gates so far described form a preparation for the study of the very complex Porta Appia (Pl. I). In literature this Gate has no important place, although it is mentioned early, by fourth-century Servius,[3] and again in the Einsiedeln List. By

---

[1] Procop. *B. G.* iii, 36.

[2] Diario Romae: *Rer. Ital. Script.* xxiv, col. 992.

[3] Servius (*nat. c.* 355), *Schol. ad Aen.* i. 296 'templum Martis in Appia via extra urbem prope portam'. Cf. *Schol. ad Ovid. Fast.* vi. 691 'templum Martis stat recta fronte contra Capenam portam' (apparently Capena=Appia here). The hill in front of Porta Appia was called *clivus Martis, C. I. L.* vi. 1270.

medieval times [1] its name had become corrupted to Porta d'Accia, or Daccia, or changed to Porta di San Sebastiano. Not far outside it, crowning the hill to the east of via Appia and overlooking the Almo, lay the old Templum Martis. Indeed, the traditional belief, since Canina's [2] time, has been that blocks of stone were robbed from this Temple in order to build the beautiful bastions of Luna marble which decorate the Gate to-day. This is, however, a pure conjecture, and it will presently be seen that the character of the blocks themselves suggests a mixed provenience.

(a) Early constructions and the east tower

The clearest traces of primary construction (fig. 20) exist behind the Gate in the back of the east tower, where a blocked door was visible in 1926. Failing a proper entrance, access to the interior had to be won by a hole, used at that time, as was to appear from remains and certain livestock within it, as a tramp's sleeping place. Thither the writer wormed his way, followed closely by Mr. M. A. Sisson, who helped throughout in the measurement of this intricate Gate, and whose kindness was only equalled by his enthusiasm. This was a truly exciting event, during which a small and uninvited audience betted upon our relative chances of sticking. There were high odds on the writer. The hole led us to a passage, roughly cut through the concrete of the Gate in aimless fashion, no doubt rather like the hole which Ficoroni [3] saw made at Porta Flaminia in 1706, by unintelligent treasure-hunters. This broke through into a staircase-well, behind the blocked door, which contained a system of stairs, preserved sufficiently to enable a complete restoration of them to be made, and so to demonstrate that the staircase had nothing to do with Porta Appia as now visible. As for their period, it is thus clear that, since the doorway leading to them is bonded into the earliest work on the Wall, the stairs must belong to the earliest Gate on the spot. And the sort of tower which they served was soon revealed by the exploration of another cavity, which led out of the stair-well to the north-west angle of the east marble bastion. The hole in question was hacked through a mass of solid concrete, and in its south side and top Mr. Sisson at once noted the vertical section and curved plan of a structure in tile-faced concrete, which ran back northwards and overlapped the east end of a travertine (not marble) curtain-wall by eight inches.

---

[1] Tomassetti, via Appia, in *Campagna Romana nel medio evo.*

[2] Canina, *Via Appia,* p. 53. C., however, did not believe in one provenience.

[3] Ficoroni, *Roma Antica* (1741), p. 286: for rumours of treasure inside Gates, cf. the amusing experience of seventeenth-century Sir Tho. Roe, in attempting to pillage reliefs from Porta Aurea, Constantinople. Van Millingen, *Byzantine Constantinople,* p. 66.

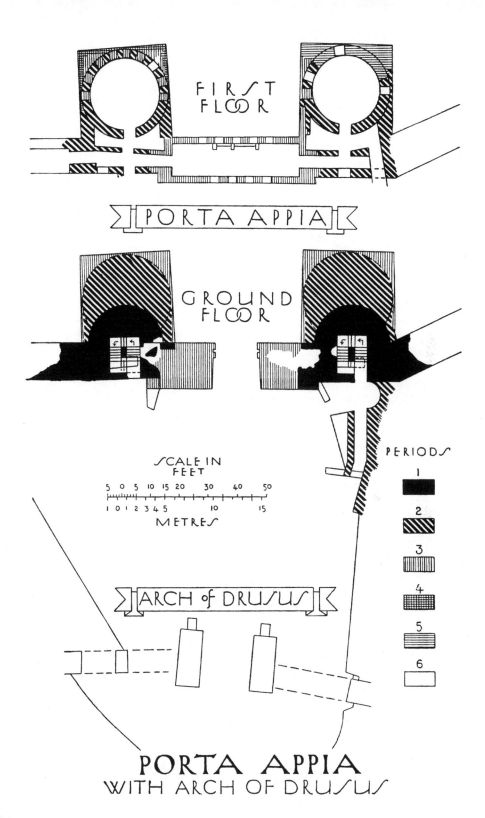

FIRST FLOOR

PORTA APPIA

GROUND FLOOR

SCALE IN FEET

5 0 5 10 15 20 30 40 50

1 0 1 2 3 4 5 10 15

METRES

PERIODS

1

2

3

4

5

6

ARCH of DRUSUS

PORTA APPIA
WITH ARCH OF DRUSUS

It was evident that these were the remains of an early tower and curtain-wall, exactly like those of Porta Ostiensis East, to which access was given by a small dog-leg[1] staircase, like that of Porta Nomentana. The size of this tower could have been determined only roughly from the small segment of its curve available for measurement; but, since it now became evident that the stairs were set centrally within the tower, it was possible to check the calculation from the segment by the distance between the axis of the central stair-newel and the edge of the tower. This gave a radius of thirteen feet to the tower, exactly corresponding to that of the towers[2] at Portae Nomentana, Latina, and Ostiensis East. The correspondence enables the confident restoration of a semicircular tower in first-period style.

The same exploration also gave, for the first time, the precise form of the staircases, of which fragments were already noted[3] at Portae Nomentana and Latina. Equally interesting is the evidence for a subsequent disuse of this example. The stairs are considerably narrowed by a later thickening wall at the back: and they are blocked completely, half-way up the second return, by a broken concrete vault (see fig. 20), which once supported the corridor leading from the Gate to the gallery of the Wall. So all access to the stairs from above was completely cut off in ancient times, and it thus becomes clear that the corridor (and all else above it) has nothing to do with the stairs, but is to be assigned to a secondary period. But with the corridor-wall is bonded the Wall-gallery: and so, at Porta Appia, as at Porta Latina, the Wall-gallery belongs to a second period in the Wall's history. In the second period access to the Gate was gained by means of a small doorway, entered from the top of a vantage-court wall, of which only a fragment now remains, bonded firmly into the upper part of the back wall of the tower, and projecting into thin air. Schultze,[4] in a most erroneous plan of the Gate, shows elaborate stairs descending at this point. There is no evidence for this and the whole matter is discussed in further detail below.

The secondary arrangements of the east tower may now be described. From its back corridor, at first-floor level, an entrance led into a staircase-well, the means of reaching the upper stories of the tower; and thence a second doorway led into a large

---

[1] Cf. Durm, *Baukunst*, p. 354, fig. 390b, for similar dog-leg stairs in the Baths of Caracalla on a 6, 3, 6, 3, arrangement.

[2] See pp. 94, 102, 115. The correspondence was unknown to the writer when surveying Porta Appia, since the other Gates had not yet been measured. It confirmed a conjecture made by him in *Discovery*, vi, p. 294.

[3] See pp. 98, 103.

[4] *Bonner Jahrb.*, Heft 118, Taf. xvii: also p. 343. This article, which is continually being used, is full of errors, especially in plans, which Schultze seems to have taken no care to verify.

circular tower-chamber, lighted by nine well-built windows,[1] grouped as follows, two at each side of the tower, and five in front (Pl. XIII*a*). Yet none of the nine windows comes through properly to the outer face of the tile-faced quadrangular bastion, and only three were adapted to do so, however awkwardly. Evidently, then, these windows have nothing to do with the quadrangular plan, but belong to a circular-fronted tower, intermediate in period between the primary semicircular tower, and the existing quadrangular tower which enveloped it. Further, not even the quadrangular marble bases now visible can be thought to belong to this round-fronted tower, as is proved by the following facts. The marble curtain, which indubitably belongs to the same period as the marble bases,[2] has an upper story of brickwork. This was attached to the round-fronted tower by an irregular bond, against a broken surface; and the style of the tower brickwork is much better than that of the curtain. So it is clear that the marble curtain, and therefore the marble bastions connected with it, belong to a later stage in the Gate's development than the round-fronted tower. In fact, three stages have been detected, and in each of them the east tower had a different form; in the first a semicircle, in the second an attached circle, in the third a quadrangle. Presently, it will be seen that the same evolution appears in the west tower.

Further facts about the round-fronted tower may now be observed. First, it is impossible to determine from present evidence how the round front was attached to the curtain at the base. The probability seems to be that its outer wall ran back in a straight line, forming thus a straight-sided and blind lower story, with semicircular front, as at Porta Asinaria;[3] the tower would then take the form of an attached circle only at a higher level. This solution is suggested by the difficulty of attaching the circle to an already existing semicircle. Secondly, the height of the tower is clear. An examination of its facing, internal and external, shows that it reached just one story above the top of the present quadrangular bastions, and similar evidence exists for the west tower. The present topmost story is a later addition. Even so, however, the over-all height obtained for the round-fronted towers is about seventy feet, considerably greater than that of the Wall at this point, which reaches on the west a maximum height of fifty-eight feet six inches from ground-level to upper rampart-walk. This was a huge tower (fig. 25), equal in size to those of Porta Asinaria in Rome, and inviting comparison with fine North-European towers like those of Porta Nigra at Trier or of the Gate of Roman London shown on the Arras

---

[1] The three central ones were loop-holes: perhaps also the four rear ones.
[2] See p. 128.   [3] See p. 145, fig. 26, and pl. XIV.

medallion[1] of Constantius I. Thirdly, the arrangements of the
stories in the tower are clear: but they have to be discussed,
as may now be done, in relation to later periods. In all there
were five floors, the topmost uncovered. The ground floor was
blind, since it was built round, or upon, the remains of the first-
period semicircular bastion. The first floor was roofed by a very
thick flat concrete vault, presumably intended for artillery. This
was removed in ancient times. But before that happened, the
quadrangular exterior had been built round the tower, and the
windows altered to suit it. Since the original construction is
secondary, this gives us three periods, while the removal of the
vault goes to a fourth period. When the vault was removed, the
effect was to make one story out of two, and so the old windows
were now blocked, and two new ones were cut, at the level
of the demolished vault. The eastern one is surmounted by a
large Rho in tile-work, perhaps part of a chrism. With difficulty,
the original window arrangements of the upper story can be
recovered. When the external walls were quadrangular, there
were two windows, now blocked, in each side: and this arrangement probably follows the earliest circular plan, since the
position of the windows does not really suit the quadrangular
form. But the circular plan would give room for more windows,
where the angles of the quadrangle tower now obtrude; and
proportion would strongly support a theory that the nine windows
in story II, and the six windows in story IV, may have been
matched by seven or eight windows in the artillery-story III.
The reason[2] for this change in levels was plainly visible on
the side of the tower before the repairs of 1927. Two large
cracks had appeared at corresponding points on both sides of
the tower, and were matched by two more, in precisely similar
positions, on the west tower. Their occurrence is explained by
the evolution of the Gate. They come just at the point where the
round-fronted tower walls pass from the foundation provided by
the first-period bastion on to unconsolidated ground. Either the
second-period builders did not provide an adequate foundation
for the new fronts, or the new work slipped a little on the soft
rock on which it was founded. Anyhow, the new fronts sank or
slipped forward, and broke off from the more firmly founded
parts behind them. This fundamental defect in the foundations,
which has nothing to do with the first settling of the concrete,
was minimized later by the erection of quadrangular bastions,

[1] Beaurains medallion, *Aréthuse*, Jan. 1924, pl. vii = *J. R. S.* xiv, p. 155.

[2] I should have liked to offer this explanation in 1926, when I first began to suspect it.
But this kind of observation cannot be made casually, before the whole history of the Gate
is examined and set forth. The methods of preservation used in 1926-7, tying back the
towers and refacing the cracks, do not touch the root of the evil. But they have checked
it. Before then the Gate appreciably rocked as traffic passed through it.

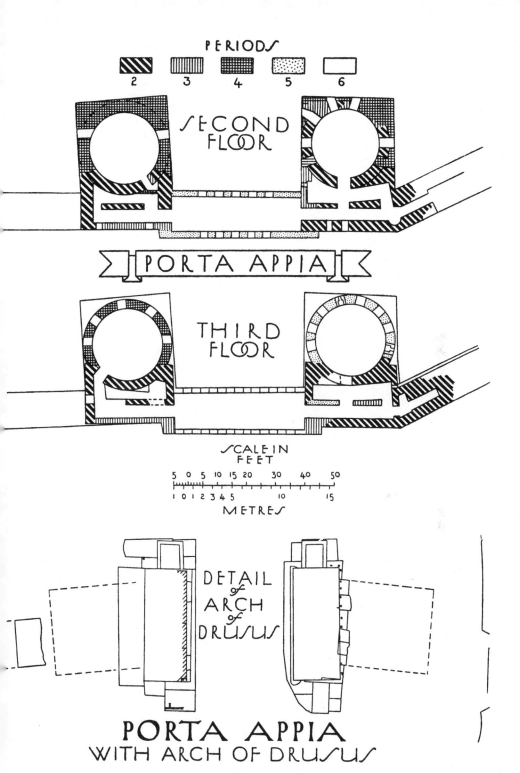

PERIODS

2   3   4   5   6

SECOND
FLOOR

PORTA APPIA

THIRD
FLOOR

SCALE IN
FEET

5 0 5 10 15 20   30   40   50

1 0 1 2 3 4 5   10   15

METRES

DETAIL
of
ARCH
of
DRUSUS

PORTA APPIA
WITH ARCH OF DRUSUS

Fig. 21

which acted as buttresses, and slowed down the cracking. But the process has never quite ceased, and the vibration of heavy modern traffic was opening the cracks until 1927. This suggests that the foundations are really slipping on the rock, and, if so, the towers are still in peril.

The topmost covered floor of the round-fronted tower, number IV, was once roofed with another great vault, and received light from five symmetrically-placed round-headed windows. Three of these have been replaced by oblong modern windows, which do not, however, wipe out entirely the voussoirs of their predecessors. The character of the roofing is proved by the blind story now visible near the top of the Gate. This can only have masked a large vaulted but flat-topped roof. Above this point the tower wall is stepped back, and so becomes thinner and much worse built, being matched in this respect by the topmost story of the marble curtain. Again, the fundamental crack does not continue beyond this point, as if it had ceased to grow by the time the addition was made, and all Roman brickwork in the rear staircase towers stops. It is therefore clear that the second-period work went no higher than this: and a completely new system of putlog-holes marks a new construction above this point.

Access to the additional and topmost story, whose place in the series of reconstructions is discussed below, was provided by stairs set in the staircase tower; but how its roof was reached is quite uncertain, for the whole of the staircase tower behind the great crack described above is at this point of Papal origin, built of the tufa-faced work associated at Porta Ostiensis East[1] with Pope Nicholas V, in 1451. Thus the oldest useful views of the gate, given by the panoramas of Tempesta[2] and Maggi,[3] show the arrangement as now. On top of this story came a flat roof with parapet and merlons, restored in 1926–7.

The additions which made this tower quadrangular comprise one high story of marble and two of brick-faced concrete. The writer penetrated, for a second time, the valuable hole leading to the north-west angle of the east marble bastion, in order to examine the concrete between the face of the semicircular bastion and the back of the marble-faced quadrangle. This was found to be all of one build, and it is thus clear that the second-period face (intermediate between the semicircular and quadrangular forms) was destroyed when the bastions were faced with marble. There is no doubt that the circular tower lost its facing elsewhere, for the outer face of the marble blocks is almost tangent to the circular bastions: here, then, the curved facing must have been removed in order to key the new marble blocks to the earlier structure.

[1] See p. 120, note 2,
[2] Tempesta, 1593.   [3] Maggi, 1625.

Yet it is obvious that the builders could not cut too deeply into the base of a seventy-foot tower; and this, among other reasons,[1] seems to have led to a curious treatment of the marble work.

Most of these blocks of Luna marble (the two skewbacks in the front arch and a block to the east thereof are *cipollino*) are provided with one boss, differing in size and projection and position on different blocks; the quoin-stones sometimes have two. Every block originally had such a boss; but very few bosses are now left either on the fronts and two inner sides of the bastions or on the curtain (see Pls. I and XII), for most of them have been knocked off, with rough chiselling,[2] while fancy sometimes prompted a workman to carve out of them a cross or a bird, presumably the Holy Dove. In short, the rough bosses were only left where they attracted little notice, as happens on the Athenian Propylaea and elsewhere.[3] What, then, was their purpose? As Lugli[4] has noted, their different size and position, and the shallowness of many, preclude the idea that they were *ancones* made for lifting: furthermore, the writer penetrated to the interior of the lower curtain, and saw that they were never matched by a companion boss on the inside of the block, as a lifting arrangement would demand.[5] Nor can the bosses be *fulcra* for crowbars, as Durm[6] has suggested. Any technician who studies them carefully,[7] in relation to tooling round them, will vouch that they are the bosses which the stone-mason leaves until the last when reducing different stones, rough or smooth, to a new and common plane, in order to calculate from them any further readjustment required.

An explanation along these lines works well. It has not been pointed out, in any explanation of the surviving bosses, that all undamaged bosses (an overwhelming majority) have a carefully tooled surface, often extremely finely and even better worked than the new surface round them. The surface on the boss must thus be all that remains of an older face of the block to which it belongs, since no one would tool exquisitely one surface of a rough boss for any purpose whatever. The blocks must therefore be

[1] e.g. the variant sizes of the blocks themselves, as shown in the curtain (see below, p. 135), Nicorescu (*Eph. Dacoromana*, i, p. 4 n.) assumes wrongly that all are of the same size.
[2] This is quite certain, and it cancels Lugli's observation (*La Z. A.*, p. 318) 'mentre non ve n'è traccia negli altri due lati'. It also cancels his whole theory about the bosses.
[3] I have noted similar bosses as far apart as Athens (Gymnasium), Segesta, and Mérida.
[4] *La Z. A.*, p. 318.
[5] Nicorescu's theory, expressed in *Eph. Dacoromana*, i, p. 4 n., that the bosses were on the *backs* of the blocks to key them into concrete on another building, from which they were robbed for Porta Appia, is supported neither by the form of the boss nor by example.
[6] Durm, *Die Baukunst der Griechen*, p. 157.
[7] I am deeply indebted to Mr. Skeaping, Prix de Rome sculptor at the B.S.R., who came with me to this Gate and discussed the whole question of workshop technique with the greatest interest and care.

old ones, robbed from older buildings,[1] set in position round
Porta Appia, and then dressed down to a common plane. This
was an old practice in the Graeco-Roman world for frame-
dressing (ἀναθύρωσις), and it may be suspected that it was used
on all buildings where speed was urgent. Finally, its employment
at Porta Appia is proved beyond doubt by inscriptions on the
blocks themselves. A half-erased inscription, NEPOS, first noted[2]
by Lugli, appears on the west side of the front main arch, on
the block west of the second voussoir. Its letters have been
almost erased by secondary trimming; and it may be added that
others letters have been made illegible in the same way on the
next block to the left. So these are two blocks, robbed from some

FIG. 22. Inscribed stone built into archway, Porta Appia.

earlier structure, and trimmed for fresh use, after being placed
in position on Porta Appia: for, if the operation had not been done
in situ, the inscription would not have been worked over, steadily
more deeply, so as to erase more and more of it, towards the west.
Here, too, may be noted a third block (fig. 22), forming part of the
vault of the gateway, cut in travertine and worked over in just
the same way, on a slightly different plane from that of its original
surface. The bastions, in fact, were built with robbed blocks,
taken from various tombs and villas, or even from the adjacent
Temple of Mars. When all of these were in position, their surfaces
were worked over, and reduced to a common plane by means of
the plumb-line, leaving bosses of different sizes and projections.
In the most conspicuous parts of the Gate the final touch was
given to the operation, but later and carelessly, by removing the
bosses. Originally, they were being treated in a different way.
Some were being carved, as at the Porta Aurea in Constantinople,
into symbols in low relief, such as a cross or the Holy Dove.
This process did not get far and was broken off. The rough
chiselling may thus be either the hasty work of the same workmen, about to be called away from their task, and anxious to
finish it, or a later attempt to improve the appearance of the Gate.
But the former opinion is perhaps preferable, since the appearance
of such bosses was not much resented in the ancient world. That

[1] It is pure conjecture to confine the source of these blocks to the Temple of Mars.
[2] *La Z. A.*, p. 318.

XII

PORTA APPIA, FINAL STAGE

Two rows of windows should be supplied in the upper stories of the curtain

is why they remain upon so many buildings away from Rome, while, elsewhere on the Wall, they appear at many Gates.

The marble bastions thus constructed stood upon two courses of travertine, and were crowned by a specially cut moulding of late-Roman pattern.[1] The fact of special cutting, and the still more valuable fact that the curtain was contemporary with the bastions, are both proved by the joggled piece, carved as a special item, which brings the mouldings into line at the west end of the curtain. The blocks of the curtain and bastions have not the same system of coursing, nor are they bonded into each other, because they were being built up against the wall of the early travertine curtain.

Above the crowning mould of the marble facing rose a two-story quadrangular tile-faced tower front, very thinly applied to the second-period round-fronted tower. The lower story of the new front masked all the windows of the round-fronted tower: the upper story converted those available to its own use. As has been seen, these upper windows were later abolished, together with the vault with which they were connected, and their place was taken by a single window in the centre of either side. The change was necessitated by the subsidence in foundations, which was threatening the stability of the fronts of both towers, and was, no doubt, intensified by the earthquake[2] of 442. The floor above this marks the top of the rectangular part of the tower. Its level is now marked outside the Gate by a florid cyma: but this must belong to a repair, since it only occurs on the dangerous side of the great crack on the east side of the tower; while on the safe side, an earlier moulding of quieter late-Roman pattern is preserved. Schultze[3] restores above this a balustrade and walk on top of the quadrangular tower, but in fact there never was room here for either feature. At this level also it should have been possible to pass from the upper rampart-walk of the Wall into the Gate. But for some unknown reason no connexion was ever made, although the walk lies just outside an appropriate half-landing, and so all the traffic between the upper rampart-walk and the Gate must have descended to the gallery at the first tower east of the Gate.

(b) The West Tower

The history of the west tower corresponds, in its main features, to that of its eastern companion. But the relation of its floor-levels to the gallery and rampart-walk of the Wall were different, and led to differences in planning, to be discussed later in their

---

[1] Cf. Strzygowski, *Jahrb. d. Arch. Inst.* 1893, viii, pp. 12, 13.
[2] See *C. I. L.* vi. 32086–32090. Paul. Diac. *Hist. Misc.* xiv, p. 961 (Migne).
[3] Loc. cit., taf. xvii.

turn. Meanwhile, the primary construction claims attention. Much is hidden by a large modern buttress which comes down on top of some ancient rooms behind the Gate proper, which continued to be used in connexion with the medieval *gabella*-offices, shown by Uggeri.[1] But, though ancient, the rooms are separated from the main gateway structure by a break in construction, and the brickwork shows them to be clearly of later date. So they may be discussed later,[2] with the other remains at the back of the Gate. From them a passage led into a narrow staircase-well, of exactly the same type and size as the eastern first-period staircase, but less well preserved, and now occupied by a modern staircase, constructed in 1926–7. Early in 1926 it was full of rubbish, and covered over, as in the east tower, by a secondary concrete floor, belonging to the back corridor of the tower. A rough hole then permitted the writer to clamber out of this staircase-passage towards the middle of the Gate; but in vain; for it was impossible to penetrate far enough to gain evidence about the size of the bastion which this early staircase served. But the position of the staircase, the fixed points given by the west edge of the early arch, and the cracks in the later tower (see below) make it possible to be sure that the early tower exactly resembled its eastern companion, being, in fact, a semicircular bastion of the now familiar type, with an external diameter of 26 feet. It is noteworthy that the doorway of the staircase is in the same relation to the stairs as that of the east tower, so that the stairs arrive in the upper chamber out of centre, as in Porta Latina's west tower.[3] As in the east tower, a second-period corridor ran above this staircase, completely cutting it off from the Gate. This was entered from the gallery of the Wall by a flight of descending steps, and under these was set the doorway which led out on to the vantage-court wall. From the corridor a doorway led into a round-fronted tower, planned and fitted with vaults on precisely the same arrangement as in the east. The whole of the tower's lower front (Pl. I), however, had been refaced, at a late period, with great and wide-set blocks of *peperino*, which completely blotted out the second-period front windows, as shown on plan. Enough remains of the side windows of this period, however, to ensure that the system, as might be expected, resembled that in the east tower. The period of this great refacing is clearly the fifth. For, on the exterior of the tower, it replaces the fourth-period brick-and-travertine reconstruction, which had repaired the dangerous cracking in the tower, altered the windows, and removed the great vault of the second story. Similar events took place at this time in the east tower, where the

---

[1] Uggeri, vol. v, pl. 4, plan.
[2] See p.138.   [3] See p. 103 and fig. 17.

brickwork used is of the same type, but has no travertine courses. Minor differences of this kind, however, did not trouble late-Roman builders. Then comes, in the west tower, the exceptional *peperino* refacing, which repairs a rent caused by the collapse of the whole front of the west tower (see fig. 21 and below). The evolution of stories II and III was thus exactly the same as that of the corresponding stories of the east tower; and then this accident happened, after they had reached final form. The facing of story IV, on the other hand, differs notably from that of story IV of the east tower. Only the smallest piece of its external facing, close in towards the staircase tower, belongs to the second period. The rest is precisely the same as that of the fifth story, so as to suggest that the upper part of the west tower had required extensive rebuilding in the sixth period, when the fifth stories were added. It may be that subsidence was still causing trouble in the west tower, even if it had ceased to do so in the east. Otherwise, the upper story exactly resembled that of the east tower, and was finished with a flat top and battlements.

The changes through which the tower passed may now be summarized as follows. It began as a small semicircular bastion, with one blind story and one open one. In a second period the open story was removed, and the solid base was enveloped by a much bigger round-fronted bastion, closely resembling those of Porta Asinaria.[1] In the third period this bastion received a quadrangular casing of marble and brickwork. Next, a cracking set up by insufficient foundations or by slipping on the soft rock became so bad that the floors and windows of the whole tower had to be drastically remodelled, making the use of artillery impossible. This repair was marked by the loss of twin side windows, and by two bands of travertine in the brickwork. In a fifth period the whole front was seriously damaged; much of the brick-faced quadrangle seems to have collapsed with a rush, happily without taking with it the upper front of the tower. This hole was repaired with *peperino* blocks in such a way as to flatten considerably the internal curve of the tower. This is, then, a repair period[2] not found on the east tower. Finally, in a sixth period, to be equated with the fifth constructional period on the east tower, the tower received a new story. The fourth story also was fitted with an entirely new system of windows. This fourth-story repair is another piece of work which is not matched on the east tower: and with it ends the constructional history of the west tower, except for Papal repairs to its roof, parapet, merlons, and staircase tower.

[1] See p. 157.
[2] The distinction is worth making: otherwise the history of the Gate becomes unintelligible.

The arrangements for connecting the rampart-walk with the tower are as follows. The walk arrived at the point where the tower became circular instead of quadrangular. But here, owing to the planning of the gallery below, a staircase inside the Gate occupied the place where the rampart-walk was planned to arrive. So it came about that one staircase descended, and another ascended, from the rampart-walk to the nearest half-landings; the brickwork of the ascending staircase is, however, late in type, although it is difficult to say whether it has been refaced (the position is exposed), or was not built until the fifth story was added to the tower, in the sixth period. At all events two entrances to the Gate from the rampart-walk were so contrived, whereas none existed on the east. Just outside the tower, on the landing at the bottom of the lower flight of stairs, was placed a small latrine, whence a shoot passed out at the angle made by the Gateway and the Wall. This was, it seems, the Gate's only latrine, until two of the front windows in the fourth story of the west tower were converted into latrines at some late period, which is to be classed, provisionally, as medieval. These were unexpectedly removed, during the restoration of 1926–7, before I could photograph them in detail, but they appear on views [1] of the Gate by Brogi, Vasari and Moscioni, of which the first two are reproduced.

(c) The Curtain

The curtain of the Gate may now be considered. Some of its earliest remains, and some important facts concerned with its evolution, have already been noted. By far the most important piece of primary construction is preserved at the west end of the back wall (Pl. XIII*b*). This is a well-built travertine impost, supporting a skew-back and three voussoirs, having an extrados carefully cut to suit the coursing of the wall. Where the archway once came, marble blocks of the later curtain form a solid mass. The voussoirs give an arch with a radius of 6 feet 3 inches, as shown on fig. 24. It is thus clear that such an arch must belong to an early two-way gate like that already considered at Porta Ostiensis East.[2] The arch was first noted by Lugli,[3] who says, however, 'non saprei indicare a quale uso servisse quest' arco più antico, che sembra infilare col selciato della via, prima dello spostamento eseguito dal costruttore dell' arco, chiamato di Druso; certamente esso era in relazione col lungo muro laterizio, della

---

[1] Brogi, fot. 16892: Moscioni, fot. 22322 (a bad one): Vasari, uncatalogued.

[2] See p. 112.

[3] 'I cannot tell the use of this earlier arch, which seems to line up with paving of the street, before it was moved by the builders of the so-called Arch of Drusus. Certainly it was related to the long brick wall, of the first half of the second century, to be seen on the opposite side of the Gate.' *La Z. A.*, p. 317.

a. PORTA APPIA: SECOND-PERIOD WINDOWS, FIRST FLOOR
OF EAST TOWER

b. PORTA APPIA
Rear impost and voussoirs of first-period W. arch

c. PORTA METROBIA

prima metà del secondo dopo Cristo, che si vede sul fianco opposto della porta.' But the remains discovered inside the east end of the gate show that the arch belongs to an early travertine curtain, of which the length can be calculated from the distance between the early towers, thus enabling the position of the vanished second arch and the size of the *spina* to be fixed. The resultant curtain is of exactly the same length and breadth as that of Porta Ostiensis East, and is fitted with the same size of arches, and it now becomes clear that at two-way Gates not only the towers, but the curtains, were at first[1] set out to a standard plan. So there can be added to the early curtain at Porta Appia decorative details, a moulding and parapet, as at Porta Ostiensis East.

In the main this curtain must have remained untouched during the second period, for it has been seen that the relation of the marble curtain to the east tower proves that the former did not exist until the third period, and there is no trace whatever of a curtain intermediate between it and the first-period curtain of travertine. Moreover, the west part of the travertine curtain was made to form part of the back of the marble curtain. It therefore seems clear that, in the second period, the first-period curtain of Porta Appia, like that of Porta Ostiensis East, remained untouched in plan and materials, and this gives a gate with a rather low curtain and high towers, like Porta Palatina, Turin.[2]

In the third period the travertine curtain was replaced by a new one with marble facing. It was possible to get behind this marble work at the east end of the curtain by means of the hole which had already yielded so much information, and so to climb down among rough blocks to the level of the bolt-hole of the gate. This visit cast much light upon the ways of Roman builders. The curtain is built extremely roughly, as at Porta Latina. No attempt has been made to reduce the blocks to any common plane inside, and, as usual, no mortar held them together, since they were presumably bonded with metal cramps. Their inner sides have neither bosses nor ornament, and no inscription appears upon them. The roughness of the east end is, however, not to be explained by carelessness. It was once built up against a courtyard wall, of which only a small piece of core now remains. The archway is well built, with marble for the portcullis-chases, and travertine for the main vault. On one of the blocks of this vault is an inscription (fig. 22), much worked over, and turned left side downwards. It is evidently part of a slab from a *columbarium*, commemorating *libertae* of the *gens Clodia*. The

---

[1] Nicorescu, loc. cit., in his study of the Tomb of the Scipio's, studies also this curtain in a foot-note. He finds it difficult to believe that the double arch can be original and gives it to Honorius, thinking it was arranged to fit a road running on either side of the so-called Arco di Druso, which he claims as Diocletianic (Forma Iobia). This is quite fanciful.

[2] See Rivoira, *Architettura Romana*, p. 61, fig. 55.

moulded string, on the back of the curtain, differs from that on
the front, and might have come from the earlier curtain.¹   On
the rear keystone is incised a Greek cross within a circle, as at
Portae Latina and Ostiensis, and round it are set the words²
ΘΕѠ ΚΑΡΙϹ | ΑΓΙΕ ΚѠΝΟΝ | ΑΓΙΕ ΓΕѠΡΓΙ . ΘΕѠ ΚΑΡΙϹ is
squeezed in above³ the cross, and looks like an afterthought.
The question whether this inscription need be Byzantine has
been discussed elsewhere.⁴   But it should be noted that, even if
the inscription is Belisarian, it does not necessarily give an initial

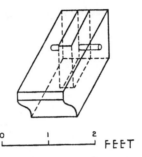

0   1   2
└─────────┴─────────┘ FEET

FIG. 23. Corbel for portcullis, Porta Appia

date to the curtain to which it belongs, for the cross is of earlier
type.
      Above the stone curtain rose a barrel-vaulted brick-faced
portcullis chamber, which received light from five round-headed
windows at the back, and from as many at the front.   All these
are blocked, but their voussoirs are still visible.   Three corbels,
which held the hoisting machinery for the portcullis, still exist
inside the chamber, and a diagram (fig. 23) of their arrangement⁵
is given herewith.   It suggests that each side-corbel held a sheaf
of pulleys, set with exactitude in a slot, and held by a large pin.
Two triple sheaves contained in these would enable the heaviest
portcullis to be raised with ease.   The central corbel would hold
ordinary pulleys for guiding to one capstan or hauling-point the
two ropes passing through the side pulley-blocks.   The machine
would thus rise and fall gently and evenly, without the slightest
danger of jamming, or of smashing the stops at the bottom of the
slots in which it ran.   These are dangers which would continually
arise if each side were pulled by a different machine or squad of
men.   The device postulated was not novel to the late-Roman

---

¹ It compares well with that of Porta Ostiensis East, which is probably original, and
only replaced in the third period.
² 'Thanks to God! Saint Konon! Saint George!'
³ Nicorescu, loc. cit., places θεω καρις below the cross: erroneously.
⁴ See p. 108.
⁵ The precise alinement of the pin-holes in the corbels is worth particular note.

Empire. As early as the Augustan age, Vitruvius [1] describes pulley-blocks with this very number of sheaves (*pentaspastos*). The brickwork of this chamber was not so good as that of the second period, and it was separated by a broken and irregular joint from the second-period brickwork in both passages leading to it. Evidently an earlier wall had been knocked back to that point in order to receive it, and what was removed was, no doubt, the first-period stone curtain together with the doorway leading into it, a removal which would leave the rough edge described.

Much worse is the brickwork of the third story. It is heavily patched inside, both at the back and the front, but enough traces of windows remain to give it for certain the five windows indicated by Vasi [2] in front, while an equal number, now converted to loop-holes, are still visible in the rear wall. The chamber at this level is not bonded into the rest of the gate, as is the story below it, and its best work compares with that of the new fifth stories of the towers. It is therefore probable that the towers and curtain were heightened at the same time. That the curtain was not heightened before would explain why its decorative moulding was not arranged to fit the top of the quadrangular stories. The new chamber was arranged to have the same height as that below it, and so the curtain-walk above it happened to come opposite a half-landing. Thus direct communication with the rest of the Gate by means of a level passage was impossible. The curtain-walk was therefore reached by a small flight of stairs, into which was built a marble slab of Christian date, inscribed L VERG XYST . Later still, an oven was built in between the stairs and the round tower. The rampart-walk slopes backwards sharply like that of Porta Ostiensis East. Otherwise its fittings are all modern, the merlons having been added between 1747 and 1821, as the engravings of Vasi and Gell prove.[3]

(d) The Vantage-Court

Behind the Gate lay a walled court (fig. 20). This existed in Nolli's time,[4] and is shown on many early engravings[5] of the so-called Arco di Druso, to which it was joined; for the Arch was made to serve as the back gate of the court, and was fitted with doors. The walls of the court joined the south-west and south-east angles of the Arch, and the west wall is still partly preserved, embedded in the modern retaining wall at the side

[1] Vitruv. *De Arch.* x, cap. 2. 16: cf. also the relief of the Haterii, *Legacy of Rome*, fig. 23, p. 305.
[2] Vasi, pl. xi. [3] Vasi, pl. xi. Cf. Rossini, tav. xv. Nibby, *M. di R.* pl. xxv.
[4] Nolli, 1748. [5] e.g. Piranesi, *Ant. Rom.* i, xix, 1.

of the Gate. Within it there ran a corridor, lit from above by shafts, which seems, by its orientation, to have led to a small private entrance, which passed through the first aqueduct Arch to the left of the stone Arch. The provision of a special entrance is matched at Porta Ostiensis East. But here there is no sign of stairs to the upper story, and it may be presumed that they existed in the demolished portion of the wall. The extant corridor, however, opens into an apsidal room, lying east and west, just behind the early west tower. This room is separated from the early gate by a building-joint, and is not built in early brickwork. Its purpose is obscure: it may be either a guard-chamber for the court—which seems unlikely, owing to its retired position—or, more probably, a room for the administration of the tax-*mancipes*[1] at the Gate. Here, at least, the site of the *dazio* remained until 1906, and this spacious courtyard, opening out from the rather narrow road, was found the most convenient place for the examination of visitors to the City. If this interpretation of this purpose is correct, it becomes clear that the courtyard was not built for military purposes, but for the convenience of customs officials. Hence the lack of precaution in providing small doors, which could easily be forced, to give access to the Gate. And the same result emerges at Porta Ostiensis East, except that here, at the most important of all the City Gates, the tax-collectors have a special office, built in permanent concrete. Elsewhere the buildings were probably wooden, like market-toll huts to-day. The wall on the other side of the court is shown roughly built of stone blocks, and may well mark a medieval restoration of the gate, although Uggeri's plan[2] shows an odd corridor with stairs, about which it would be interesting to know more. The original construction of the vantage-court is dated, however, to the second period of building at the main Gate, owing to the staircase arrangements opening on to it.

To a limited extent these new buildings affected the so-called Arch of Drusus. The style of this Arch belongs to an age much later than that of Drusus, and the heyday of its type is assigned by Curtis[3] to the opening of the third century. The present Arch, moreover, is planned to fit the Aqua Antoniniana, which crosses it, and it once had two wings, orientated with the aqueduct. The existence of the wings is proved by a set of blocks, meant to fit behind the voussoirs of flat arches, on both sides of the Gate; while the west footings have the same orientation as the west aqueduct pier, showing that this wing was built to suit

[1] For these *mancipes*, see Lanciani, *B. C.* 1882, p. 101.
[2] Uggeri, vol. v. pl. 4.
[3] Curtis; *Suppl. Pap. Amer. Acad. Rome*, ii, Arch 53, pp. 63-4. Some errors may be noted. The impost mouldings do not continue 'around the piers': the columns are not fluted, nor are the caps white marble.

the aqueduct and not the main Arch. The east footings are hidden by a great medieval battered counterfort. The position of the west aqueduct pier is governed by the north edge of a tomb against which it was built; and part of the tomb remains, while there are block-marks in the concrete of the pier. This respect for a tomb explains why the aqueduct piers on each side of the road were not set opposite each other.

Once the Arch was built, its decoration was never quite finished. This is proved, as has been noted many times, by the roughness of its keystones, which were to have been carved, as at the Arch of Septimius Severus. Yet the main work was done, and side wings were certainly built; and this is proved by the plug-holes for marble-facing on the side of the Arch, which cover everywhere but the point where the side wings made contact with the main pier. The precise dimensions of these wings are unknown, but the arrangement suggested on the plan clearly cannot be very unlike the real one, which must have been designed to suit the aqueduct piers. The general result is an interesting Arch, not unlike that of Gallienus[1] in plan, but built in more florid style, resembling that of the Arch of Septimius Severus. Its plan shows, too, beyond dispute, that it was built specially to accommodate the aqueduct.

There were later alterations. At some time or other the west wing was removed and some new structure was fitted on to the central pier by means of a great notch cut in the west impost moulding. This new construction must have been connected with the aqueduct, since it falls precisely beneath the *specus* on the aqueduct-arch and is of the same width as a normal aqueduct-pier. It looks, then, as if the whole wing had been taken down, and a new aqueduct pier built in its place. The date of this change is uncertain; but, since it is connected with the aqueduct, it cannot have occurred later than 537, when the aqueduct went out of use. It would also be natural to suppose that it did not take place until after the building of the City Wall, which so obscured the view of the Arch that its disfigurement by the destruction of its wings mattered little. Was this alteration, then, the work of Diocletian that later earned for the Arch the name[2] of Forma Iobia? Or was it connected with the building of the courtyard behind the Gate, or with that great pillaging of stone required for the third-period building? These questions cannot be answered in the present state of knowledge, but a chance discovery may solve them some day. It is enough now to have stated the problem.

[1] Arco di Gallieno, Curtis, R. *Monumental Arches, Suppl. Papers Amer. Acad.* ii, p. 76; no. 71.

[2] Forma Iobia, *Itinerarium Einsiedlense*, 11, 2; 13, 22. For a similar re-naming cf. *C.I.L.* xii. 2229, the Gates of Grenoble.

(e) Conclusions

Thus closes the architectural story of Porta Appia, and the so-called Arch of Drusus. The stages may now be connected in a summary.

(i) The Gate began (fig. 24) as a two-way entrance, with two-story travertine curtain, built throughout on the same main lines as the earliest gate at Porta Ostiensis East, and flanked by tile-

PORTA APPIA

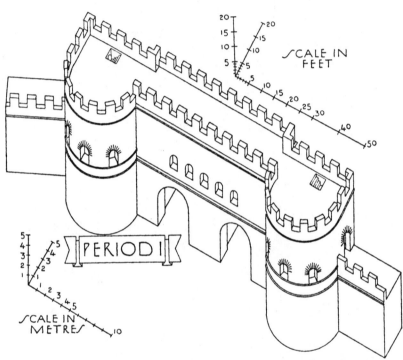

FIG. 24

faced towers of the standard semicircular type which occurs not only at Porta Ostiensis but also at Portae Nomentana and Latina. Its design was frankly utilitarian. But this does not prove, as Schultze states,[1] that it was erected by a frightened and poverty-stricken City. On the contrary, the scheme behind the design seems to have been neither nervous nor hasty, but the result of very deliberate and careful thought. This point will be considered in the final chapter.

(ii) The place of the first Gate was taken, when the gallery was being added to the Wall, by a mighty new structure, in

[1] *Bonner Jahrb.* 118, p. 343: 'Der Baucharakter dieser Torbauten ist also der eines von der Furcht beeinflussten, auf ärmliche Mittel beschränkten reinen Nutzbaues.'

PORTA APPIA

PERIOD II

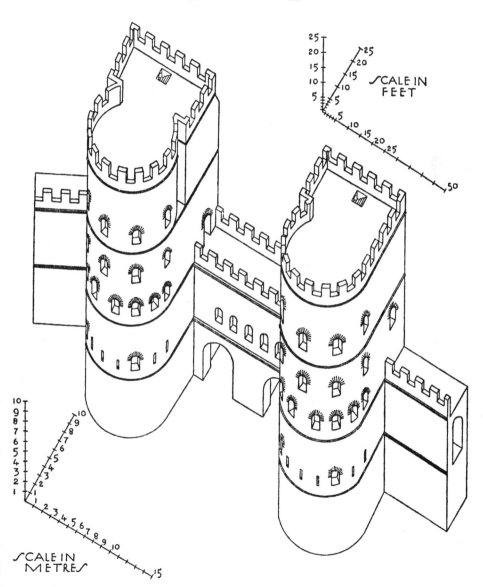

SCALE IN FEET

SCALE IN METRES

Fig. 25

which the old curtain was embodied, and flanked by new tile-faced round-fronted towers on the North-European scale (fig. 25). This type of Gate appears elsewhere on the Wall only at Porta Asinaria, but Porta Palatina at Turin provides a close analogue. At the same time an inner court was erected at the back of the Gate, giving access to the new towers by flights of stairs, and perhaps enclosing new guard-rooms or offices for the City tax-collectors. The ornamental Arch of Aqua Antoniniana was made to serve as the rear gateway to this courtyard.

(iii) The third period, as elsewhere, was marked by the use of stone. Opportunity was taken to strengthen the cracking towers of the second period by building round them magnificent quadrangular marble and brick bastions, matched by a marble and brick curtain, which set Porta Appia in the very front rank of notable Roman gateways. At the same time, Porta Flaminia received the same distinction. Consciously or not, the designers thereof achieved an artistic triumph, quite as great as any other of the new and stately Constantinian fashion, which had been the starting-point of all the new art of Christendom. Ten years later, the design of these Gates appears on the Wall of New Rome, a significant fact about which more is noted below.[1]

(iv) In the fourth period the internal arrangements of the towers were altered. For their vaults were substituted wooden floors, and stories II and III become one, for which new windows were cut. The cause of this was either insufficient foundation or a slip in the soft rock beneath the round-fronted second-period towers, which had produced large and dangerous cracks in the structure. By removing the heavy vaults the towers were lightened, and the Gate has held together until our time. The next repair was demanded by a disaster. Much of the front of the west bastion collapsed, and was newly patched with blocks of *peperino*.

(v) The fifth constructional period, which followed, was marked by the addition of another story to the towers, and one more to the curtain; and this completed the architectural evolution of the Gate in classical times.

§ 5. PORTA METROBIA

This Gate, whose name is obscure, but given here in the best authenticated form,[2] is now represented by a half-buried arch in the Wall. Behind this, at the back of the Wall, is attached a

[1] See p. 260.
[2] The forms are metrovi: metropi: metrovia: mitrobi: mitrobiensis: metrobi: mitrovi: metrobii. Metronia is always late, e.g. Leo VIII ? authentic. See Tomasetti, *Via Latina*, pp. 6–8. The origin of the name is uncertain: but Metrobius and Metrobianus are classical names, vide *C. I. L.* iii. 972, 973, 1028, from Apulum in Dacia.

gate-tower (Pl. XIIIc), which cannot be original since it is bonded neither with the Wall nor with its additional gallery, and is built of poor brickwork. So the tower must be at least a third-period addition, though the matter is far from settled. The object of the tower is uncertain, but the building may have housed a portcullis, or served as a guard-house. In 1157 the tower was repaired, as is recorded by a well-known inscription,[1] still affixed thereto: and it should be noted that, since the facing associated with the inscription is of *selce*, its date may fit the whole series of *selce* repairs on the Wall. By way of the Gate passed the Marrana stream which drained the Decennae marshes:[2] and in classical times this must have been contained in a conduit. But in the fourteenth century it was coming through the Gate as an open stream, the Marrana, and the gate-tower then belonged to SS. Quattro Coronati.[3] The stream had already been given an artificial channel as far as the Lateran[4] by the great peace-loving Pope Callixtus II. So not much is known about this Gate, but it prepares the way for the description of a different type of Gate from those hitherto considered (fig. 27), the archway set in an ordinary Wall-curtain between two towers, for this must have been the original form of Porta Metrobia. Later, when the gallery was added to the Wall, there was no fundamental change in the Gate's form, and the guard-house tower was added only in or after the third period. The type with guard-house tower, though infrequent on Walls so important as those of Rome, was an old one, widely used for simple needs all over the Roman world: and it may be observed that it occurs at the entrance of big roads into the Empire where a tax was levied and an examination of travellers made. There may be compared with this entrances to the Empire as far apart as Britain[5] and Africa.[6] The Gate here may therefore have served the needs of tax-collectors just as much as those of soldiers or of City militia-men. Finally, some special precautions were taken to guard the great re-entrant in which this Gate lay. Artillery was posted on strongly reinforced towers so as to rake the whole approach with heavy fire.[7]

Conclusions.—The gate started as a simple arched portal in an ordinary wall-curtain. Later, it received a guard-house tower

---

[1] The Ward of Sant' Angelo. In the Year of the Incarnation of Our Lord Jesus Christ, 1157, the Senate and People of Rome restored these walls when ruined with age. Senators Sasso, Giovanni di Alberico, Rovere Buccacane, Pinzo Filippo, Giovanni di Parenzo, Pietro Dominetesalvi, Cencio di Ansoino, Rainaldo Romano, Nicola Mannetto.

[2] *B. C.* 1891, pp. 343, 355.

[3] Tomasetti, *Via Latina*, p. 12: 'Marrana ... que venit ad turrim sanctorum iiiior.'

[4] Boso, *apud Rer. Ital. Script.* iii, pars 1, col. 420: 'Hic etiam derivavit aquam de antiquis formis et ad portam Lateranensem (i.e. Asinarium) conduxit.' Lanciani, *F. U. R.*, applies this statement, wrongly, to the portion between Porta Metrobia and S. Sisto.

[5] Britain: G. Macdonald, *R. Wall in Scotland*, pp. 247 sqq., pl. xiii. 2.

[6] Africa: Cagnat, *Mém. Acad. Inscr. et B–L.* xxxix, p. 87, figs. 2, 3.   [7] See p. 89.

which bestrode the rear of the archway and may have served to contain a portcullis. This did not happen, however, until after the second-period gallery had been added to the Wall.

§ 6. PORTA ASINARIA

The name of Porta Asinaria is derived from *Via Asinaria,* a by-road[1] leading to Viae Latina and Appia. It has nothing to do with the family of the Asinii;[2] for the road, in spite of Platner's objections,[3] and Short's terse pronouncement,[4] may well have been called the 'ass-track'. It has been thought[5] that a marble relief, now in the Lateran, gives an ancient representation of the Gate. But the condemnation[6] of this idea by Matz and Duhn seems decisive. They observed that

'die Deutung auf die Porta Asinaria,—wohl nur durch den Esel im Thore verbunden mit Unklarheit über den Fundort veranlasst—und somit der Gebäude auf *S. Giovanni in fonte* und der alten lateranischen Basilica, ist sicher falsch. Abgesehen von der Technik im Allgemeinen weisen die Form der Säulen, sowie die Art der Ornament und der Mauereintheilung—dem sog. ersten pompeianischen Stile entsprechend—das Relief in viel frühere Zeit; keinesfalls darf es später als in's erste Jahrhundert der Kaiserzeit gesetzt werden.'

It is equally more relevant to note that neither the City Wall nor Porta Asinaria ever had an aspect in the least like that shown on the relief. The Gate was closed[7] by Pius IV (1559–65), presumably at the same time as Porta Nomentana, and replaced by Porta S. Giovanni, in 1574. Since then it has remained untouched, and its front is still well preserved (Pl. XIV) although the

[1] See Festus, s.v. 'retricibus', 282: '"Retricibus" cum ait Cato in ea quam scripsit cum edissertavit Fulvi Nobilioris censuram, significat aquam eo nomine quae est supra via Ardeatinam inter lapidem secundum et tertium, qua irrigantur horti infra viam Ardeatinam et Asinarium usque ad Latinam.'

[2] The Asinii did not come into Rome, from Teate Marrucinorum, until the end of the Republic, when the via Asinaria already existed. *Vide* Pauly-Wissowa, vol. i, pp. 1583–6.

[3] *Gesch. Roms.,* p. 633.

[4] Lewis and Short, *Latin Dictionary,* s.v. 'Asinarius': cf. Salaria.

[5] *Vide* Stevenson, *Ann. Inst.* 1877, p. 367, n. 2: figured badly by Fleury, *Le Latran,* pl. LVI, and Rossini, tav. x: better by Lauer, *Le Latran,* p. 19, fig. 7: but the slab is certainly not part of a sarcophagus, as Lauer suggests. The relief was found in 1750 during the rebuilding of SS. Marcellino e Pietro, *vide* Bianchini, *Historia Chalcographica.*

[6] *Antike Bildwerke in Rom,* iii, pp. 47–8, no. 3533: cf. Fucine Lake relief, Lehmann-Hartleben, *Die Traiansäule,* p. 129, Abb. 19. 'The reference to Porta Asinaria (only, indeed, induced by the ass in the gate, which was obscurely connected with the findspot), and also the reference to S. Giovanni in fonte and to the old Lateran Basilica, are certainly false. Apart from the general technique, the form of the pillars, the kind of ornament, and wall-panelling (belonging to the so-called first Pompeian style), prove that the relief is much earlier in date. It cannot be put by any means later than the first hundred years of the Empire.'

[7] It is usually held that the gate was finally closed by King Ladislaus in 1408 (cf. *Diar. Rer. Ital. Script.,* xxiv. 992) but this was only temporary. Audebert says 'qui fut condemnée et bouschée par Pie iv'.

PORTA ASINARIA

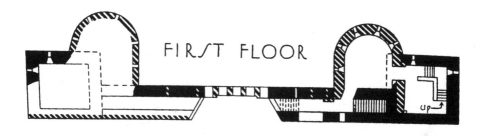

SCALE IN
FEET

5 0 5 10 15 20   30   40   50

1 0 1 2 3 4 5   10   15

METRES

FIRST FLOOR

GROUND FLOOR

■ PERIOD 1
▨ PERIOD 2
▤ PERIOD 3

STAIRS BETWEEN
FLOORS

FIG. 26

back has suffered much damage (Pl. XV). No reasoned attempt seems to have been made to analyse its structure. Artists have, indeed, been considerably attracted by its picturesque, half-ruined appearance. But the wealth of detail has usually tempted them to gloze over its real architectural form, and their representations therefore add to the confusion. By far the best picture of the Gate, if tested by present remains, is Gell's engraving:[1] Rossini's plate of 1829 is bad,[2] but the view in his *Vedute*[3] is better. No engraving, however, is accurate.

The whole Gate is not now (1929) accessible (fig. 26) and still less of it could be explored[4] early in 1926. Then, however, cracks were becoming dangerous, and the Municipio decided upon a restoration, which undoubtedly came just in time to save the east tower's top[5] from collapse. The writer was frequently present while this work was in progress, and received valued consideration from those in charge, and from individual workmen. The lower stories of the west tower were excavated to ground-level, and the curtain was half emptied of earth. Most important of all, the lowest floor of the west round-fronted tower was probed, and an early wall was found therein. This investigation was made to see whether the tower had a solid base, and was visible for one morning only (April 6, 1926), when the writer measured its contents for the accompanying plan. So from this tower a study of the Gate's evolution may fitly begin.

(a) The first Gate

The tower in which the discoveries just described were made consists of two elements.[6] The first is a side staircase-tower of rectangular plan, projecting from the line of the curtain-wall. The second is a rather narrow tower, with semicircular front, which is attached to the east side of the staircase-tower, and also covers the whole width of the rampart-walk at the back. The staircase-tower is hollow down to ground-level, and is entered from the west by a small door, leading into substructures of an ancient building, which form part of the Wall for some distance westward. The semicircular-fronted tower has a solid base, which is built up against a finished front to the staircase-tower,

---

[1] *M. di R.* tav. xix.

[2] Rossini, tav. xi *a*. xii.

[3] Rossini, *Vedute*, ii, tav. xxxii; earlier editions are unnumbered.

[4] I am grateful for help in measuring this gate to Messrs. G. H. Wedgwood and G. A. Butling, of the B. S. R. In other respects the *capogiardiniere*, of the Giardini S. Giovanni, showed me much kindness.

[5] But the removal of the elaborate eaves cornice, with modillions, was mistaken zeal: it could certainly have been saved, and was unique on a Gate.

[6] Amusing is Grisar's plan of the Gate (*R. alla fine del mondo antico*, p. 127, fig. 32) where it is considered as an ordinary section of Wall, with an exceptional type of tower.

PORTA ASINARIA

Only the quadrangular towers belong to period I

without being bonded with it. But above the level of the first
stringcourse on the staircase-tower this relation is reversed,
and the wall of the staircase-tower is applied to a finished face of
the semicircular tower without a bond.[1] This is an odd arrangement, and it raises the question whether the two elements are
not of different dates. This point is answered by the discovery of
the outer face of an east wall belonging to the staircase-tower in
the round-fronted tower's floor: and it may be added that the
face comes opposite a constructional break in the back wall of
the round-fronted tower, and the end of a vault in the passage
behind it, and so explains why the steps leading from the base of
the staircase-tower to the curtain begin where they do. They are
set exactly half-way through the early east wall. Again, to
postulate two periods is to explain the difference of brickwork in
the independent part of the staircase tower; this is not wide, but
sufficiently marked to demonstrate that the staircase-tower was
not erected by the builders of the round-fronted tower. So the
staircase-tower existed independently at first: and one story
is left to us of the independent structure. No doubt the tower
once had one story more, as a Wall-tower has. But the upper
part of such a tower could not be easily made part of the
new semicircular-fronted tower; it may therefore be presumed
that it was demolished,[2] while the new second story was built
up against the new tower, as visible to-day.

Further evidence for the aspect of the Gate connected with the
rectangular tower comes from the curtain. Any one who examines
the front of this curtain closely can see that the lower arcade of
five windows in the curtain breaks across an earlier row of merlons,
built[3] in block-and-brick work. Four merlons appear east of the
windows, and three (a fourth has been knocked away) to the west.
They stand on a parapet, protecting a rampart-walk, which still
serves as a floor behind the later windows; and its level is marked
externally by a much-damaged string-course of tiles. Below this
level are four loop-holes, two on each side of the arch, each pair
covering ten feet. And these must be early, because they are
set out on their ten-foot interval from the east wall of the west
rectangular tower. The ten-foot unit does not work between the
two sets, for they are separated by twenty-four feet, no doubt to
give room for a central gateway arch. But on the east side of
this gap it continues, though it did not fit the space accurately
any longer. It looks, then, as if not only the west group, but
the whole series, of loop-holes was set out from the west
tower.

[1] See p. 145, fig. 26.   [2] Cf. p. 148.
[3] This facing is very bad and might be a late refacing of the merlons, when they were
long walled-up: for they would still fall off as separate pieces.

The type of wall which these loop-holes served appears best in the sixth and seventh Wall-curtains east of the Gate. It has already been described[1] in detail, but main features may be recalled here. A gallery ran below the rampart-walk, as in the second-period Wall, but the loop-holes are not spaced in relation to the bays of the gallery, as in the later Wall, since there are no transverse arches. This was the arrangement at Porta Asinaria, and one gallery-arch is still preserved at the back of the Gate. Its relation to the early curtain is quite clear, and so it becomes evident that the first Porta Asinaria was a small postern, set in a galleried wall. The springing of the gallery-vault is marked externally by the lower edge of a block-and-brick belt; and the remains of the vault itself were retained and worked into the body of the later Gate in a manner described below. Here it must be noted that the gateway arch must have interrupted the gallery floor; but the arch itself has disappeared, and only a filling of rubbish marks its destruction by Pius IV. It is not set quite centrally between the rectangular towers, but this fault was disguised when the round-fronted towers were added, while the original position of the Gate no doubt was determined by the already existing *via Asinaria*.

Only the east tower of the early Gate now remains for discussion. Here, unfortunately, ancient vaults cut off all access to the two lower stories where evidence for the early history of the tower must exist. But this very lack of connexion suggests, as at Porta Appia, that the tower passed through changes, which would explain still further oddities in its plan. These have not been noted before, since all existing plans are based upon the Uggeri-Rossini group,[2] which are inaccurate when tested by information available on the west. Measurement reveals that the early east tower was a smaller thing than its companion on the west. It projected a foot less far from the Wall, and it may therefore be suspected that its width was correspondingly less great. A decrease of two and a quarter feet gives an arrangement which explains the odd building of the internal west wall of the round-fronted east tower, and shows that the two stairs leading upwards from its third story are probably founded on top of the older tower-wall. It is also evident that the same curious method of bonding united the new tower with the old tower-wall on each side of the Gate.

It is important to note that, despite this tower's smaller size, there is sufficient space for the same arrangement of stairs as in

---

[1] See pp. 63, 65, fig. 8.
[2] See Uggeri, vol. xxx, planche vi; elevation poor: premier étage is guesswork. Rossini, tav. xxxii. It may be doubted whether the east tower was completely accessible at this time. It must have been half-filled with earth and unpleasant to enter.

PORTA ASINARIA

PERIOD I

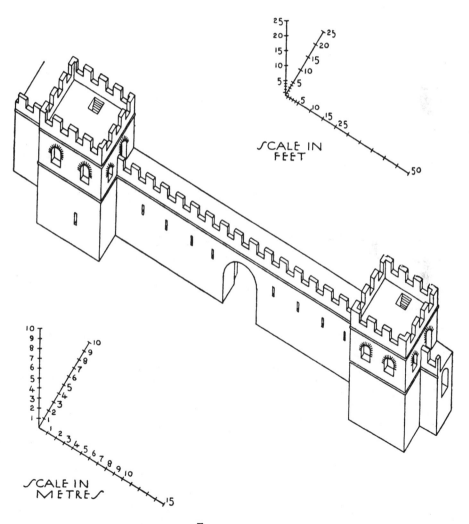

SCALE IN FEET

SCALE IN METRES

Fig. 27

the west tower, and that the space between the towers is now exactly one hundred feet, the standard elsewhere. Otherwise, no further certain detail emerges about the plan of the early tower. Only the loop-holes visible externally prove that its plan in front was the same as that of the west bastion. Therefore it may be surmised that the resemblance extended to the plan of the whole lower story of the tower, giving a hollow staircase-tower and a bastion with solid first story. The Wall-gallery's floor no doubt ran straight into the tower, though it must be regarded as uncertain whether there was an extra set of stairs at the back, as in the west tower, running straight up to the curtain. Short flights of stairs must have existed, however, in the curtain in order to surmount the gateway arch, and their presence no doubt accounts for the drop in the level of the third-story floor in the curtain, as on the west.

So the earliest gate at Porta Asinaria (fig. 27) was a simple postern, set not quite centrally in an arcaded wall of the earliest period, and flanked by two ordinary wall-towers to east and west. It resembled Porta Metrobia closely; indeed, both may have been set in a galleried Wall.

(b) The Second Gate

In a second period, this postern was converted into a mighty Gate of heavy northern type which had an extremely long curtain and depended entirely upon its enormous size to disguise its odd proportions and lack of symmetry. This Gate (fig. 28) is still one of the most impressive, and quite the most forbidding, of the Gates of Rome. In describing it the method used for other Gates may be employed once more, beginning with the east tower, passing thence to the west, and finally, dealing with the curtain.

The east tower as now planned consisted of two elements: the old wall tower, destined for use only as a staircase-tower and a new round-fronted tower, very like the second-period towers of Porta Appia and the west tower of Porta Pinciana. The lowest story of the staircase-tower has been considered already: that of the round-fronted tower undoubtedly was, as at Porta Appia, a room with loop-holes, whence observations could be made, and where 'snipers' could be stationed. Its floor-level is marked externally by a triple string-course of tiles, as on the west tower, and it may be surmised that access thereto was gained as in the west tower also. Connexion between the tower and the rampart-walk of the early Wall, which had now become the gallery of the later Wall, must have been carried out by

PORTA ASINARIA

SCALE IN FEET

5 0 5 10 15 20 30 40 50

1 0 1 2 3 4 5 10 15

METRES

SECOND FLOOR

Up
RUINED STAIRS

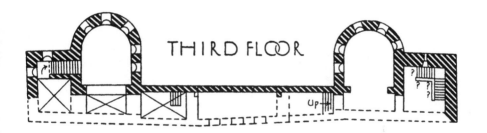

THIRD FLOOR

Up

? ?

MEZZANINE PASSAGE

Up
Down

PERIOD 2

PERIOD 3

PERIOD 4

FIG. 28

another flight of stairs, for which various positions might be suggested. That which suits the old scheme best has been chosen here, on the assumption that the builders of the second period changed the older arrangements as little as possible. Above this point there was no connexion between the second and third stories of the towers, except by passing along the curtain, climbing one story in the other tower and returning by the curtain once more. This grave fault in planning [1] is entirely due to the changed type of staircase made by the new builders farther up the staircase-tower. Instead of using the old style of staircase-well, they decided to arrange the stairs to climb in two long flights from west to east, and east to west, as in Porta Appia's east tower. This arrangement begins at the back of the third story of the bastion and gives access to the fourth: but it cut off all communication with the stories below.

The third story of the new tower was provided with five round-headed windows, of which three are contained in the semicircle, and two in the west side. These windows have similar dimensions [2] to those of the corresponding period in Portae Appia, Ostiensis East, and Pinciana. The staircase-tower wall is built up against the finished side of the bastion at this point, and the stairs receive light from a loop-hole at the top of the rear flight in the east end of the tower. In front is a small landing, a blind alley which serves to defend the front of the staircase-tower, and was lit by a front window, later blocked by medieval filling. A plain triple string-course of tiles marks the floor-level of the bastion at this point, and is continued, for ornament's sake, round the staircase-tower, where it marks no floor-level at all. The springing of the vault of the semicircular chamber is marked by a similar string-course, which is continued round the square tower to landing-level. The string-course, which should correspond to this on the west tower, occurs at the floor-level of the next and topmost story, and the glaring lack of correspondence gives a very odd appearance to the Gate. Just above this string-course the east staircase-tower is slightly set back, but the walling above the set-back clearly belongs to the original building.

The method of connexion between the third and fourth stories has already been described—a long flight of stairs from west to east, with two north-to-south stairs at the bottom. These led up to an intermediate landing, where a doorway gave access to the curtain, in order to make connexion with the rampart-walk of the second-period Wall. From the landing an east-to-west stair once more climbed to the floor-level of the top chamber in

---

[1] The fault could have been remedied by making a door in the rearward walk.
[2] i.e. 2′ 11″–3′ 1″.

a. PORTA ASINARIA. A GLIMPSE OF THE STAIRCASE-
ARRANGEMENT

b. PORTA PINCIANA

the bastion, being lighted by two windows, one in the landing's east wall, the other half-way up the stairs.

At the entrance to the top chamber of the new tower the wall of the rectangular tower once again abuts without a bond. The chamber is fitted with five windows, not arranged exactly above those of the story below, another carelessness which went to mar the appearance of the Gate. Otherwise they were of exactly the same size and type. Before the repairs of 1926 they were badly damaged, for the sills of most of them had been pushed out at some time (possibly in defence of the Gate). Large cracks were also appearing above them, probably because the bastion had settled where it left the older foundations of the staircase-tower. To-day all the cracks are mended, and the Gate is safe for the time being.[1] The roof of the tower was not vaulted in stone, but hipped in wood. This is proved by its height, and by the existence of squinches at the back of the chamber which supported the two main rafters of the hips. Outside the tower there also existed, until 1926, the little corbels, or modillions, for supporting an elaborate eaves-cornice. This gives a long and low roof with hipped back and curved front. On the east side rose the roof of the staircase-tower, set at a lower level, and possibly screened by crenellations. But the roof was not flat since no staircase led up to it, and there may be restored a low sloping roof, with rafters coming to a central point.

Such, then, was the east tower of the second period. A word may now be added about its structure. It was well built, and much care seems to have been devoted to both its facing and foundations. A great deal of the original facing remains, and what is newer has been applied to the top story in a style that might well belong to the fifth century.[2] The foundations must have been particularly well laid, since they have escaped the subsidence that took place at Porta Appia, where new towers of this period were also built partly off and partly on older foundations. To-day the appearance of the lowest story is much spoilt by a medieval battered facing,[3] and the misplaced string-course above the third story must always have given an unnecessarily top-heavy look to the tower.

The west tower, now to be described, has escaped the blemishes just noted, and has, therefore, a finer appearance, even though it is less well preserved. Much better also is the planning of the staircase-tower. Its base was hollow, and was entered from the west by a small doorway, now blocked, leading into the rooms of

---

[1] The real need, as at Porta Appia, is underpinning for the newer bastions.

[2] i.e. short tiles with much black pozzolana in the unwashed mortar, also tiles with the white glaze ; see p. 88.

[3] This could probably be removed without in any way endangering the stability of the structure.

an ancient building, which the Wall blocked and made useless. On the east another doorway led to a flight of thirteen steps, which rose to a landing behind the lowest chamber in the round-fronted bastion. It may be suspected that this was not an original arrangement, for the tower was supplied with another set of original stairs, and two separate sets would hardly be wanted. These rose round a square well inside the tower by two flights, situated on the west side and front of the tower, and thus reached the level of the gallery floor of the early Wall. The staircase-tower floor here is supported on a low barrel-vault, which makes the room below small but extremely strong. The original east wall of the tower does not exist now, except as a core in the back wall and floor of the round-fronted tower. In the floor, as has already been noted, its outer face was visible for a few hours on an April morning. The precise position of the inner face is unknown, but it can be fixed with reasonable probability by comparison with the known thickness of the two other outside walls: it is therefore shown by a broken line.

The lowest chamber in the round-fronted tower is thus entered either from a back landing or from the staircase-tower. It has five loop-holes, four being contained in the semicircle, and one in the straight portion of the east side. The loop-holes resemble those[1] of Portae Appia, Ostiensis East, and Pinciana. Quite a considerable field is visible through each; through that in the straight side, for example, can be seen the whole west wall of the east tower. Its floor-level, as has already been noted, was marked by a shapely string-course of tiles. Access to the next floor was gained by returning through the west door, and ascending two flights of stairs in the staircase-tower, arranged above the two already described. They ran straight up into the round-fronted tower, without any return. Light reached them from two loop-holes, situated on the landing between the two flights.

The chamber thus accessible had an open back, as at Porta Pinciana,[2] provided with the usual five windows, arranged, as in the east tower, with three windows in the semicircle and two on the long straight side. Externally, as in the east tower, there was the usual type of tile string-course, marking the floor-level of the tower, and joined by one in the curtain. This level is 2 ft. 11 in. higher than the corresponding floor in the east tower, but the difference is not very pronounced over so wide a curtain. The string also corresponds to that which marks the top landing level in the staircase-tower. From the westernmost window of the round-fronted tower a fragment of stamped tile, extracted by one

---

[1] See figs. 19, 20, 21, 30.　　　　　　　　[2] See p. 160, fig. 30.

of the workmen, was seen by the writer. This read   NISOP·DOL·
                                                                    L·PRIMIT·
and is to be identified with the stamp[1] EX PR · AIACIANIS OP ·
DOL · EX OF · CAL · PRIMIT ·. Another example of this stamp
was found in the sixth curtain[2] east of the Gate, and it belongs
to the close of Hadrian's reign, as do so many tiles used to
build the Wall.[3] At this story also the arrangement of bonding between the staircase-tower and the bastion changed. Up
to this point, as has been noted, the round-fronted tower has
been built up against the staircase-tower; now the order is
reversed, so as to give a complicated locking-joint between the
two towers, in which one story is toothed into the other like a
course of masonry. Here too the system of staircases changed
abruptly to the other side of the staircase-tower, which was not
now entered from the front, as before, but from a round-headed
door at the west end of the landing which continues the curtain.
Of this door only the south jamb and springing remain. The
position of the vanished staircase, beyond this level, is given by
that of the little window on the front of the tower, which will
not suit any other plan than that shown. So there may be restored
a staircase leading to a top story in the staircase-tower, which
was, no doubt, carried originally to the same height as the east
tower and roofed in the same way. And from the top story of
the staircase-tower a doorway, once more at the west end of the
rearward landing, leads into the top story of the bastion. Except
for the absence of side-doors, and the difference in level of the
external string-course, this story resembles its twin in the east
tower. It has five round-headed windows of the usual type, not
set quite accurately above those of the story below, and its rearward angles held two squinches for hip-rafters.

The second-period curtain between the two towers may now
be considered. Here the first problem which faced the builders
was the adaption of the early curtain. Certain alterations are
self-evident. In the centre of the curtain the merlons were
demolished in order to accommodate the arcade windows, which
have been built on top of the older parapet, as might be expected.
Inside the Gate only fragments of the early gallery were kept in
use. Its floor was now made to form that of the landing behind
the west tower's lowest story. Its vault held the walk behind the
central arcade, but has been removed elsewhere, in order to give
room for a staircase rising in two flights (lit by a new loop-hole
in the front wall) to this level from the landing just mentioned.

---

[1] *C. I. L.* xv. i. 10. ᴗ. 'From the Aiacian estates: *dolium* manufactory: workshop
of Calvus Primitius.'
[2] *Suppl. Pap. Amer. Acad. Rome*, i, p. 12. Pfeiffer, Armstrong, and Van Buren.
[3] See p. 58, note 1.

The stairs thus shut off completely the dead ends of the old gallery, which came to the edge of the gateway arch, and they also put out of use a large gallery-arch in the back wall, of which it was possible to measure the top in 1927, when the curtain had been partially cleared. Outside the curtain, but intimately connected with its plan, the straight rear staircase, leading from the ground floor of the staircase-tower, seems best explained as an addition, made to suit the Gate of the second period. It may be suspected that the arrangement on the east side was much the same; but it would be possible to keep there a little more of the original vault, owing to the slightly different arrangement of the junction of bastion and curtain. So it can be seen that the scheme of adaptation was not ill-conceived, for it evolved the least change in the old fabric, and the least building in the new. Returning once more to the centre of the curtain, we can see that the new arcade, built on the old parapet, consisted of five windows, three set very close in a specially built rearward niche, and one set on each side of them in the ordinary curtain-wall. Above and behind them were three corbels, rather like those used in Portae Appia and Ostiensis East to support pulleys for moving a portcullis. But these are not pierced for holding pulley-blocks, and it seems better to consider them as corbels for centring the new barrel-vault above the arcade. This vault was a short one, and dropped in level almost immediately over the new staircases coming up on each side. The southern springings of the arches that covered the heads of the stair-cases can still be seen on each side of the recess with three windows.

The continued use of the old rampart-walk, which was situated slightly above the level of the chambers in the new bastions, dictated that the curtain-walks on this gate should never be at quite the same level as the chamber floors until the top of the Gate was reached. And the different levels always had to be reconciled by small flights of steps in the curtain. This accounts for the presence of steps on the next floor. Here there were six windows, asymmetrically placed in relation to those below. Only three of these were original, and one to the east and two to the west were inserted later, in order to light the stairs better. Even when blocked they give the Gate an odd appearance, and the effect when they were open, and conspicuous, must have been startling. The string-course, which seems, from outside the Gate, to mark the bottom of this level, has, in reality, no connexion with any level in the curtain, except the landing behind the third-story chamber of the west bastion; it is merely a continuation, for decorative effect, of the string-course at that chamber's floor-level. But its value as decoration is somewhat reduced by the

PORTA ASINARIA
(WITH · SUBSEQUENT · ADDITIONS)
ISOMETRIC · RESTORATION

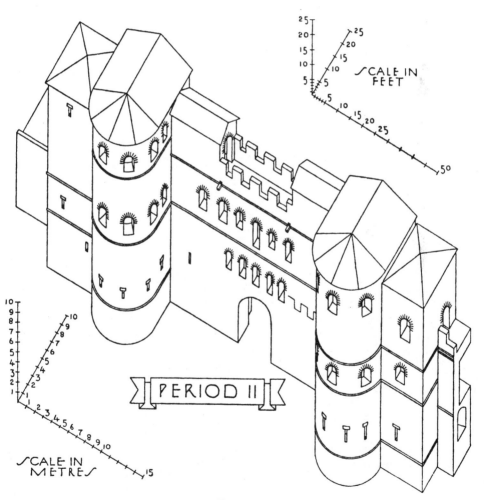

SCALE IN FEET

SCALE IN METRES

PERIOD II

Fig. 29

fact that it does not coincide with the corresponding string-course in the east bastion.

The next, and topmost, level is accessible from the east by a doorway in the half-landing on the stairs between the third and fourth stories. This opens into a straight passage along the curtain, and thence a short staircase leads up to the real level. These stairs were lit by a tiny window with a flat travertine lintel, and their head was covered by a small sentry-box, as at Porta Ostiensis East (Pl. X),[1] of which the roof has now disappeared, though the south springing of its barrel-vault remains. There also remains the first merlon of an uncovered rampart-walk, which has now broken away beyond this point. Two drain-spouts from its floor are still visible, piercing the front wall. A similar sentry-box existed on the west, and was entered, not by steps from below (which would not fit the staircases of the west tower), but directly from the landing behind the topmost storey of the west bastion. The roof-line of the sentry-box is still marked on the west bastion, and so the top of the Gate can be restored with complete certainty as shown in fig. 29. The whole scheme is mainly due to the logical construction of roof upon roof and stair upon stair above the earlier remains. But it should be added that to finish the curtain in this way also gives due weight to the towers, less prominence to the great width of the curtains, and a pleasantly irregular sky-line: and these aesthetic considerations may well have influenced the designers of the second Gate.

Later alterations to the Gate as a whole were few. The battered counterfort[2] at the base of the east bastion and staircase-tower is medieval. The windows added in the upper arcade of the curtain are not late in style, and might easily be of fifth-century date. During that century also, to judge from the brickwork, the gate seems to have received a good deal of refacing. Otherwise it continues to retain much the same form as it received in the second period of its history. Why the Gate was ever rebuilt in this magnificent style is obscure. *Via Asinaria* was never an important road. And the scheme which reconstructed the Gate thus splendidly, together with Porta Appia and the west tower of Porta Pinciana, might have been expected, if general in application, to have included more Gates, or if special, to have omitted Porta Asinaria. At least two explanations are possible. Firstly, Portae Appia and Asinaria may have been selected as a pair for rebuilding because they spanned the main roads from populous parts of the City to the Circus Maxentii: for it will be seen that

[1] See p. 114.
[2] Battered counterforts first appear on the eastern frontier under Justinian: in Italy they had been a feature of Etruscan work, but disappeared in classical times.

there are other reasons for connecting this work with Maxentius.[1] Or, secondly, an intention to reconstruct all Gates magnificently may not have been realized, thus explaining why the other Gates rebuilt in this period did not receive anything like so magnificent a form. Both views, indeed, may well be concurrently true: and the question is discussed in relation to historical contexts in the final part.[2]

Conclusions. The early Gate (fig. 27) closely resembled the first Porta Metrobia. It was a simple archway, set not quite centrally between two normal wall-towers. The wall which it pierced was galleried, and its loop-holes and merlons are still partly to be seen.

In a second period the whole aspect of the Gate was changed (fig. 28). A tower with a round front was added to the side of each wall-tower nearest the gateway. The height of the new combined tower thus obtained was increased to four stories, while the curtain was made three stories high, and crowned with sentry-boxes of the type visible at Porta Ostiensis East.

No important alterations took place after this time, but the third story of the curtain received some additional windows.

§ 7. PORTA PINCIANA

This little Gate, which Procopius[3] calls πύλις, now appears one of the most complete in Rome (Pl. XV*b*). But, in reality, it has been much transformed in modern times, and has lost its ancient aspect in the process. It was shut for the same reason as Porta Latina in 1808,[4] and reopened in 1906. The two entrances on either side of it, cut through the Wall to take the increasing traffic of *Quartiere Pinciano*, are, of course, entirely modern. In ancient times the Gate was never of great importance; it spanned *via Pinciana*, which derives its name from the *mons Pincius*. But the hill, in turn, did not receive the name until the fourth century,[5] when it was all owned by the *gens Pincia*,[6] only to pass[7] from them, with the heiress Anicia Faltonia, to Petronius Probus, consul of 371. It is therefore uncertain[8] whether the original Gate of 271 was called Pinciana. But that the structure goes back to the third century, and is not later in origin, is proved by

---

[1] See pp. 232–6. [2] See pp. 232–6.

[3] *B. G.* i. 23. For the name Belisaria see Porta Salaria, p. 185: it is quite uncertain whether the name ever existed and still more so whether it was applied to this gate: this cancels Lanciani's purple passage in *R. & E.*, p. 75.

[4] See p. 100.

[5] Before then it was *collis hortulorum*: Suet. Nero. 50.

[6] The Domus Pinciana lasted, cf. Cassiodor. *Var.* iii. 10, and Procop. *B. G.* ii. 9, τὸ παλάτιον.

[7] See Hülsen, R. *Mittheil.*, 1889, p. 269, note 2. Faltonia, *C. I. L.* vi. 1754: Petronius Probus, *C. I. L.* vi. 1751.

[8] Cf. Ashby, *P. B. S. R.* iii., p. 10: Tomasetti, *Via Salaria*, p. 5.

the planning of the Wall, which is specially set out in order to accommodate the road, as at other Gates and posterns. At present the Gate has two brick-faced towers, equalling the second-period Wall in height and flanking a curtain with a lower story in stone. Only the curtain and west tower are accessible:[1] connexion

PORTA PINCIANA

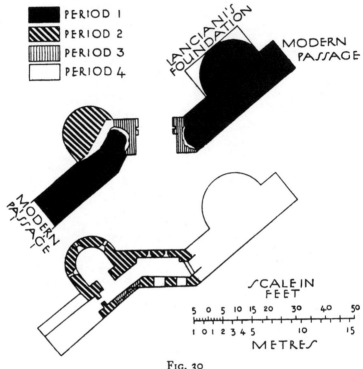

PERIOD 1
PERIOD 2
PERIOD 3
PERIOD 4

LANCIANI'S FOUNDATION

MODERN PASSAGE

MODERN PASSAGE

SCALE IN FEET

5 0 5 10 15 20   30   40   50

1 0 1 2 3 4 5   10   15

METRES

FIG. 30

with the east tower is blocked, and access to its back is impeded by a War Memorial erected in 1925.

All the peculiarities of the ground-plan (fig. 29) are explained by the position of the road, which accounts equally well for the skew curtain-wall, or for the small size of the semicircular east tower, which has a diameter of twenty-three feet, like the west tower of Porta Ostiensis East. For, no doubt, the tower, like all others of the same plan known on the Wall, stood upon a rectangular foundation, which, if built larger, would have impinged too much upon the road. As it was, there were only five feet to spare between the road and the foundation, and ten between

[1] I am glad to acknowledge the help of Mr. Russell Meiggs, sometime Pelham Student at the B. S. R., and now Tutor of Keble College, Oxford, in measuring this Gate.

the road and tower. It may be observed, however, that Lanciani, dealing with this Gate in general and the east tower in particular, notes: [1] 'Nel recinto di Aureliano e di Probo non vi fu una porta pinciana, ma una posterna di secondo o terz'ordine. Essa è di origine prettamente onoriana. Infatti nel recinto primitivo la posizione delle porte rispetto alle torri è sempre questa:

mentre la porta pinciana onoriana è stata costruita fuori d' ogni regola nel modo seguente, mediante la trasformazione della torre da quadrata a semicircolare, e l'aggiunta della seconda torre semirotonda B.'

The argument, which would have been clearer if the second diagram had been drawn to scale, is that Porta Pinciana began as a postern, set in a curtain of normal length, and flanked on the east by a rectangular wall-tower, and that Honorius [2] substituted a semicircular tower on the west, thus creating a Gate set abnormally in the Wall. There is, however, nothing exceptional about the position of the original postern, which is matched by the arrangement of the two south of Porta Nomentana and of that west of Porta Appia. And, in view of this, the most remarkable point in the passage is the casual, yet unique, [3] allusion by Lanciani to the change in plan of the east tower, as if such changes were common elsewhere on the Wall. Presumably he must have seen, perhaps during the road-making operations at the gate in 1888 (see below), some square foundation-work. But it does seem likely that what he saw was nothing more than the rectangular foundation of a semicircular tower, either faced, as at Porta Nomentana, or rough, as at the first remaining tower west of Porta Salaria. Quite certainly, there can have hardly been a square tower here; it would have impinged too much upon the road line,

[1] B. C. 1892, p. 102, and unnumbered figure. 'In the Wall of Aurelian and Probus there was no Porta Pinciana, but a second or third-class postern. The former is essentially Honorian. In fact, in the original wall the position of Gates in relation to the towers is always thus; . . . While the Honorian Porta Pinciana has been built exceptionally, as follows, by changing the tower from a rectangle to a semicircle, and adding the second semicircular tower, B.'

[2] In the end L. tacitly dropped this dating, and in 1897 assigned the Gate's present form to Belisarius, R. & E., p. 75.

[3] By the kindness of Mgr. G. Mercati, Prefetto della Biblioteca Vaticana, I was able to consult all Lanciani's MS. notes on the Wall: there I found no allusion to Porta Pinciana's history, so far as architectural changes were concerned.

and would have seriously restricted the range of both vision and fire from the curtain of the gateway. Also, the alteration from rectangular to semicircular ground-plan is not known elsewhere on the Wall, though the reverse occurs. But that this is not the reverse is shown by the size of the rectangle, which exactly fits the semicircular tower, and is not built round it, as an added rectangular tower would have been (cf. Portae Latina and Appia). So Lanciani's discovery is more easily interpreted as the foundation of a semicircular tower, especially since it lay below modern road-level, which is only just above the road-level of Roman times.

Above ground, this east tower had a battered base of medieval origin until the restoration of 1888. None of its original facing now remains; the base is completely modern, at middle height there is block-and-brick work of the kind associated with the Gothic siege of 536, while the top is a mixture of late Roman and nineteenth-century work. Whether any original work exists inside the tower has been impossible to ascertain, but it should be noted that Lanciani records[1] a staircase arrangement typical of the early towers. In the seventeeth and eighteenth centuries, as is proved by the Cadastro[2] and Vasi,[3] there existed a third story, with two large front windows (fig. 31); but by Vasi's time these had almost disappeared, and at some time during the nineteenth century a gun-emplacement was constructed in the second story of the tower. The data for the evolution of the east tower, though clear so far as they go, are insufficient. It began as a semicircular tower, with rectangular foundation, and, no doubt, it was less than three stories in height. When the uppermost story was added is unknown. In the sixth century, apparently after the heavy fighting of the Gothic siege of 536, the Gate was refaced in block-and-brick-work. There is thus no reason for supposing that the tower owed to Belisarius even the form which it retained until the eighteenth century, and the question whether the Gate ever was called Porta Belisaria depends upon a variant reading in the manuscripts of Procopius, which may equally well be applied to Porta Salaria,[4] as a fuller discussion below will demonstrate.

The west tower is a little semicircular-fronted bastion, some five feet smaller in diameter than the round-fronted west tower of Porta Asinaria, but otherwise closely resembling it in design. It had originally three stories,[5] the lowest being solid, the second connected with the gallery of the second-period Wall, and the third reached by a door from the upper rampart-walk, as is

---

[1] F. U. R. 2.   [2] Cadastro, Archivio dello Stato.
[3] Vasi, pl. iii.   [4] See p. 185.
[5] The eastern straight piece of the lowest story was built slightly convex, giving an odd appearance to the junction between tower and curtain.

FIG. 31. Porta Pinciana, c. 1747: engraved by Vasi

shown by the careful drawing (fig. 32) of the back of the Gate, made not long before 1746 by Alexander Cozens and now in the British Museum.[1] The rough drawing in the Cadastro shows the same arrangement, but mistakes the door which leads out to the rampart-walk for a window. The tower is unquestionably part of the second-period Wall-gallery, since it is built of exactly the same material and bonded into it. The fact that its walls, loop-holes, and string-courses are of precisely the same type as those of the second period at Porta Asinaria corroborates this dating, and even suggests that both Gates may have owed their form to the same builder. There is therefore no evidence whatever for the existence of a tower here in the first period.

The second story of the tower is entered from the Wall-gallery, which is closed off to the west by a partition-wall and door, and which was once filled in behind with a thin brick-faced wall, carried across the angle in the Wall behind the tower by a little stone squinch. This is not an original arrangement, and is dealt with below in discussing the curtain. The tower chamber received light from three loop-holes, of the same size and type as those of Porta Asinaria, and the doorway behind it was planned in the same style, as a wide-arched opening, a feature wholly absent from first-period towers on the Wall. Its roof was once vaulted, and there is now no trace of any stairway inside: it looks as if communication must have been made either through the tower to the west or across the gateway-curtain from the east tower, unless there was a wooden ladder of which no trace now remains. Modern merlons crown the surviving shell.

Above this point once rose the third story. This was demolished between the time of Cassini[2] (1779) and Gell[3] (1821), when the merlons now to be seen were built. It is painted in the Cadastro; drawn by Cozens (1746), and engraved by Vasi (1747) and Cassini (1779). At the back it received light from a fairly large window, shown by the first two sources, and was entered from the upper rampart-walk through a doorway on the west. In front it had two windows, shown by Vasi and Cassini (the Cadastro misses out the west one), and symmetry demands a third on the west side, which is not visible on any of these views.

The curtain is now built almost entirely of stone, which is left with toothed edges on each side, as if the addition of stone facing to the lower stories of the towers had been contemplated when the curtain was added. And the idea that this was indeed the intention of the builders of the curtain receives some corroboration from the fact that the span of the main arch (12 ft.

---

[1] A facsimile thereof was procured by Dr. Ashby for the exhibition of 1911 in Rome; = Roman Scenes by British Artists, 1715–1850, London, 1911; pl. iii = V. and A. 1867. 10.12.7.   [2] Cassini, no. 58.   [3] Gell, pl. v.

FIG. 32. Porta Pinciana, rear view; Alexander Cozens, *c.* 1746.
(From the facsimile of a drawing now in the Victoria and Albert Museum.)

5 in. as against 12 ft. 3 in.) pairs with that of the contemporary curtain at Porta Latina, where stone-faced towers certainly were to have been built. Again, the portcullis arrangements are exactly the same. Another pairing of this kind, between Portae Appia and Ostiensis East, has already been noted, and one more is yet to be described, between Porta Tiburtina and La Porta Chiusa. The stonework exhibits bosses, indicating, as at Porta Appia and elsewhere, that it was dressed *in situ*. On the front key-stone (fig. 18) is incised a Greek cross, within a circle; and on the rear one is cut in relief a Latin cross with foot-rest (*suppedaneum*). These crosses are usually assigned to a Belisarian restoration, but their type is at least a century earlier, and they would go better[1] with work by Honorius. On the block behind the second and third west voussoirs a half-erased inscription N (or R) IS is visible; and when diggings were made[2] through the Gate, while laying water-pipes, the ancient sill of the Gate was found, and turned out to be partly composed of an inscribed slab, read as EROTID, clearly part of a funerary inscription of a woman named Erotis. Evidently, then, inscribed tombs were being robbed here, as at other gates, to build the stone curtain. The elaborate moulding with dentils, which decorates the top of the stonework, is no doubt also stolen from some such source. It may be added that in its earliest form the curtain must have run as shown with broken lines on the plan (fig. 30), and not in a straight line behind the west gate-tower, as Lanciani thought. Only thus is it possible to secure a standard width for the Wall: and it can be seen how the later tower was fitted round the shape thus formed, and took therefrom its internal diameter. But neither the form nor the age of the curtain now visible are in doubt. It must have been added after the building of the second-period tower, otherwise its stones would not have been cut down specially to fit the edge of the tower, but would have been toothed behind it. Again, it would have fitted the back of the gate properly, whereas, in actual fact, at the time of its addition a large archway which had spanned a sharp re-entrant in the early Wall at the back of the west tower was filled in, and the filling-wall had to be carried across on to the stonework by means of a squinch.[3] This archway was part of the second-period gallery structure, as its identical brickwork and a continuous bonding-course show. So the stone arch is everywhere associated with third-period work. It is clear, however, that the stonework is no more than a facing, inserted to replace an earlier

---

[1] See p. 107 for a full discussion.

[2] *N. Scav.*, 1888, p. 60 = *B.C.*, 1888, p. 41. The entry in the first source—le cui pietre furono adoperate nella prima costruzione della porta—suggests that this was the one and only sill found; it might, then, be Aurelianic.

[3] For such another squinch cf. the re-entrant in curtain no. B 5: omitted by *F. U. R.* 2.

surface of brickwork, for the brickwork of the west side of the
front wall of the curtain's upper story is separated by no break
in construction from the second-period gallery and west tower.
The centre, a front wall 2 ft. 6 in. thick pierced by loop-holes
and recessed to receive the third-period portcullis, is of worse
brickwork, of fifth-century type, and was no doubt built at the
same time as the arch below it. The east side, once again, is one
with the Wall-gallery. The rear wall is all of the same age as the
gallery, as is proved both by the similarity of its brickwork and
the presence of a continuous bonding-course joining both structures. In the Wall two small windows set over the gateway and
a great archway spanned the original irregularity in the Wall,
which still existed behind the gate, although in front it had been
corrected and disguised by the addition of the second-period
tower. The whole structure was covered by a barrel-vault. But
even in its final third-period form it was very much narrower
than the ordinary gateway with a stone arch. In fact it never
lost the long and narrow proportions associated with its earlier
functions, whether rampart-walk (first period) or gallery (second
period).

There once rose to crown the curtain, as at the towers, a third
story. This is shown best[1] from the front by the Cadastro,
Vasi, and Cassini, and from behind by the Cadastro and Cozens.
It had two front windows, arranged over the loop-holes, of which
the level, as shown by Vasi and Cassini (but not by the Cadastro),
was slightly lower than that of the tower windows. The arrangement at the back is doubtful; but it seems that the back wall had
become ruined at the time of the Cadastro, which is, unfortunately,
hazy at the critical point; and more still was gone when Cozens
drew his sketch. Whether this third story belongs to the second
or third period is not certain; but it seems more likely that it
belonged to the third, when the lower room would be almost
completely occupied by portcullis machinery, and could not be
used effectively by defenders of the gate.

Behind the gate was a courtyard. This had disappeared
before the nineteenth century, and has escaped the notice of
Lanciani; but it is marked on Nolli's plan,[2] and appears in the
drawings of the Cadastro and Alexander Cozens (fig. 32). It is
also mentioned by Audebert,[3] who describes the two curtains as
follows:

'Le bastiment de la porte Pinciana est composé d'une haulte archade de
pierre Tyburtine, qui paroist fort antique, et n'y a aulcune inscription, ny

---

[1] All these sources have already been cited, see notes pp. 162, 164.

[2] Gianbattista Nolli, 1748.

[3] Audebert, fol. 267. 'The building of Porta Pinciana is composed of a high travertine
arch, which appears very old and is uninscribed and unmarked except for a cross at the

aultre marque sinon une croix sur le haulte de la vouste, toutesfoys par comparaison d'aultres bastymens il semble à la fabrique qu'elle soit du temps de l'empereur Iustinian et de pareille matiére et structure que le pont Saincte-Clare ou Salarius basty par Narses: aussy L. Faunus est d'opinion qu'elle a esté bastye par Bélissaire, lieutenant de Iustinian. Plus avant dedans la ville y a un aultre grand portail, et une vouste, qui semblent estre plus modernes.'

Audebert's dating may be taken with a pinch of salt, but it is evident that he felt the rear arch was less well built than that of the front, which certainly is of quite high standard. How little this need mean is shown by the structures at Porta Ostiensis East. It is therefore unfortunate that he does not say of what material the arch was built. Among other sources, the Cadastro shows something indeterminate, which might be a rough brick or plaster facing of medieval date, while Cozens draws with some care a good stone arch, of the type common elsewhere on the Wall, crossed by a rampart-walk with pointed merlons, and embellished with a Papal stemma. It is clear, however, that the merlons drawn by Cozens replaced those which are shown on the Cadastro, and these were no doubt at least part of the repair commemorated by the Papal arms. But it is uncertain whether the arch, which is shown to be rather carefully built in stone, is Papal or earlier. Behind it came two Renaissance customs houses, heightened since the drawing of the Cadastro was made. These features are all delineated on the small but very careful plan by Nolli, who is careful to differentiate, by varied hatching, what was ancient work and what was not. He shows an extensive ancient court, no doubt supplied with staircases behind the present gate, which joins the Wall on the west just behind the original east side of the first tower (this tower has extensions both to east and west not marked on *F. U. R.*) west of Porta Pinciana, and on the east behind the west side of the semi-circular tower. With the junction of this wall and the staircase arrangements is no doubt connected the little door behind the Gate below gallery level, shown by Homo;[1] and this door proves that there must have been a vantage-court wall of some kind. It may be supposed, then, that here, as at Portae Latina, Ostiensis East, Appia, and Tiburtina, a courtyard was added behind the Gate. The period of this addition is as uncertain as its character, but analogy suggests that it must have been added in the second period, and its existence cannot well be doubted, since it is in

top of the arch. Yet, on comparison with other buildings, it seems that the construction is of the time of Emperor Justinian, and of similar material and build as the Ponte Santa Chiara or Salaria built by Narses. L. Faunus, too, is of the opinion that it was built by Belisarius, a lieutenant of Justinian. Further inside the town is another great gate and arch, which seem to be more recent.'

[1] *Essai*, p. 264, fig. 3.

XVI

a. PORTA TIBURTINA. FRONT VIEW

b. PORTA TIBURTINA. INSCRIPTION OF
HONORIUS AND ARCADIUS (*C. I. L.* vi. 1190)
The inscribed arch in the rear is the Aqua Marcia

fact the method of access to the ground demanded by the door in the back of the second-period tower. Like the court of Porta Ostiensis East, this one may have had a rather clumsily built rear arch, which would account for Audebert's observation as to date, or it may have received a medieval arch before his time.

Conclusions. So the periods at Porta Pinciana emerge in an order that is now familiar. The Gate started as a minor entrance, to be classed with the early Portae Metrobia and Asinaria. It was flanked on the east by a semicircular wall-tower and no doubt it had an ordinary wall, set askew across the road which it spanned. The early name of this road is quite uncertain, and so, therefore, is that of the Gate.

The second period coincided with the addition of the gallery to the Wall. Now the Gate received for the first time a west tower, closely resembling the second-period bastions of Porta Asinaria, although the site demanded that it should be built on an altogether smaller scale than these. Its size seems to have been dictated by the angle in the early wall on to which it was fitted. The Gate was, in fact, thus promoted from a third-class to a second-class entry. And it received a courtyard behind it, perhaps for customs administration.

In the third period, by which time it was no doubt called Porta Pinciana, it received a new stone curtain, of the same dimensions as that of Porta Latina, protected from human foes by a portcullis, and shielded by crosses from such assaults of the Devil as lightning. Whether it was now or in the second period that its towers and curtain received new upper stories is uncertain, but analogy suggests that this happened now. The ill-arranged communication with the top story of the west tower also supports this view. But the absence of the elements under discussion effectively prevents any final decision.

Later alterations were few. The Gate saw some heavy fighting in 536, and it received a rough block-and-brick work refacing, whose distribution coincides with the siege area. At the time when the Einsiedeln List was compiled the Gate was shut.[1] But it was apparently open in the eighth century, when the source[2] of William of Malmesbury described cemeteries accessible through the Gate. It was open again before 1454 when, as Tomasetti points out, the *gabella* receipts from this gate form an item in the accounts of Ambrosio Spannocchi, the Pontifical Treasurer.[3] In 1808 it was shut for a century, and it is likely now to remain open for long, since it carries a road far busier than *Via Pinciana* ever can have been.

---

[1] See p. 44 for a discussion of the bearing of this point upon the dating of the Einsiedeln document.
[2] *C. U. R.* p. 87 = Tomasetti, *Via Salaria*, p. 12. Porta Portitiana or Porciana looks like dittography.　　　　　[3] *Vide* Tomasetti, loc. cit.

§ 8. PORTA TIBURTINA

This imposing, if somewhat gloomy, Gate was built in front
of an earlier aqueduct arch,[1] constructed by Augustus in 5 B.C.
to carry *Aquae Marcia–Tepula–Iulia* across *Via Tiburtina*.[2]   In
the Middle Ages[3] the Gate was called either Porta San Lorenzo,
after the great church outside it, or Porta Taurina, with reference
to the *bucranium* which decorated each keystone of the aqueduct
arch. As it stands to-day (Pl. XVI*a*) the Gate, facing east, consists
of two towers, much altered in the Middle Ages, the south much
taller than the north. Between them runs a well-preserved
travertine curtain, upon which is carved the important inscription[4] of Arcadius and Honorius (Pl. XVI*b*).

Behind the Gate lay a courtyard with a magnificent stone
rear arch, which is photographed complete by Parker. Sad to
say, the Risorgimento did not come in time to prevent Pius IX
from demolishing the arch, in 1869, in order to build with its
stones a triumphal monument on the Janiculum, although it
prevented the monument from being erected. A study of the gate
is further complicated by the Acqua Felice, the high-level
aqueduct of Sixtus V, which used the City Wall for support, and
was here taken through the Gate without regard for the ancient
structure. This makes it impossible to examine either the south
end of the curtain or the lower stories of the south tower, which
might have shed much light upon the earliest history of the
Gate. Yet, apart from this, an accurate plan of the Gate helps to
elucidate its architectural history. With these preliminary remarks the description[5] of the actual remains (fig. 33) may begin.

The north tower is now inaccessible except at the level of the
top of the curtain, and was not to be measured without some
exacting climbing. Its two lower stories are solid, and its front
is entirely refaced with medieval work. The character of this is
best shown by the view in the Cadastro, drawn when the Gate
was in better repair than now. Behind the battered lower story
in front there is Roman work on the north side of the tower, of
a type earlier than the fifth century, attached to the City Wall at
its west end. The southern wall is later, but comes into line with
some earlier work inside the stone curtain. The medieval work
probably belongs to the fifteenth century,[6] and is matched by

[1] *C. I. L.* vi. 1244: repaired in A.D. 79 (loc. cit. 1246) and 212–13 (loc. cit. 1245).

[2] Certainly Via Tiburtina by the Augustan age, see below p. 180.

[3] *C. U. R.*, p. 88, source of William of Malmesbury, *Porta Sancti Laurentii*: p. 92,
Descr. plenaria: Porta taurina, que dicitur sancti Laurentii vel tiburtina: p. 115, *Graphia
aureae U. R.* Porta taurina, vel tiburtina, que dicitur sci laurentii.

[4] *C. I. L.* vi., 1190.

[5] For help in this work I am indebted once more to Mr. G. H. Wedgwood.

[6] *M. di R.*, p. 341, assigns it to Nicholas V, and notes some travertine underneath it,
'fabbricato sulle rovine di travertino dell' antico bastione.'

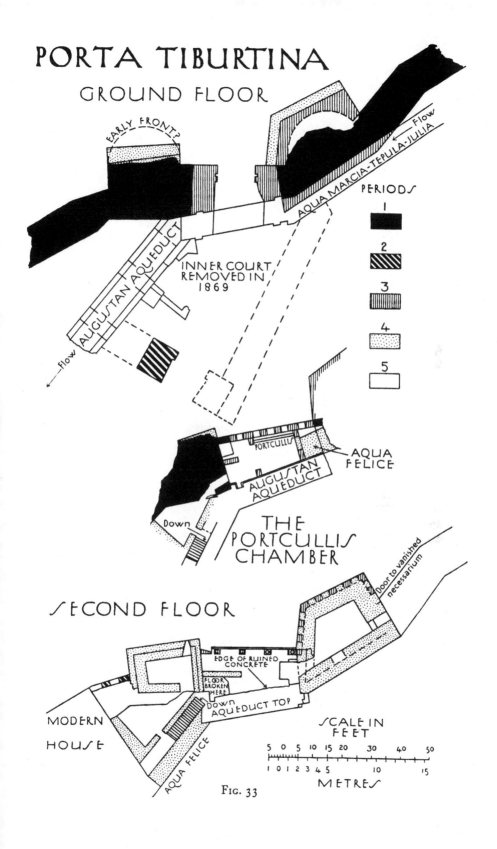

PORTA TIBURTINA

GROUND FLOOR

EARLY FRONT?

Flow

AQUA MARCIA-TEPULA-IULIA

AUGUSTAN AQUEDUCT

INNER COURT REMOVED IN 1869

Flow

PERIODS

1

2

3

4

5

PORTCULLIS

AUGUSTAN AQUEDUCT

AQUA FELICE

Down

THE PORTCULLIS CHAMBER

SECOND FLOOR

Door to vanished necessarium

EDGE OF RUINED CONCRETE

FLOOR BROKEN HERE

Down

AQUEDUCT TOP

MODERN HOUSE

AQUA FELICE

SCALE IN FEET

5 0 5 10 15 20 30 40 50

1 0 1 2 3 4 5 10 15

METRES

FIG. 33

similar work on the south tower, commemorated by two cardinal's *stemmata*; these belong to the families of Carafa and Farnese, and are assigned by Tomassetti[1] to the sixteenth century. They are discussed in further detail below.

The upper part of the tower is reached by a little staircase cut behind the aqueduct piers. This is certainly of medieval date, probably contemporary with the Acqua Felice. It leads to an irregularly-shaped medieval chamber, which has a Roman front wall, of which the south end is now broken, but originally continued straight through to the north end of the Augustan aqueduct arch, thus linking the latter to the wall. This is the rear of the ancient Gateway at this point, and it is built in good brickwork, better than that associated with the fifth century. It will be seen that it turns through an obtuse angle, and that the section south of the turn exactly corresponds to the width of the tower. The south end was broken through in medieval times, and the breach was reopened in 1916[2] in order to reach the inside of the portcullis-chamber, to which the original entrance (perhaps not from the north) could not be found.[3] But the continuation of the wall in ancient times is certain, and is still visible, in section, among a great deal of medieval rubble, which carries the medieval staircase up to the top of the curtain built on the aqueduct arch. It may be assumed that the tower itself was originally approached from behind by walking through the first aqueduct arch north of the Gate, which later was used to house a little chapel, decorated with frescoes of the twelfth century. Above this rose the back of the medieval tower, now completely broken away, but still intact in 1795, when J. Smith painted a pleasing view of the Gate, now in the South Kensington Museum.[4] In the sections provided by the butt-ends of the broken side-walls, it is possible to see that both were thickened in medieval times, the thickening being added on the inside. The tower was not vaulted, but roofed with a flat wooden floor and protected by battlements. These were ruined in the days of the Cadastro (1657–66), and had completely disappeared by Vasi's time; since then all have been renewed, between the time of Cassini and Gell.[5] Not much, then, is known of the Roman tower on this spot. Its side-walls exist, but only for the shortest distance; just far enough to establish that it was

---

[1] *Via Tiburtina*, p. 11.

[2] L. Mariani, *B. C.* 1917, p. 215, fig. 13. The angles in my plan do not agree completely with those of this figure, but they have all been verified and are the result of rigid triangulation.

[3] Since, however, this curtain is Honorian, an earlier entrance may have lain at a lower level.

[4] A reproduction thereof is now in the *B. S. R.*; it was acquired by Dr. Ashby for the exhibition of 1911. See Ashby, *Top. Dict. Anc. Rome*, p. 416, fig. 44.

[5] They are out of sight in Smith's drawing, which is of intermediate date.

twenty-five feet in width. The brickwork of the north wall looks older than the fifth century. The slight projection of the existing tower, and the fact that the end of the straight north wall comes into line with the curtain, prompt the query whether this is the back of a Roman semicircular tower (like the west tower of Porta Ostiensis East) from which the semicircular front has been removed. This question is discussed more fully later.

The south tower is considerably better preserved. Like its companion it has a medieval battered front: and the batter extends also along the north side of the tower, right up to the Honorian stone curtain. The south side, however, is free, except for a modern latrine of simple form, set in the angle between the tower and the walls. Behind the medieval batter, on the south side, can be seen two stories in Roman work, the lower faced with stone blocks, the upper with tiles. Above them, but lower than the top of the City Wall, the Roman work is replaced by medieval tufa work. One of the blocks of the stone wall, in the third course from the top, is turned upside down and inscribed [1] INV · Ⅎ · Ɔ · SΛⅠ⅂⅂Iᖷ0. If the line of this blockwork is continued round the tower on the same plane as its true face (not that of the battered walls), its end exactly coincides with that of the Honorian stone curtain. And on a level with the top of this curtain merlons, now embedded in later masonry, run round the tower. Above them the whole tower is built in bad medieval block-and-brick work, and there is no sign whatever of Roman work in it. Even the lower parapets seem medieval, although they existed before the Cadastro, the oldest large-scale drawing of the gate. On Tempesta's map [2] (1593), however, the towers are shown equal in height, and representation would not seem to be schematic. It shows the whole east Wall of the City as it existed just before the building of the Acqua Felice, and therefore must have been engraved before 1586. Sixtus also repaired the curtain south of the gate, which Tempesta shows as ruined. On the tower itself the Carafa and Farnese *stemmata*, which are of this period, [3] may well belong to Cardinals Antonio Carafa and Alessandro Farnese, both active builders during the pontificate of Sixtus. [4]

---

[1] *C. I. L.* vi. 23381: the fact that the block is upside down is omitted, although it proves that it is not *in situ*: no letter is now visible before OFILLIVS: I am inclined to think that the stone has been dressed down in its present position.

[2] The great arch of the Acqua Felice, north of the Gate, is shown. But such discrepancies are not uncommon. Cuts could be brought up to date, cf. a cut of Jo. Jacobo di Rubeis, Cartaro's view, now in the B. S. R., called Urbis Romae Novissima Delineatio, MDCL. Here MDCL is cut over MDCXXXVII, the Walls of St. Peter and Urban VIII inserted, together with new houses in Via Sistina, Via Lungara, the Palatium Burghesiorum, and obelisk of Piazza del Popolo. Excudebat Romae ad Pacem, 1650. 1650 *in litura* of 1637.

[3] Tomasetti, *Via Tiburtina*, p. 11.

[4] Pastor, *Geschichte der Päpste*, x, p. 477.

It is, indeed, highly probable that the upper story of the tower was added now, when the lower one was blocked by the Acqua Felice.

Up to the height of the lower parapet and merlons there is some ancient work in the back of the tower. This is not early, and it has been considerably patched with rather coarse block-and-brick work, but there is no doubt that it belongs to the Roman age. In it was a small door, which must have led out on to the top of the aqueduct-*specus*, upon which the back of the tower was originally built. The *specus* was later removed, possibly piecemeal, and was replaced by medieval facings of tile and of block-and-brick work: the line of the top of the *specus* is marked by the top of these rough and varied facings. The south angle is masked by a little control chamber, connected with the Acqua Felice, and depicted in the Cadastro with a domed roof. The north angle plainly is all refaced with medieval work, set at a new angle and provided with prominent quoin-stones; but the north side runs straight through on to the end of the Honorian curtain, and fits on to one of the Honorian merlons, and therefore must be on lines at least as old as the fifth century. It was not, however, the earliest outer wall of this tower, as will presently appear.

The upper chamber of the tower is now accessible from the top of the aqueduct arch, reached by a continuation of the little medieval staircase that leads up to the space behind the north tower. And from the roof of the portcullis-chamber, built in front of the aqueduct arch, it was once possible to enter the tower by a north door. In medieval times an external staircase at the front of the curtain, protected by specially high parapets and merlons, led up to the next story in the tower, at the level of the top of the Honorian parapet, now embedded in the tower. Above this level no trace of stairs exists in the tower, but this whole additional story is medieval, and it seems likely that communication was achieved by means of wooden floors and staircases. The upper story is therefore inaccessible; and in view of its unquestionably late date (see above), it did not seem worth while to go to the trouble and expense of procuring ladders in order to measure it in detail.

The doorway leading from the aqueduct top into the tower has been cut through the tower wall, and provides some important evidence for the tower's evolution, for straight joints on each side of the passage show that the outer wall of the tower, at the end of the Honorian curtain, is applied to an earlier brick-faced wall as an outer thickening. Yet it is certain that this outer thickening, though not now faced with ancient material, is on ancient lines, for the Honorian stone merlon fits it, and it comes into line with the stonework [1] of the tower. The inner wall must therefore belong to an early brick-faced tower, earlier than the Honorian period. And it should be noted that, while the line of the Honorian stonework is slightly splayed, as at Porta Appia, the earlier line, which can be determined by joining the two sections, is at right angles to the curtains. From this fact it may be concluded that, as at other Gates, a tower with stone-faced lower story was being built round a tower of earlier date. It is also clear that something of the same kind happened at the north tower, where the stone curtain is left toothed, and stops short of the edge of the tower in order to be keyed into stone facing; the space allowed for this is exactly the same as that between the stone curtain and the earliest north wall of the south tower. Some of this facing was seen by Nibby, [2] in 1821, although he does not define its precise position. The fragments of brick wall now visible therefore belong not to this stone Honorian Gate, but to an earlier structure, of which the aspect may be considered now. The stone curtain is entirely Honorian and can be left until later.

The outlines of the plan of the Gate reveal that, in order to cross *Via Tiburtina*, which did not run through the Wall at right angles, the Wall-builders adopted the device used in dealing with *Via Pinciana*.[3] The Wall to the north of the road was set forward twelve feet, and the Gate was fitted in the skewed shape thus gained. But at Porta Pinciana, at first, the difficult problem of fitting towers to the skewed shape did not arise. At Porta Tiburtina, on the other hand, as at Porta Ostiensis East,[4] gate-towers had to be fitted somehow, and so the Wall was set back on each side of the Gate, in order to gain the extra space required. What kind of towers were then built?

The south tower may be considered first. Here there is clear evidence that the Honorian tower in *opus quadratum* was built round an earlier tower. No doubt this later facing was of uniform thickness, and by peeling it off we get a tower with a base-line of approximately twenty-six feet, but a tower of very awkward proportions, if its lines resembled those of the tower built round it, and also quite unlike other early Gate-towers on the circuit. Yet its base-line, twenty-six feet in length, corresponds to the diameter of those semicircular towers which we have come to recognize as associated with the early gates. A complete semicircle is, however, an impossibility here, and so the following arrangement is put forward as feasible. It is clear that the curve,

---

[1] There can be little doubt that if the medieval battered wall below were cleared off, Honorian stonework would appear on this line at the base of the tower.

[2] *M. di R.*, p. 341.

[3] See p. 160, fig. 30.   [4] See p. 111, fig. 19.

once granted, must have been set out from a centre, situated
somewhere on an extension of the line taken by the Wall approaching from the south, since otherwise there would have been no
point in skewing the Wall to meet it. Then, using the standard
radius for early towers (13 ft.), a centre on this line may be chosen,
so as to make a tangent of the line of the newly discovered early
wall (which is set at right angles to the gateway curtain). We
can thus project a shapely tower, which reconciles the awkward
orientations associated with the skew shape, and gives on the
south side of the Honorian tower just the same amount of room
for blocks as on the north. Furthermore, the resultant shape,
though odd as a whole (as that of any tower in this position must
have been), does not appear odd in elevation, as a small-scale
tower on Honorian lines would have done. It may be suspected,
then, that this solution of the problem approaches the truth; and
it may be claimed that it satisfies the present state of knowledge.

The remains of the early north tower are also explicable if
treated on similar lines. The straight north wall stops level with
the curtain, and a semicircular bastion may be postulated set out
on this line. Its diameter is one and a half feet less than the normal
twenty-six feet, but it is impossible to escape from the lines laid
down by the Roman brickwork, and the decrease from the standard
has its parallels at Portae[1] Ostiensis East and Pinciana. Otherwise the tower would have a quite normal aspect from the
front of the Gate, and round it can be fitted, with much the same
room to spare as on the south and with not dissimilar frontal
aspect, a rectangular Honorian tower. The reconstructed Gate
thus comes as close to the standards associated with the relevant
periods at other Gates as its awkward situation will permit.

The curtain (Pl. XVIb) is the only Honorian inscribed curtain
now left standing in Rome, and is therefore of great importance.
The inscription has already been discussed elsewhere, but it
is worth emphasis here that the curtain was never repaired, as is
suggested in the Corpus of Latin Inscriptions.[2] The original
stones still are there, with the erasure of the names of Stilicho
and Macrobius Longinianus on them. Also, a large M exists on
the south transon of the central window, proving that this curtain,
like all other stonework on the Gates of Rome, was built with
stolen material.

The position of the gateway arch was not central. It is
determined by the line of the Flavian *Via Tiburtina*, which lay
at 49.49 m. above sea-level, compared with the Augustan level
of 48.12 m. and Honorian level of 49.50 m. The facts were
ascertained by Ingegnere Bonfiglietti,[3] when the arch was exca-

[1] See pp. 111, 160.   [2] See *C. I. L.* vi. 1190.
[3] See L. Mariani, *B. C.*, 1917, p. 209, n. 3.

a. LA PORTA CHIUSA, 1925. THE FRONT

b. LA PORTA CHIUSA, 1868. THE REAR (Parker)

vated in 1916. The whole discovery was of considerable importance, for it disproved completely Lanciani's statement[1] that
the Honorian pavement here was three metres above the level of
the age of Augustus, which he equates with that of Aurelian;
and the reduction of three metres to one centimetre makes
impossible his interpretation of the phrase 'egestis immensis
ruderibus'. The Honorian builders, however, narrowed the width
of the roadway from the south, though whether they were
following an earlier arrangement in so doing cannot be said. The
north side was kept alined to the north side of the Augustan
arch, and thus the Honorian arch was thrown one foot nine
inches south of the centre. On the south side is preserved, in
bad condition, a little cross, with the following inscription,[2]
BACIANDO LA SS. CROCE CIÈ│CENTO GIORNI D'INDULGENZA,
a record of vanishing standards of faith and hygiene. The portcullis slots are still there, but are so irregular that one doubts
whether any machine ever ran in them. The width of this arch
is 13 ft. 2 in., as compared with the 13 ft. 6 in. of Porta Chiusa.
It therefore looks as if a pair of Gates entrusted to the same
builder was in question.

The upper story is now reached by the little flight of stairs
leading to the north tower. It is entered through a small rough
passage, which was cut through the Roman wall at the back of
the curtain in medieval times, and was reopened and refaced in
1916. There does not seem to have been an original entrance on
the north side at this level. The front wall of the stone curtain
does not come right to the end of the portcullis-chamber: it is
met, at 4 ft. 2 in., by a brick-faced wall, the remains of an earlier
brick-faced curtain, which is bonded in to the north wall of the
chamber, also composed of good brick-faced concrete, which
might easily be of third-century date. The back wall of the
chamber was formed by the attic of the Augustan aqueduct arch.
The south wall is inaccessible, for the whole end of the curtain
is blocked by the concrete conduit of the Acqua Felice, which
is directed through the south tower, and enters the Augustan
arch at this point. Between these limits, then, the portcullis-
chamber is divided into a small north compartment and a large
south compartment; and the latter was once the central compartment of the curtain and still contains the portcullis-slot over
the archway. The north and south windows were set rather
farther apart from the others, in order to give room for dividing
walls, which supported barrel-vaults, arranged in exactly the
same way as at Porta Latina. The other dividing wall, on

---

[1] B. C. 1892, p. 111. Equally erratic are his statements about levels at other Gates, see
pp. 176-7, 214, 220.
[2] 'By kissing the most Holy Cross we get 100 days' indulgence.'

the north side of the chamber, is modern, and its function is to support the broken vault of the roof. The arrangements for hauling up the portcullis are not preserved. In the north-east corner of the north compartment was a block of concrete, of which the meaning is not now clear: it might well be the foundation of a corner pier for the roof, which the modern dividing wall has replaced. The roof overtops the aqueduct arch, which may not have been considered as part of the ancient Gate at all.

To-day the only way of reaching the top of the curtain is by the medieval flight of steps which leads up to the top of the Augustan arch. It is then possible to mount the curtain from the south side of the aqueduct top. At the back of the curtain is a partly preserved late parapet, and on the front are still to be seen four Honorian merlons, each standing upon a base, set in turn above a decorative moulding that marks the top of the stone curtain, and looks as if it had been stolen from some earlier tomb, like that of Ofillius. The merlons, useless for defence, are thin rectangular bollards of travertine, with tapered tops, and the southernmost is formed of a sawn moulding stood on end, and is cut to half size in order to fit against the wall of the tower. Such battlements belong to the old decorative type, which appears, for example, on the Colosseum as shown on the Relief of the Haterii.[1]

Evidently, then, the top of the Gate was to be treated in decorative fashion. And this gives a clue to the disposition of the *simulacra* of Arcadius and Honorius, which are stated, in the inscription on the Gate, to have been set up by the Senate and People of Rome. The question of the distribution of these statues and inscriptions has been discussed already,[2] but the position of the former remains to be ascertained. Actually, it can hardly be in doubt. There is no place for statues of two Emperors on the sheer façade of the Gate, and they would be quite out of place on towers which were wanted for artillery. So they have to be placed, perforce, on the top of the curtain, between the merlons, above the side look-out chambers in the curtain below. There they stood, representing the Ever-victorious and Triumphant Emperors, All-powerful Protectors of the Sacred City. This imaginative conception is one more proof, if such be needed, that Art in the fifth century was not dead, but had found new forms of expression. Nothing could symbolize better than these stately figures the outlook of the late-Roman Empire on the function of the Emperors: they have become superhuman knights, champions of Civilization against Barbary. Nor did this striking artistic idea escape notice. It was caught

---

[1] See von Gerkan, R. *Mitth.* 1925, p. 26.   [2] See pp. 33–5.

in the stream of influences from West to East, and formed not
the least fair embellishment of the Golden Gate at Constantinople,[1] soon to be the last home of both the pageant and the
realities of Empire.

When the statues disappeared is not clear. Not all the Gates
were supplied with them, and we do not hear that they were
thrown down in any siege. At all events, they had vanished by
medieval times, when the decorative merlons had become the
core of a defensive parapet, crowned by serviceable merlons of
more normal outline, and rising in a great step at the south end,
as already noted, in order to protect the entry to the upper tower.
At the same time the top of the Augustan aqueduct was supplied
with merlons and parapet, and embodied as part of the gate. The
character of the work and its freshness, as shown in the Cadastro,
rather suggest that this may have been an improvement by
Cardinals Carafa and Farnese;[2] anyhow, the work on the front
merlons cannot be earlier than the heightening of the tower, for
it was not needed before them.

Behind the gate lay a court, a magnificent structure, only
destroyed by Pius IX in 1869. Fortunately, Parker photographed
it before its disappearance, and there is also a good large-scale
plan by Uggeri.[3] There may be added a view in the Cadastro
and a painting by J. Smith, dated 1795, now in the British
Museum. These and the few existing remains make it possible
to get an accurate idea of the type of the court.

The rear arch was built of stone blocks, and alined with
the road, which bent round to the north after passing through
the Augustan arch. Even in Uggeri's day there was little more
left than the rearward arch. The top thereof was approached
from behind by a flight of steps, which ran into a room in
the north pier. Some brickwork of this pier still remains, belonging to a date certainly not later than the fifth century and
possibly earlier. The space between it and the Augustan arch
was filled up in the Middle Ages with a little chapel,[4] customs
houses, and lodgings for the guard of the Gate; the altar of the
chapel and a few rough walls are all that now remain of these
buildings. It is, therefore, not clear exactly where the walls
joined the back of the aqueduct, but it might be suspected that
the south wall joined the south end of the aqueduct arch, and
that the west wall ran straight into the adjacent pier of the
aqueduct, while the aqueduct itself formed the north wall. Presumably the structure was crowned with merlons, but the

[1] Theophanes a. 6332. Edn. Bonn. l. 634: ref. to the statue of Theodosius on the Golden
Gate, Constantinople. Cf. also the extant statue-bases on Porta Aurea, Split.
[2] See p. 173.
[3] Uggeri, vol. vi, pl. 1 = B. C. 1917, tav. xviii.
[4] Apparently of XIth cent. date; Muñoz quoted, B.C. 1917, p. 214.

Cadastro shows nothing, and J. Smith drew only the remains of a machicolated parapet. This means that the ancient work had disappeared long before his day. At no point is it possible to trace any contact between the vantage-court and datable structures on the Gate, owing to the interposition of the aqueduct. The date of the court therefore remains doubtful. All that can be said is that its brickwork proves it to be ancient, and would not deny it a position among second-period structures. In other words, it may be contemporary with the courts of Portae Latina, Ostiensis East, and Appia.

It should be added that excavations were made within the area of the court in 1916. These were chiefly valuable for the history of the aqueduct and of *Via Tiburtina*, of which Honorian, Flavian, and Augustan levels were exposed, as noted above. But the presence of a Republican tomb or *aediculum*, in alinement with the road, proves that this road to Tibur was in full use in late-Republican times. A detailed account of these discoveries has been given by L. Mariani,[1] to which readers are referred, since the matter does not concern the history of the court.

Conclusions. Such, then, is the architectural history of Porta Tiburtina. It is important chiefly because it provides a definite date for the period of stone-faced towers and curtains on the Wall. But it is possible also to divine something about its earlier form. The first Gate had a curtain and towers in tile-faced concrete, and it seems highly probable that these towers conformed, as best might be in so awkward a site, to the standards set for other first-period towers on the Wall. To strip the medieval battered counterforts off the north tower and to excavate would, however, solve the problem, for the foundations of the Roman towers are likely to be still *in situ*.

Of the history of the Gate in classical times nothing is known after the age of Honorius. The curtain (cf. fig. 16) was then faced entirely in stone, with large quadrangular towers, of which the lower stories were also faced in stone. The only decorative elements were the merlons and the two statues of Arcadius and Honorius. It is clear that these towers were ruinous early in the Middle Ages,[2] like the whole tract of wall on this side of the City, and that extensive repairs had to be made, perhaps by Pope Nicholas V, as Nibby suggests. At the end of the sixteenth century, the building of the Acqua Felice completely blocked the lower open story of the south tower and the south end of the curtain, and the south tower was rebuilt about this time, so as to reach the immense height that it has to-day. After that, the few repairs were chiefly confined to the battlements, and later, the

[1] *B. C.* 1917, 207–14.
[2] Here Ladislaus effected an entry to the City in 1408.

Honorian merlons were freed from medieval encumbrances. In conclusion, it may be repeated that this is a Gate where the judicious and valuable excavations already made by the Municipio behind it might be carried on with advantage at the front, and might yet produce useful corroborative *data* for the early history of the Wall.

§ 9. LA PORTA CHIUSA

This Gate is now hidden behind the Cantiere Castro Pretorio del genio civile per construzione governative, on the south side of the Caserma Castro Pretorio, and is not accessible to the public. The back of it forms part of an annexe to the Barracks of the Castro Pretorio, which the writer was able to visit, through the kindness of Generale di Giorgio and Tenente Bitocco, when studying the ancient Castra Praetoria. Nothing of note is now left at the back, and the front is difficult to reach, owing to the risk of being engulfed by the sump of a clay-pit. The Gate itself is blocked, but in good condition (Pl. XVII).

The earliest Gateway on the site has now disappeared, and that which exists is of Honorian type (fig. 31), built entirely of travertine, with an arch slightly bigger (13 ft. 6 in.) than that of Porta Tiburtina (13 ft. 2 in.). These are the widest stone-built gateway arches in the city; and, although double arches were supplied to even bigger roads, this width demonstrates the importance of the road which the gate spanned. The road in question shared with *Via Tiburtina* the traffic to Tibur, Sulmona, and the Adriatic, and may have been the earliest road for the purpose. The matter is discussed in detail by Dr. Ashby,[1] who concludes that there certainly were alternative routes to Tibur as far as the modern *Via Cupa*, west of the bridge across the Tiber-valley railway, and that, in and after the age of Augustus, the southernmost was the most important, and was called *Via Tiburtina*. Above the arch are six blocked[2] windows, the largest number in any Gate of this type in Rome, and the whole curtain is crowned with a moulding which returns at either end, showing that the Gate was a little higher than the Wall at this point. But this difference in level is not to be properly appreciated now, since the present Wall on both sides is of Renaissance type, with battered face, made[3] by Urban VIII in 1628. Audebert, who saw the gate before these restorations, describes[4] it thus:

'250 pas plus loing on veoit, tout en un recoing, une PORTE ANTIQUE,

---

[1] *P. B. S. R.* iii, pp. 85–7.

[2] Two northernmost and one southernmost blocked, the three remaining are converted to loop-holes in block-and-brick work.

[3] Inscription *in situ*, Nibby, *M. di R.*, p. 338.

[4] Audebert, fol. 260: '250 paces further on, one espies in an angle, an ancient gate, built with a high arch of travertine. It has a similar appearance both inside and outside the town,

bastye d'une haulte archade de pierre Tyburtine, laquelle paroist semblable tant par dedans que dehors la ville, et est murée de fort vieille massonnerie et située sur un hault et tertre, dépendant du mont Viminalis: toutesfoys elle paroist peu, estant en un recoing, et en lieu peu frequente pour le jour-d'huy ... A la sortye de ceste porte y avoit anciennement un grand chemin pavé, duquel on veoit encores les restes et vestyges, mais je n'en trouve point le nom.'

This account may be compared with the photograph (Pl. XVII*b*) of the back of the gate by Parker, and with the drawing made, according to his instructions, by Ciconetti (fig. 35), reproduced in *Archaeologia.*[1] These record an excavation made behind the

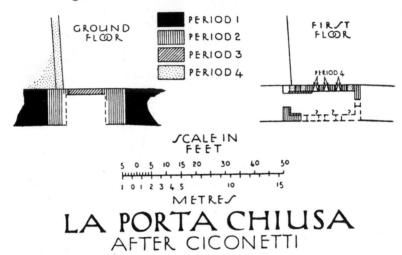

GROUND FLOOR

■ PERIOD 1
▦ PERIOD 2
▨ PERIOD 3
▢ PERIOD 4

FIRST FLOOR

PERIOD 4

SCALE IN FEET

5 0 5 10 15 20   30   40   50

1 0 1 2 3 4 5   10   15

METRES

LA PORTA CHIUSA
AFTER CICONETTI

FIG. 34

gate in May 1868 by the British Archaeological Society of Rome. It revealed nothing of great importance, and the results were misinterpreted by Parker, who took the tufa blocks of a conduit of the Acqua Felice to belong to the Anio vetus, despite the fact that they were almost level with the springing of the gateway arch. Actually, the drawing demonstrates quite clearly that Parker did not even reach late-Roman ground level. It is therefore meet to be thankful that work of this standard was, as Parker says, 'conducted quietly and without much show'. Ciconetti's drawing does demonstrate, however, the valuable fact that the stonework of the Gateway originally went right round its four sides. So the coarse block-and-brick facing shown inside the Gate by Parker cannot be original; nor, again, could it have

and is walled up with very ancient masonry. It lies on a height and knoll belonging to the Mons Viminalis. Yet it is not conspicuous, being in an angle, and in a spot little frequented nowadays. At the exit of this gate there was in ancient time a great paved road, of which traces and remains can yet be seen, but I cannot discover its name.'

[1] *Archaeologia*, xlii, 1869, pl. ii, p. 18. Cf. Parker photographs 1056, 1057, 1058.

led Audebert to observe that the Gate *paroist semblable tant par dedans que dehors la ville.* Audebert probably saw much or all of a west façade in travertine still standing and used as a wall-tower; and this, no doubt, was considerably damaged in laying the duct from the Acqua Felice, and has been robbed of its stone-work since that time.[1] At some date after the main vault had

FIG. 35. La Porta Chiusa; Parker's excavations, 1868. Drawing by Ciconetti, reproduced from *Archaeologia*, xlii, pl. ii.

disappeared, the Gate was supplied with a wooden floor. But this would not seem to have been done before the block-and-brick internal thickening wall was already half-ruined, for the holes for the floor-joists are cut partly in the block-and-brick work, where it survives, and partly in the stonework. The block-and-brick wall, therefore, may have partly collapsed with the vault. Whether this had happened before Audebert's time is not certain, since he wrote nothing about the interior of the Gate, and recorded only what an intelligent gazer could see from outside. The block-and-brick repair may therefore well be late-Roman, although it

[1] That it was removed late is proved by the fact that its blocks were left *in situ* up to the level of the Acqua Felice pipe.

barred any arrangement for a portcullis. In short, the Porta
Chiusa conforms to the same type as third-period Porta Metrobia,
which has a gate-house tower. It was not a first-class, perhaps
not even a second-class Gate, and originally had not been considered much more important than any other postern. But in
the age of stone building on the Wall it received stately form,
and was clearly designed to carry a considerable volume of local
traffic.

It should also be noted that this Gate has sometimes been
thought to lead into the *Vivarium*, the quarters of beasts kept
in readiness for the amphitheatre. Obviously, it cannot have
done so, for it is certain, as Jordan [1] notes, that the *Vivarium* was
near Porta Praenestina: otherwise the clear statement of Procopius,[2] which says *(Οὐίτιγις) ἀμφὶ πύλην Πραινεστίναν ἐπὶ μοῖραν τοῦ
περιβόλου, ἣν Ῥωμαῖοι βιβάριον καλοῦσιν,* is incomprehensible. True,
Bufalini, Du Pérac, and Nolli mark some form of fortified enclosure
outside the Wall at this point: but both its purpose and its date
are quite uncertain.[3] Also, what the medieval topographers, including Audebert, thought to be the *vivario*, or *vivaiolo*, was the
Castra Praetoria:[4] for they mistook the praetorian *contubernia*
for beasts' dens.

The name of the Gate is modern. Its ancient name is quite
unknown, for the Gate is omitted from the Einsiedeln List, in
common with Portae Ardeatina and Septimiana. The List therefore belongs [5] to a time after these Gates had been shut, but not
later than the ninth century. The date when the other Gates
passed out of use is unknown, but this one is of Honorian type
as it stands, and so must have been shut later than 402. It is
thus certain that the original text of the List cannot be as old as
Honorius, and this conclusion is entirely confirmed by the analysis
of the text given in the chapter on literary sources.

[1] Jordan, vol. i[3], p. 365-7.

[2] *B. G.* i. 22: 'Vitiges near the Praenestine Gate, on that part of the circuit which the
Romans call *Vivarium.*'

[3] Audebert, loc. cit., fol. 260, notes: 'Hors de la ville y a au devant de ceste porte une
grande place quarrée, autour de laquelle ou veoit encore les murailles ruinées que l'on tient
avoir jadis esté Castrum Custodiae.' No further description is given.

[4] Cf. Flav. Blondus ed. Venet. 1511, lib. ii, sect. 89, fol. 21, Fulvius, Pomp. Laetus, all
cited by Jordan i[3], p. 392, n. 48. Cf. also Audebert, fol. 260. 'Tout joignant icelle (la
porte antique) commence une grande estendue du costé de la ville, laquelle est aujourd'huy
appellée *il vivario*, . . . on ne veoit maintenant que des vignes et jardinages, où y a en quelques
endroicts des cavernes soube terre, bastyes avec voustes, que l'on dict qui servoyent pour
retirer les bestes saulvages'. These were the praetorian *contubernia* !

[5] See p. 44.

XVIII

a. PORTA SALARIA, BEFORE DEMOLITION IN 1871 (Parker)

b. PORTA SALARIA, 1821 (Sir William Gell)

III. DEMOLISHED GATES

§ 1. PORTA SALARIA

THE ancient Porta Salaria was severely damaged during the bombardment of Rome in 1870, and was removed in the following year. In 1873, its place was taken by a new Gate, designed by Vespignani, which in turn was demolished in 1921. Few can regret the loss of Vespignani's Gate, and that of the ancient Gate is less serious than it might be, since its aspect is well known from a photograph by Parker (Pl. XVIIIa), engravings by Vasi[1] (1747), Gell[2] (1821), Rossini[3] (1829), and Ricciardelli[4] (1832), and a drawing in the Cadastro[5] (1655–67). Yet the older structure must have contained valuable information about the evolution of the Gates, and we may regret that no record was made while it was being demolished. All attention, as at Porta Praenestina in 1838, was diverted to the tombs known[6] to exist underneath the towers. On discovery, these were left *in situ* until the restoration of 1927, when they were removed farther to the right and left. They are described in detail by Henzen,[7] and claim no further attention here, since they never interfere with the plan of the Gate, being curtailed wherever they projected beyond its limits. The ordinary name of the Gate, Porta Salaria, is certain, and is derived from the ancient road which it spanned. It is uncertain however, whether it ever was called Porta Belisaria, as the majority of readings[8] in the manuscripts of Procopius might suggest; for even if such a name ever existed, its acceptance in the text always cancels the word Salaria in connexion with it; and, as Jordan[9] notes, the name Belisaria is just as likely to have been applied to Porta Pinciana, which Belisarius also held,[10] and near which his head-quarters were situated, in the Domus Pinciana.

Parker's photograph of the Gate may now be analysed. The face of the east semicircular tower is shown reduced to just above the springing of the gateway arch, and above this point the core of solid concrete has been trimmed to the shape of a half-cone. This demolition is as old as the Cadastro of Alexander VII (1655–67), and the mass was already tree-covered in 1820. Then at some date, obviously not when the first floor of the tower was in use,

---

[1] Vasi, vol. i, pl. 3: and ex Vasi, Cassini, 1779.   [2] *M. di R.*, pl. 8.
[3] Rossini, pl. iv.   [4] Ricciardelli, pl. 23.
[5] Archivio dello Stato.
[6] Nibby, however, mistook these for the remains of rectangular towers, just as the towers at Porta Latina were mistaken for tombs.
[7] *Boll. Inst.* 1871, pp. 98–115.
[8] Procopius, *B. G.* i. 18. W, v, V (the Vatican group) are the exceptions.
[9] Jordan, i¹, p. 354, note 23.   [10] Procop. *B. G.* i. 19.

the whole of the back wall, through which an entrance must have once existed, has been completely refaced. So no information emerges from this part of the gate, except that the tower, like all other semicircular towers on the circuit, had a solid base.

The west tower is shown standing as high as any part of the Gate. For two-thirds of its height there rises a blind story, no doubt solid, as in the east tower, and the lowest part of this is covered with heavily-mortared facing, as old as Vasi's time (1747). This facing gives way to extremely short bricks, set in narrow belts, which is a treatment characteristic of much early nineteenth-century restoration on the Wall. And the dating cannot be far wrong, because the brickwork in question has wiped out a distinctive feature that appears on the careful drawings of Rossini [1] and Gell [2] (Pl. XVIII*b*), namely, a double string-course of ornamental bricks, of which the lower member lies at first-floor level, while the upper is shown by the Cadastro (1655–67) to pass right round the tower, and to form a sill to its windows. The feature appears in first-period work at Portae [3] Latina and Nomentana, and is without doubt to be recognized as typical of that epoch. The story which it distinguished was fitted with wide round-headed windows, turned with large tiles (no doubt *bipedales*). The west window was perfect; only half of the central one existed in the time of Parker, Gell, and Vasi; but both it and the east window are shown in the Cadastro (1655–67). From Vasi's engraving, indeed, it can be seen that by his day the whole of the east side of this story had fallen out, disclosing the top of the vaulted roof of the chamber. The damage had been mended by Gell's time, but further cracks were appearing, and these in turn had been patched before Parker made his photograph. It is possible, then, to restore three symmetrical windows in the towers of Porta Salaria, exactly as at Portae [3] Nomentana and Latina. The facing of this story is mostly block-and-brick work of poor quality, clearly of late date. But a small patch of better work is left, near the junction of tower and Wall, on a level with the top of the west window, and this gives an idea of what once covered the whole surface. The west window has been blocked, and fitted with a narrow loop-hole, with travertine top, exactly like the loop-holes used in the great reduction of window openings all along the Wall.

Vasi's engraving (1747) and the Cadastro (1655–67) also show that the west tower had a second floor. This was lit by a window in its west side, shown by Vasi: and the Cadastro also shows two windows in its back wall, arranged like staircase-windows. These had collapsed before 1747. No merlon is shown

[1] Rossini, tav. iv. This drawing is rather better than Gell's.
[2] Gell, *M. di R.*, tav. 8.   [3] See pp. 96, 102.

on the tower by any drawing, and by Parker's time the topmost story had been cleaned right off, and replaced by smooth concrete. Thus there is now no evidence to prove whether the second upper story of the Gate was an addition to the original or not. But the towers in this final form were so very like those of Portae[1] Pinciana and Ostiensis East that it seems fair to assume their history to have been the same; and at both these Gates there is the clearest evidence that the uppermost chamber was not original. Again, although it is now unknown how the roofs of towers were finished, it seems safe to assume that they resembled those of Porta Ostiensis East: in other words, that they were flat roofs, provided with merlons.

Between the towers ran a two-story curtain wall, of which the lower part was faced with travertine,[2] while the upper part was built in brick-faced concrete. It was pierced by a single arch, of the same proportion as those of Portae Ostiensis East, Appia, Latina, Tiburtina, Chiusa, Pinciana; and any one who focusses a magnifying glass upon Parker's photograph can detect bosses on the stones of the same kind as appear at Portae Appia, Latina, and Pinciana. The blocks, then, as their odd arrangement in relation to the voussoirs on the west side of the arch might suggest, are robbed tomb-blocks.[3] And on the west side of the curtain they have clearly been related not to the edge of the arch, but to the other end of the curtain, no doubt in order to fit them against the already existing edge of the bastion, where they finished off regularly, as shown by Vasi. This accounts for the small pieces of stone inserted between the voussoirs of the main arch and the coursed blocks. Six voussoirs of this arch remain, enough to show that their bed-planes had a dangerously slight taper. The place of the rest is taken by a poorly built arch of *bipedales*,[4] which is shown on all existing engravings or drawings of the Gate, and is mentioned by Audebert in 1575, who describes the main arch as an 'archade de pierre Tyburtine fort antique, dont le dessus est seulement de brique'. The brick arch is therefore of respectable age, and may well be classical. Above it is a patch of mixed but fairly homogeneous material, reaching up to a band of white stone fragments, either marble or travertine, which are shown, but less accurately than in the photograph, by Gell, and finish on a clean horizontal break. All this brick and tile work, then, is an ancient patch which took the place of the

---

[1] See pp. 117, 167.

[2] Audebert, fol. 267: archade de pierre Tyburtine, fort ancienne dont le dessus est seulement de brique. 'A very old arch of travertine, of which the upper part is only brick.'

[3] Parker's photograph, turned upside down, reveals a much reduced inscription on the third block from the top on the west side of the Gate. I read ░AR░. On the block below this and on the west skewback there are also traces of illegible letters. Cf. p. 196.

[4] See n. 1, p. 188.

top of the stone curtain. As for the causes [1] of the collapse, it is clear that the bed-planes of the voussoirs had far too slight a taper; and they could not be keyed in to the back of the Gate, because they were completely separated from it by the portcullis-slot. No doubt the stone curtain was finished originally with an ornamental string-course, as were all single-story stone curtains on the Wall; and this would be formed either by a stolen cyma, as at Porta Pinciana,[2] or by a string-mould specially cut for the purpose, as at Porta Appia.[3] It would run at the level of the lower string-course on the towers, and would mark the floor-level of the portcullis-chamber. The slots for the portcullis are not visible either in Parker's photograph or in Gell's engraving, but they are plainly shown by Vasi and in the Cadastro, when the medieval doors were set behind them. By Gell's time these had been replaced by newer doors set farther forward. Behind the portcullis the whole archway became wider, as at other surviving gates. The Cadastro and Rossini show that at some time or other the back arch had also fallen; but there is no reason to think that its fall was contemporary with that of the front or that either fall brought down the long voussoirs of the main vault. If so, the upper part of the curtain hardly could have stood; whereas the straight horizontal break, between its good brickwork and the worse filling, which takes the place of the stones, shows that it unquestionably did stand firm amid all these shocks.[4] This may seem incredible to those unfamiliar with the monolithic qualities of Roman brick-faced concrete, when it has set hard, but a glance at plate I will show that risks far greater than any involved here were taken freely during repairs, with perfect safety.

The period of this curtain is not to be determined by any evidence from the Gate, but the very precise comparative material for its form gives no uncertain testimony. All existing curtains like it go to the third period of construction in the Gates to which they belong and all are of a standard type.[5] It cannot therefore be doubted that, as Audebert [6] thought, the stone curtain of Porta Salaria belongs to the same epoch as these. This fits the evidence from Porta Latina, which is the largest single-arched Gate of the first period, and yet had at first no travertine curtain.

The brick-faced first floor is of still greater interest. Most of its facing is the same rather poor block-and-brickwork as occurs

---

[1] Compare the precautions taken against such a collapse at Porta Latina, p. 105.
[2] p. 166.   [3] p. 131.
[4] Cf. a smaller but analogous case of replacement at Castra Praetoria; *P. B. S. R.* x, p. 17, pl. vii B.   [5] See p. 257.
[6] *Fort ancienne* or *fort antique* are the adjectives applied as a standard to these curtains by Audebert, who thought them, however, Belisarian.

on the west tower of the Gate. But a large piece of very much better facing exists at the west end of its base, and contains, stretching almost half-way across the gate, one of those tile bonding-courses which are rare on the Wall after the first period and disappeared after the second. It is, for example, vastly superior to the brick-faced story above and contemporary with the stone single arch at Porta Ostiensis East,[1] which in turn is contemporary with the stonework of Porta Salaria. This suggests that, as at Porta Pinciana,[2] stone facing was inserted here in the lower part of an early brick curtain, of which the top was left untouched. Such a process has also been noted at Porta Appia, where the marble facing is inserted in the towers and it is theoretically a possible process, for the upper wall, left *in situ* while the alteration was being made, was built of practically monolithic Roman concrete, of which the downward stress is distributed very widely in suspension. Further, its feasibility here is amply proved by evidence quoted above, which shows that the whole upper half of the front arch fell out, and left a large portion of this identical curtain wall standing upon nothing until the repair was finished.

It may also be noted that a first-period date for the upper story seems demanded by the type of its windows. These are carefully built to match those of the towers exactly, which are of undoubted first-period type. Moreover, they are very exceptional windows for a Gate in Rome, being extra wide in themselves and separated by intervals much wider than those of any other such arcade on the Wall. But the fashion of great windows for low positions in gateways did not continue anywhere along the Wall, even in the second period of construction, when wide windows all along the Wall were made to disappear, except at a height where the normal projectile would have lost much of its power. It is therefore reasonable to think that the windows of Porta Salaria were built in the first period, when wide windows were the rule, and designed thus in order to harmonize with the semicircular bastions. The alternative explanation would be that the windows were built thus in later times either with a wish to archaize, or in stupid neglect of the better windows at other Gates. But this will not fit the evidence of the brick-facing with bonding-course, which once must have extended over the whole curtain; and on general grounds it would be folly to think that archaizers refitted the most vulnerable Gate in the City with out-of-date windows of a type that had been carefully removed from every Gate and tower and replaced by loop-holes or narrower closer-set windows of improved pattern. So it seems best to conclude that at Porta Salaria there existed, until 1871, the only

[1] Cf. pl. XI*a*. [2] See pp. 166–7.

upper story of a first-period curtain which had survived the extensive restorations through which the Gates have passed.

Certain minor questions about the arrangement of this earlier curtain remain to be noted, although all cannot be answered. Its depth was doubtless the same as that of the stone one, since this is shown by Lanciani [1] to be governed by the width of the Wall. The top would come not far above the windows, with breastwork and merlons protecting a walk. The vault supporting this walk did not reach as high as the wider-spanned vault of the towers, so the top of the curtain comes slightly lower than that of the towers, which would be crowned in turn with a flat embattled roof. It is not possible, however, to be sure about the form of the arch, or to know whether there was a portcullis. For while first-period posterns had travertine imposts and a flat arch, and the arches of the two-way curtain were round, these one-way curtains of brick-faced concrete are intermediate in type between the two. So it is impossible to know for certain which they followed, although there is strong support for the round arch in tradition.

Conclusions.   Such is the information now available about Porta Salaria. The Gate started as a one-way Gate, with twin semicircular towers,[2] ornamented exactly like those of Portae Nomentana and Latina, and obviously built to the same standard pattern.[3] Each had three large windows, and was covered with a vaulted concrete roof, which was flat on top and therefore no doubt crowned with merlons. So much is quite certain. And it may be regarded as extremely probable that the triple windows of the brick-faced curtain belong to this period also. The only important element whose form is obscure is the gateway arch.

At a later period in the history of the Gate two notable changes were made. The towers were heightened, and the lower part of the curtain was faced with travertine. Analogy for the heightening of the semicircular gate-towers suggest that this improvement belongs to the third period, as at Portae Pinciana and Ostiensis East. And there can be no doubt about the travertine curtain. This is certainly dated to the third period, when every single gate whose form can be analysed was treated in this way.

There is little light on subsequent periods. But an extensive refacing in block-and-brick work at no very late date should be noted, and this was followed by the collapse of the travertine arch as far back as the portcullis slot. The block-and-brick work is of the type associated elsewhere with Belisarius.[4]

---

[1] Lanciani, *F. U. R.* 3.
[2] Du Pérac's restoration of 1557 probably comes very near the truth.
[3] See p. 244.   [4] See p. 89.

§ 2. PORTA FLAMINIA

It must be admitted that the sacrifice of the marble towers of Porta Flaminia was demanded by the needs of modern traffic; it may be conceded that the remodelled Gate still remains one of the stateliest entrances to the Eternal City; yet few will fail to deplore the passing of the ancient Gate in 1877–9. This destruction is to be regretted particularly since no adequate account of the Gate was published either before or at the time of its demolition. Had archaeologists of fifty years ago been alive to the problems outlined below, it is highly probable that they could have solved them by a glance at the structures which were then swept away.

The outward aspect of the Gate, not long before its demolition, is preserved in a photograph by Parker (Pl. XIX*b*). The curtain was pierced by the existing central arch, designed by Vignola [1] for Pius IV in 1561–2, and it was flanked by two large quadrangular towers. The lower stories of these were ancient, and faced with marble blocks; the topmost stories and the attic of the curtain belonged to a later restoration by Bernini,[2] under Alexander VII, in 1655. When the quadrangular towers were demolished, in 1877, a semicircular tile-faced bastion was found inside each of them. Visconti's account [3] of the discovery is important enough to quote in full:

'La porta Flaminia ebbe anticamente due torri rotonde, di quella forma e

[1] See Pastor, *Geschichte der Päpste*, vii, 601–2. Audebert, fols. 269–70. For a plan of the Gate, see Rossini, pl. xxxiii.

[2] Muñoz, *Roma Barrocca*, p. 355.

[3] *B. C.*, vol. v, p. 210. 'The Porta Flaminia once had two round towers, of that shape and size which all the towers of gates on Aurelian's Wall reconstructed by Honorius once had. This circumstance, which completely cancels all doubt about the original position of that gate, was necessarily unknown to all those scholars who had dealt with the argument. But, on the demolition of the bastions of Sixtus IV, we found inside them the two towers mentioned below, which were scabbed from top to bottom in the way called 'button-holed', in order to bind and unite them with the new structure of the marble bastions. We only knew the inner right-hand tower when we wrote, on page 192 above, that it was of bad brickwork, which might be thought later than the fifth century. In the meantime the demolition of the other bastion was largely completed, and the other tower discovered therein, similar to its companion in shape and size, appeared built with much more regular work, and faced in yellow and red bricks, like those used for facing by Honorius in repairing the Wall of Aurelian. Its diameter, equal to those of other Honorian towers, measures seven and a half metres. The tower discovered first is to be considered as restored in later ages. In order to be satisfied that the construction of the said towers compares in detail with the Honorian towers, it suffices to compare it with that of those which still remain in the circuit of the Imperial walls. These may be attributed with certainty to the said Emperor, either because they are part of the structure of gates solemnly declared as his by the well-known inscription of Flavius Macrobius Longinianus, prefect of Rome, which stood on high, built therein; or because it corresponds to the construction of those deprived of the said inscription. In past time there were many such towers, but now they are reduced to very few. These are, those of Portae Latina and Pinciana, and the one remaining of Porta Nomentana, the other having been destroyed long ago in order to discover a sepulchral monument enclosed therein. And this last is, perhaps, the best of all for a comparison, being completely preserved in its original construction.'

grandezza, che nel recinto di Aureliano ebbero una volta tutte quante le torri delle porte rifatte da Onorio. Una tal circostanza, che toglie affato di mezzo qualunque dubbiezza circa la primitiva situazione di essa porta, restò necessariamente ignota a tutti quegli eruditi, che primi di noi aveano toccato sifatto argomento.[1] Ma caduti a terra i bastioni di Sisto IV, noi vi abbiamo trovato dentro le suddette due torri, le quali erano tagliate dall' alto a basso nel modo che dicono "ad asola", a cagione di collegarle et incorporarle colla nuova struttura dei marmorei bastioni. Noi conoscevamo soltanto la interna torre destra allorquando più sopra, alla pag. 192, abbiamo scritto, ch' essa era di cattiva opera laterizia, la quale potea credersi posteriore al secolo quinto. Ma compiutasi frattanto in gran parte la demolizione dell' altra bastione, l'altra torre quivi scoperta, simile alla compagna quanto alla forma ed alla grandezza, è comparsa edificata con opera molto più regolare, e rivestita di mattoni gialli e rossi quali furono quelli adoperati esternamente da Honorio nelle sue riparazioni del recinto aurelianèo. Il suo diametro, pari a quello delle altre onoriane, misura sette metri e mezzo. La torre scoperta prima è da credere che fosse stata ristaurata in epoca recente. Ad accertarsi che la costruzione di dette torri si raffronti a capello con quella delle torri di Onorio, basterà compararla con alcuna di queste che nel giro delle mura imperiali si conservano ancora: e che sicuramente attribuisconsi a detto imperatore, o perchè inerenti alla struttura delle porte dichiarate solennemente per sue dalla nota incrizione di Flavio Macrobio Longiniano, prefetto di Roma, che sull'alto delle medesime stava incastrata: ovvero perchè di struttura onninamente conforme a quelle minute della incrizione suddetta. Negli andati tempi ve ne avea parecchie di torri cosifatte, ma nel presente son ridotte a pochissime: cio sono, quelle della porta Latina, quelle della Pinciana, e l'unica superstite della Nomentana, essendo l'altra stata distrutta, è gia gran tempo, per iscuoprire un monumento sepolcrale che vi stava racchiuso: e quest' ultima è forse, per un confronto, la più idonea di tutte, essendosi per intero mantenuta nella sua cònstruzione originale.'

The discovery was one of great importance, but the description is inconsistent, for the following reasons. No semicircular tower with which an Honorian inscription could be connected has existed since 1838, and it may be seen to-day that there is no real similarity between the mass of brickwork in the semicircular towers cited. Again, no semicircular tower belongs to the age of Honorius. That at Porta Nomentana, claimed as 'per un confronto, la più idonea di tutte', is certainly Aurelianic.[2] So these observations provide no reason for supposing the newly discovered towers to be Honorian: as far as they go, they suggest them to be Aurelianic. Secondly, if the diameter of the towers was $7\frac{1}{2}$ metres, it was not the same as that of the other towers,[3] which is almost exactly eight metres. More regrettable are the omissions. No indication is given of the distance between the

---

[1] It is necessary to observe that Visconti refers to a theory that the Gate was nearer the Pincian Hill; based upon Procop. B. G. i. 23 ἐπεὶ ἐν χώρῳ κρημνώδει κειμένη οὐ λίαν ἐστὶν εὐπρόσοδος.

[2] See p. 97–8.   [3] See figs. 15, 17, 19, 20.

a. PORTA FLAMINIA, *c.* 1650, by Silvestre

b. PORTA FLAMINIA, BEFORE DEMOLITION OF THE TOWERS,
IN 1877–9 (Parker)

two towers. There is no hint of a fragment of early curtain preserved between the faces of the semicircular and quadrangular towers. It is not observed whether the footings of the two types of tower were on the same level, nor how far that level lay below the modern street, nor, indeed, whether those parts of the towers, which were below modern street-level, were demolished at all. Yet there is much that is useful in the account. It emerges that two tile-faced semicircular towers originally flanked the Gateway, each having a diameter of 7½ metres. Their surface had been scabbed, in order to unite it with the concrete of the later marble towers. The westernmost of the two was faced in worse style than the eastern. But Visconti's remarks about the bad quality of the brickwork cannot be taken seriously,[1] in view of the analysis of his pronouncements given above. Even in the second phase of construction on the Wall the deterioration in quality was very marked.[2] All that can be deduced from his remarks is that the westernmost tower had evidently been refaced before it was made to serve as the core of the marble structure.

The marble towers, too, present their own special problem, much discussed and recently reconsidered by Dr. Ashby.[3] The common belief about their date is based upon the following statement by Flaminio Vacca:[4]

'Mi ricordo, al tempo di Paolo III (1534-1550, I. A. R.) aver nella piazza di S. Maria del Papolo veduto un gran massiccio di selci assai alto da terra. Parve al detto papa ruinarlo, e fu spianato al pari della piazza. Accanto alla Porta del Popolo dalla banda di fuori vi sono due bastioni fatti modernamente di belli quadri di marmi gentili, quali sono tutti buccati all' usanza dei Goti, per rubarne le spranghe che così ne fanno fede gli altri edifici antichi; ed ho osservato, che buccavano tra un sasso, e l' altro, dove era la commessura, per essere quello il luogo della spranga, e così veniva buccato il marmo di sopra,

---

[1] Theoderic's tile, C. I. L. xv. i. 1665 b. no. 27=Visconti, B. C. v (1877), p. 224, no. 61, cannot decide the question, since it was 'trovato in opera o nelle torri antiche della Porta Flaminia o nella parte laterizia dei bastioni'. The failure to distinguish the two categories has lost us some valuable evidence.

[2] See p. 69.

[3] T. P. R., Dec. 1924, vol. ix. 2, pp. 76–9.

[4] Memorie di Flaminio Vacca, 1594=Fea, Memorie, pp. c–ci. 'I remember, in the time of Paul III, to have seen, in the square of S. Maria del Popolo, a great mass of blocks notably high above the ground. The said Pope decided the ruin it, and it was reduced to the level of the square. On each side of the Porta del Popolo, outside the town, there are two bastions, built in modern times of beautiful blocks of fair marble which are all bored in the manner of the Goths, to extract therefrom the clamps, as other ancient building witness. And I have noted that they bored between one block and another, at the joint, for that was the position of the clamp; and thus the upper block of marble and that below were bored, otherwise they could not extract it. But, in the said bastions, the said holes do not come opposite each other, a manifest sign that they are despoiled from other buildings. And Sixtus IV, a great builder, having built the church of S. Maria del Popolo, to the longer perpetuation of his memory, seeing that the church was attached to the said gate and might one day be devastated by some accident of war, built there the said bastions for its defence, using the said marbles, robbed from that great mass, which cannot be anything but a Mausoleum.'

e quella di sotto, altrimenti non la potevano cavare. Ora in detti bastioni dette bucche non affrontano. Dunque è segno manifesto che sono spoglie d'altri edifici; ed essendo Sisto IV, gran fabbricatore, edificata S. Maria del Popolo (1477, I. A. R.), accio più eternamente durasse la sua memoria, essendo la chiesa attaccata a detta porta, che un giorno per qualunque accidente di guerra poteva essere desolata, egli vi fabbricò detti bastioni per sua difesa con li detti marmi, de' quali spogliasse quel gran masso, che altro non poteva essere, che un Mausoleo.'

This seems a straightforward and circumstantial account, but there are reasons for doubting its fidelity. It had already been questioned by Ficoroni,[1] who observed levels in 1706, and made the following comment.

'Nell' anno 1706 fu fatta da alcuni una cava per trovar tesori a fianco del bastione sinistro della porta del Popolo, della parte, che riguarda il Tevere. I pezzi di marmo, che si vedono nel detto bastione, erano più di venti palmi sotto il piano moderno: segno evidente, dice il Ficoroni, non essere stato fabbricato da Sisto IV, come pensò il Vacca; ma forse da Belisario'.

Twenty palms are equal to 4·66 metres. It can now be added that the highest Roman street-level, that of Honorius, was found just behind the Gate, as recorded by Lanciani,[2] at 3·29 metres below the present street-level, which has changed very little since 1706, as is proved by engravings of the Gate showing the height of the road in relation to the pillars decorating the archway and to the steps of S. Maria del Popolo. It is therefore quite certain, if Ficoroni's statement is exact, that the bastions went 1·37 metres below the latest Roman level: and even supposing that, since the excavation was made on the side near the Tiber, there may have been an accumulation[3] of earth round the tower, reducing this figure, no accumulation of this kind will explain away 4·66 metres of earth. The fact adduced by Visconti, that there was a difference of 12 metres between modern and ancient road surfaces at the Meta, is quite irrelevant; for this was a Republican monument, lying at a much earlier and lower level than that of late-Imperial times. Ficoroni's observation, that Sixtus IV would be quite unlikely to lay his foundations so deep, if he built the towers, therefore remains valid, and is a penetrating criticism of Vacca's statement.

But there are two earlier sources than this, earlier even than Vacca, which have not been fully used in discussing the problem.

[1] Fea, *Misc.* 1, 168 = mem. 106, *R. Antica* (1741), p. 286. 'In 1706 some people made a hole to look for treasure on the side, facing the Tiber, of the left-hand bastion of Porta del Popolo. The blocks of marble, which are visible on the said bastion, were more than twenty palms below the modern level. A clear sign, says Ficoroni, that it was not built by Sixtus IV, as Vacca thought; but perhaps by Belisarius.'

[2] *F. U. R.* 1.

[3] Cf. Porta Appia, west side. But not reducing the figure to anything like zero, otherwise Ficoroni would have had to qualify his *piano moderno*.

The first is a sheet of sketches (Pl. XXII*b*) of the Gate by Van Heemskerck,[1] drawn not later than 1537—that is, sixty years after the supposed building of Sixtus IV, and nearly as long before Vacca wrote. These show from the east (side), and from the south (behind), a Gate provided with quadrangular stone towers in front, which were decorated with a large stone over-sailing course at the same height as that of the marble towers. This feature establishes their identity with those swept away in 1877. The upper stories were built on the same plan, and behind them were high rectangular towers, evidently containing upper-floor staircases, and meant to connect with external stairs in a rear court, or ward, which had disappeared by Van Heemskerck's time. The back of the curtain projected still farther towards the City, and had a stone arch much sunk in level. The state of the Gate is as interesting as its plan. The east staircase tower is derelict, with a tree growing in the topmost south-eastern corner. And this is a most important point, in relation to the date of the bastions. For, if the tower was new in 1477, such ruin cannot have come about by 1537. Or again, supposing the bastions only to be new and the staircase tower to be old, Sixtus IV cannot have built bastions and left the staircase towers behind them in such bad repair that they were ready to fall in on top of his new structures at any moment. From the implications of this fact there is no escape; and the more reliance may be placed on Van Heemskerck's work since he had no interest in falsifying the evidence, and gives the same decisive facts from two different points of view. His drawings form an independent testimony of the most valuable kind, and they should put Vacca's statement out of court.

The second source is Audebert's description[2] of the Gate,

---

[1] R. *Ved.*, taf. 2=Egger, *Krit. Verzeichniss* (1903), p. 29, fig. 7=Hülsen-Egger, *Das Skizzenbuch von Marten van Heemskerck*, (1913), vol. i, pl. 8, Text zum ersten Band, p. ix= Lanciani, *Destr. Anc. R.*, fig. 36. H. was working in Rome in 1534-6.

[2] Audebert, fols. 269, 270 ᵣ and v. 'Then begins another wall, less old, which is made in little blocks of stone, and finishes, at 100 paces, against the Porta del Popolo, which was once called Porta Flumentana, because it was near the Tiber bank, and subject to flood. Then it changed its position and name, being called Porta Flaminia, from the name of Flaminius the Consul, who laid out and paved Via Flaminia . . . Not long ago this gate had the form of a triumphal arch, in which form it was built, making use of the arch which existed on the spot. The latter arch belonged, according to common opinion, to the time of Belisarius, who, as we may note in view of what we had seen before, was very attentive in rebuilding the gates of the town of Rome. One may add, too, that the walls of the two sides of the gate, in contact therewith, were built by him, just as they are to-day, quite entire. Having been rebuilt later, then, the Gate is now a beautiful, lofty arch of travertine, decorated with four great rich columns of polished marble, two on each side outside the town. And above the gateway there is a great slab of marble, between two cornucopiae, on which is engraved this inscription: PIVS IIII PONT MAX PORTAM IN HANC AMPLITUDINEM EXTULIT VIAM FLAMINIAM STRAVIT ANNO III., which witnesses that the Gate ha been rebuilt by Pius. It took the name

written twenty years before Vacca's. The traveller approaches from the Muro Torto:

'Puis commence une aultre muraille moins antique, qui est faicte de pierre à petits carréz, et a 100 pas finist contre la Porta del Popolo, qui estoit jadis appellée Porta Flumentana, à cause qu'elle estoit proche du fleuve du Tybre, et subjecte aux débordements: laquelle depuis changea et de place et de nom, estant nommée Porta Flaminia du nom de Flaminius Consul, qui fit dresser et paver la via Flaminia ... Ceste porte estoit n'y pas longtemps en forme d'Arc Triomphal, sur lequel elle avoit esté bastye se servant de l'archade qui se trouva en ce lieu; qui fut, selon la commune opinion, du temps de Bélisare, que nous puvons remarquer par ce qu'avons veu cy-devant, avoir esté fort curieux de rebastir les portes de la ville de Rome: Joinct aussy que les murs des deux costéz de cette porte touchant à icelle ont esté par luy bastyz, tels qu'on les veoit encores aujourd'huy fort entiers.

'Ayant donc depuis esté rebastye, elle est maintenant d'une belle et haulte Archade de pierre Tyburtine, ornée de quatre grandes et riches colonnes de marbre poly, dont y en a deux de chacun costé par le dehors da la ville: Et audessus du portail y a une grande table de marbre entre deux cornes d'Abondance, où est graveé ceste inscription PIVS IIII PONT MAX | PORTAM IN HANC AMPLITUDINEM | EXTULIT | VIAM FLAMI-NIAM STRAVIT | ANNO III, qui tesmoigne que la porte a esté refaicte par le pape Pie IV. Et a pris le nom qu'elle a maintenant à cause d'une église qui est joignant icelle au dedans de la ville à costé gaulche en entrant, laquelle est appellée Santa Maria del Popolo.'

This is an extremely valuable check on Vacca's account. It gives a careful description of the Gate as designed by Vignola and some details about the arch of travertine, which he built from the spoils of an older one, clearly the same as that shown by Van Heemskerck at so low a level. The description of the towers is terse. For these must be meant by *les murs des deux costez de ceste porte touchant a icelle*; since *icelle*, as used by Audebert, always refers to the main subject of discussion, which in this context is *archade*. But the most noteworthy point is that Audebert, who habitually includes the minutest points in his description, had full opportunity, in mentioning both the Gate and the Church of S. Maria del Popolo, to introduce the story of Sixtus IV, the church, the Gate, and the Meta. The fact that he wrote nothing about it, even after having embodied in his account *la commune opinion* about the origin of the gateway arch, places Vacca's ascription of the quadrangular towers to Sixtus IV under the very gravest doubt.

After this, it is less surprising to learn that when these marble towers were demolished it was discovered that the great majority of the blocks came from early Imperial tombs [1] and not from the

which it now has, because of a church which joins it inside the town on the left as you go in, and is called S. Maria del Popolo.'

[1] *B. C.* v (1877), pls. xx–xxi: viii (1880), pls. xii–xiii: ix (1881), pls. vi–ix.

Meta, the source mentioned by Vacca. Visconti has used[1] the fact that a few blocks from the bastions were of 'Byzantine style' to corroborate Vacca, but, as Dr. Ashby[2] has noted, these can be considered just as well as patching. Indeed, as Dr. Ashby[3] observes, a certain case of precisely this kind of patching is provided by Fabretti,[4] who saw an inscription in the Orti Giustiniani sometime before 1702, which was found mutilated in the bastions in 1877; and no one has yet suggested that the bastions were built after 1700. Visconti also wished the tomb of the charioteer Gutta Calpurnianus, from which a fragmentary inscription[5] was copied for the Sylloge Einsiedlensis, to be considered as the source of the fine *quadrigae* reliefs[6] and a broken inscription,[7] mentioning race-horses (which, however, corresponds with no part of the Einsiedeln text), found inside the towers. He intended to prove by this fact that the towers could not have been built until after the Sylloge Einsiedlensis was compiled, about the ninth century. But no part of the inscription of the Sylloge was found in the towers; and since it was damaged when copied there is no difficulty in believing that, if the reliefs from the towers belong to the same tomb at all, they may have been robbed to build the Gate before the inscription was copied, thus accounting for the fragmentary state of the inscription when the pioneer epigrapher saw it. So the argument is not affected, even if the identification of the *quadrigae* reliefs with the tomb of Gutta is right. Again, as Dr. Ashby points out, it is odd, if Sixtus IV built the towers, that no inscription found in them, except that from the Orti Giustiniani, should have found its way into epigraphical records before the end of the fifteenth century. It may therefore be concluded that the inscriptions inside the towers do not prove them to be of Renaissance date, and they demonstrate quite decisively that the towers were not built with spoils from the Meta, the source specified by Vacca. In fact, analysis has now proved Vacca's whole statement to be worth nothing, and only the evidence of Van Heemskerck and Audebert remains, telling that until Vignola's time the Gate, though becoming increasingly ruined, remained substantially as it had been for centuries.

There are also other drawings which shed light upon the architectonics of the Gate, since they show approximately where alinements come. Valuable are those of Israel Silvestre[8] (Pl. XIX*a*)

---

[1] *B. C.* v (1877), p. 194: illustrations were never published.
[2] *T. P. R.*, Dec. 1924, p. 79. [3] loc. cit., p. 79, n. 4.
[4] Fabretti, *Inscr. Antiq. Explicatio*, 290, 222 = *B. C.* vi, p. 182 = *Not. Scav.* 1878, p. 84 = *C. I. L.* vi. 21657 = Ashby, loc. cit., see n. 5.
[5] *C. I. L.* vi. 10047 = Syll. Einsiedl. 53-5.
[6] *B. C.* ix (1881), pls. vi-vii.
[7] *C. I. L.* vi. 33954. [8] Ashby, loc. cit., pl. 12, figs. 12, 13.

(*c.* 1650), Jan Asselyn [1] (1610–52), and Johannes Lingelbach,[2] which show a small staircase-tower of early type behind the marble tower. This does not belong to the marble tower, and must be connected with Visconti's semicircular tower. This gives the approximate position of the semicircular tower, and also shows by its relation to the Wall-gallery that the rectangular bastions were not added until after the gallery had been built. The plan which can be reconstructed by their aid is, of course, only approximately accurate, but it shows how the elements fit together; and by its means it can be recognized with ease how the small and early Gate was hidden away inside the great quadrangular bastions. It should also be noted that these bastions stand in exactly the same relation to the later plan as that which will be suggested for Porta Praenestina.[3] The back windows of the small towers show that the early staircase arrangements were normal, while on Jan Asselyn's important drawing it can be seen that an extra flight of stairs was later added on the Wall, exactly as at Porta Ostiensis East.[4] So there are two stages, as at Porta Appia, before the addition of the quadrangular bastions.

Conclusions. At this point the evidence may be re-stated, with comparisons with other Gates. Every one after Visconti has agreed that the semicircular bastions of the earliest Porta Flaminia were of the same type as those of the earliest Portae [5] Appia, Ostiensis East, Latina and Nomentana. But some additional facts may be noted. The two early towers lay (fig. 33) immediately inside the inner face of the blockwork of the marble towers; and the space between them, 49 ft. 6 in. between the marble towers and something extra for the bastion walls, comes very close to the 53 ft. of Portae [6] Appia and Ostiensis East. It is therefore highly attractive to think that the curtain of the first Porta Flaminia was indeed the same as those which spanned the three other first class main roads into Rome, for Porta Portuensis [7] may be added here. Again, in view of the complete similarity between all the normal semicircular towers, it seems likely that those measured by Visconti were really of the same size as the others, as he says, and therefore had a diameter of eight metres, instead of seven and a half metres, which he gives: the '*taglio ad asola*' [8] would account for the discrepancy in measurement. The proved instances of standard planning, which occur elsewhere on the Wall, give great strength to these probabilities; but, even if there was no precise correspondence in size, there can be

---

[1] *R. Ved.* taf. 3.
[3] See p. 207.
[5] See figs. 15, 17, 19, 20.
[7] See pp. 200–5.

[2] *R. Ved.* taf. 4.
[4] See p. 119.
[6] See figs. 19, 20.
[8] *B. C.* v. (1877), p. 210.

no doubt whatever about the similarity of form. So the first Porta Flaminia may be restored with certainty as a two-way Gate of simple but not ungraceful form, flanked by well-proportioned semicircular bastions, fitted with the small staircases characteristic of the first period of construction at so many Gates.

The second phase involved a refacing of the western tower, but it seems that no change was made in its form, while the eastern tower apparently remained as before. This comes into line with

PORTA FLAMINIA
VANI/HED GATE

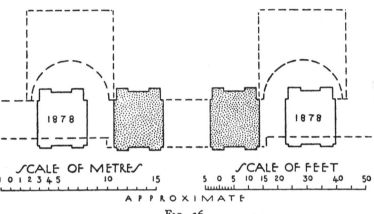

/CALE OF METRE/

1 0 1 2 3 4 5   10   15

/CALE OF FEET

5 0 5 10 15 20   30   40   50

APPROXIMATE

FIG. 36

repairs of the second period at many Gates,[1] when the walls of their towers were thickened internally in order to support a higher story. It is not comparable, however, with the second phase of construction at Porta Appia,[2] which was treated in a special way. Asselyn's drawing shows how the gallery was attached, just as at Porta Ostiensis East.

But the resemblance between Portae Appia and Flaminia again becomes striking in their third phase. This time both Gates received marble quadrangular towers, built from old tomb-blocks fitted together as well as might be. Parker's photograph and two beautiful engravings by Uggeri[3] show how strikingly close the similarity was, not merely in the uncommon material, but in the whole technique. For example, the same type of bosses appear thereon, with technical implications which have

[1] Cf. Portae Ostiensis East (fig. 19), Latina (fig. 17), Nomentana (fig. 15).

[2] See fig. 20.

[3] Uggeri (1828), vol. xxx, pl. x. These and all other constructional details are plagiarized by Rossini, *Vedute* (1829), pl. xxxiv.

already been discussed at length in the account of Porta Appia.[1] By now, too, as at Portae Appia and Ostiensis East, the double arch must have been removed, and replaced by the single opening set in the travertine curtain drawn by van Heemskerck. And there are also demanded the large staircase-towers, although this addition may have been made already in the second period, if the semicircular towers were heightened then. This gave to the Gate a plan of third-period type, precisely resembling that of Porta Appia. The resemblance between the two gates probably ceased in elevation at the fourth story, for Porta Flaminia had no round-fronted towers of the type that caused subsidence and repairs at Porta Appia. Accordingly, there may be restored on Porta Flaminia not the Appia's round top, which was quite abnormal and only existed there because of special circumstances, but a flat embattled roof, such as must have graced the very similar Porta Rhegii (Mevlevi Hane Kapou) at Constantinople, built in 412.

It is clear, then, that the Gates spanning Rome's two most important roads had on the whole a similar architectural history. This had been vaguely suspected by antiquaries of Ficoroni's school, and these suspicions, after a temporary eclipse following the discoveries of 1877–9, were thoroughly resuscitated by Dr. Ashby in 1924. At that time, however, the comparative material was not employed, and now the remarkable cross-correspondences, which comparisons provide, discredit Vacca's idle but much-repeated story, and restore to favour the earlier and more trustworthy evidence of Van Heemskerck and Audebert.

§ 3. PORTA PORTUENSIS

This little-known Gate passed out of use in 1643, when Urban VIII built entirely new fortifications for Trastevere, in anticipation of trouble from the North Italian coalition, which he had brought into being by his attack on Parma in 1642. It was, however, a Gate with twin arches, and it bore an inscription of Honorius,[2] arranged exactly as at Porta Tiburtina, in four long lines, with a widely separated S. P. Q. R. over the top. This is made certain by the copies of Pighi,[3] Audebert,[4] and Smetius,[5] which are better than the earlier uncritical versions derived from the Sylloge Signoriliana. As has been noted already, Pighi's copy (fig. 37) shows that the last line of the inscription was cut

---

[1] See p. 129.

[2] C. I. L. vi. 1188.

[3] Pighi, Preussische Staatsbibliothek, Lat. Cod. 61, fol. 118. Through the kindness of Dr. Guido von Kaschnitz-Weinberg of the Institutum Archaeologicum Germanicum of Rome I was able to secure a copy of this valuable drawing.

[4] Audebert, fol. 237.   [5] MS. Neap. 10. C. I. L. ad loc. cit.

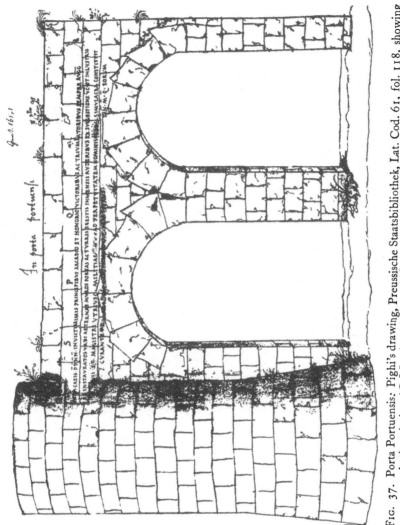

FIG. 37. Porta Portuensis: Pighi's drawing, Preussische Staatsbibliothek, Lat. Cod. 61, fol. 118, showing the inscription (*C.I.L.* vi. 1188). By courtesy of the Preussische Staatsbibliothek.

on the voussoirs of the arches in a manner which suggests that
it was an addition. The inscription was not carved on the second
story of the building, and is only placed there by Nardini[1] in
order to fill up space in his sketch. This is corroborated by
Maggi's tiny but accurate view of the Gate (fig. 38) in his
prospective plan[2] of Rome, which shows that in the sixteenth or
seventeenth century no upper story existed from which the inscription could have been copied. Both Maggi and Pighi are obviously
reproducing carefully the actual state of the Gate at the end of the
sixteenth century, and their testimony may be substituted for
Nardini's diagram as a basis of study without hesitation. Both
drawings agree completely about the form of the Gate. It had a
double entrance and semicircular towers; and the western arch
(not the eastern, as shown by Nibby) was blocked. This seems
to agree with Bufalini's tiny plan[3] (1551), which shows a longer
curtain wall on the west side of the Gate. The lower story
of the curtain was built completely in travertine, as Pighi's
drawing shows. But there is no evidence for the character of its
upper story. This may have been either brick-faced, like that of
Porta Ostiensis East, or entirely composed of travertine. It had
completely vanished by the time of Maggi and Pighi, and its
nature is not described by Audebert. The curtain was flanked
by two semicircular towers, of which the east was reduced to the
level of the top of the stone curtain by the time of Maggi and
Pighi, while the west was standing three stories higher, with some
parapets intact. Both towers had by then received a great battered
reinforcement round their base. Behind the Gate, amid a maze
of small houses (doubtless connected with levying the lucrative[4]
customs), Maggi shows the back wall of an embattled court.[5]
Further indications about the character of the Gate are to seek.
Its site is not in doubt, since the number[6] of towers between it
and the river is known, and the line of the City Wall and of the
road behind it was hit[7] during sewer-digging in 1892. The
intersection of these lines should mark the centre of the Gate.
In 1892 remains of a portico and other buildings were also
found,[8] across which the Wall must have passed very much in

---

[1] Nardini, *R. Antica*, ed. 1660, p. 36=Nibby's ed. p. 68.

[2] Dated *c.* 1625: published 1744. I owe this reproduction to the kindness of Dr. Ashby.

[3] Bufalini, *Urbis Icnografia*.

[4] See Tomasetti's remarks, *Via Portuense*, p. 10.

[5] Tempesta (1593) may be trying to indicate the same thing: but his viewpoint is not
chosen to suit an exposition of this gate, which is distorted badly.

[6] See Appendixes I & II; Jordan, however, is wrong in supposing (i, p. 371) that
these towers had anything like the normal interval. One was no doubt a gate-tower.

[7] Lanciani, *B. C.* 1892, p. 286–7; irrelevantly, the article is headed 'Porta Portuense di
Aureliano'.

[8] D. Marchetti, *N. Scav.* 1892, pp. 116–17.

the way shown on the *Forma Urbis*.[1] The plan of the Gate given on this survey is derived from Nolli's *Rione Ripa*, compiled in 1747. Lanciani's own notes on the Wall, which are now in the Vatican, and which, thanks to the kindness of Mgr. G. Mercati, I have examined in detail, do not indicate that he was

FIG. 38. Porta Portuensis, from Maggi's Prospect of Rome, *c.* 1625; by courtesy of Dr. Ashby.

in the possession of any special source of information, which confirmed Nolli's plan.

From the pictorial records, however, it is possible to fix the type of Gate in relation to structures elsewhere on the Wall. Clearly it was the double-arched type with semicircular bastions which decorated the three other important roads into Rome, the *Viae Appia, Flaminia* and *Ostiensis*. So in the earliest period of their existence the Gates of the North and South and the Harbour-Gates of Ostia and Portus conformed to a common type, specially reserved to distinguish the arterial roads through

[1] *F. U. R.* 39.

which pulsed the rich, full life of the Urbs Sacra. These had two-story travertine curtains and low semicircular towers of the standard dimensions common to all the early Gates. In the next phase, when the Wall was heightened, resemblance between them ceased.[1] Porta Appia was completely remodelled; and at one phase later still [2] Portae Appia and Flaminia received marble-faced rectangular bastions, while Porta Ostiensis East received an additional story and stone-casing of travertine, which followed the semicircular form of its towers. At Porta Portuensis the heightening of the towers certainly took place, but its date is uncertain. And it must also remain uncertain whether a stone facing ever strengthened the base of the towers, although it may be noted that it might easily have been concealed beneath the great battered bases given to both towers by medieval restorers. The precise nature of the work of Honorius, which is com-memorated here by the great inscription, is also uncertain. It cannot have been the blocking of the west arch (a creation of unsightly asymmetry with which no Emperor would wish to associate his name), nor can it have involved anything beyond slight repairs to the upper part of the tower, or the addition of a stone face to their base. It may be suggested, however, that the important operation of removing the upper part of the curtain, and erecting there a new portcullis-chamber, may have taken place at this time; for since the two other analogous Gates had first-period curtains built completely of stone, it may be regarded as certain the Porta Portuensis was originally so fitted. If Honorius, however, had left intact an upper story of stone he would have placed his inscription much higher up, as at Porta Tiburtina, between the arches and the arcade of windows. The architects who heightened the Wall in the second period are not likely to have removed the story, since they did nothing of the kind at the other Gates; so the work may well have been done by the Honorian builders, who would then have to squeeze in their commemorative inscription between the top of the archways and their new stringcourse, which marked the place where they had cut off the stonework and established the floor of their new portcullis chamber. This at least seems the simplest way to account for the awkward position of the Honorian inscrip-tion.

This is twilight; and darkness follows. It would be of great interest to know just when the west arch was blocked: but it is of at least equal importance to note that Porta Portuensis was the only Gate where a front double-arch seems to have lasted beyond the time of Honorius. Doubtless this was due to the

[1] See p. 254.
[2] Cf. Cassiodor. *Var.* vii. 9 (c. 500) *His primum faucibus Romanae deliciae sentiuntur.*

great economic value of Portus[1] in relation to the fifth-century traffic, and to the existence, on this side of the Tiber, of an extremely important tow-path, as valuable as a modern railway.[2] The secure strategic position of the Gate, which was safe from all invasions except those coming from the sea (and therefore escaped attack all through the Gothic sieges), must surely have been another factor that prompted the Honorian builders to retain the double arch. In fact, the blocking of the Gate is on the whole more likely to be associated with the decline of Portus after the sea-borne Saracenic invasions of 846, and with the contemporary precautions of Pope Leo IV at this very point,[3] than with any earlier events in the decline of Imperial Rome.

§ 4. PORTA PRAENESTINA-LABICANA

This twin gateway was built in front of the magnificent Claudian aqueduct arch[4] which carried *Aquae Claudia* and *Anio Novus* across *Viae Labicana* and *Praenestina*. It was removed by order of Pope Gregory XVI in 1838–9, and the only part pre-served was the upper story of the curtain of Porta Labicana, which carries the inscription[5] of Arcadius and Honorius. This was reassembled at the west side of the Gateway, where it still remains (fig. 39). The cause of the demolition was neither road-widening, as at Porta Flaminia, nor the unsafe condition of the antiquarian gateway, as at Porta Salaria, but desire to unmask the Claudian aqueduct-arch and to reveal the late Republican tomb of Eurysaces embodied in the Gate. The lack of photo-graphs of the Gate is hardly compensated by a very numerous series of pictorial records; engravings by Ricciardelli,[6] Rossini,[7] Sarti,[8] Gell,[9] Vasi,[10] Cassini,[11] Piranesi,[12] Dosio,[13] and Du Pérac;[14] drawings in the Cadastro of Pope Alexander VII (1555–67) and by Van Heemskerck[15] and Sangallo;[16] and a water-colour painted during the demolition by Marchese Giuseppe Melchiorri.[17] Nor did the excavations[18] of 1917 shed light on any problem except the important one of road levels.

---

[1] See the valuable chapter, Procop. *B. G.* i. 26. Ostia was now in decay, and the *Via Ostiensis* out of repair: cf. the brilliant study of G. Calza, *Mon. Ant.* xxvi, pp. 410–30, 'La decadenza di Ostia e la sua crise edilizia', in his article 'Gli scavi recenti nell' abitato di Ostia.'　　　　　　[2] See pp. 245, 248.　　　　　　[3] See p. 52.

[4] *C. I. L.* vi. 1256.　　　　　　[5] *C. I. L.* vi. 1189.

[6] Ricciardelli, pl. 5.　　　　　　[7] Rossini, pl. 9.

[8] Sarti, R. Calcografia, 1224: engraving in the possession of Dr. Ashby, see pl. XXI.

[9] Gell, pls. 14, 15.　　　　　　[10] Vasi, pl. 7.

[11] Cassini, pl. 54.　　　　　　[12] Piranesi, Hind, no. 119; Rome, 49.

[13] R. *Ved.*, 69.　　　　　　[14] Du Pérac, 25.

[15] Hülsen-Egger, *Das Skizzenbuch von Marten van H.*, ii. 40 b.

[16] Sangallo, 1549, Cod. Barb. fol. 5.

[17] *Estratti dall' Album*, anno V, p. 217, Roma, 1838, 'Intorno al monumento sepolcrale di Marco Vergilio Eurisace.'　　　　　　[18] Mariani, *B. C.* 1918, 193–217.

The name of the Gate used most frequently in the ancient literary sources was Porta Praenestina,[1] but the name Porta Maior Sessoriana appears in William of Malmesbury,[2] and Labicana in the *Mirabilia*.[3]   In the fifteenth century the Gate was also known[4] as Porta Dominae or della Donna, a name possibly suggested[5] by a representation of the Virgin Mary on the Gate.

The general aspect of the Claudian aqueduct-arch[6] and of

FIG. 39. Porta Labicana; inscription of Honorius (*C. I. L.* vi. 1189).

the defensive Gate which was to mask its front appear from Rossini's engraving (Pl. XX).   The Gate, as can be seen, had a small central tower, built round the tomb of Eurysaces.   And it was flanked by two tall quadrangular towers, which went right back to the aqueduct-arch, and considerably overlapped its outer edges (see below).   Between these towers ran two stone curtains, the east short, with four windows, the west longer, with five; and on the west, as Audebert noted,[7] was an inscription of Arcadius and Honorius,[8] described in detail above.   The curtains, like the towers, were orientated to suit the diverging roads[9]

[1] Procop. *B. G.* i. 18; *C. U. R.* p. 78: Einsiedeln List.
[2] *C. U. R.* p. 88: cf. *Lib. Pont.* Silvester, c. 27, Bd. i, 102. Vign. Sosoriana.
[3] *C. U. R.* p. 126.
[4] *Rer. Ital. Script.* xxiv, col. 981=*Diario di R.* 1407.
[5] Jordan, i[1], p. 357–8, note 29, rightly points out, however, that *Maior* need have nothing to do with S. Maria Maggiore in ordinary accounts of the Gate.
[6] I may note here, since it does not seem to have been pointed out before, that the original scheme was to build this rusticated arch *smooth* and highly decorated. This is shown by (1) unfinished architrave mouldings on both archways, front and back: (2) unfinished columns: (3) a leaf-pattern, incised ready for carving, upon the east archivolt moulding of the Praenestine archway.
[7] Audebert, fol. 254, 'l'inscription qui est au dessuz de la vouste bouschée'=*M. di R.*, p. 349.
[8] *C. I. L.* vi. 1189.
[9] If Strabo's statement (v. 3. 9) about *Viae Labicana* and *Praenestina* is correct, ἡ Λαβικανὴ ἀρχομένη μὲν ἀπὸ τῆς Ἠσκυλίνης πύλης, ἀφ' ἧς καὶ ἡ Πραινεστινή· ἐν ἀριστερᾷ δ' ἀφεῖσα καὶ ταύτην καὶ τὸ πεδίον τὸ Ἠσκυλῖνον, πρόεισι . . ., there may have been a gate called

which they spanned, and this accounts for the irregular plan of
the Gate.

The towers may now be considered in detail (fig. 40). The
great projection of the central tower is accounted for by the
position of the *panarium* tomb of Eurysaces, which offered a
tempting core to the builders of the tower, who accordingly
incorporated it, after demolishing its front. This tower was
semicircular, as was noted by all who described its demolition,

PORTA PRAENESTINA-LABICANA

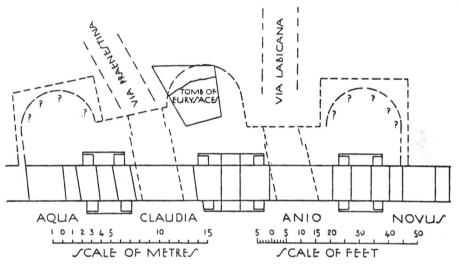

FIG. 40

and can be seen in the engravings of Vasi (1747) (fig. 41), Rossini
(1829), and Ricciardelli (1832). But in medieval times, as appears
from the Cadastro, its upper part had been replaced by a small
rectangular turret, perched high up on the ruins of the *panarium*,
whose front and sides were then almost completely disclosed;
hence it was possible to read most of the inscription [1] on the tomb
before the whole monument was uncovered in 1828.

The early date of the semicircular tower is attested by the fact
that almost the whole of the front [2] of the *panarium* was found to

Porta Esquilina in the customs-barrier of Augustan Rome close to Porta Praenestina.
This is preferable to the supposition that the roads diverged at the Servian Porta Esquilina
and rejoined each other before Porta Praenestina (see Ashby, *P. B. S. R.* i, p. 150): it is
also better than admitting the complicated guesswork embodied on the maps of Kiepert
(*Latium*) and Hülsen (*Forma Urbis Romae*, taf. 1).

[1] *C. I. L.* i. 1013, 1014, 1015.

[2] (1) Inscription, Canina-Jahn, *Ann. Inst.*, 1838, p. 226=Melchiorri, *Cenni intorno
al sep. di M. V. Eurisace*, p. 19=Grifi, *Bull. Inst.* 1838, pp. 143–44=*C. I. L.* vi. 1958.
(2) Statues, Grifi. (3) Cornice, volutes, Canina, *Mon. Aggiunti all' Opera di Desgodetz*, pp.
38–40=*Ann. Inst.* 1838, p. 226. One 'bread-roll' volute was found in the vault of Porta

have been embodied in its concrete. This must have been done by the first builders of any kind of defensive Gate here. For, firstly, even if it is supposed that the Aurelianic builders contented themselves with adding doors to the Claudian arch, they could not then have left the tomb standing and providing cover so near the Gate, but would have demolished it, just as they destroyed the tomb of Cornelia Vatiena at Porta Salaria.[1] Since, then, the tomb was in fact left standing, the tower built round it must belong to the first period in the Gate's history; for if the tower were later the tomb must either have been demolished, or must have been embodied in some earlier defensive structure, so that its complete front would not be available to form part of the concrete of a late tower. Finally, the Cadastro shows the semi-circular tower encased with blockwork built in rectangular form, which has nothing whatever to do with the medieval turret, and must therefore be contemporary, as is such blockwork elsewhere, with the stone curtains. The semicircular tower, therefore, certainly goes back to the first stage of the Gate's history, and it may be thought that when the Gate received stone curtains this tower also was encased in stone.

The west tower is shown by Vasi (fig. 41) considerably reduced, and its construction is described by Nibby as *cattiva costruzione* of the *epoca del secolo XIV*. This, however, proves no more than that it was much refaced. It is shown by Van Heemskerck [2] in an advanced stage of ruin; only its rear half was in existence, and the top of that was badly cracked and about to fall. For the tower, like the bastions of Portae [3] Appia and Flaminia, was divided into two parts, the rear for staircases and the front for defensive chambers, and owing to the difficulty of arranging stairs in connexion with the Claudian arch the staircase tower had to be set in front of the aqueduct. Since the aqueduct occupied the line of the Wall, this created an exceptionally prominent tower. Van Heemskerck's side-view also agrees with all the later illustrations in showing that the edge of this tower, like that of the east tower, came only a little way beyond the end of the Claudian arch; and this is decisively confirmed by the remains of the brick-faced upper walls of these towers which are still to be seen, bonded in to the upper part of the aqueduct filling; while photographs of the west tower exist which show traces of the stone facing of the lower story keyed into the aqueduct, and left when the tower was taken down. This contradicts Lanciani's plan [4] of the Gate, which carries each flanking

Praenestina (Canina, loc. cit., p. 38), but this was right at the top of the tomb and may easily have been lying about: it does not invalidate the general argument.
[1] See p. 185.   [2] Hülsen-Egger, *Das Skizzenbuch*, vol. ii, fol. 40 b.
[3] See pp. 123, 195.   [4] *F. U. R.* 32.

Fig. 41. Porta Praenestina-Labicana; engraved by Vasi, *c.* 1747.

tower as far as the first stone aqueduct pier beyond the Claudian arch. This plan, however, does not seem to be the result of direct observation. It is based upon that of the imaginative Canina,[1] who does not represent clearly, any more than Lanciani, the semicircular round tower the tomb of Eurysaces. Furthermore, there is a plan of 1829, by Rossini,[2] which shows almost the same arrangement as the engraving, although it is not quite accurate in dealing with the Labican Gate. So the contradiction is not a serious matter, and the unanimous tradition of the careful engravings may be accepted without demur. This gives a tower of quite normal width, provided with a stone-faced lower story, like those of Portae Appia and Tiburtina. The tower had not less than three open stories and a blind one at the base, and the first floor is shown by the Cadastro to have had three loop-holes in the front. The top of the tower thus reached to the top of the Claudian arch, and was no doubt flat and embattled, like that of the east tower. Its original appearance must therefore have had much in common with Portae Appia, Flaminia, or Tiburtina. The staircases inside it were, no doubt, arranged well in front of the pillars of the Claudian aqueduct, but little is known of their arrangement. It can be seen from Rossini, Nibby, Gell, Vasi and the Cadastro that at least three doorways were preserved until 1821.

The East tower was standing to full height until Vasi's time (1747), but by 1821 it had lost its parapet and merlons, and had been very thoroughly patched at the top. Vasi also shows a considerable patch half-way up the west side of the front and a large patch spreading westwards from the east corner. These, no doubt, are the repairs which mended some ominous cracks shown at those points in the Cadastro. Gell drew a very much patched surface. Vasi and the Cadastro show a large wall-shrine of the Madonna and Child, affixed to the front of the tower: perhaps this is connected with *Porta Dominae* or *Porta della Donna*, the name of the Gate in the fifteenth century, although another cause, as Jordan [3] notes, may be sought in the fact that the road inside the Gate led to S. Maria Maggiore, which may have prompted the erection of the wall-shrine. By Gell's time the old wall-shrine had been replaced by one of an elaborate type. A *necessarium* is shown by Vasi attached to the west parapet, but only the corbels of this remained in Rossini's day. The internal arrangements of the tower are unknown, but its similarity to the western tower in type, size, and plan no doubt implies that both towers were planned very much alike. Sparsely-scattered windows and loop-holes are shown in the Cadastro, but Rossini [4] shows two blocked

---

[1] Canina, *Edifici di R. iv*, pl. ccxxv=*Ann. Inst.* 1838, tav. i.   [2] Rossini, tav. xxxiii.
[3] Jordan, i¹, p. 357–8, n. 29.   [4] Rossini, tav. viii.

XX

PORTA PRAENESTINA-LABICANA BEFORE DEMOLITION IN 1838 (Rossini)

round-headed windows on the front at a slightly higher level than the curtain windows, a late square-headed window on the west side, and a round-headed one on the top story close to the aqueduct. The last may have been a staircase window. The Cadastro shows that the west side of the tower stood on a stone plinth, like that of the bastions of Porta Appia. As has already been noted, traces of the junction of its upper brick-faced wall with the aqueduct filling appear to the east of the Claudian arch.

The curtain of the Gate was arranged as follows. There was an upper curtain, formed by the top of the unused conduit of the Claudian arch, which was supplied with a low parapet all round and with merlons in front. The walk thus formed was level with the top of the towers, and may be considered as an upper fighting-platform. This feature follows entirely from the peculiarities of the site, and in permanent form is perhaps unique. But its advantages are well illustrated in the description by Hirtius [1] of a not dissimilar temporary erection:

'Haec (castra) imperat vallo pedum duodecim muniri, loriculam pro haec ratione eius altitudinis inaedificari, turris excitari crebras in altitudinem trium tabulatorum, pontibus traiectis constratisque coniungi, quorum frontes viminea loricula munirentur, ut ab hostibus . . . duplici propugnatorum ordine defenderentur: quorum alter ex pontibus quo tutior altitudine esset, hoc audacius longiusque permitteret tela, alter, qui proprior hostem in ipso vallo collocatus esset, ponte ab incidentibus telis tegeretur.'

The date of the arrangement at Porta Praenestina is almost certainly classical. Its merlons were badly ruined in 1536: and the classical builders, who must have fortified the aqueduct conduit to east and west, can hardly have failed to espy the obvious advantage of that at Porta Maggiore, especially since they allowed it to govern the height of their towers.

The main lower curtain served in two distinct Gates, divided by the central tower built on the *panarium*; and it was built in two distinct pieces, of which the eastern may be examined first, since it remained in use until the end, in 1838. This was all in travertine, and its front is well drawn by Gell; [2] it was rather narrow, and had a single arch and upper story, lighted by four windows provided with arcuate lintels. Whether there was a portcullis is unknown, but since one appears at the precisely similar Porta Tiburtina the existence of one here seems

---

[1] *de Bello Gallico*, viii. 9. 3. 'He orders the camp to be fortified with a rampart of twelve feet, and a breastwork to be built thereupon in proportion to its height; to erect frequent towers three stories high, joined with gangways with boarded floors and a front protected with an osier breastwork, in order that they might be protected from the enemy by a double row of defenders. One would be able to hurl its missiles all the more boldly and all the farther from the gangways according as its height rendered it safe; while the other, which was ranged nearer the enemy on the rampart itself, would be protected by the overhead gangway from falling missiles.' [2] *M. di R.* pl. xiv.

almost certain. The top of the curtain was decorated with an elaborate moulding, best shown by Rossini, and this in turn was probably surmounted, as at Portae Tiburtina and Latina, with a parapet and pointed merlons of stone. But, by the time of the Cadastro, parapet and merlons had disappeared, and the level of the curtain top had been raised by the addition of a badly-built embattled story, level with the top of the medieval central turret. By Vasi's time these merlons had been replaced; and another renewal, marked by the extremely ugly merlons of the early nineteenth century, had taken place when Gell engraved his illustrations. The whole turret and upper curtain-wall had also been roughly refaced with uncoursed tufa or *peperino*.

Behind the curtain-front the Gateway expanded, and continued without interruption to a point slightly beyond the rear of the Claudian arch. There was no courtyard between the Gates and the aqueduct as Lanciani suggests;[1] and to suit the arrangements of this Gateway the two main passages of the Claudian arch had been lined, to half height, with a stone-faced arched passage, whose flat top formed the floor of a chamber which reached from the back of the aqueduct-arch to the windows of the stone curtain, and was doubtless used as a portcullis chamber. For the rest of its height the Claudian arch was carefully lined with brick, which did not project beyond the end of the arch. All this is shown by the careful engraving (Pl. XXI) of the architect Antonio Sarti,[2] which seems to have been made while the demolition of the Gate was in progress in 1838; for Gell, in 1821, was able to see only the back of the stone arch. The brickwork at the higher level was masked by a stone back-wall of the upper chamber, which was added outside the brickwork on top of the projecting stone-filling, and reached right up to the top string of the lowest inscribed panel[3] on the aqueduct-arch. When Sarti made his record this, and the sheds behind the Labicana entrance, had already been removed. Originally this back-wall was crenellated like a tower, and it is a feature of respectable age. It appears in the views of Tempesta (1593) and Maggi, is missed out by Du Pérac[4] (1575) (who assumed that the east and west arches were treated alike), and then turns up again in the Cadastro (1655–67), where the artist, oddly enough, misses out the whole east bay of the aqueduct arch. What Du Pérac shows, presumably based on the west arch, is almost the same as Sarti's evidence, but he omits to give the horizontal break in construction between the stone and the brick-lining, and shows the end of the chamber filled up

[1] *F. U. R.* 32.   [2] Sarti, R. Calcografia, 1224.
[3] *C. I. L.* vi. 1256; Vespasian.
[4] Du Pérac, pl. 25. Mariani (*B. C.* 1918) may be right, however, in thinking that Du Pérac's work is guesswork.

with a wall. Whether this filling wall was part of the little tower, or an earlier construction contemporary with the stone arch below it, is not certain. The Cadastro shows it to be built of much better stone than the tower and as part of the stone arch: Gell records the reverse. Obviously, however, there must have been a wall of some kind there originally, otherwise the stone arch would not have projected. Rossini shows [1] three small windows in the west back: these had vanished by 1829. So it seems possible that the wall is not original, and that there were once three windows in the east room too.

Behind the aqueduct lay a court-yard, entered by one arch, out of the centre. This feature is not noted by Lanciani, but it is marked by Nolli (1748) on his valuable plan of Rome, is drawn by Cassini [2] (1779), and it forms the inset for Gell's view of the back of the Gate: it also appears on the prospective views of Tempesta (1593) and Maggi. All four authorities agree in showing that it was built to fit both Gates, and its single arch was no doubt set asymmetrically in order to span the junction of *Viae Praenestina* and *Labicana*, which lay just behind the Claudian arch. This suggests that the vantage-court existed before the closing of Porta Labicana; for, otherwise, the Gate would have been set immediately behind Porta Praenestina. Despite prolonged search, I have failed to find any description of this court belonging to an age when it was still [3] standing; and it would seem that topographers' descriptive powers usually became exhausted after they had dealt with the quantities of material in the main Gate and aqueduct arch. Even the reliable Audebert fails here. The reason why the court appears so rarely on the drawings of the Gate is that artists always took up a standpoint just inside it (and no doubt leant against it!) in order to draw the picturesque aqueduct-arch, or passed right through and drew the front of the Gate.

Between the east and west curtain-walls the whole of the space behind the tower on the *panarium* was filled up solid. This is shown by Nolli's plan (1748), and corroborated by the little water-colour frontispiece to Melchiorri's account of the discovery of the *panarium*, which shows the west curtain-wall half demolished and composed of stolen material, among which were inscriptions, not all from the *panarium*.[4] Whether the semicircular central tower ever had a staircase of its own, or was always reached from either of the side towers by way of the curtain, is not now to be ascertained: the chance to find out was missed in 1838.

[1] *R. Vedute*, 1822, vol. ii, plates unnumbered.
[2] This is the only detailed view of size: it agrees with Maggi's in showing only the arch itself of stone ; cf. Porta Ostiensis East (fig. 19) for the plan.
[3] It is noted, however, by Mariani (*B. C.* 1918, p. 198, note).
[4] *C. I. L.* vi. 1958=Canina, *Bull. Inst.* 1840, pp. 19–20=*C. I. L.* i. 1017–18.

The west curtain-wall of Porta Labicana is always less well shown in the views than the east, because it was blocked as early as 966,[1] and the tower which flanked it was out of commission long before Van Heemskerck's time (1536). The upper part of the Gate, with its five round-headed windows and its inscription of Arcadius and Honorius, is still preserved by the side of the road, although the ornamental moulding which formed its top was not replaced. Attention has already been drawn to the nature of the blocks of which it was composed. Above the stonework rose a further story, with two blocked square-headed windows, shown on the Cadastro; but this had disappeared by Vasi's time, when the structure was neatly trimmed. It was not fitted with parapets, nor did it ever receive the ugly refacing that appears on Gell's drawing of the east curtain. Behind the curtain the internal arrangements, as shown by Du Pérac (1621) and Sarti (1838), were apparently the same as those of the east curtain, but it is not clear how the Claudian archway was filled in at the back. Tempesta (1593) shows some rough tree-crowned blocking, and this is also shown by the Cadastro (1655–67). By Gell's time (1821) it had been removed, doubtless during the construction of some of the small private buildings which were beginning to cluster behind the disused arch as early as the time of the Cadastro, and which increased in number until the Gate was demolished.

Such then is Porta Praenestina-Labicana. It is one of the vanished Gates whose loss is most to be regretted both by the archaeologist and artist, and it is the irony of fate that antiquarian zeal should have swept it away. When excavations were made in 1917 no trace was noted of the ancient gate, and the only point established was about road-levels. The late-Republican level at the tomb of Eurysaces was 3·50 metres below the modern road, and the latest Roman road-level (*ultimo piano stradale*), thought by the excavators[2] to be certainly not later than Honorius, followed at 1·50 metres below the same *datum* line. The fact, then, that the rise between the time of Augustus and Honorius was only two metres effectively disposes of Lanciani's fiction,[3] that between the time of Aurelian and Honorius the level rose 3·50 metres. Here again, in fact, as at Portae[4] Ostiensis and Tiburtina, Lanciani took the Augustan level as equivalent to that of Aurelian's day, and the modern to that of Honorius.

---

[1] Tomasetti, *Vie Labicana e Prenestina*, p. 16, quotes *Reg. Subl.*, pp. 166–7, 'portam quae nunc aperta est: viam quae exiit a porta quae est clausa.' What Jordan means (i[1], p. 357) by 'Die Labicana trägt *noch jetzt* die Ehreninschrift des Honorius und Arcadius: sie ist jetzt offen, die Praenestina geschlossen, früher war es umgekehrt,' I do not understand, unless this was some temporary Customs arrangement.

[2] Mariani, *B. C.* 1918, p. 198.

[3] *B. C.* 1892, p. 111.   [4] See pp. 176–7, 220.

Conclusions. The development of the Gate now may be considered. This is a particularly valuable gate, since the west curtain is inscribed in the name of Honorius.[1] The east one, of exactly the same type, must belong to the same reconstruction, although it never received an inscription, for reasons considered in detail elsewhere.[2] Honorius, then, fitted the gate with completely new stone curtains. Presumably brick-faced curtains existed there before, as at Porta Latina,[3] for, otherwise, there would have been no need to rebuild entirely in stone. With the stone fronts were indissolubly connected both the stone facing of the semicircular tower and also the large chambers built within the Claudian archways, which must be connected with the working of a portcullis, as on the other Honorian gates. The brick lining of the upper story, however, may suggest, though it certainly does not prove, that a similar scheme in brick had been evolved at an earlier date, of which the lower remains might easily be hidden by the lower arch. For why should Honorius, who was building completely in stone, and gave a stone front and stone back to this upper story, have chosen to line these stories with brick sides?

With the stone curtains, as at all other Gates,[4] no doubt also went the two large quadrangular towers, with their solid bases matching the central stone-faced tower built round the semicircular tower. Their elaborate staircases must have emerged through the arcades of the Claudian arch, which are shown open by the Cadastro and Cassini; for there is no trace of any staircase entrance emerging inside the gateway passage, and these are the only ways through to the back of the Claudian arch. Probably, too, as at Portae[5] Appia, Ostiensis, Latina, and Tiburtina, the staircases of this age emerged at a high level on the wall of the rear court, through the very top of the Claudian arcades. These, then, are the arrangements which facts and analogies suggest for the Porta Praenestina of Honorius, a Gate with a great stone-faced front and three quadrangular towers.

Of the earlier stages in the Gate's development there are few traces. But it has been seen the central tower had a semicircular form in the first phase of the Gate's history, a conclusion that facts about semicircular towers elsewhere on the Wall amply confirm.[6] So it becomes clear that the first constructors of a Gate at the Claudian arch did not confine themselves to closing that arch with doors but built a large gate with a semicircular central tower, using for its core the tomb of Eurysaces. This granted, it

---

[1] *C. I. L.* vi. 1189.
[2] See p. 34.
[3] See p. 106.
[4] See pp. 102, 115, 128, 173, 199.
[5] See figs. 20, 19, 17, 33.
[6] See p. 245.

becomes necessary to suppose that there existed earlier curtains which Honorius replaced, or incorporated in his structure, and these cannot have been of travertine since we still have the whole width of the Labicana curtain and that incorporates nothing. This implies that the earlier work was in brick-faced concrete, and so an early brick-faced Gate begins to emerge.

Had the earliest gate semicircular side towers, matching that in the centre? This is a question which cannot be answered for certain, but analogies[1] from Portae Appia, Latina, and Flaminia, coupled with the fact that the central bastion at this very Gate received a quadrangular stone casing when the stone curtains and side towers were built, form the strongest presumptive evidence for supposing that such bastions were here encased by the great stone flanking towers. Again, such a hypothesis would admirably explain two peculiarities in the planning of the stone towers. Firstly, why did their builders choose to attach their stonework to the brick aqueduct arches (in which they had to cut special beds for the stones) rather than to the ends of the stone-built Claudian arch, which was only two feet (a wall's width) away, and which would have given them a far better joint? No builder beginning *de novo* would have neglected this opportunity of securing a really good bond. Secondly, why did they plan their towers asymmetrically, when their whole plan depended upon the staircases going out through the pierced centres of the Claudian arch piers? If it is postulated, however, that semicircular bastions, planned in precise relation to the ends of the Claudian arch, existed already and were now to be enclosed in stone, these peculiarities are explained at once. For in both cases the edge of the stone bastions would not then be governed by the Claudian arch, but by earlier towers. The case for assuming that there were three standard early semicircular bastions at Porta Prae-nestina is therefore worth attention. And it remains to observe that little importance attaches to the fact that such towers were not noted when the demolition took place: men were no less apt to miss what they were not seeking in 1838 than nowadays.

The later stages of the Gate's history are quite obscure. But it seems likely that the west entrance, of Via Labicana, was closed not very long after Honorius' day. It was shut by A.D. 966, and its great flanking tower was in complete ruin by 1536, and must have been out of commission for most of the Middle Ages. An adequate occasion for the blocking of one Gate would be the Gothic siege, when Belisarius temporarily blocked Porta Fla-minia.[2] By this time also one entrance would amply suffice for the need of normal traffic. Nor is it clear at what epoch the central rectangular tower was replaced by the medieval turret. The Gate,

[1] See figs. 20, 17, 36.   [2] Procop. *B. G.* i. 19.

XXI

PORTA PRAENESTINA-LABICANA BEFORE THE ISOLATION OF THE AQUEDUCT-ARCH

A view of the rear of the gate, by Antonio Sarti, 1820–38

therefore, is chiefly valuable, like Porta Tiburtina, for the fact
that its stone facing is dated by an inscription to Honorius.

§ 5. PORTA ARDEATINA,[1] (? LAURENTINA)

This Gate disappeared in 1534, when the Bastione di Sangallo
was built for Paul III. All that is known about it has been
summarized by Hülsen,[2] who discovered in Florence[3] a sketch-
plan of the Gate and its surroundings, drawn by Sangallo while
preparing to build the Bastione (fig. 42). The Gate lay in the
second curtain absorbed by the west end of the bastion, that is,
between the twelfth and thirteenth towers west of Porta Appia.
It should be noted that the width of the Gate is not clearly given,
but the length of the curtain in which it lay is given as 132 *passi*
as compared with lengths of 118, 125, and 127 *passi* to the east
of it, and the Gate may, therefore, well have been included in
this length; at all events it is not likely to have been wide. Its
form and relation to the Wall are not very clear from the rough
drawing; either it lay just to one side of a salient angle, as did
Porta Ostiensis West, or it cut through a straight curtain, when
it would have resembled Porta Metrobia and the earliest Porta
Asinaria. The actual Gate no doubt had travertine jambs, projecting as shown, and must have looked very like the postern
south of Porta Tiburtina. In fact, this is one more instance of a
Gate set between two normally placed Wall-towers, which seems
to have been the standard arrangement on the Wall for Gates of
third-class main roads. And it should be noted here that, although
the angles cannot be worked out adequately from Sangallo's *data*,
the Wall changed direction steadily from the east, in order to
let *Via Ardeatina* pass through it at a suitable angle, a point
appreciated neither by Rauscher[4] nor by Lanciani.[5] If the
bird's-eye view by Kartarius,[6] which shows the Bastione finished
and the Wall half demolished, is accurate, the Wall turned
through a considerable angle here. At an early but unknown
date in its history the Gate was blocked; it is not mentioned in
the Einsiedeln List, and it was closed when Poggio Bracciolini
made his examination of the Walls in 1431.

Poggio[7] records that he saw on this Gate an inscription of

---

[1] In connexion with this name it should be noted that Ashby (*Topog. Dict. s. v. Via
Ardeatina*) considers it a matter of doubt whether this road was called *Via Ardeatina* at all.
Via Laurentina vetus is as least as probable, for *Via Laurentina nova* branches from *Via
Ostiensis* near the *bivio di Tre Fontane*, just as *Via Ardeatina* branches from *Via Appia*.
Via Laurentina vetus* must therefore come in between.
[2] R. *Mittheil*, 1894, pp. 320–7.
[3] Uff. 1517 = R. *Mittheil*, 1894, p. 326, line-block = Rocchi, *Piante*, pl. xxxii.
[4] R. *Mittheil*, loc. cit.: Rauscher was responsible for the drawing.
[5] F. U. R. 45, 46.   [6] *Novissimae U. R. Accuratissima Descr.* = Rocchi, *Piante*, pl. xvi *bis*.
[7] *De Varietate Fortunae* = C. U. R., p. 242.

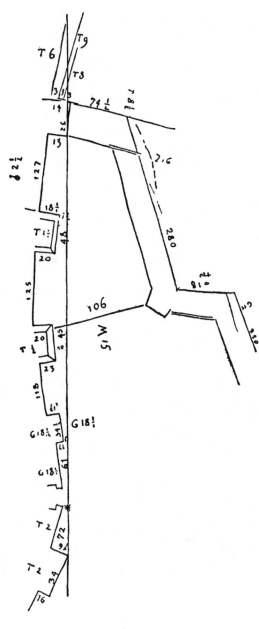

FIG. 42. Porta Ardeatina (Laurentina ?); Sangallo's plan, *c.* 1534. (Reproduced from Hülsen, *Mittheil. d. K.D. Arch Inst., Röm. Abt.,* ix, p. 326).

Arcadius and Honorius. This, as Hülsen has observed,[1] is highly improbable. In the first place, if the inscription continued to exist until 1431, it should have been copied by other antiquaries than Poggio. Secondly, Poggio is certainly wrong in his similar statement about Porta Ostiensis. Lastly, the time during which these inscriptions were set up has been shown to be so short that no more inscriptions than have survived are likely to have existed.

§ 6. PORTA OSTIENSIS WEST

This Gate was demolished in 1888, in connexion with an abortive scheme for straightening Via della Marmorata. Lanciani saw [2] and measured it while the demolition was in progress, and soon afterwards produced a general plan. This was inaccurate, and was tacitly corrected by him in his *Forma Urbis Romae*,[3] in accordance with a detailed measured drawing preserved among his notes in the Vatican Library.[4] From these measurements a drawing (fig. 43) has been prepared to the scale used throughout this book; and it agrees in every particular with the details described by Lanciani in the text [5] attached to his original but less reliable plan. 'Essa (cioè, la porta, I. A. R.) misura 3·60 m. di luce, ed ha le spalle murate con massi di travertino, grossi metri 0·67. I battenti della porta sono formati da cornici intagliate, poste verticalmente: la soglia monolite di travertino è lunga oltre a 4 m., e si trova nell' istesso piano della piramide.' So Porta Ostiensis West was a small postern, spanning the old and important road from the Porta Trigemina, and serving the needs of traffic from the adjacent warehouses (*Horrea Galbana*) on the Tiber bank. In appearance the little Gate must have closely resembled the postern south of Porta Tiburtina, but there was one notable difference. The Gate itself was recessed and the architraves were moulded.[6] This must have given it a pleasantly rich appearance from outside, but since the other Gates of this type are all blocked up flush with the face of the Wall it is unascertainable whether they were similarly treated or whether this was a special feature.

[1] *R. Mittheil*, 1894, p. 326; cf. also *C. I. L.* vi. 31257=1188. In a private letter to me Hülsen reiterated this opinion; he also adds that Poggio quotes no Gate-inscription in his own collection of inscriptions (*C. I. L.* vi, 1, pp. xxviii–xl).

[2] *Mon. Ant.* i. (1889), p. 513: fig. 9, pp. 511–12.

[3] *F. U. R.* 44.

[4] I was able to consult these by the kindness of Mgr. G. Mercati, *Prefetto della Biblioteca Vaticana Apostolica.*

[5] 'The opening measures 3·60 metres wide, and the sides are walled in travertine blocks, 0·67 m. in size. The doorposts are made of cornices cut down and set on end. The monolithic travertine threshold is over four metres long, and lies at the same level as the Pyramid.' *Mon. Ant.* i, p. 513.

[6] Cf. Πύλη τοῦ πέμπτου, Constantinople.

Whether these architraves were in fact bed-moulds stolen from cornices, as Lanciani suggests, does not, of course, affect their rich aesthetic value in their new position.

There is also evidence for the date when the Gate was closed. In another source[1] Lanciani observes that the Gate was found blocked by a wall more than two metres thick, built with a mixture of Hadrianic tiles, and of large tiles stamped OF·S·OF·DOM· DECEMB. The last stamp[2] dates to A. D. 307+, and gives the

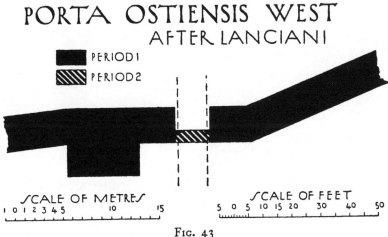

FIG. 43

terminus post quem for the blocking of the gate, assigning it to the time of Maxentius,[3] and certainly not to that of Honorius, as Lanciani assumed.[4] The early blocking is not at all surprising, for Maxentius had to deal with two sieges of the City, and it will be seen that he was certainly responsible for much more work on the Wall than this.

Some points may also be added about levels at this road junction. Firstly, the footings of the curtain in which Porta Ostiensis stands do not go down to the level of the base of the pyramid. This disproves Lanciani's statement[5] that the level of the pyramid base was the same as the threshold of the Gate. In fact, the threshold must have lain at least half a metre above it, as is suggested by *data* in the Cimiterio degli accattolici, where the road that passes through the Gate is recorded upon an inscription of 1824, *in situ*, to be *tribus circiter palmis* (0·699 m.) *platea lapidis tiburtini quae puramidem ambit altior*. Secondly, the level at Porta Ostiensis East was even higher. The road con-

[1] *B. C.* 1892, p. 93.   [2] *C. I. L.* xv. 502, 1315 a, 1578 a, 6.
[3] See my observations in *P. B. S. R.* x, p. 21.
[4] *Mon. Ant.* i, p. 513.
[5] Illustrated by a completely false diagram, *Destr. Anc. Rome*, p. 54. Cf. *B. C.* xx, p. 111.

necting the two Gates behind the Wall was found 2·31 m. below the modern tramway line. Since, then, the tramway lies 4 metres above the base of the pyramid this is a rise from 0·699 to 1·69 (i.e. 4·00—2·31) metres. And it involves the assumption that the Porta Trigemina road, which was about to meet the road passing through Porta Ostiensis East just outside the Wall, must have been rising too. Lanciani, on the other hand, has produced a widely known diagram of levels at Porta Ostiensis East, which assumes that while the Aurelianic level coincided with the Augustan, the Honorian corresponded to that of to-day. Why he should have thought so is difficult to imagine, and the view, as has been demonstrated, is quite certainly mistaken. The fore-going statement was written in 1927. Two years later, excavations at Porta Ostiensis East proved that the original level there was about one metre below the modern tramway line. The rise in the road therefore continued quite steadily, as had been surmised.

§ 7. PORTA AURELIA-PANCRAZIANA

This Gate was destroyed by Urban VIII in 1644 in connexion with the same rebuilding as Porta Portese; and when the seventeenth-century Gate was destroyed by the French [1] in 1849, Pius IX built the present uninteresting arch in its place. Pope Urban's Gate was built a few yards in front of the older Gate— it may be suspected that the old one was not removed until the new one was ready—and no large drawing was made of the old Gate before it disappeared. Bufalini (1551), however, shows that it had quadrangular towers, and this is confirmed by Tempesta (1593), and by the excellently clear view (fig. 44) of Maggi (1625), who, however, does not show the undoubted straight extension which the Wall made northwards beyond the Gate before it turned eastwards to descend the hill towards Pons Aurelius. The archway was single and built in stone, and Aude-bert's description thereof [2] is notable.

'Ceste porte a deux portaux en archade dont le premier estant du costé de dedans est tout de brique, et bastye par le pape Paule 3, comme se voit par les armes qui y sont eslevées et ses mots gravéz soubz icelles: P A P A P A V L O I I I . . L'aultre portail de dehors est fort antique, basty de grosse pierre de taille: joignant lequel il y a plusieurs vieilles inscriptions qui pour

---

[1] An engraving showing the damage is published by Lanciani, R. and E., fig. 36, p. 87.
[2] Audebert, fol. 237 v. 'This gate has two portals, of which the first, inside, is all brick and was built by Paul III, as may be seen by the arms engraved thereupon and the inscription beneath them P A P A P A V L O I I I: the other, outer, portal is very old, built with large dressed stones, adjoining which are several old inscriptions, which are so worn and defaced by age and time, that one can only read part of them, and even then with extreme difficulty.'

leur ancieneté sont tellement minées et effacées par le temps, qu'il ne s'en peult lire qu'une partye et encores bien malaisement.'

Unfortunately, Audebert does not give the text of what he thought he could read, but the whole account of these inscriptions is strongly reminiscent of the curtains built with half-effaced inscribed blocks from tombstones, which occur at Portae [1] Labi-

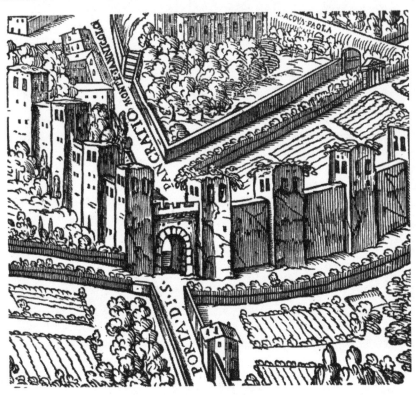

FIG. 44. Porta Aurelia-Pancraziana; from Maggi's Prospect of Rome, *c.* 1625. (By courtesy of Dr. Ashby).

cana, Appia, Pinciana, and Salaria. Evidently, too, the Gate had an inner court, which, in view of the facts from the other Gates, is perhaps more likely to have been rebuilt by Paul III than built by him as an entirely new structure.[2] The front gate would appear to have been of the type common in the third phase of construction, with a stone curtain and square towers. There is no reason to think that it ever had more than one arch, since Via Aurelia was not a road of first-class importance.

---

[1] See pp. 32, 130, 166, 187 n. 3.
[2] Procop. *B. G.* i. 28, refers to a double gate, ἐκτὸς δὲ πυλῶν Παγκρατιανῶν, αἱ ὑπὲρ Τίβεριν ποταμόν εἰσι.

The name of the Gate was Porta Aurelia, but Procopius [1] calls it Porta Sancti Pancratii, Porta Pancraziana, and 'the Gate [2] beyond the river Tiber'; and on the second occasion when he uses the last title, he does not distinguish the Gate from any other Gate across the Tiber. The name Aurelia is derived from *Via Aurelia vetus*, and appears in the Einsiedeln List; it is also used by William of Malmesbury.[3] There can be little doubt about the name's antiquity, and Procopius probably avoided using it simply in order that his readers, in Byzantium, might not confuse it with Porta Aurelia-Sancti Petri. No doubt the old name continued in Rome, and it may, indeed, have been revived when Porta Sancti Petri completely replaced Porta Aurelia as the name for the Gate at Pons Aelius.

§ 8. PORTA SEPTIMIANA

This Gate was entirely rebuilt [4] by Pope Alexander VI in 1498, as is established by the following statement of Fulvius [5] (1527). Portam vetustate iam collabentem Alexander VI nuperrime a fundamentis instauravit et in meliorem formam redegit, ubi Septimii antea legebatur inscriptio. The statement is confirmed by Audebert [6] (1575): ceste porte n'est point l'antien bastiment mais est bien en la mesme place, ayant esté toute refaicte de nouveau par le pape Alexander 6, en forme d'archade de pierre quarrée, aussi qu'on le veoit à present. Et au lieu de l'inscription de Septimius, cestecy y est maintenant, ALEXANDER VI, PON. MAX. OB UTILITATEM PUBLICAM CURIAE P.Q.R. A FUNDAMENTIS RESTITUIT. No big view of the older Gate exists, and it does not occur in the Einsiedeln List.[7] *Portam*

---

[1] Procop. *B. G.* i. 18 ἣ ὑπὲρ ποταμὸν Τίβεριν ἐστι Παγκρατίου ἀνδρὸς ἁγίου ἐπώνυμος οὖσα: i. 23 τὴν ὑπὲρ ποταμὸν Τίβεριν, ἣ Παγκρατιανὴ καλεῖται: i. 19 τὴν ὑπὲρ τὸν ποταμὸν Τίβεριν.

[2] If this is a translation of Transtiberina, as Nibby (*M. di R.* p. 381) and Comparetti (Ed. vol. 1, p. 141) think, and not a locality-qualification supplied specially by Procopius, it may be that before Porta Aurelia was called Pancraziana, it was called P. A. Transtiberina, Porta Aurelia Sancti Petri being, by implication, P. A. Cistiberina.

[3] *C. U. R.* p. 88.

[4] The form of Alexander's gate does not suggest that it replaced anything large, but rather something of the third class in a wall-curtain: cf. Lanciani, *F. U. R.* 27 and Bufalini, *Urbis Icnografia*, 1551. B. was just in time to record a normal wall-tower just west of the opening which had been incorporated in houses by Tempesta's day.

[5] Fulvius (ed. 1545), p. 45. It is odd that no transcription exists: did Fulvius mean *quondam* when he wrote *antea*? 'Alexander VI recently restored the gate, already in ruin with age, from its foundations and gave it a better appearance. Here could be read before the inscription of Septimius.' See Pinardo, *U. R. Descr.* (1555)=Rocchi, *Piante*, pl. iv.

[6] Audebert, fol. 236. 'This gate is not the ancient building, but is in precisely the same place, having been rebuilt anew by Alexander VI, in the form of an arch of squared stone, as is now to be seen. And in place of the inscription of Septimius, this one is there now, ALEXANDER VI, PON. MAX. OB UTILITATEM PUBLICAM CURIAE P.Q.R. A FUNDAMENTIS RESTITUIT.'

[7] Jordan, i¹, p. 373, wishes to argue that this proves a medieval date. This is in order

Septimianam, however, is mentioned in a Papal Confirmation of 1123 in the passage *S. Iohannis prope portam, S. Silvestri iuxta portam Septimianam*: and the church of S. John was still called *ecclesia Sci. Iohannis de porta* in 1492.[1]

In the ordinary medieval sources for Roman topography the name is badly corrupted. When it occurs in the twelfth-century *Descriptio plenaria*,[2] and in the thirteenth-century *Graphia Aureae Urbis Romae*,[3] it has taken the odd form '*septem naides iuncte Iano*', destined to give rise to some ingenious legends. The fourteenth-century *Mirabilia*[4] invents a new story, '*porta Septimiana, ubi septem laudes fuerunt factae Octaviano*'; here the last clause is obviously a new reading of *Septem naides iūcte iano*, i.e. *septem laudes octaviano*. The fable thus started is further embellished by Anonymus Magliabecchianus[5] early in the next century, '*Septignana adhuc porta est: quae per Octavianum denominata fuit Septignana, quando voluit visitare templum in monte Ianiculo, reverentia Iani, quia septem vices genuflexit antequam veniret ad templum illud: et ideo septem Iano laudes datae sunt per Octavianum.*' So far was it possible to wander from the original *septem naides iuncte iano*. What then was the real sense of the original? Evidently, *Septem naides* arises from *Septimiana*. The last half, then, must embody some gloss,[6] as Urlichs points out; and it may now be suggested, on the basis of the list of 1123, *S. Iohannis prope portam, S. Silvestri iuxta portam Septimianam*, that the gloss read something like *iuxta sc̄m̄io* (i.e. *iuxta sanctum Iohannem*), which would be mistaken as easily for *iucteiano* as was *septimiana* for *septem naides*. This explanation of the name is more convincing, if also more prosaic, than the amours of Janus.

Why, however, was the Gate called Septimiana? The reason for this is somehow embodied in an extract from 'Spartian's' life[7]

to bolster up his own view about the high antiquity of the Einsiedeln List, a view which becomes harder to maintain at every omission admitted.

[1] 1123, Cod. Vat. 8951, fol. 26: *C. U. R.* p. 172. All=Hülsen, *Le Chiese di Roma nel medio evo*, p. 275.

[2] *C. U. R.* p. 92.   [3] *C. U. R.* p. 115.

[4] *C. U. R.* p. 126.

[5] *C. U. R.* p. 149. 'Porta Septignana still exists. It was called Septignana because of Octavian Augustus, when he wished to visit the temple on Mons Janiculus, out of reverence to Janus; for he genuflected seven times in succession before he came to the temple. Thus seven praises were given to Janus by Octavian.'

[6] Urlichs, *C. U. R.* p. 92, note 15. Jordan, on the other hand (ii. p. 608, n.), suspects an origin in Ovid, *Met.* xiv. 785 'Iano loca iuncta tenebant Naides Ausoniae'. This is an ingenious tribute to the humanistic tendencies of the writer of the *Mirabilia*. But it has nothing to do with any Gate, and, despite the medieval penchant for Ovid, is much less likely to have suggested the etymology of Septimiana than the reading of the longer gloss about to be suggested. Again, if the Classics inspired this gloss, why are there no more such glosses in the *Mirabilia*?

[7] *Vit. Sev.* 19, 5. 'Notable public works of his still exist; the Septizonium and the Baths of Severus (*eiusdemque etiam ianus*=and also the Ianus-arch of the same), in the Trastevere

XXII

a. POSTERN OF THE LICINIAN GARDENS

b. VAN HEEMSKERCK'S DRAWING OF PORTA FLAMINIA, 1534

of Septimius Severus in the *Historia Augusta*: Opera publica
praecipua eius extant Septizonium et thermae Severianae, eiusdemque etiam ianus (ianae, iane, ianuae, *codd.* Iani, C.) in
Transtiberina regione ad portam nominis sui, quarum (quorum
C) forma intercidens statim usum publicum invidit. This corrupt
passage has been interpreted in various ways, which may be
summarized as follows.

(1) The Renaissance topographers, familiar with the *Mirabilia*
tradition, chose *Iani . . . quorum . . .* and connected with it the fact,
which is stated for the first time by Fulvius (1527), and accepted
by Audebert (1575), that Porta Septimiana itself was a Ianus-
arch of Severus, which existed until 1498, with an inscription of
Septimius on it, forming part of the City Gate. But *iani* (plural)
means portico, and at all events the text here says nothing about
the *porta* being a Ianus-arch; it states that the *porta* was a Gate
in Trastevere, called after the Ianus-portico; for this meaning, and
not the interpretation 'after Severus', must be the force of *sui*,
when Severus has been represented by *eius* twice in the same
sentence. Nor does the awkward phrase *eiusdemque etiam* explain
itself satisfactorily. It is also very odd that no one (not even
Fulvius) gives the text of the inscription of Severus, which
is first mentioned by Fulvius, being copied later by Audebert.
Fulvius could, of course, have invented the whole story out of
portam nominis sui; but the demolition of the Gate happened
only twenty-nine years before he wrote, and, unless he is using
antea quite loosely, in the sense of *olim*, it can hardly be supposed
that he was in error.[1]

(2) *Ianuae . . . quarum* has been accepted by Peter.[2] This
might do. But to what did the *ianuae* belong? Again, *quarum . . .
invidit* is now either separated from *Thermae Severianae* by a
clumsy interpolation, or *forma* refers to *ianuae* and has either its
extremely rare transferred meaning of arch (and in that case why
should the arch not have been repaired?), or its more ordinary
meaning of plan, which might indeed admit of an explanation
given below. But here again the awkward phrase *eiusdemque
etiam* remains to be explained; and the work is even less worthy
than a portico of the title *opus praecipuum*.

(3) Becker[3] proposed *balneae*. This gives better sense and
forma might then mean water-main, or aqueduct, or plan. But
eiusdemque etiam still remains; and, although *balneae* form an

Ward at the gate of the same name (*quarum* = of which: pl), the arch fell in and promptly
hindered the public from using it.' There is no need to enter here into the controversy about
the date of the *Historiae Augg.* It suffices that all commentators hold them no earlier than
the Constantinian Age.

[1] Jordan, i[1]. 373, states flatly 'so muss wohl die Annahme . . . irrtümlich sein.'
[2] Teubner text. *Ianuae . . . quarum* = the doors . . . of which.
[3] Becker, *Ant. Rom.* i, p. 213. *Balneae* = baths.

opus praecipuum, the name Septimiana, which the medieval tradition giving the name of the Gate shows to be the essential point of the whole passage, never emerges. This failure is shared by the first two suggestions.

(4) Very much better, then, is Zangemeister's suggestion,[1] *eiusdemque Septimianae*, which attaches admirably to the previous clause, gives excellent sense, and is certainly covered by *opus praecipuum*. Furthermore, the last phrase now can be simply explained. *Forma* will mean neither aqueduct nor arch, for the building of Thermae in the Capital of the Empire is not likely to have been held up by a blocked water-main, or by the collapse (*intercĭdens*) of an arch. Instead it will mean 'plan', and the plan will have gone to limbo (*intercĭdens*), not because of any accident while the building was in progress, but because Aurelian's Wall cut right through it, as it cut through the *Cellae vinariae nova et Arruntiana* [2] just east of the gate. And quite a small subtraction from the plan of Thermae, whose whole organization depended upon the full use of an intricate and symmetrical plan,[3] would make them obsolete immediately. This last point would be the force of *statim*.

To the history of the defensive Gate, however, it makes no difference which interpretation is chosen. For it is certain that *porta* is not itself one of the buildings which lie hidden behind the corruption, but was called after them. Again, the interpretation does not affect the truth of the unanimous agreement that the source in which it occurs was compiled in or after the Constantinian age. And at such a time *porta* (even if it embodied a Severan structure, as Fulvius states) could mean, when Rome was in question, nothing else than a City Gate, since the City Wall was already some fifty years old. So the earliest mention of Porta Septimiana does not occur in the Papal document of 1123, but in the Vita Severi, and this shows that the Gate goes back to classical times. Exactly how far it goes back depends upon the dating of the *Historia Augusta*.[4] But if the results of the study

---

[1] Zangemeister, *Rhein. Mus.* xxxix. 'And the Septimian baths of the same'.

[2] Lanciani, *B. C.* 1892, p. 111, states that there was a big rise in level here between Aurelian and Honorius. This is untrue: the rise existed before the Wall was built, as he himself was first to note, *N. Scav.* 1880, p. 141. The reason for this drastic treatment here was that the wall had to reach Ponte Sisto, for strategic reasons, no matter what important buildings it wrecked.

[3] Cf. E. Pfretzschner, *Die Grundrissentwicklung der Römischen Thermen*, 1909, Strassburg, taf. i–xi. Also Kramer, *Die Kaiserthermen von Trier*.

[4] Von Domaszewski has discussed this whole passage in his monograph 'Die topographie Roms bei den Scriptores Historiae Augustae (*Sitzungsberichte der Heidelberger Akademie der Wissenschaften. Philosophisch-Historiche Klasse*, Jahrgang 1916, Abhandlung 7). He believes that the source used is a glossed edition of the Chronograph of 354 and of Hieronymus, and, further, that the glosses were drawn from a map of A.D. 145–61. Suffice it to note that the ground for dating the source to A.D. 145–61, that *Templum Faustinae* is so called instead of *Templum Faustinae et Antonini*, is erroneous. *Templum Faustinae*

of Baynes [1] are accepted, which date the *Historia* to the time of Julian, the Gate becomes as old as any in the Wall: and one more proof is added to those which demonstrate that the Wall on the west bank of the Tiber was built earlier than the fifth century. In short, if nothing is known of the form of Porta Septimiana, its age need not be in doubt, and it may be added to the number of City Gates omitted by the Einsiedeln List.

§ 9. PORTA AURELIA-SANCTI PETRI

This Gate is mentioned by Procopius,[2] as follows: τήν τε Αὐρηλίαν (ἣ νῦν Πέτρου τοῦ τῶν Χριστοῦ ἀποστόλων κορυφαίου, ἅτε που πλησίον κειμένου, ἐπώνυμός ἐστι), and its position is given in another passage [3] by the same author: Ἀδριανοῦ τοῦ Ῥωμαίων αὐτοκράτορος τάφος ἔξω πύλης Αὐρηλίας ἐστὶν ἀπέχων τοῦ περιβόλου ὅσον λίθου βολήν. The common-sense reading of the latter passage would interpret the Gate as being in the περίβολος, where a Gate certainly must have existed in order to forestall attacks by boat. In continuation, the same passage [3] describes the Mausoleum as ἔοικε γοῦν (ὁ τάφος) πύργῳ ὑψηλῷ πύλης τῆς ἐκείνῃ προβεβλημένῳ, and this is equally ambiguous, since προβεβλημένῳ is here used to mean 'set as a bulwark'. So it could be maintained that the Gate mentioned by Procopius was that in the river-defences of the Mausoleum.

The Einsiedeln List raises further problems. There the Gate has no other name than *Porta S. Petri*, used thrice. But the third time it occurs as PORTA SCI PETRI, with the addition on the next line of IN HADRIANIO, all written in red majuscules.[4] Jordan[5] has rightly noted that the phrase *in Hadrianio* must go with the next passage, so as to read *in Hadrianio sunt turres VI*. He does not attempt, however, to explain the phrase *Porta Sci Petri*, which has no connexion with the rest of the text if it is isolated from the phrase *in Hadrianio*. Here the fact that the whole phrase is written in red majuscules seems to give a clue to how the words first became isolated. As commentators on the *Descriptio Murorum* have not noted, a particular kind of item, emphasized with red majuscules, recurs frequently throughout the sixteen-folio Einsiedeln Itinerary, which precedes the *Descriptio Murorum*, and is written in the same hand. In the Itinerary the

---

retained its simple name even so late as the Notitia. Again, how could anything connected with Severus be drawn from a source of this date? And what is the proof that the edition was glossed? Why should the *Urquelle* not have contained this information? This excessive *Quellenforschung* brings its special manifestation of Nemesis.

[1] Baynes, *Historia Augusta*, Oxford, 1926.

[2] *B. G.* i. 19, 'Porta Aurelia, which is now called after Peter, the Chief of Christ's apostles, who is buried somewhere near'.

[3] *B. G.* i. 22, for trans. see p. 20, n. 3.

[4] Cf. Hülsen, *Atti. Pont.*, ser. ii, vol. ix, pp. 384, 385.

[5] Jordan, ii. 580, 166.

majuscules are used to distinguish headings and directions, taken originally from a detailed map.[1] Examples of these items are, ARCUS SEUERI, FORUM ROMANUM. SUBURA, FORMA UIRGINIS, IN SINIŜT A PORTA SC̄I PETRI USQUE PORTA ASINARIA, DE PORTA APPIA USQ SCOLA GRECA IN UIA APPIA. PORTA SC̄I PETRI, which was a favourite starting-point, occurs four times in the Itinerary. Now in the *Descriptio Murorum* there was no such system of directions or headings, but it happens that the passage PORTA SC̄I PETRI IN HADRIANIO is the only item which breaks the monotony of the ordinary paragraphs with their uniform phraseology. It is possible, then, that when the scribe reached this title, after copying sixteen items of the ordinary kind, he mistook this phrase for the old sort of direction-rubric which he had only just left behind, after using it for sixteen consecutive folios of his work. Thus he came to write the whole exceptional phrase in red majuscules: furthermore, it may be thought that, since he had often omitted prepositions in such rubrics, and in other passages in the *Descriptio Murorum* itself, he left out an *ad* in front of Porta Sc̄i Petri. So we should get a paragraph beginning *Ad porta sc̄i petri, in Hadrianio, sunt vi turres*, &c. Even then, however, it remains doubtful whether Porta Sc̄i Petri is really one of the Gates of the Mausoleum fortress.

One more name is added to the complex by William of Malmesbury[2] (1126), who mentions, in his list of Gates, Porta Cornelia: *Prima porta Cornelia, quae modo dicitur porta Sancti Petri, et via Cornelia*. The *Via Cornelia* branched off from *Via Aurelia nova* and *Via triumphalis*[3] in Trastevere, not far from Hadrian's Mausoleum; so it looks as if Porta Cornelia were indeed part of the Mausoleum fortress. But, then, if the name Aurelia, which belongs to a Transtiberine road, could be applied to a Gate on the east bank, so could Cornelia. So, in the end, the following facts emerge. There existed in the time of Procopius at least two Gates connected with Hadrian's Mausoleum, the first at the east end of Pons Aelius, guarding the entry to the City through the River wall, the second in the western τείχισμα of the Mausoleum.[4] And not impossibly Totila's fortifications[5] round the Mausoleum may have introduced yet another Gate. Which of these was the Porta Aurelia-Sancti Petri is quite uncertain. The problem of nomenclature is therefore very complicated, and the present evidence will not permit any solution thereof.

[1] But Hülsen (loc. cit.) has proved that the map was not in the hands of the writer of the MS. [2] *C. U. R.* p. 87.
[3] It is perhaps worth note that the Peutinger Table marks the road across Pons Aelius as *Via triumfalis*; cf. Hülsen, *Atti. Pont.* ser. ii, vol. ix, p. 391, fig. 2.
[4] See above, p. 23. [5] Procop. *B. G.* iv. 33.

IV. EXISTING POSTERNS

THE existing posterns are six in number, including two wickets. Their distribution is quite irregular, for it depends in no way upon strategical considerations, but upon the incidence of by-roads which were thought important enough to require a Gate. All the posterns (and perhaps the wickets too) seem to have been blocked at an early date, and it may be suspected, although it is in no way proved, that they were closed at the same time as Porta Ostiensis West, an event dated by Diocletianic tiles to early in the fourth century.[1] In this connexion may be noted the blocking of the Postern of Castra Praetoria: this gave access to the road which formed a glacis round the outside of the Fortress, and which was blocked and partly removed in the Maxentian age.[2] With this event must apparently be associated the blocking of the Gate, which was connected with the road; and at all events the blocking cannot well be later than the dismantling of the Fortress in 312, when the road must have been deprived of all possible use. Of the four existing posterns all conform to a definite type, but two are modified in order to permit their insertion into earlier structures. Since none is now open, it is impossible to obtain an idea of their vaulting arrangements, but their external aspect is clear. They had imposts and a flat lintel (in two places a flat arch) of travertine, and these were surmounted by two relieving arches, set in the body of the Wall, the lower segmental, with much lowered centre, the uppermost semicircular. Analogy from East-Roman fortifications at Constantinople,[3] Salonika,[4] and elsewhere,[5] would suggest that the semicircular arch continued right through the thickness of the Wall, and that the lower arch and travertine lintel are infilling, forming a tympanum. This arrangement facilitates the fitting of doors, and is easy to repair if damaged, since the collapse of the door-casing, through accident or assault, does not entail the ruin of the whole wall above it. At all events in frontal aspect these posterns anticipate in remarkable fashion the East-Roman gates of the fifth century and later, and they may now be described in detail.

[1] *P. B. S. R.* x, p. 21 ; see p. 220.
[2] *P. B. S. R.* x, p. 19=*N. Scav.* 1888, p. 734.
[3] See Lietzmann, Die Landmauer von K., *Preussische Akademie der Wissenschaften,* 1929: *Phil-Hist. Klasse* 2. Taf. ix.
[4] Personal observation.   [5] e. g. Nicaea.

§ 1. THE POSTERN OF VIA NOMENTANA

This postern lies [1] at the end of the first curtain south of Porta Nomentana, where the Wall, by means of a zigzag, permits a small but important road to pass from the Viminal to Via Nomentana. The arrangement of the zigzag, with a tower on the unshielded side in the re-entrant, closely resembles that of the postern in Vigna Casali;[2] but it should be noted that here the tower is given a full-sized front with two windows, in contrast to the half-front usually provided [3] at sharp angles in the Wall. The windows seem to have been left open, like those of a large Gate, if this is the right conclusion to be drawn from the fact that the window now surviving is blocked with filling no earlier than the late Middle Ages, or the Renaissance. The salient angle in the Wall, which is the weak point, has been buttressed with a battered medieval counterfort, which gives it a misleading tower-like appearance. It also hides the east impost of the postern, so that only the lintel and the west impost are visible, but a measurement from the centre of the opening gives an entrance 8 ft. 10 in. wide. The width is not so great as is usual, and it was perhaps determined by the length of the monolithic lintel that was available at the time of building, for the lintel and imposts in each postern seem to be built up from robbed blocks.[4] Above the lintel come two relieving-arches, built with *bipedalis* voussoirs, which are of good quality, but widely spaced; and the lower and flatter arch is separated from the travertine lintel by three courses of brick. Twenty-eight courses above the top of the uppermost (semicircular) arch there is a single string-mould of *bipedales*. This no doubt marks the site of the original rampart-walk, as is suggested by the position of the window in the adjacent tower. There follows, twenty-four courses higher, another double string, above which comes much poorer work, with dark mortar; so the string was probably added after the removal of first-period merlons. The character of the blocking of the Gate is difficult to determine, since it has been much patched and is in bad condition, but its appearance does not seem to warrant a late date.

§ 2. THE POSTERN OF CASTRA PRAETORIA

The significance of this postern has already been noted in general terms. It gave egress to the road which passed round the Castra, forming a glacis in place of the ditch common in frontier fortifications. This road was bodily removed in the

---

[1] *F. U. R.* 3, 4.   [2] Cf. *F. U. R.* 46.

[3] Cf. towers nos. L 35, K 13.

[4] Here the visible blocks are 1 ft. 3½ ins. and 1 ft. 1 in. wide respectively. The fact that the blocks are robbed is quite certain in the Posterula Hortorum Licinianorum.

last period of the history of the Fortress, which at the same time had its gates blocked, while its wall was heightened by removing earth at foundation-level:[1] so it might be expected that the postern associated with this outer defence was blocked then too. This is strongly suggested by the character of the brickwork used for the original blocking, the surviving part of which became visible in 1928 during levelling for an electric sub-station of the City Tramways. It is good brickwork, to be classified with the second-period work on the Wall. There is thus clear evidence for very early disuse of this gateway. The early date of the gateway itself is, moreover, amply demonstrated by its construction. It is set in a beautifully-built piece of Wall, indubitably of early date: and the high quality of the voussoirs of its semicircular arch date it equally certainly to the first period of the Wall's existence. Only the semicircular relieving-arch is now to be seen, however, for the tympanum has been stripped of all facing. It is therefore uncertain whether a segmental lower arch ever existed. Otherwise the gateway does not differ fundamentally from its neighbour, just described. The travertine lintel, once monolithic, but now terribly cracked and fragmentary, and the two travertine imposts, each in two pieces as now visible, are still to be seen. The threshold is not visible, but excavation would quickly reveal it: and the Gateway, situated in land appropriated by the Municipio, may be commended to the proper authorities as well worth examination, both for its structure and for its historical importance.

§ 3. THE POSTERN OF THE LICINIAN GARDENS

The next postern is situated in the eighth curtain south of Porta Tiburtina,[2] and may be suspected to have served a road passing through the Horti Liciniani, in front of the *nymphaeum* known as the Temple of Minerva Medica. The character of the filling of this Gate led Nibby to believe [3] that it was begun, but closed before it was ever used. The writer, however, does not share this impression, since the filling differs from the Wall round the gateway, and prefers to conclude that this filling in question is good work of the second period. Anyhow, this is, once more, adequate evidence for an early closing of the postern. The name of the road which passed through it is unknown, but Dr. Ashby's researches [4] have rendered it safe to say that the road in question was not Via Collatina, as Nibby conjectured.[5]

Only the upper half of the postern is visible to-day, for the threshold has disappeared amid modern refacing (Pl. XXII*a*).

[1] See *P. B. S. R.* x, p. 19.
[2] See *F. U. R.* 24.
[3] Nibby, *M. di R.* 344.
[4] *P. B. S. R.* i. 138–9.
[5] Nibby, loc. cit.

Again, although the general aspect of this postern is similar to that of the others, it differs therefrom in detail, owing to the employment of an odd set of travertine blocks for the stonework. Two stones are used for the key-stone of a flat arch (which takes the place of the normal monolithic lintel), and two for the long voussoirs, which project exceptionally far beyond each side of the gate, rather as at the Postern of Vigna Casali. The imposts are also built up with many blocks, arranged as headers and stretchers, in a different system[1] for each. Above the stonework, the arrangement of relieving arches is almost the same as at the Postern of Via Nomentana; but the uppermost of the three courses of bricks, which lie between the travertine flat arch and the segmental relieving arch of *bipedales*, is made to project as a string-course. The topmost, semicircular, arch is separated, as at the Postern of Via Nomentana,[2] by twenty-seven courses of brick from the string-mould of the original parapet.

§ 4. POSTERN OF VIGNA CASALI

This Gateway lies in the eleventh curtain west of Porta Appia.[3] As has already been noted, its ground-plan is strikingly like that of the Postern of Via Nomentana. But there the resemblance ends, for the Gateway has been inserted in an earlier entrance connected with a tomb. The remains of the tomb, a high structure with travertine casing and mouldings and *opus spicatum* floor, are clear behind the Gate, for the Wall has been built over part of them (Pl. II*a*). Just in front of the tower are traces of another small tomb, in two tiny stories, as at Ostia, like two sarcophagi placed one on top of the other. The earlier entrance, in which the Gateway is inserted, is a beautiful door in brickwork, flanked by pilasters with caps of terra-cotta. Its arch is formed by tile voussoirs of excellent quality, and once had a moulded terra-cotta key-stone, of which damaged remains appear in a photograph by Parker. Its extrados was decorated by a terra-cotta moulding, almost perfectly preserved in Parker's day, and grievously damaged during the restorations of 1927. Above the arch came a terra-cotta cornice, of which the lowest member is shown *in situ* by Parker, suggesting a treatment in the manner of the Via Latina tombs, while the other members have been shaved off to carry the Wall. The structure does not seem to have extended further than the south pilaster on the south side, but it extends on the north beyond the north pilaster, so as to pass behind the tower with which the builders of the Wall protected

---

[1] South impost, from top downwards, H·S·H·S·H·S·H·S·H·: North, ditto, H.H·S·H·H·S·H·H·H·.

[2] See p. 230.　　　　　　　[3] *F. U. R.* 46.

it. The north pilaster, moreover, as Parker's photograph shows, stood upon a moulded travertine base, which passed under the tower, and no doubt belonged to the tomb visible behind the tower. Nevertheless, the original aspect of the converted structure is not easy to imagine. Was the entrance an ornamental precinct gateway, or was it the façade of the tomb? If the former, its relation to the tomb beneath the tower seems oddly disjointed and difficult to understand, unless the tomb happened to be one of the many enclosed by a cemetery wall. If the latter, why do not portions of the tomb to which it belongs appear in the back of the Wall? These are difficult questions, which even excavation, though very desirable, might not solve.

In order to convert the gateway into a postern of standard type, the builders of the Wall equipped it with a tower based on the early tomb, reduced the opening to nine and a half feet, and provided it with travertine imposts and flat arch. The latter was cut through in comparatively modern times by a flat-headed window, and blocked still earlier. So it comes that we can see only the front of the Gate and two voussoirs, one on each side, each cutting deeply into the early brick pilasters. The imposts were cleared to road-level by Parker, and are built with two long blocks of travertine each, which do not follow the line of the edge of the earlier arch, although they are bedded therein. Above the level of the pilaster-caps the ornamentation of the early arch was shaved off, and the first Wall was built up to the level now marked by second-period loop-holes. These were cut through the line of merlons, as is shown not only by their relation to the string-course which marks old rampart-walk level, but by the filling of the embrasures, which remained visible until 1927, although the merlons themselves had long been swept away by the loop-holes. This arrangement continues, however, only over the Gateway: to the south all has been covered by an ancient refacing, almost as disastrous to the historian as the refacing of 1927, which treated this Gateway harshly,[1] although time may tone down the effect.

§ 5. WICKET OF GIARDINO CARDELLI

This little-known doorway is situated in the nursery gardens of Cardelli, in a deep re-entrant formed by the wing of the ancient Lateran Palace, now buried in the Orto dei Penitenzieri, and its relation to the City Wall is obscure. It seems clear, from present-day observation, that the segmental relieving arch, with

---

[1] I do not wish to decry the restoration in itself; but it was harsh, and no attempt was made really to understand the structure being restored. Slower work, combined with skilled assistance, would have given a better effect.

two rings of voussoirs, which are neither well chosen nor very well laid, and are related to the brickwork of the Wall, must belong to the Aurelianic age, or later. But, when the opening was excavated [1] by Parker in 1868, remains of the east impost of an earlier door were found at a lower level, associated with a wall in reticulate work, and therefore not likely to be later than the last quarter of the second century. This early door must have formed part of the Domus Lateranorum. It had then been filled up, after a considerable rise in ground-level, to nearly half-way between its threshold and the arch, and a new and narrower travertine threshold had then been inserted amid new brickwork jambs and foundations. This brickwork, to judge from Parker's detailed view,[2] is moderately good in standard, and might easily be Aurelianic. Then the entrance which it formed had in turn been blocked, and Ciconetti's drawing [3] suggests that at the time of the blocking, the lintel had been thrown down on to the threshold and so abandoned. The filling, as it appeared in Parker's day, at least, was work of the very roughest kind, which it would be rash to attempt to date.

It would not appear then that the Doorway of Giardino Cardelli was of any importance among entrances to the City. In its first days its purpose was apparently domestic, connected with the internal [4] economy of the Domus Lateranorum: it was then reduced, perhaps from the very first days of the fortifications of the City, to the size of a wicket-gate. Precise dates for its reconstruction and its closing are, however, to seek, for Parker seems to have left neither description nor survey of the structure.

§ 6. THE DOORWAY OF VIGNA CASALI

This tiny doorway lies in the thirteenth curtain to the west of Porta Appia, the last before the Bastione di Sangallo, close beneath the shelter of the twelfth tower.[5] It was noted by the keen eyes of Audebert [6] so early as 1575, but has since almost disappeared amid refacings. But a semicircular arch of *bipedales* still marks its top, set in a piece of Wall which is typically of the first period. Below it, on a projecting piece of *tufo* rock, are to be seen traces of concrete, which may be connected either with stairs or with some structure to which the little door led. The opening is blocked up with rough uncoursed tufa-work of quite uncertain date.

---

[1] Photograph, 4to, 1097, 1096: 1149 (drawing by Ciconetti).

[2] Photograph, 1097.

[3] Ciconetti, photograph Parker, 1149.

[4] The *Domus*, of course, originally projected beyond the Wall, see *F. U. R.* 37. And there would seem to have been a large internal courtyard.

[5] Tower no. L 12: see *F. U. R.* 46.

[6] Audebert, B. M. Lansdowne MS. 720, fol. 244: see above, p. 55 (ii).

What was the purpose of this little doorway? An adequate solution is rendered the more difficult by the fact that nothing is known of the archaeology of Vigna Casali at this point; and the puzzle is greater because the Postern of Vigna Casali is so near (two curtains to the east). The purpose of the gate therefore remains quite uncertain; but it is perhaps worth while to state possibilities. The gate may have been connected purely with the construction of the Wall, being used for the passage of supplies, and then blocked when the construction of the section was complete. It may have led to a tomb, cistern, private cemetery, gardens, or market-gardens. Anyhow, it is an example of a rare type of gate found only once elsewhere on the existing Wall, and in that case connected with an important mansion behind it. So it is tempting to think that the doorway of Vigna Casali, situated close by a full-sized postern, was constructed in order to respect some private right. The date of its disuse is to seek.

V. DEMOLISHED POSTERNS

PRESENT-DAY knowledge of posterns which have disappeared is based entirely upon the Einsiedeln List. This mentions [1] five *posterulae*, all of which gave access to the Tiber (east bank), and remained open, owing to the relatively increasing importance of river-traffic, after all the landward posterns had been closed. Two of them are assigned to the sector Pons Aurelius—Porta Aurelia (Sancti Petri), and three to the sector Porta Aurelia—Porta Flaminia. These are all for which ancient literature gives warrant, but it is impossible to deny that there may have been more in the early days of the Wall's history. Later, at least, there were six, as Corvisieri [2] has shown, and Lanciani [3] adds a possible seventh. So the real question at issue is how far the medieval posterns represent ancient gateways, or, in other words, whether some of them may not be additions, due to the enhanced importance of river-traffic and of the Vatican Quarter.

The questions raised are not now answerable for certain, but some striking facts emerge from Corvisieri's researches. Out of the six posterns which he was able to trace four are mentioned in tenth-century or early eleventh-century documents, and one, the Posterula di San Martino, già di Sant' Agata, was known [4] as ancient in A. D. 962. So at first sight it looks as if these four at least might be ancient. But there is another line of approach (fig. 45). Some of the Posterulae are known to be on the line of ancient streets to river-ferries. The Posterula di San Martino (A.D. 955–A.D. 962) lies at the head of an important branch-road, which led from Via Lata (now Corso Umberto Primo) to the river, and passed the main front of the Mausoleum of Augustus.[5] The two adjacent Posterulae, Della Pila [6] (A.D. 955– A.D. 1010) and di S. Lucia—Quattuor Portarum [7] (A.D. 1002), must be close to the *Ciconiae Nixae*,[8] where *vina fiscalia* [9] were landed after Aurelian's

[1] The number is certain: see the reproduction of MS. by Hülsen, *Atti. Pont.* Ser. ii, vol. 9, p. 424, tav. xiii. Corvisieri, *Archiv. di Stor. Patr.*, vol. i, p. 90 n., raises a mare's-nest by comparing the editions of Mabillon and Haenel.

[2] *Archivio Romano di Storia Patria*, vol. i, pp. 79–121, 137–71.

[3] *F. U. R.* 14.

[4] Corvisieri, p. 98. Site fixed by church of S. Rocco and S. Martino, bulls of Agapitus II (955), and John XII (962).

[5] *F. U. R.* 8.

[6] The origin of the name is a ruin on the river-bank, mentioned in a Bull of Agapitus II of 955 (Corvisieri, p. 94): site uncertain, meets medieval road from Trevi fountain (Corvisieri, p. 101).

[7] Inscr. Bibl. Chigiana, Cod. Sign. 558, p. 313 (Corvisieri, pp. 108–9): site fixed by S. Lucia della Tinta; see Forcella, *Inscr. delle Chiese di R.* xi, p. 237, no. 374; and Hülsen, *Chiese di R. nel medio evo*, p. 303.

[8] Hülsen, *B. C.* 1895, pp. 49–51: *C. I. L.* vi. 1785.

[9] Vopisc. *Aurel.*, c. 48.

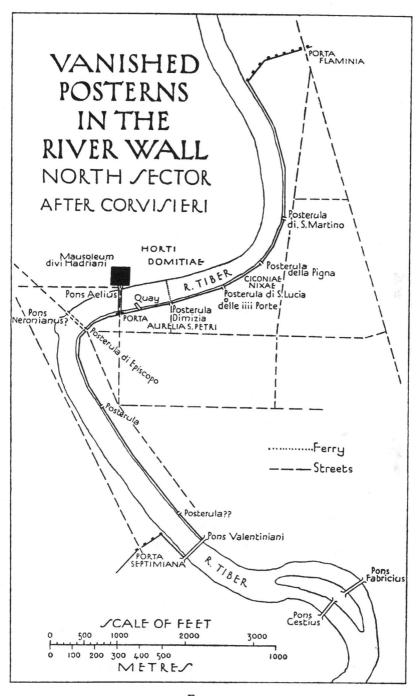

VANISHED
POSTERNS
IN THE
RIVER WALL
NORTH SECTOR
AFTER CORVISIERI

PORTA
FLAMINIA

Posterula
di. S.Martino

Mausoleum
divi Hadriani

HORTI
DOMITIAE

R. TIBER

Posterula
della Pigna

CICONIAE
NIXAE

Pons Aelius

Quay

Posterula di S.Lucia
delle iiii Porte

Pons
Neronianus?

PORTA
AURELIA S.PETRI

Posterula
Dimizia

Posterula di Episcopo

Posterula

..........Ferry
— — —Streets

Posterula??

Pons Valentiniani

PORTA
SEPTIMIANA

R. TIBER

Pons
Fabricius

Pons
Cestius

SCALE OF FEET

| 0 | 500 | 1000 | 2000 | 3000 |

| 0 | 100 | 200 | 300 | 400 | 500 | 1000 |

METRES

FIG. 45

day, and conveyed to the portico of Templum Solis. So it is
necessary to think of at least one of these as ancient. Again,
Posterula Dimizia,[1] which is not mentioned in extant documents
before A.D. 1177, is situated at the head of an ancient road[2] leading
to important marble quays, substituted in medieval times by the
Tor di Nona, and excavated in 1890. Opposite came a ferry,
leading to the Horti Domitiae; and so Corvisieri's suggestion,
that the street and gate alike were anciently called Domitia, is
not without attractions, although unproven. The next Posterula,[3]
de Episcopo (A.D. 1012), lies at the Trigarium, a point important
enough to be taken as an early boundary in connexion with river-
embankment, perhaps because there was anciently a ferry there.
The existence of a road is not substantiated; but the point lies [4]
on the production of a line from the Ara Ditis et Proserpinae to
the change in direction of the Via Porticus Maximae.[5] Finally,
strategy demands an opening near Ponte Sisto; and Corvisieri's
association [6] of such a gate with the Vicolo del Polverone may
well be nearer the truth than his case suggests. Here no early
medieval view, however, gives any help.

It is possible, then, to arrive at the following conclusions. Of
Corvisieri's posterns, Posterula di San Martino is mentioned in
early sources, and is on the line of an important ancient road.
Posterulae della Pila and delle Quattro Porte are of early date,
and are near *Ciconiae Nixae*: one of them must therefore be
ancient, if not both. Posterula Dimizia is mentioned only in 1177,
although this may be pure chance, but it lies on an important
ancient road. Posterula de Episcopo is situated at an important
ancient landmark on the river. Posterula del Vicolo del Polverone
is barely substantiated, but an ancient gateway is demanded
somewhere near it by strategy. This gives a number which
corresponds with the Einsiedeln List, if one posterula instead of
two be postulated at *Ciconiae Nixae*, although to be sure, it would
be unwise to attach great weight to the correspondence. So it
seems clear that the Posterulae di San Martino and Dimizia
represent ancient gates for certain, while Posterulae de Episcopo
and del Polverone may be added as probable identifications.

There is no evidence whatever for the form of these Posterulae,
and the plans suggested by Lanciani,[7] with semicircular towers,
seem improbable. Indeed, if all these gates had two towers
apiece, only five towers would be left for the Wall between Pons
Aurelius and Porta Aurelia-Sancti Petri and eight between
Portae Aurelia-Sancti Petri and Porta Flaminia, which eight

---

[1] Cod. Vat. 6196: full text in Corvisieri, pp. 164–7.
[2] *F. U. R.* 14. The quays are still visible when the river is low.
[3] Corvisieri, pp. 152–3.   [4] *F. U. R.* 14, 20.
[5] *F. U. R.* 14.   [6] Corvisieri, pp. 156–60; *F. U. R.* 20, 27.
[7] *F. U. R.* 8, 14, 20, 27.

are already known to exist between Porta Flaminia and the river. These numbers, then, apart from the question of types, seem to invalidate Lanciani's hypothesis. It seems much more likely that the river-gates resembled the other posterns in being simple gateways, unprotected by towers, and planned without regard to the vicinity thereof.

PART FOUR

HISTORICAL INTERPRETATION OF THE REMAINS

I. AURELIAN'S WALL AND GATES

THE literary tradition about the Wall and its architectural development have now been considered in turn, and the relation between them may be defined. There is, fortunately, no doubt about the correlation of the first periods of both, and the inscriptions of Honorius [1] provide another certain cross-correspondence at a further stage. So the earlier schemes at least become clear.

The first period is marked by the erection of a twenty-six foot Wall, provided with Gates, and passing all round the City. It followed the standard type of Roman defensive wall, except in one or two sectors, where, for obscure reasons, perhaps best ascribed to individual taste, it copied a less common type, provided with an arcaded gallery of Hellenistic antecedents. [2] The Gates were of standard type, designed in two main sizes, double and single. And there were also numerous postern gates of a pattern which later spread all over the East-Roman world. Such, in summarized form, was the character of the first defensive Wall of Imperial Rome. The date of this Wall is not in doubt. It can be assigned to Aurelian without hesitation, not only because literary tradition unanimously asserts that Aurelian gave Imperial Rome a Wall for the first time in A.D. 271, but because the Wall itself embodied or destroyed monuments, which existed independently at least as late as the fourth decade of the third century. Again, the work closely resembles in technique the dated repairs of Aurelian at the Thermae Antoninianae. So the work may be taken as Aurelian's, and may now be examined in greater detail.

The historical circumstances fit its character admirably. During the long years of dynastic troubles and of disorders within the Empire which had preceded Aurelian's reign, the Upper Danube frontier had been broken; and Italy, after more than three centuries of quiet, had again to experience devastating inroads from beyond the Alps. [3] The horrors of the Cimbric and Teutonic invasions had renewed themselves under Gallienus, when the Alamanni reached Lake Garda and the Apennines; and fierce riots had taken place among the nervous and defenceless

---

[1] *C. I. L.* vi. 1188, 1189, 1190.
[2] See pp. 67–8, where the type is discussed.
[3] Zos. i. 37.

ii

populace of Rome. Gaul had elevated the house of Tetricus; and Odenaethus, with Zenobia, had set the Near East in a ferment. To meet these troubles, the Imperial Army had not yet been re-organized, as it was to be some forty years later, in order to acquire mobility and a reserve striking force; for the older theory of Imperial Defence (to stud a wide area with small garrisons, and a legion as reserve) was only proved inadequate by the events of these bitter years. Thus the problems which Aurelian had to solve were two. How to protect with least effort the unfenced cities of the Empire if a great horde of barbarians happened to burst right through the frontier defences; and how to ensure that such provision should be adequate while the surplus troops of the Empire were campaigning against Zenobia in the East.

The solution adopted for Rome was simple and effective. The Eternal City received a Wall, not very large, but sufficiently big to keep out barbarians unprovided with siege-machinery. And the matter was treated as urgent. The new fortifications had to be built at high speed and by non-military labour, for when soldiers were urgently needed for the Palmyrene campaign against Zenobia it was impossible to spare the large staff needed to build twelve miles of Wall. These factors induced the employment of the City guilds for the work, as attested by John Malalas,[1] and they might be expected to give the following special characteristics to the design and its execution. The main lines of the scheme would have to be laid down with accuracy and precision, by specialist military architects,[2] such as the contemporary Cleodamus and Athenaeus, and then the details could be trusted to take care of themselves. Further, a Wall and Gates, designed to be built in haste, would have to be kept simple, yet architecturally worthy of the great City which they were encircling, not as an ornament, but as a work of necessity. Thus the requirement was not a barrier which would attract notice and overawe by its enormous scale, like the then newly-built Porta Nigra in Trier, but one which was efficient and self-effacive, like the anti-aircraft defences of a modern Capital. The problem in itself was nothing new to Roman architects, who commonly adopted simple functional designs for their most grandiose utilitarian buildings, and so, if only by chance, often achieved real distinction.

That these conditions were in fact imposed upon the building of the Wall is strongly suggested by the character of the remains. The Wall was built to a standard size and pattern, and was made to follow, in part at least, the well-known Customs boundary.

---

[1] John Malalas, *Chron.* xii, p. 299 (Dindorf).

[2] *Vit. Gallienor.* xiii 'inter haec Scythae per Euxinum navigantes Histrum ingressi multa gravia in solo Romano fecerunt. Quibus compertis, Gallienus Cleodamum et Athenaeum Byzantios instaurandis urbibus muniendis praefecit'.

Only on certain sectors, where a special type of Wall was provided, did the arrangements behind it vary, and even then the front had almost the same aspect. Here and there great buildings were embodied in the Wall; and in many places larger edifices must have dwarfed the Wall by their size, even if they did not form part of it. Nevertheless, the Wall formed everywhere an impenetrable obstacle, however little it attracted notice. The towers followed a rather old-fashioned and simple pattern, much more akin to the examples carved upon Trajan's Column [1] than to those which grace the frieze of the Arch of Constantine or the medallions of Arras [2] or Moguntiacum.[3] But they were built to house an elaborate park of artillery, to deal with a massed attack. In short, the whole design was notable for its simplicity and uniformity. There were few exceptions, and for the most part the City workmen, not used to building fortifications as such, could go straight on with their work. Yet nowhere does the planning of this earliest Wall evince really carefully or detailed thought for the problems of defence, and in some places it falls far short of good strategic requirements. Instances may be selected. Few plans could be more awkward than the junction [4] of the Wall with the north-west angle of Castra Praetoria, and with Aqua Antoniniana;[5] or the arrangement of the postern [6] of Vigna Casali, or, again, of the great re-entrant between it and Porta Ostiensis.[7] Nothing could be more impracticable than the complete lack of communication along the Wall at the Pyramid of Gaius Cestius,[8] or at the tenement house south of Porta Tiburtina.[9] At Portae Ostiensis East [10] and Flaminia [11] there are glaring cases of bungling in the setting out of the gate in relation to the Wall. Considered separately, these are not bad mistakes: collectively, they suffice to emphasize not only the speed at which the structure was erected, but the lack of experience in such work that handicapped its builders. These mistakes could hardly have been made by military labour.

Finally, the use of stock sizes of material may be noted everywhere. The Wall is of the same thickness and height, the towers have the same type of staircases, and the windows are arranged to fit the standard *bipedalis* tile. Only here and there does individuality emerge, in the treatment of the ornamental string-

---

[1] Trajan's Column ; Rodenwaldt, *Die Kunst der Antike,* 579; cf. also J. Ward, *Romano-British Buildings and Earthworks.*

[2] *J. R. S.* xiv, p. 155=*Aréthuse,* Jan. 1924, pl. vii.

[3] Blanchet, *Enceintes romaines de la Gaule,* pl. xxi, 4.

[4] Curtain D 4.

[5] Curtain K 6.   [6] Curtain L 11.

[7] Curtains L 34–6.   [8] Curtain M 1.

[9] Curtain F 6.   [10] See p. 111, fig. 19.

[11] See *F. U. R.* 1.

course,[1] in the tiling of the extrados of a window arch,[2] or in the provision of an ornamental plaque on a tower,[3] to give it a name. The arrangement of the merlons, and choice of material from which they are built, is, indeed, left within fairly wide limits; but this only emphasizes more sharply the fact that in other matters standards were being strictly followed. The economy in preparation of material gained by this standardization must have been very great. An order could be issued for so many thousand *bipedales*: and, once assembled, the aids to building, such as shuttering and scaffolds, could be used anywhere and any number of times. The initial organization must have been immense; but the *collegia* were available, and in 271 Aurelian personally attended to the detailed arrangements; that is the force behind the observation *transactis igitur, quae ad saeptiones atque Urbis statum et civilia pertinebant, contra Palmyrenos . . . iter flexit.*[4] He was able to leave for the East confident that the work would proceed smoothly and well, and that Rome would presently be protected by an adequate barrier against any sudden invasion from the north.

These, then, were the utilitarian considerations which entered into the building of Aurelian's Wall. What of the aesthetic? It is clear that neither the epoch nor the labour (the one disastrous, the other non-military) invited the erection of a monumental work. Also, the scale of the work did not offer a field for a grandiose artistic scheme. The World was not to know that its greatest City had become a fortified castle; two more centuries were to pass before it became used to that view about Constantinople. The essential part of the plan was to build a wall which was strong, but inconspicuous. But at a limited number of places something more elaborate might be expected, namely, at the points where roads passed through the Wall. The Gates are the buildings in which the aesthetic conceptions in the design of the Wall can best be discerned.

Once again it is evident that the sense for standardization was strong. Of the nine principal Gates that survive, Portae Ostiensis East,[5] Appia,[6] Latina,[7] and Nomentana[8] are known to have standard plans, to which also conform Portae Portuensis,[9] Labicana-Praenestina,[10] Salaria,[11] and Flaminia,[12] among those which have disappeared. Details of the earliest Gates[13] at Portae

---

[1] See p. 61.

[2] Towers A 21, B 16, M 22.

[3] Tower L 36.

[4] *Vit. Aurel.* 'After transacting the business of the Walls, and the ordering of the City and civil affairs, he turned his course against the Palmyrenes.'

[5] Fig. 19.   [6] Fig. 20.

[7] Fig. 17.   [8] Fig. 15.

[9] p. 202.   [10] Fig. 40.

[11] p. 186.   [12] Fig. 36.   [13] See pp. 175–6, 222, 227.

Tiburtina, Aurelia-Pancraziana, and Aurelia-Sancti Petri are lacking, but there is nothing suggestive of an exceptional treatment, and there are fairly strong reasons for supposing that Porta Tiburtina [1] at least was true to type. Portae Septimiana,[2] Ostiensis West,[3] Metrobia,[4] Ardeatina [5] (Laurentina?), Asinaria,[6] and Pinciana [7] were minor Gates, built to a much simpler plan, also following a recognized standard. So, in spite of the fact that the earliest form of three Gates remains unknown, it seems safe, on the evidence of eight out of eleven, to assume that the whole scheme was organized on standard lines.

The group of eleven main Gates was treated in two ways, in order to mark the importance of the roads which they spanned. Double arches were given to four first-class Gates, spanning Viae Flaminia and Appia, the great roads to north and south, and Viae Ostiensis and Portuensis, which led to the great harbours of Ostia and Portus. All the Gates of both classes had towers built to one size, but at least one exception survives, the west tower [8] of Porta Ostiensis East; and it looks as if the north tower [9] of Porta Tiburtina may have been another.

The general aspect of these Gates is not doubtful. The decorative details of the first-class Gates may be extracted [10] from Portae Appia and Ostiensis East. They had semicircular towers, with one covered chamber, lit by three round-headed front windows, and reached by a small 'dog-leg' staircase from behind. On the top of the towers were flat crenellated roofs, and between, at the same level, came a long, embattled curtain, built entirely of stone, and crowned with a graceful moulding. The other decorative features of this curtain are less certain; but there were two arches below, and five windows, provided with simple mouldings, have been chosen to grace the upper story. This scheme is suggested by the Porta Praetoria [11] at Regensburg (Castra Regina), which closely resembles these gates, although it is entirely built in stone. That there was no more elaborate treatment is made quite certain by the parts of the curtain still preserved, which allow no room for the elaborations of Verona [12] or Turin.[13] Aurelian's first-class Gate was therefore a simple structure, in keeping with the Wall to which it belonged; and it defined by its larger scale

[1] p. 176.   [2] pp. 223–7.   [3] p. 220, fig. 43.
[4] pp. 142–5.   [5] p. 218, fig. 42.
[6] Fig. 27.   [7] Fig. 30.
[8] See p. 118.   [9] See p. 176.
[10] See pls. X, XI, fig. 24.
[11] Personal observation.
[12] The Veronese gates are very close in date, see C. I. L. v. 3329.
[13] It seems highly probable that the towers of Turin are to be considered as late, although this has no bearing upon the date of polygonal R. gateway-towers as a whole. The town-wall was cut back to receive them, and their foundations are also at a higher level than those of the wall. I hope to publish these observations in detail shortly.

the four arterial roads of the Capital, roads of unrivalled importance, to which there was no alternative method of travel.

The second-class Gates were built to much the same pattern as the first. But their curtains were made of tile-faced concrete, and were much shorter than those of the first-class Gates. What their single arches were like is uncertain: it seems likely that they would be made of travertine; but it is quite uncertain whether this material was confined only to the jambs of the gateway, or whether there was a flat arch of travertine,[1] with tile or travertine relieving arch, or a round-headed arch,[2] with voussoirs of travertine or tile. At two of these Gates at least, however, it is proved that the lower part of the curtain was not made of travertine, for at Portae Latina[3] and Tiburtina[4] the edges of the brick-faced curtains remain. These are the largest of the second-class Gates, and so the conclusion might be expected to hold, *a fortiori*, for the other Gates. The upper story of the curtain was lit by three large front windows, as is proved by the remains of Porta Salaria, recorded in a photograph by Parker, and it was no doubt surmounted by a battlemented walk. The towers were of exactly the same plan and aspect as those of the first-class Gates, and all were built with the same stock sizes of material and tackle. The importance of this discovery is not small: not only does it make the cross-correspondences much more certain and numerous, but it shows that the design of the Gates had been carefully thought out before the building began. This procedure is, of course, neither surprising nor unique in its time, and is to be compared with events like the complete reconstruction of the Moesian city-fortifications, under Gallienus.[5] But it is interesting to establish this important case.

Finally, there were the seven third-class Gates, equal in number to those of the second-class. It is uncertain whether these were considered originally to rank higher than posterns. But it is clear that their importance qualified them in later times to be counted as normal City Gates, so that they were not closed when the other posterns passed out of use. Thus it came about that most of them rank as regular City Gates in the Einsiedeln List, or in the eighth-century list given by William of Malmesbury in his *Historia Anglorum*. In their first stage, however, all but one consisted of a simple archway set in an ordinary wall-curtain. The exception was Porta Pinciana, perhaps not called thus at first, which was arranged in a sector of skewed wall,[6] as were Porta Tiburtina[7] and the posterns[8] of Via Nomentana

---

[1] As at posterns.
[2] As at Porta Metrobia, see p. 142 and pl. XIIIc.
[3] See pl. IXa.   [4] See p. 177
[5] See n. 2, p. 242.   [6] See fig. 30.
[7] See fig. 33.   [8] See *F. U. R.* 3, 4, 46.

and of Vigna Casali. The form of the arch is preserved only in two places. Porta Metrobia [1] has an arch with *bipedalis* voussoirs: Porta Ostiensis West [2] was treated in richer fashion, with moulded stone architraves, in a manner which anticipated by about a century and a half that of the Πύλη τοῦ πεμπτοῦ at Constantinople.

Posterns also conformed to a standard style. They had travertine jambs, supporting a flat arch of travertine, surmounted by a tile-relieving arch. The type is dated definitely to the Aurelianic age by Porta Ostiensis West, which passed out of use [3] in the second period of the Wall's history, and by the associations with early brickwork of the other three.[4] Four of these postern gates are now preserved. The Einsiedeln List [5] mentions none of these, but adds five in the River Wall, bringing the total up to nine, and the number of entrances through the Wall to twenty-six (excluding two wickets). This was a generous allowance, and compares well with the earlier Customs gates mentioned by the elder Pliny.[6] But the posterns are chiefly interesting for their architectural type, which came into vogue for the main Gates of Constantinople a century and a half later, and passed from Byzantine and military architecture to ecclesiastical uses. In them may be seen the beginnings of the great Romanesque doorways with their decorated tympana, which still rank high among the decorative triumphs of Western Europe. The type was perhaps chosen because it would stand much more damage than an ordinary arch, and because it was cheap and easy to repair. This fact was certainly recognized in the Wall of Anthemius at Constantinople and in many other East-Roman fortresses, where multiple relieving arches, superimposed upon a flat arch and set in a stone frame, are a regular feature.

The types of the Gates are of great interest in relation to the roads and their economic value. They do not shed light upon how the road-system of Rome grew—a story of which the main outlines are already known—but upon the relative importance of the roads when new ones were being built no longer, and when the whole system was in full working order. They give us the classification of Roman times: and it is particularly gratifying to observe that this entirely corresponds to the arrangement divined by Dr. Ashby [7] in his articles on the roads of Rome. First come the four arterial roads of paramount importance, *Viae Appia* and *Flaminia*, serving both local and long-distance traffic to south and north, and *Viae Ostiensis* and *Portuensis*, connecting

[1] pl. XIIIc.
[2] p. 219.
[3] See p. 220.
[4] See pp. 230, 231, 232.
[5] See Appendix I.
[6] Pliny, *N. H.* iii. 5. 66.
[7] See *P. B. S. R.* vols. i, iii, iv, v.

Rome with her sea-ports. Next in order follow roads important for local needs, and for the Italian countryside; first among them *Via Latina*, elder sister to *Via Appia*; then *Via Tiburtina*, the trunk road to the fertile Abbruzzi and the Adriatic; the busy *Via Nomentana*; and the age-old *Via Salaria*. Across the Tiber stretch *Via Aurelia vetus*, with which connected *Viae Cornelia* and *Triumphalis*, and *Via Aurelia nova*. The rest of the roads are strictly local, carrying no long-distance traffic, but sometimes, like *Viae Pinciana* and *Asinaria*, providing useful short cuts to the arterial roads. If this classification were translated into the terms of modern railways, it would mark the difference between express-routes to Paris, Berlin, or Brindisi, the direct line to Naples, Sulmona, or Genoa, and the light rail-road to Civita Castellana or Albano. And just as modern architects might design for these a different kind of station, so Aurelian planned for his roads different types of entrances to the City. The analogy, too, becomes closer when it is remembered that the Customs' service was located at the Gates, and that travellers, like Juvenal's Umbricius,[1] were wont to start from the Gates on their lengthy journeys.

The large number of the Gates has also a tactical significance. It shows that the danger foreseen by the builders of the Wall was not really formidable. No tactician who visualized a definitely serious siege would have provided so many openings; and the point is proved by the blocking of these entrances when times had changed and serious siege warfare was the order of the day.[2] Both the Wall and its Gates were built to meet strictly the needs of the third century. The danger was a force of barbaric horsemen, unprovided with siege-machinery or commissariat organization, who could pillage an undefended city at their ease. Given an obstacle of reasonable size, and of ordinary, and in no way exceptional, strength, such raiders could be held off until they melted away or a relieving force[3] hurried up to disperse them. This requirement was fulfilled admirably by the Wall and Gates of the first period. Furthermore, the design of the works throughout was kept simple and uniform, suiting the employment of non-military labour, and it was no doubt executed in the minimum amount of time. Only in details do the failings emerge: and this is not surprising, for, however simple the design, the fact remained that the City corporations had never in all their experience had to build fortifications. Small wonder, then, if they occasionally failed to realize tactical possibilities. There is evi-

---

[1] Juv. *Sat.* iii. 12. Umbricius, of course, was starting from the *Augustan* customs-gate at Porta Capena.

[2] Cf. the survey of Procopius, *B. G.* i. 24.

[3] For the expression of this theory of defence, compare the names of certain corps in the Notitia Dignitatum.

dence, too, already considered, that they were allowed some considerable margin. Indeed, on one sector[1] at least, between Porta Asinaria and the Amphitheatrum Castrense, they built an altogether different type of Wall from that in erection elsewhere, and this same gang of men can be traced by their peculiar construction at the Lateran, at Porta Metrobia and east of Porta Pinciana.[2] On the whole, however, the requisite margin of freedom was not misjudged or misused, and the work was well performed, if with varying standards of technique and execution.[3]

Parallels for the Wall and Gates have already been noted. But here it should be emphasized that these structures are not out of keeping with those of their time,[4] despite their simplicity of plan. The age of really complicated Roman fortifications, as now becomes steadily clearer, had hardly begun in the West, even in the third century. During the long quietude which followed the establishment of *Pax Augusta*, the art of fortification, almost confined to the frontiers of the Empire (where it had most to learn), only freed itself rather slowly from an earth-work technique, although in Italy town-wall builders had been learning a good deal from Hellenistic tradition, while in Arabia and Bosnia, both unsuitable for earthworks, stone fortress-building began early.[5] It was not, however, until late in the second century, that freestanding masonry walls came into universal vogue for defences. Then the disasters of the third century, and the ever-increasing military activity of the fourth, gave the requisite impetus to the study of defensive tactics and poliorcetics, and thenceforward knowledge and understanding of such work advanced rapidly, producing mighty gates like the Porta Nigra, fortresses like Anderida (Pevensey) or Cardiff, and City Walls like the later stages of this one, or like the threefold defences of Constantinople. Invention, too, went steadily forward, and culminated in Greek fire, the *Flammenwerfer* of the ancient world. Finally, the Crusades brought back the art of fortress-building, now fully developed, to western Europe, and so is explained the likeness between the defences of Roman Cardiff, Edwardian Carnarvon, and Theodosian Constantinople. Aurelian's Wall takes its place in the earlier stages of this evolution, and it may be claimed that its design and execution demonstrate that the Roman genius for

[1] Curtains G 15-27.

[2] Curtains H 2, J 1, B 1-7.

[3] We may compare with this the character of Hadrian's Wall in Britain: here also a great scheme was magnificently designed but often spoilt through insufficient attention to details by subordinates.

[4] Cf. p. 66.

[5] For Italy cf. the walls of Pompeii, Ostia (Sullan period), Aosta, and Turin; Arabia, Dmêr, El Lejjun, Bosnia, Morgojelo.

straightforward construction was as capable, and even brilliant, in the third century, as in epochs associated more commonly with Roman architectural or tactical achievement. Once built, moreover, it did not remain unchanged. It was brought up to date with later developments, and was even destined, in its newer form, to set the pattern for other important Walls.

II. FROM AURELIAN TO HONORIUS

IN the second period a great change came over the Wall, and it assumed its present form, copied from the first-period galleried sectors. On the rampart-walk of the first period was built a mighty gallery, making a covered passage, provided with a varying number of loop-holes towards the country, and open arcades towards the City. On top of the gallery ran an upper rampart-walk, open to the sky, and protected by a frontal parapet and merlons. In many sectors the towers were also heightened, being entirely rebuilt in much grander style, illustrated by *turris omnium perfectissima*;[1] where they were left untouched the newly-heightened Wall equalled them in height. The new Wall was in truth a mighty bulwark, probably bigger than any other in the Roman world at the time when it was built.

Great changes also took place at the Gates. All were remodelled to suit the new Wall. But two, Portae Appia and Asinaria, were entirely rebuilt in the sombre and stately style of Turin, Spalato, and Trier, or of the towering portals shown on the medallions[2] of Arras and Moguntiacum. This experiment was not repeated in Rome, and it has an individuality which would mark all its products as contemporary, even if this dating was not proved by their relation to the new Wall.

Who was responsible for this important change? It is quite clear that it was not Honorius, whose work at the Gates, as the inscriptions[3] of Portae Labicana and Tiburtina prove, was quite a different type of stone construction, associated with a third period whenever it occurs. Furthermore, activity on the Wall at an epoch between those of Aurelian and Honorius is proved by remains at three different points and by one literary source. The level of the ground outside the north-east angle of Castra Praetoria was altered,[4] and on the new level were found tiles stamped OF·S·OF·DOM·DECEMB which belong to the first decade of the third century. Again, similarly stamped tiles, mixed with some of the Hadrianic age, were found in the filling which blocked Porta Ostiensis West.[5] Finally, the only tiles later than Aurelian recorded to have come from the heightened first curtain east of Porta Ostiensis East belonged also to this Diocletianic series.[6] All three are then defensive measures, and their age and character alike associate them with the statement[7] contained in the

[1] Tower B 14, see also towers B 4, 18, G 15–20.
[2] Medallions, Beaurains, see p. 126, n. 1. Moguntiacum, Blanchet, *Enceintes romaines*, pl. xxi, 4.
[3] *C. I. L.* vi. 1189, 1190.
[4] Lanciani, *N. Scav.* 1888, p. 734.
[5] Lanciani, *B. C.* xx (1892), p. 93.   [6] *N. Scav.* 1889, p. 17.
[7] Mommsen, *Chronograph: Abhandlung d. K. Sächs. Ges. d. Wissensch.*, ii, p. 648. Lactantius, *de morte persecutorum*, 27.

Chronograph of 354, 'fossatum aperuit, sed non perfecit (Maxentius)'. They are direct proof of a Maxentian restoration of the Wall.

Is, then, the great second-period restoration to be associated with this minor work and with the ditch-digging which was not completed? There is no direct evidence for this conclusion, but some very strong presumptive proof can be adduced. In the first place, historical circumstances in no way demand a rebuilding of the Wall between the time of Maxentius and Honorius, while, on the other hand, a Maxentian restoration is appropriate. The City Wall was threatened[1] three times during the reign of Maxentius; and only on the last occasion, as Seeck[2] acutely notes, did Maxentius make the unwise blunder of rejecting its shelter. This was due either to pressure from the City populace, which understood nothing of strategy, or to the feeling of Maxentius that treachery might make it impossible to endure a siege. The two first invasions, of Severus and of Galerius, had come early and late in 307, when Maxentius had been Emperor for barely a year. Yet, after they were over, it must have been abundantly plain that, although a breathing-space might occur, the offensive from the north certainly would be renewed. To this time, then, may be very suitably assigned the determination to rebuild the Wall, so as to make it fit to withstand serious attack. For Aurelian's Wall had not been constructed to withstand a determined attack with siege-machinery, such as was bound to come from Constantine or Galerius in the north. These circumstances thus demand a reconstruction with a cogency that can be claimed by no others between the third and fifth centuries. The scope of the work has already been discussed in detail: in general, it is clear that the Wall became such a barrier as no besieging army could hope to cross without the most elaborate preparations, which could be adequately thwarted by a minimum garrison. It is, in fact, just the expression that Maxentius might have been expected to give to his strategical policy.

The character of the work in general therefore accords well with the view that it belongs to Maxentius. Detail supplies still more remarkable confirmation. The brickwork of the new Wall is not only strikingly like that of the Basilica of Maxentius, but it cannot be much later, since it contains tile bonding-courses, which went out of fashion in Constantine's reign.[3] Again, the scope of the rebuilding has peculiar features which once again lead us to Maxentius. Not only was the rebuilding never com-

---

[1] Lactantius, *de morte persecutorum*, caps. 26, 27, 40; Eutrop. x. 2 (4).

[2] Seeck, *Untergang der Antiken Welt*. i, p. 124.

[3] The apse of the Basilica Maxentii contains none: Arco di Malborghetto very few, see Töbelmann, *Abhandl. d. Heidelberger Akad. d. Wissenschaften*, 2, 1915, pls. vii, xiv; cf. also Dr. E. Van Deman, *A. J. A.* 1912, p. 425.

pleted, like the ditch of which the Chronograph speaks, but it started on grandiose lines, which had soon to be modified. This appears in all sections of the work, but it is perhaps clearest in the treatment of the new Wall-towers. On the sector between Portae Pinciana and Salaria some mighty new towers [1] were built, of the type given by Lanciani's *turris omnium perfectissima.* And similar towers [2] once existed on the sector between the Lateran and the Anfiteatro Castrense. But these towers are rare, and their erection cannot be squared with the fact that, at the west end of the Pincian sector, some of the little towers, [3] designed to fit a first-period galleried Wall, and wholly unfitted for use with the Wall as increased in height, were allowed to remain unaltered. For the most part the older towers elsewhere also were adapted as well as might be in the ways described in a former section. But the possibility enunciated there, that the new towers were built in order to gain effective outlook, will not explain their distribution. They are not placed where that outlook is most needed; and, at all events, good outlook is required upon every sector of a military work. This consideration suggests that all the towers originally were intended to have additional stories, but that the scheme of refitment broke down, whereupon the newly-heightened wall had to be attached to the older towers as well as might be. Some of the towers thus received no alteration whatever.

Similar facts emerge on the Wall. It has been noted that, although the predominating type of wall in use at this period is a galleried wall (copied from the little galleried wall of the first period which appears in the sector of San Giovanni), there are numerous sectors [4] where this arrangement is abandoned for the very awkward type of thin wall, without gallery, which crowns the older wall of the first period. This is well shown in the sectors of San Saba and of the Caserma di Artiglieria pesante campale. Again, the River Wall never can have been heightened at all if Procopius's description [5] of it is correct; and the same observation applies to the river walls of the Mausoleum [6] if these belong to this age at all. Another sector is that between Porta Tiburtina and Porta Maggiore. There were thus considerable sections of the Wall, though not preponderatingly large ones, which had no gallery and were heightened by means of an altogether inferior device, which was much quicker constructed than the gallery, with its elaborate arrangements for centring. But does not this once more look like the abandonment of a vastly superior scheme for one which could give the same external effect, but would require for its erection much less time, skill, and money?

[1] Towers B 4, 14, 18. [2] Towers G 15, 20. [3] Towers B 1-3, 5, 6.
[4] Sectors E, F, L 36-50. [5] *B. G.* ii. 9. Sectors Q and R. [6] Procopius, *B. G.* ii. 9.

Finally, the restoration at the Gates also started with grand and bold conceptions. The new Porta Appia,[1] with its tremendous towers of lofty outline, comes to rank with the other great gates of the age, such as Porta Nigra at Trier and Porta Palatina at Turin. It is matched, if not surpassed, by the new Porta Asinaria,[2] where two ordinary wall-towers were converted, with great cunning, into enormous flanking-towers for a Gate of exceptional width and height. But there the grandiose scheme ends. On the other Gates the work of this period amounts to nothing more than a matter-of-fact alteration of first-period gates in order to fit the arrangements of the newly-heightened wall. Portae Latina[3] and Ostiensis East,[4] for example, were strengthened and received inner courts, but their external aspect did not change very much. A similar arrangement seems also to have existed at Portae Pinciana[5] and Praenestina.[6] Again, then, there is evidence for a magnificent scheme of re-building, meant to provide the City with new gates on the northern model. This proceeded so far, and then was continued on a much less imposing scale. To the breakdown of the original plan is owing both the preservation of so many Aurelianic outlines and the fact that all the necessary work was finished in the same epoch: and about this final point there is no room for doubt, since the character of the building is the same throughout.

This state of affairs harmonizes completely with the career of Maxentius. Historical documentation for this Emperor's reign is unfortunately scarce, for not only his armies but his religion happened to be beaten, and the result was that he received no panegyric from secular historians, and much concentrated vilification from ecclesiastics, who forgot to be merciful in the moment of triumph. Nevertheless, certain features of his Home-policy remain clear. The reign opened with some splendid architectural projects,[7] the Basilica Nova, the rebuilding of the Temple of Venus and Rome, and the construction of the huge Circus along the Via Appia, outside the Wall. Programme-coins,[8] with the reverse CONSERVATOR URBIS SUAE, are issued to accompany this splendid embellishment of the City. Yet danger is pending, and how admirably the beginnings of the Wall-building would fit in with the need. On this hypothesis the great Gates come into being; and perhaps they too are advertisements,[9] like the coins, for they span the roads to the new Circus,

[1] See p. 141, fig. 25.
[2] See p. 157, pl. XIV.
[3] See fig. 17.
[4] See fig. 19.
[5] See p. 167.
[6] See p. 213.
[7] See Rivoira, *R. Arch.*, pp. 211–19, figs. 258–67.
[8] Cohen, *Médailles Impériales*, vol. vi. Aurélien, 216–22. Cf. the action of Severus.
[9] Cf. the fountain of Commodus, on Via Appia, built to gloze over the confiscation of the Villa Quintiliorum.

and remind the populace of the watchful care of their *Conservator*. This, at least, would explain (as no other hypothesis will) why Gates so different in importance as Portae Appia and Asinaria should have been selected for first and similar treatment. The new Wall and Towers also began to rise, destined to be an especially magnificent mural crown for Royal Rome. But the reign, which began so brightly, clouded over towards the end. After 310, when Maximianus[1] deserted from Maxentius, and presently died, it became clear that an attack from Constantine would not be so long in coming. This factor in itself might be thought sufficient to account for the abandonment of the more elaborate scheme of reconstruction, and for the concentration upon the erection of an efficient barrier, as ugly in design as might be so long as it was strong. But an equally valid reason for the change may well have been the fact that the other large and costly building-schemes already mentioned were in progress at the same time, and that the drain upon the Treasury had to be met by heavy extra taxation, as recorded by the Chronograph[2] of 354.

Then comes the final scene. When Constantine descends from the north not all the towers are ready, and a ditch is being dug;[2] but the Wall is in fighting trim. Yet, to every one's surprise, Maxentius comes outside the Wall, and trusts his luck at the battle of Saxa Rubra. As Seeck[3] acutely notes 'blieb er noch ruhig stehen, wie er es in den Kriegen gegen Severus und Galerius gethan hatte, so müsste auch Constantins Unternehmen zweifellos scheitern.' The Emperor, however, had been led by the uproar in the City[4] to defend it in more spectacular fashion. It looks as if his hand had been forced. Perhaps the people had not sufficient faith to withstand a siege, or perhaps, as the Constantinian historians[5] assert, they were tired of oppression, and Maxentius could no longer count on their support. The building-programme, among other things, may well have cost too much in extra taxation and labour.

This reading of the evidence is attractive, and its appropriate relation to the historical facts seems difficult to evade. To sum up; it is clear from the character of the building that the reconstruction belongs to the early fourth century. A date after Constantine will not suit it. This granted, and taken in connexion with the fact that both archaeology and literature hint at a restoration by Maxentius, it seems impossible not to connect the second period of construction on Aurelian's Wall with the last great Italian

---

[1] Eutrop. x. 3. 2: Zosimus, ii. 11.   [2] *Chronograph*, see p. 30.
[3] O. Seeck, *Untergang der Antiken Welt*. i, p. 124.
[4] Lactant. *de morte persecutorum*, 40.
[5] Ibid. *loc. cit.* Eusebius, ix. 9 ; *vit. Const.* i. 39; Vict. 40, 24.

Emperor. The circumstances suit the rebuilding and its character-istics so well. Finally, a Maxentian restoration would explain completely the silence of Constantinian historians on the subject of this rebuilding. They could hardly be expected to mention a reconstruction which threatened to nullify all Constantine's efforts to capture Rome. Under the circumstances, then, the case for associating this thorough but hurried restoration with Maxentius seems strong enough to be worth emphasis.

III. THE RESTORATION OF HONORIUS

THIS restoration is attested by inscriptions,[1] and mentioned by the poet Claudian,[2] and it is noteworthy that the poetry refers to nothing more than a repair, and not to a great reconstruction such as has just been considered. The lines [3]

'Erexit subitas turres cinctosque coegit,
Septem continuo colles iuvenescere muro'

cannot be taken to mean anything so elaborate. The inscriptions, which record the erection of statues as a thank-offering to Arcadius and Honorius, are equally precise; they state in simple terms that the statues [4] were voted, 'ob instauratos Urbi Aeternae muros portas ac turres, egestis immensis ruderibus'. Clearly, this need not refer to such an operation as doubling the Wall in height, and entirely rebuilding many Gates.

With the third-period work on the Wall, however, these statements agree very well. The Wall and towers were restored; the towers received, wherever possible, loop-holes instead of windows; while the structure of the Wall was not altered, but refaced and repaired where this was required. The Gates received new stone curtains, of a type which has been inscribed at Portae Labicana [5] and Tiburtina,[6] but which appears uninscribed at Portae Praenestina [7] (Porta Labicana's twin), Latina [8] and the Porta Chiusa.[9] These were two-storied travertine curtains, built in Syrian fashion,[10] with arcuate window-hoods, and it is not clear whether they were something new in Rome or whether, as is equally possible, they were copying the windows of Aurelian's stone curtains, which have all perished. There were also single-storied stone curtains, added at Portae Appia,[11] Ostiensis East,[12] and Pinciana.[13] And it is likely that the similar curtains at Portae Flaminia,[14] Salaria,[15] and Aurelia-Pancraziana [16] belong to this epoch too. Aurelian's double Gates (except Porta [17] Portuensis) were now reduced, by curtains with one story of stone, to Gates with a single arch only, in order to facilitate defence. All the new gateways were fitted with a portcullis.

More important was the choice of the old quadrangular type of gateway tower. This choice had nothing to do with the

---

[1] *C. I. L.* vi. 1188, 1189, 1190.   [2] Claudian, *de VI Consulatu Honorii,* 529–34.
[3] Ibid., lines 533, 534.   [4] They were therefore not in the original scheme.
[5] p. 206, fig. 39.   [6] p. 170, pl. XVI*b*.
[7] p. 214.   [8] Pl. IX*a*.   [9] Pl. XVII*a*.
[10] For the fashion, cf. Butler, *Architecture and other Arts,* pp. 37, 166–7.
[11] p. 135, pl. XII.   [12] p. 113, pl. X.   [13] p. 166, pl. XV*b*.
[14] p. 195, n. 2.   [15] p. 187, pl. XVIII*a*.
[16] p. 222.   [17] p. 204.

contemporary return of these solid towers to fashion[1]. It resulted from the decision that if the semicircular gateway towers were to be thoroughly strengthened and faced in stone, the best and cheapest way to do so was to build quadrangular towers round the curved forms, using the latter as a core. The intention seems to have been to surround the semicircular towers of most Gates in this way. But at one Gate at least, Porta[2] Ostiensis East, the semicircular form was retained, and followed by the new facing, while the towers received an extra story: they also received the serrate tile cornices which were now becoming common—the bands of decoration which are sparingly used, but with such splendid effect, on the plain walls[3] of Hagia Sophia, Salonika, or Hagia Paraskeva, Sofia, or, in Rome itself, on the drum of S. Stefano Rotondo. At Portae Salaria[4] and Nomentana[5] the semicircular form was also left, apparently without any stone facing whatever. Porta Salaria received an extra story now, like Porta Pinciana,[6] and this brought them into line with Porta Ostiensis East.

The next point to note is that not all the work of this period was finished. This incompleteness is not really connected with the odd distribution of the inscriptions, which is due to another factor in the same chain of historical events. As Claudian[7] notes, the restoration of the Wall began at the end of the year 401, *audito rumore Getarum*, with which is to be connected the entry in the Chronicon Cuspiniani, *et intravit Alaricus in Italiam ad XIV Kal. Dec.* To this time, as has already been noted[8] in detail, belong the inscriptions on the Gates, of which the main text must have been cut before the beginning of March 402, since it does not mention Theodosius II, the new Emperor created in February. After the accession of that Emperor no more examples were cut, but the vow which they recorded was later carried out by the City Prefect of 403, Flavius Macrobius Longinianus. No doubt the work was pressed on with desperate haste until the spring of 403, when Stilicho's victory at Pollentia, on Easter Sunday, freed Rome from the impending terror. Then the work was dropped, with the result that sixteen months of building had been done on the Wall, without sufficing to complete the whole

---

[1] This is a difficult question. It looks, indeed, as if in NW.-European *military* work, the evolution was, *exceptis multis excipiendis*, from square to semicircle or polygon ; not so in the towns, or in Hellenic building areas, whether military or civil. Here all the types stand side by side.

[2] p. 115, pl. XI*b*.

[3] Hagia Sophia, Rivoira, *Lombard. Arch.* p. 9, fig. 2. Hagia Paraskeva, personal observation. S. Stef. Rot., Rivoira, loc. cit. pp. 25–6. See also, above, p. 114.

[4] Pl. XVIII.

[5] Fig. 15.

[6] See p. 164, fig. 31.

[7] Claudian, *de VI Cons. Hon.*, l. 230.

[8] See p. 34.

reconstruction. Porta Latina[1] still required towers: the north tower of Porta Tiburtina[2] may have been also unfinished: the final touches were not given to Porta Appia.[3] Yet the achievement was not small for so short a time. The whole Wall was now in good repair, and the towers had been converted[4] from *ballista*-casemates into castles for archers. Almost every Gate was completely refurbished. The whole task must have taxed the resources of even so great a City, and is to be compared with the speed inspired at Constantinople by the 'Scourge of God' in 447, when five miles of Wall were built[5] in sixty days.

In this reconstruction, hurried though it was, certain important constructional facts deserve note. Uniformity of design stands out as clear as in former schemes. The stonework follows a standard type—it is all stolen from earlier structures, and fitted together as well as may be. The sizes[6] of the arches in the surviving gates pair off; Porta Appia goes with Porta Ostiensis East, Porta Latina with Porta Pinciana, Porta Tiburtina with the Porta Chiusa. This suggests that the Gates were let out in pairs to different building *collegia*, as would be done in modern times, except that the labour would be done under contract and not under compulsion. Interesting, too, is the appearance[7] for the first time of the Cross and Chrism on the Gateway arches, or in the brickwork of Gate-towers, as if for protection against such crafts and assaults of the Devil as lightning. It is perhaps worth while to emphasize here once more the fact that these symbols all have their earlier forms. They have usually been associated with Belisarius, but by his time richer and more elaborate forms had appeared, and were abundantly used elsewhere in Rome.

The origin of the type of curtain used in this period remains for the moment obscure. The arcuate hoods for windows, usually monolithic, are strongly reminiscent of Syrian architecture.[8] And the whole aspect of the structure, sheer and bare, devoid of all but the most elementary decoration, is very like that of the early Syrian stonework, before it becomes fantastically elaborate. But it may well be that the resemblance is fortuitous, for both in Syria and Rome the effect is produced entirely by the material used, and by the utilitarian conception of functions involved; in either place the stone was built into position, and ornamentation followed, according to the means and wishes of

[1] See p. 102.
[2] See p. 176.   [3] See p. 130.
[4] On the strategical significance of this see p. 80, also *D. U. J.* xxv, p. 404.
[5] *C. I. L.* iii. 734.
[6] See pp. 113, 166, 181.
[7] See pp. 107-8, fig. 18.
[8] See Butler, *Princeton Expedition to Syria*, vol. ii, *passim*.

the constructing party. And the usual result—a plain unbroken surface, conceived in simple quadrangular forms—possessed a quiet dignity and serenity of its own. To a fortified gateway-curtain this style of building was especially suited. At Rome attackers saw before them a precipitous frowning wall-face, to which the cornice which crowned it, gave a top-heavy threatening appearance. And above all, between pointed merlons, and in heroic guise, stood the two Unconquered Augusti, in attitude of ever-watchful repose, or with spear poised to hurl against impious assailants of the Eternal City. The result is a noble Gateway, which has as much in common with the statue-bedecked medieval gateways [1] as with the Roman triumphal arch. But the majestic conception was the result of chance rather than design, for it must be remembered that the statues were only put there by a vote of the Senate, which probably took no account whatever of the design of the gateways. There is, however, one feature of this restoration, which was apparently a new and noteworthy artistic discovery. That was the use of marble towers, for decorating a principal entrance. It was an old notion to build specially ornate gateways for the main entrances of a City. It was something new to face the severe form of their bastions with gleaming marble, and the design was so successful that Portae Flaminia and Appia, which were treated in this way, have never ceased to excite admiration. The scheme was thoroughly in keeping with the artistic feeling of the age, which was in full reaction against the over-elaboration of classical forms that had crippled expression in the Capital since the age of the Antonines. Furthermore, it had far-reaching influences, which are discussed below.

Especially noteworthy is the tactical conception which fits the Wall as reconstructed at this time. The conception is that of a sea-wall, a mighty barrier from which no powerful offensive attack is ever conducted, but which repels assailing forces by sheer weight and massive bulk. The towers no longer harbour *ballistae*, but shelter bowmen; and artillery can be fitted on top of the towers as an exceptional,[2] and not as a permanent, defence. This is an important distinction, to be contrasted with the defence of Aurelian's day, when the towers were obviously meant to be fitted habitually with *ballistae*. Nor were the Gates very numerous. The character of the brickwork which blocks most of the surviving posterns does not suggest a later date for their disuse than this epoch, and they seem rather to have been filled up, like Porta Ostiensis West, in the second period.[3] This reduced the entrances

---

[1] e. g. Alnwick Castle, Bothal, Chepstow, and London Bridge.
[2] See Procop. *B. G.* i. 21.
[3] See p. 220.

to the City from twenty-eight to twenty-two. And so Rome became an impregnable and well-stocked castle, around which besiegers might surge for a year and a day, without making much impression on the defences, while citizens could go their ways unhindered behind the ramparts. The policy is the logical development of Maxentian tactics; but, while Maxentius adopted this strategy only because he was not full Augustus, it now governs the whole fortification of the Capital of the Empire, at a time when the relations between Augusti were never so cordial. Yet no one can deny that in itself (given a healthy Empire) the device was successful, and only explosive artillery was to breach the Wall. The assaults of Bixio[1] and Garibaldi,[2] in 1849 and 1870, did greater harm than all previous erosions of Time.

The new Wall of Rome was ready for the triumphal entry of Honorius in 404. Eight years later, in 412, Constantinople[3] was equipped with a magnificent Land Wall, which was built on entirely free ground. There was nothing to prevent the latest plan being chosen. It is therefore interesting that its plan should have very closely resembled that of Old Rome's Wall, with some minor differences and new ideas here and there. The new Wall was a sixty-foot structure, without a gallery (but the gallery on the Rome wall was only a device for increasing its height), reached by ramps at very rare intervals, and defended by great rectangular towers which were provided with loop-holed windows, and built to the same height as the Wall. Its gates were stone-faced structures, with single arches and quadrangular towers, which had covered upper stories and battlemented tops. The likeness between these gates and Portae Appia, Flaminia, Latina (as it was meant to be), or Tiburtina is very striking.

But the resemblance did not end here, for there may be added the Golden Gate, first identified by Strzygowski[4] as the mighty marble structure which overlooks the Roumelian railroad. It was once assumed that this Gate was built by Theodosius I, in order to celebrate his victory over Magnus Maximus in 388. But E. Weigand[5] has recently pointed out that this dating was groundless, and that the structure was pretty certainly built in 412 by Theodosius II, who later gilded[6] Gates both at Constantinople and Antioch, in 425. The tops of its marble bastions were finished off with a balustrade or parapet, and the gate was decorated with various statues, among which was one

[1] Bixio, at Porta Aurelia-Pancraziana, see p. 221.
[2] Garibaldi, at Porta Salaria, p. 185.
[3] See Van Millingen, *Byzantine Constantinople*, 1899, *passim*.
[4] J. Strzygowski, *Jahrb. d. Arch. Inst.*, 1893, article 1.
[5] E. Weigand, *Athen. Mittheil.* xxxix (1914), article 1.
[6] John Malalas, ed. Bonn, p. 362.

of Theodosius.[1] The entrance itself was triple, with one large central arch and two smaller side arches, of simple design, with lintels, and relieving arches above them, in stone. The striking similarity of this structure, with its great marble bastions and statue of Theodosius, to the marble Gates of Rome is not to be disputed. Not only does the same general idea appear, but many points in the execution are exactly the same. The same type of voussoir, giving an evenly curved extrados, was chosen for the arches. The proportions of the bastions, and their relation to the gateway curtain was similar, and the decoration of the top, by a simple moulding of late-classical type, was almost identical. These resemblances are not strong enough to prove that the same architect was responsible for both Walls: but they seem to be altogether too many and too close, both in time and type, to have been the product of completely independent designers. In short, whether the resemblance be the result of official co-operation, or of community of ideas, it leads to the same general conclusion. The builder of the Wall of Anthemius in Constantinople was clearly inspired by the same ideals as the Honorian restorer of Aurelian's Wall in Rome.

Such, then, were the effects of the Honorian restoration. An imperfect thing in itself, carried through in feverish haste, while Alaric was on the march, it ranked in magnificence with the Wall of Anthemius in Constantinople, and thus embodied the ideas which influenced military architecture for a thousand years. Its architect is unknown, and his very scheme is much hidden in a tangle of earlier and later remains. But the main line of his policy emerges crisp and clear. It involved the introduction of stone Gateways, flanked by quadrangular stone-faced towers and crowned by statues of the Augusti: the earlier double-arched Gates were abolished, except at Porta Portuensis: marble towers were built to decorate *Viae Flaminia* and *Appia*: and the Wall-towers were finally adapted to suit archers rather than artillery. These were the changes which brought the Wall of Rome into the forefront of late-Roman barriers. The offensive days of the Empire were over: thenceforward came centuries of dignified defence.

[1] Theophanes, a. 6332; ed. Bonn, l. 634.

IV. FROM HONORIUS TO NARSES

§ 1. PERIOD IV

THE date of Period IV is obscure. Its clearest traces occur at Porta Appia,[1] and on the Wall-towers between there and Porta Metrobia.[2] They are marked by bands of travertine blocks, set between mediocre tile-facing. At Porta Appia the whole repair is connected with the great cracks which continued to appear in the second-period towers, threatening the total collapse of the gateway. Without this fact it would be rash to connect Period IV with the repairs envisaged in the decree[3] of Valentinian III, 'de Pantapōlis ad Urbem' dated to A.D. 440. These repairs must have come after the earthquake[4] of A.D. 442, which damaged the Colosseum and other City buildings. It must necessarily have seriously increased the cracking in Porta Appia, and no doubt made its action felt not only there, but at every point on the Wall where stress existed.[5] The travertine bands which distinguish this repair occur, moreover, in just such work as would be required after an earthquake, namely, in buttressing and refacing of prominent sections of the Wall and towers, and they are used in brick-faced concrete where courses of tiles would normally be used in a stone structure. It is therefore reasonable to recognize in this type of construction the results of the earthquake of 442, and to assign it to Valentinian III.

Perhaps the most noteworthy repairs in this series, excepting Porta Appia, which was important, and is discussed below, were the buttresses east of that gate, where the tower[6] at the angle of Aqua Antoniniana was made into an exceptionally large angle-*ballistarium*; the buttressing system east of Porta Latina,[7] which gave extra solidity to the important angle there involving the construction of a special *necessarium* shoot (see pl. VIIIa): and the buttressing of two towers,[8] situated at the tips of a weak re-entrant, east and west of Porta Metrobia, which converted them into large *ballistaria*, completely covering the approaches to the Gate. Probably all these towers had been converted into the great *ballistaria* before this restoration, and the primitive core formed by Aurelian's structure was unequal to the strain. The restorations of Porta Appia[9] were more important. It would seem that

---

[1] See p. 127, fig. 21. [2] Towers J 2, 3; curtain J 19.
[3] *Novellae Val.* iii, tit. v, see p. 36.
[4] *C. I. L.* vi. 32086–32090: cf. also Paul Diac., *Hist. Misc.* xiv, p. 961 (Migne).
[5] The distribution of this suggests that the earthquake affected the southern side of the defences only, between Porta Tiburtina and the river.
[6] Tower K 7. [7] Curtain J 19.
[8] Towers, H 10, J 3. [9] See pp. 126, 133.

opportunity was taken now, not only to alter completely the heavy vaulting system of the interior, which was badly cracked, but to add extra stories to the towers, giving them the full height which they now possess. But the proof that the increase in height belongs to this period depends entirely upon the resemblance between the facing of the new stories and that of the quadrangular towers as repaired in this period: and this might, after all, be a fallacious resemblance, since the tile-facing of this date, and for some time beyond it, becomes indistinct in style.

With this heightening certainly went also the addition of an extra story to the gateway-curtain. But if a critic were to suggest that these improvements were the work of Theoderic, it would be impossible to deny it in the present stage of knowledge. The story of Porta Appia's evolution may therefore be slightly more complicated than a straightforward interpretation would allow, and Valentinian may only have repaired the Gate, while Theoderic added to it. Future research may provide a more satisfactory answer to the riddle.

§ 2. PERIOD V. THEODERIC'S RESTORATION

A general restoration of buildings in Rome during the first decade of the sixth century is attested by Cassiodorus.[1] But his language is loose, and it is not plain whether his phrase 'moenia' means City Wall or buildings in general. It is certain, however, that the Wall was included in the restoration, since tiles [2] of Theoderic have been found therein, both near Porta Asinaria and in Porta Flaminia. But it is far from certain whether this restoration included any schemes of rebuilding. It should be noted, as evidence for the date of the fortifications of Hadrian's Mausoleum that it was now [3] called 'carcer Theoderici'. If Theoderic was using it as a state prison, there can be little doubt that it had been fortified before his time. On the whole, however, the evidence for the character of Theoderic's work on the Wall is extremely shadowy.

§ 3. PERIOD VI. BELISARIUS IN 536

The reconstruction by Belisarius in 536 is to be carefully distinguished from two others with which he was associated. It was the prelude to the Gothic siege of 537, after the capture of the City for the East-Roman Empire, upon the downfall of the Ostrogothic kingdom of Theoderic, in the hands of the Queen-regent Amalasuntha. Procopius [4] tells us, in passages quoted at length in an earlier section, that Belisarius paid great attention

---

[1] Cassiod. *Variarum* i. 25, ii. 33 = *Excerpt. vales.* 67: see above, p. 37, for full quotation.
[2] *Suppl. Pap. Amer. Acad. R.* i. 1905; *C.I.L.* xv. i. 1665b, 27, see p. 37.
[3] Carcer Theoderici, Borgatti, Castel di Sant' Angelo, pp. 31–2: the question is, however, far from certain.   [4] *B. G.* i. 14.

to the City Walls, which were damaged in many places, and that he fitted them with a new kind of merlon, with a side wall which gave protection on the left side of defenders. The new feature was gamma-shaped in plan, but it was really an old device.[1] It occurs on the Wall of Pompeii, and was a Hellenistic invention, which Belisarius borrowed for his own purposes. Sections of parapets like these are to be seen[2] south of Porta Tiburtina. No doubt the Wall was also refaced. But Belisarius did not trust to the Wall alone for defence. He dug a large ditch[3] (or ditches, according to one graphic passage of Procopius) all round the City, and it would be greatly to the interest of the study of late-Roman fortifications if this ditch were to be discovered. Its position, as a securely dated structure, which would be quite certainly distinguishable from the ditch of Maxentius (if that happened to turn up in the same trench), would throw great light upon the late-Roman theory of entrenchment. At the Gates great 'dead-fall' mantraps[4] were arranged, in addition to the ordinary gateway defences.

Of great interest also was the arrangement of machinery on the sectors of the Wall, from Porta Pinciana to Porta Prae-nestina, which were in danger of direct attack by the Goths. The towers were provided with *ballistae*, which are described as great machines with steel springs,[5] improvements on the older Augustan models, so powerful that at the range of two bow-shots they would easily pierce a tree or a stone. And on the parapet, fixed to the merlons, there were little machines,[6] called *onagri*, which projected small stones, and kept up what modern tacticians would call a 'curtain-fire' or a 'creeping-barrage', in addition to the much heavier missiles thrown by the *ballistae* (a case is recorded, not in this siege, where one of the *ballista*-shot pro-jectiles transfixed and pinned together five men). In another interesting passage[7] Procopius notes that *ballistae* οὐ . . . πέμ-πουσιν ὅτι μὴ ἐξ ἐναντίας . . . τὰ βέλη. This passage is something of a puzzle: it can hardly mean that the machines only shot straight ahead, for they were habitually mounted upon platforms for swivelling. The context[8] suggests that it is more likely to mean that the machines would not shoot downwards, so as to hit objects immediately below the Wall. And this would explain the motive of Belisarius in digging a ditch, in order to keep attackers away from the dead ground just in front of the Wall.

[1] Durm, *Baukunst der Römern*, p. 439, figs. 494, 495.
[2] Curtain, F 12.
[3] Ditch, *B. G.* i. 14 τάφρον βαθεῖαν; Ditches, *B. G.* iii. 24: τάφρους βαθείας : . ; ὀρύξας.
[4] *B. G.* i. 21.
[5] *B. G.* i. 21.   These are the same as the Übergeschütz of Schramm.
[6] *B. G.* i. 21.   [7] *B. G.* i. 21.
[8] See p. 22.   See also *D. U. J.* xxv, pp. 399–405.

When the siege came, the preparations proved a great success; and it was to them, and not to the prowess of Roman arms (Belisarius ascribed Roman ill-luck to lack of mounted mail-clad archers [1]—an invention from the East), that the Imperial forces owed their victory. The *ballistae* wrecked [2] the Gothic siege-machinery at the edge of the ditch, and kept all but long-distance weapons away from the Wall. The operations throughout were a great credit to the ingenuity of Belisarius, and a thorough vindication of the policy of Maxentius, which he was following.

§ 4. PERIOD VII. 537 to 546

The retreat of the Goths was followed by a refacing of the Walls, carried out in rather rough block-and-brick work extending only to those parts [3] of the circuit which had been the object of Gothic attack, and it is therefore to be distinguished from the former period. This refacing was particularly lavish between Portae Salaria and Pinciana, where the heaviest fighting had been. It is not recorded in literary sources. The work was identified as Belisarian by Nibby [4] and Parker, [5] but the inference has not hitherto been drawn that it must represent repairs of the years 537 to 546. The repairs of 536 must have included the whole circuit, and are not now to be certainly identified.

§ 5. PERIOD VIII. BELISARIUS IN 547

The next repair is accorded considerable space in literature. In December 546, the City was betrayed to Totila by Isaurian soldier-traitors, stationed near Porta Asinaria. [6] Porta Asinaria was burst open, and the Goths began a reign of terror and destruction, which was only checked by their superstitious fear, and by the courage of Deacon Pelagius in facing Totila. Totila's declared policy was to dismantle the Walls, and to make them useless; and in one passage [7] Procopius definitely states that τοῦ μὲν οὖν περιβόλου ἐν χωρίοις πολλοῖς τοσοῦτον καθεῖλεν ὅσον ἐς τριτημόριον τοῦ παντὸς μάλιστα. This, as has already been noted, is an exaggeration, if it is considered in terms of length; and a subsequent passage of Procopius [8] proves that what was damaged was the face of the Wall. It may be, then, that Totila did not demolish the Wall, but half undermined it, by picking away the face; and this Belisarius sought to repair, on recapturing the City in 547 by a *coup de main* from Portus, when Totila had

[1] *B. G.* vi. 3.
[2] *B. G.* i. 22.
[3] Sector B, *passim.*
[4] Nibby, p. 319.
[5] Parker, see p. 89.
[6] Procop. *B. G.* iii. 20.
[7] *B. G.* iii. 22.
[8] *B. G.* iii. 24 ὅπως μόνον τὸ τῆς οἰκοδομίας σώζοιτο πρόσωπον.

moved southwards into Apulia. In twenty days, by the aid of palisades [1] at critical points, he put the Wall in defensive order. His repair, as has already been noted, was distinctive enough to be still recognizable. Its technique is that which often must have been applied to City Walls in the days when the Empire was crumbling,[2] and Procopius himself mentions another example from Pisaurum.[3] In Rome many stretches of Wall [4] and many towers [5] were refaced with ill-selected blocks of *tufo* or *peperino*, probably stolen from ancient tombs. Evidently the Wall's face had been torn away to a great depth, and these blocks were inserted to fill the gaps. Their joints are now roughly filled with mortar and scraps of tile, but, obviously, this pointing was later in date than the erection of the blocks, for which mortar cannot have been contemplated, owing to the extreme width of the joints. At the towers the blocks were usually grouped round the older work, forming an external buttress, but many of these have been removed in recent years. Parker, however, made a speciality of photographing them, under the odd impression that they represented the City Wall of the Tarquins, and records of many are thus preserved. The whole reconstruction is of great interest and considerable archaeological value, since it gives a cross-correspondence between architectural and literary evidence at the very close of the classical age.

Before this repair, tradition records that Rome was empty for forty days. The subsequent history of the City is therefore not that of an Imperial Capital, but of the small metropolis of a Byzantine exarchate. Furthermore, the repairs on the Wall drop to their lowest level after this time, and become quite undistinguishable from one another for the historian's purpose. The old tradition of building has disappeared, and in its place comes the botching associated with unskilled labour of any age, and only resembling earlier work by its use of older materials in the most indiscriminate way. Most of these repairs have since been replaced by Papal work, and several disappeared beneath new coats of mortar in 1926–7. But Poggio [6] saw many, and his description is worth remembering here: 'Sunt praeterea muri fragiles ac putridi, ut, nullo impellente, labantur, quorum structura ex variis marmorum contritorum &c. tegularum frustris conglutinata est.' From such material as this it would be vain to attempt the extraction of historical facts.

---

[1] B. G. iii. 24 σκολόπων τε μέγα τι χρῆμα ἔξωθεν ἵστησιν.
[2] Cf. Arles, *J. R. S.* xvi, pp. 186–7, 189.
[3] Pisaurum, Procop. *B. G.* iii. 11; see p. 42.
[4] Curtains, D 22; E 10; G 12; L 24, 34; M 11.
[5] Towers, G 5, 6, 11, 13; K 8; M 8, 10.   [6] See p. 53, n. 4, for ref. and trans.

APPENDIX I

TEXT OF THE EINSIEDELN LIST

THE text given here is based upon the facsimiles of the MS. published by Hülsen in *Atti Pont.* ser. ii, vol. ix, p. 424 and tav. xiii. The leaves of the original codex are Einsiedeln MS. 326, fols. 85 *r.* & *v.*, and 86 *r.*

A porta scī petri cū ipsa porta usq portā flamineā turres xvi propugnacula dcclxxxii posternas iii necessariae iiii fenestrae maiores forinsecus cvii minores lxvi.

A porta flaminea cū ipsa porta usq ad portā pincianā clausā turres xxviiii propugn̄ dcxliiii necess̄ iii fenest̄ maiores foriñs lxxv minores cxvii.

A porta pinciana clausa cum ipsa porta usq ad portā salariā turr̄s xxii ppḡ ccxlvi necess̄ xvii fenest̄ maiōr foriñs cc minōr clx.

A porta salaria cū ipsa porta usq num̄tanā turr̄ x ppḡ cxcviiii nēc ii fēn maiōr foriñs lxxi mīn lxv.

A porta num̄tana cū ipsa porta usq tiburtinā turr̄ lvii ppḡ dcccvi nēc ii fenest̄ maiōr foriñs ccxiiii mīn cc.

A porta tiburtina cum ipsa porta usque ad p̄nestina* turr̄ xviiii ppḡ cū porta p̄nestina cccii necess̄ i fēn maiōr foriñs lxxx maior* cviii.

A porta p̄nestina usq asinariā turr̄ xxvi ppḡ diii nēc vi fenst̄ maiōr foriñs clxxx minōr cl.

A porta asinaria usq m&roviā turr̄ xx ppḡ cccxlii nēc iiii fenest̄ maiōr foriñs cxxx minōr clxxx.

A porta m&rovia usq latinā turr̄ xx ppḡ ccxciiii nēc xvii fēn maiōr foriñs c minōr clxxxiii.

A porta latina usq ad appiā turr̄ xii ppḡ lxxiiii necess̄ vii fēn maiōr foriñs lxxx minōr lxxxv.

A porta appia usq ad ostensem turr̄ xlviii ppḡ dcxv nēc xxviii fēn maiōr foriñs cccxxx minōr cclxxxiiii.

A porta ostense usq ad tiberim turr̄ xxxv ppḡ dccxxxiii nēc xvii fenest̄ maiōr foriñs cxxxviii minōr ccxi.

A flumine tyberi usq ad portā portensi* turr̄ iiii ppḡ lviiii fenest̄ maiōr foriñs x minor xv.

A porta portensi usq aureliam turr̄ xxviiii ppḡ cccc necess̄ ii fēn maiōr foriñs cxxxvii mīn clxiii.

A porta aurelia usq tiberim turr̄ xxvii ppḡ cccxxvii necess̄ xi fēn maiōr foriñs clx mīn cxxi.

A flumine tiberi usq ad portā scī p&ri turr̄ viiii ppḡ ccccclxxxviiii fēn maiōr foriñs xxi & minōr vii posternae ii.

PORTA SCĪ PETRI IN HADRIANIO*. Sunt turres vi ppḡ clxiiii fenest̄ maiōr foriñs xiiii mīn xviii.

Sunt simul turres ccclxxxiii propugnacula v̄īīxx posternae v necessariae cxvi fēn maiōr foriñs n̄lxvi.

* The asterisk denotes mistakes in the original MS.

APPENDIX II

INDEX TO THE TOWERS AND CURTAINS OF THE WALL

Sector A. Porta Flaminia to Porta Pinciana. (*F.U.R.*, 1, 2, 9.)
The Einsiedeln List has xxviiii towers. Only nine of these now show ancient work. But fifteen more exist, no doubt upon ancient sites. So we number backwards in this sector, west from Porta Pinciana. Towers, A 24–16. Curtains, A 25–16. xxiiii should presumably be substituted for xxviiii.

Sector B. Porta Pinciana to Porta Salaria. (*F.U.R.*, 2, 3.)
The Einsiedeln List has xxii towers, including the Gate. This is correct. There are twenty towers, and 20 is missing. Towers, B 1–20. Curtains, B 1–21.

Sector C. Porta Salaria to Porta Nomentana. (*F.U.R.*, 3.)
The Einsiedeln List has x towers, including the Gate. There are ten, excluding the Gate, but 4, 5, 6, 7, 8, and 9 are rebuilt and 8 is missing. Either the ancient arrangement was different, or the List is wrong, as is more likely. Towers, C 1–3, 10*. Curtains, C 1–3, 10*, 11*.

Sector D. Porta Nomentana to Porta Chiusa. (*F.U.R.*, 3, 4, 10, 11.)
The Einsiedeln List, going on to Porta Tiburtina without a break, has lvii towers. There are eighteen towers between Porta Chiusa and Porta Tiburtina. This leaves thirty-nine, of which twenty-one are known, numbers 5, 6, 7, 15, 16, 17 being missing. But it is quite unlikely that there were eighteen on the south side of Castra Praetoria, and an x has probably fallen from the text, i.e. xlvii. Anyhow, we number: Towers, D 1–20. Curtains, D 1–21.

Sector E. Porta Chiusa to Porta Tiburtina. (*F.U.R.*, 11, 18, 24.)
The Einsiedeln List does not run. Towers, E 1–18. Curtains, E 1–19. Towers 1–3 and curtains 1–3½ have disappeared.

Sector F. Porta Tiburtina to Porta Praenestina. (*F.U.R.*, 24, 25, 32.)
The Einsiedeln List gives xviiii towers. Eighteen towers are known, but tower 14 and curtain 14 have been swept away by the railway. Towers, F 1–18. Curtains, F 1–19.

Sector G. Porta Praenestina to Porta Asinaria. (*F.U.R.*, 32, 38, 37.)
The Einsiedeln List gives xxvi towers. Twenty-six are known. Towers, G 1–26. Curtains, G 1–27.

Sector H. Porta Asinaria to Porta Metrobia. (*F.U.R.*, 37, 36, 42.)
The Einsiedeln List gives xx. Thirteen towers are known, and an emendation to xv would be easy, Gate-towers being included. Towers, H 1–13. Curtains, H 1–14.

Sector J. Porta Metrobia to Porta Latina. (*F.U.R.*, 42, 46.)
The Einsiedeln List gives xx towers. Nineteen towers are known, but it is just conceivable that the break-forward in curtain 20, or, again, a Gate-tower, may have counted as the twentieth. Towers, J 1–19. Curtains, J 1–20.

Sector K.   Porta Latina to Porta Appia. (*F.U.R.*, 46.)
The Einsiedeln List gives xii towers. Eleven towers are known, or twelve, counting the turret at Aqua Antoniniana: 4 is missing. Towers, K 1–11. Curtains, K 1–12.

Sector L.   Porta Appia to Porta Ostiensis East. (*F.U.R.*, 46, 41, 44.)
The Einsiedeln List gives xlviii. This is too little, for fifty towers are known, though five, 11, 13, 29, 30, and 34 are missing, 34 perhaps in ancient times. Towers 13–21 and curtains 14–21 were removed, together with Porta Ardeatina, when the Bastione di Sangallo was built in 1539. Towers, L 1–50. Curtains, L 1–51.

Sector M.   Porta Ostiensis to the Tiber. (*F.U.R.*, 40, 44, 43, 39.)
The Einsiedeln List gives xxxv. Twenty-three towers are known, and twenty-four curtains, but many of the towers on the river-bank are missing. Towers, M 1–23. Curtains, M 1–24.

Sector N.   Porta Portuensis to the Tiber. (*F.U.R.*, 39.)
The Einsiedeln List gives iiii. Maggi shows four, including the eastern Gate-tower.

Sector O.   Porta Portuensis to Porta Pancraziana. (*F.U.R.*, 39, 33, 27.)
The Einsiedeln List gives xxviiii. Fifteen are known, and there may well have been more: Tempesta shows thirty, Maggi twenty-two.

Sector P.   Porta Pancraziana to the Tiber. (*F.U.R.*, 27, 20.)
The Einsiedeln List gives xxiiii. Seventeen are known; but Maggi marks sixteen and Tempesta twenty; adding two for Porta Septimiana and two on the river to Tempesta's total, we get twenty-four.

Sector Q.   The River-wall to Porta Aurelia. (*F.U.R.*, 27, 20, 14.)
The Einsiedeln List gives viii. None is now known.

Sector R.   Porta Aurelia to Porta Flaminia. (*F.U.R.*, 1, 8, 15, 14.)
The Einsiedeln List gives xvi. Eight are known between Porta Flaminia and the River, and along the river there is room for many more than the residuum of eight. But see p. 19 for the discussion of the relevant passage of Procopius. Tempesta and Maggi show a piece of the Wall running along the River as far as S. Maria dei Miracoli.

INDEXES

I. ANCIENT LITERATURE, ARTISTS, AND MODERN AUTHORITIES

II. GENERAL INDEX

Loop-holes: connexion with *fenestrae*, 47; in Wall I, 66; in Wall II, 68; in towers, 80, 257, 260; tactical value, 66, 68.

Malborghetto: Arch at, compared with period II, 88.

Mausoleum: called *carcer Theoderici*, 264; decoration, 23; enlargement by Totila, 22; foundation, 23; gates, 23, 228; Gothic attack, 23–4; lower story, 23; τείχισμα, 22, 253; towers, 24–5.

Mausoleum Divi Augusti, relation to river-postern, 236.

Maxentius : building - programme, 254; coin-issue, 254; evidence for work on wall, 251; extra taxation, 255; new wall and towers, 251–6 ; strategical policy, 252, 255; three invasions of rivals, 252.

Maximianus, deserts Maxentius, 255.

Merlons: Belisarian, 38, 72, 89, 265; in Einsiedeln List, 45; of Wall I, 58, 62; of Wall II, 69.

Moenia, meaning of, 37, 264.

Moguntiacum, gate on medallion, 243, 251.

Naples, church of St. George at, 108.

Narona, wall at, 72 *n.*

Narses: arrives A.D. 552, 43; possible repairs, 90.

Necessaria: analogies, 84 *n.*, 85 *n.*; at Porta Appia, 85 ; at P. Praenestina-Labicana, 210; at P. Tiburtina, 171; derivation, 84 *n.*; supplied with shoots, 84; type, 85, criticism of, 85–6.

Otto I, captures Rome A.D. 967, 50.

Paludes Decenniae, Wall circumvents, 9.

Pantapōli, edict *de pantapōlis ad Urbem revocandis*, 36.

Papal destructions:
Alexander VI: P. Septimiana, 44, 223.
Gregory XVI: P. Praenestina-Labicana, 205.
Paul III: P. Ardeatina, 217.
Paul IV: P. Ardeatina, 44.
Pius IV: P. Asinaria blocked, 144; P. Nomentana blocked, 93.
Pius IX: P. Tiburtina, 170.
Urban VIII: P. Portuensis, 31, 200; P. Aurelia-Pancraziana, 221.

Papal repairs:
Eugenius IV: Mausoleum, 25.
Gregory II: 43.
Gregory III: 43.
Hadrian I: 43, 52.
Leo IV: 43, 52, 205.
Nicholas V: P. Ostiensis, 25 *n.*, 90, 120; P. Appia, 128; merlons, 89 *n.*; P. Tiburtina, 180.
Paul III: 55.

Pius IV: 93.
Sissinius: 43.
Sixtus V: 173.
Perge, wall of, 67.
Pisaurum, Belisarius repairs, 42, 267.
Pomerium, relation of Wall to, 8–9.
Pons Aelius: gate at, 23; τείχισμα at, 24.
Pons 'Neronianus', relation to Wall, 25.
Pope, *see* Cadastro, Papal repairs, Papal destructions.

Porta Appia:
Name: corrupted or changed, 121–2.
Early Gate: discovery of E. tower, 122; E. staircase, 122, 124; dimensions, 122–4, 132; relation to later work, 124; endangers collapse, 126; W. staircase, 132; double-arch, 134–5; curtain intact in period 2, 135; standard plan, 244.
East Tower: staircase-well, 124; stairs and rampart-walk, 131; circular chamber, 125; windows, 125; relation of circular plan to square, 125; original plan, 125; height, 125; flat vault, 126; two stories made one, 126, 264; artillery story III, 126; danger of collapse, 126; story IV, 126–8; story V additional, 128; Papal repairs, 128; marble facing, 128; treatment of marble blocks, 129–30, 259; moulding, 131; earthquake damage, 131; repair to mouldings, 131.
West Tower: compared with east, 131, 133; *peperino* refacing, 132; windows, 132; two stories made one, 132, 264; fifth period defined, 132, 133; relation to rampart-walk, 134; latrine, 134; medieval latrines, 134; oven, 137.
Curtain: marble curtain related to period II, 125; re-used inscriptions, 32, 130, 135; specially cut moulding, 131; block-work, 135; portcullis, 135, 136–7; Christian tombstone, 137; oven, 137; stairs to W. tower, 137; third story, 137, 264.
Vantage-court: relation to Arch of Drusus, 137; W. wall and corridor, 138; apsidal room, 138; function, 138.
Comparisons with: P. Asinaria, 125, 133, 150, 152, 154, 156, 158, 254; P. Flaminia, 142, 198, 199, 200, 244, 261; P. Latina, 102, 103, 104, 107, 124, 132, 135, 136, 261; P. Nomentana, 96, 98, 124; P. Ostiensis, 124, 136, 162, 166, 168; P. Portuensis, 203, 204, 244; gate at London, 125, 254; P. Nigra, Trier, 125, 254; P. Palatina, Turin, 135, 142, 254; P. Aurelia-Pancraziana, 222.

Porta Ardeatina: blocked, 217; form and plan, 217; inscription, 217, 219; name, 217 *n.*; standard plan, 245; travertine jambs, 217.
Comparisons with: P. Asinaria, 217;